A Dangerous Mind

A Dangerous Mind

Carl Schmitt in Post-War European Thought

Jan-Werner Müller

Yale University Press
New Haven and London

Designed by Adam Freudenheim
Set by Alliance Phototypesetters, India
Printed in Great Britain

Library of Congress Cataloging-in-Publication Data

Müller, Jan-Werner, 1970–
A Dangerous Mind. Carl Schmitt in Post-War European Thought / Jan-Werner Müller.
p.cm.
Includes bibliographical references and index.
ISBN 0–300–09932–0 (handcover : alk. paper)
1. Schmitt, Carl, 1888—Political and social views. 2. Liberalism.
I. Title.
JC263 .S358 2003
320.51—dc21
2002014897

A catalogue record for this book is available from the British Library
10 9 8 7 6 5 4 3 2 1

For

B. B.

1913–1999

and

E. M.

1908–2001

Tho' much is taken, much abides . . .

(Tennyson, *Ulysses*)

Contents

viii   Contents

I am bored by reading people who are allies, people of roughly the same views. What is interesting is to read the enemy, because the enemy penetrates the defences.

Isaiah Berlin

Acknowledgements

My first, hesitant engagement with Schmitt was greatly helped by Mark Philp, John Burrow, Andy Rabinbach, Harold James and Patrick Gavigan. Andy Rabinbach also first encouraged the idea of a critical history of 'what Schmitt has meant' in the twentieth century. Peter Pulzer, on the other hand, tried to restrain me at the right moments, albeit often unsuccessfully. Nevil Johnson kept provoking my interest in Schmitt over the years and, often inadvertently, gave me a feel for just what makes a British conservative so different from a German one, while Erika A. Kiss revealed the difference between political and philosophical conservatism. Also, in the spirit of 'conversing with the adversary' (rather than the enemy), Andreas Kalyvas and I conducted numerous exchanges about Schmitt over the years – which, yet again, proved Isaiah Berlin right.

Sinkwan Cheng, Jerry Cohen, Peter Ghosh, Nevil Johnson, Erika Kiss, Peter A. Kraus, Andreas Kalyvas, Leszek Kolakowski, Elliot Neaman, Theodor Paleologu, Peter Pulzer and Hew Strachan read parts of the manuscript at various stages and did much to improve them and to save me from errors. Special thanks are due to Mark Lilla and Galin Tihanov, who read entire drafts and provided many ideas on how to improve them. The responsibility for all shortcomings – and, above all, the responsibility for writing *this* kind of problem-based series of reception histories – remains of course mine.

For kindly answering queries about Schmitt and his many echoes in Europe (and elsewhere) I am grateful to José Maria de Areilza, Daniel Arenas-Vives, Olivier Beaud, Ernst-Wolfgang Böckenförde, Giovanni Capoccia, Richard Faber, Roberto Farnetti, Evelyn Goodmann-Thau, Jürgen Habermas, Wilhelm Hennis, Ellen Kennedy, Reinhart Koselleck, Dirk van Laak, Günter Maschke, Heinrich Meier, Theodor Paleologu, Pasquale Pasquino, Gianfranco Poggi, Ulrich K. Preuss, Nicolas Roussellia and Nicolaus Sombart. Theodor Paleologu and Frieder Günther very kindly allowed me to read their unpublished dissertations on the *Katechon* and the 'Westernization' of German public lawyers after 1945 respectively. I also wish to thank

Professor Dr. Jürgen Becker for giving me permission to access the *Schmitt Nachlaß* at the Nordrhein-Westfälisches Hauptstaatsarchiv in Düsseldorf. There Dr. Dieter Weber proved to be extremely friendly and efficient in locating material. Thanks are also due to Elisabeth Dutartre of the Centre de Recherches Politiques Raymond Aron, who expertly and beyond the call of duty helped me to make sense of the Schmitt-Aron correspondence and other materials in the Archives Privées Raymond Aron.

Parts of Part I were originally published in 'Carl Schmitt – an Occasional Nationalist?' in *History of European Ideas* (Vol. 23, No. 1 [1997]). Material in 'Dangerous Liaisons' has previously appeared under the heading '1968 as Event, Milieu and Ideology' in the *Journal of Political Ideologies* (Vol. 7, No. 1 [2002]). I am grateful to the editors of the journals, John Burrow and Michael Freeden respectively, for permission to use the material here. I also wish to thank Professor Becker for permission to quote from Schmitt's *Nachlaß*, Dominique Schnapper for permission to quote from Raymond Aron's letters, and Martin Forsthoff for permission to quote from Ernst Forsthoff's letters. Every effort has been made to trace copyright holders of other materials and any failure to cite them will be corrected in future editions.

I am grateful to the Warden and Fellows of All Souls College, Oxford, for providing a wonderfully congenial environment for work and in particular for two grants to undertake interviews and archival research in connection with this project. Thanks also to Humaira Erfan-Ahmed and Doris Lehmann, who provided crucial help in managing an increasingly complex manuscript and a sometimes even more complex correspondence. *Terminer la recherche*, as anybody who has worked in this area knows, can be a serious challenge to Schmitt scholars. Adam Freudenheim, with both patience and persistence, did much to help meet it.

This book is dedicated to two remarkable women. It was completed with the help of another, Erika Kiss, who provided a home, philosophical foundations and a title. More importantly, she also, with passion and scepticism, put it all in perspective.

Introduction

Such indirect influences, which elude any documentation, are the strongest and by far the most authentic.

Carl Schmitt, in a letter to Ernst Jünger, 1947

Somebody is always waiting on the other shore for your messages in a bottle – even if he remains silent.

Jacob Taubes, in a letter to Carl Schmitt, 1958

. . .seeing things as similar and making things the same is the sign of weak eyes.

Nietzsche, *The Gay Science*

'Liberalism', declared José Ortega y Gasset in 1930, 'announces the determination to share existence with the enemy'.[1] At around the same time, Carl Schmitt professed his determination not to share existence with liberalism. Instead, he sought to unmask and undermine liberalism, the supposed 'enemy of enmity' – a task to which he dedicated most of his long and extremely fruitful intellectual life. Many of his liberal opponents, however, were not only prepared to share existence with Schmitt. They also tried to learn from the century's most brilliant enemy of liberalism.

Schmitt's frontal and 'general attack on liberal modernity' had a large and lasting intellectual fallout.[2] It left arguments and theoretical fragments which were subsequently picked up by political thinkers of many – often contradictory – intellectual stripes in Europe and beyond. In fact, it might not be an overstatement to say that no twentieth-century thinker has had a more diverse range of readers. The thought of the man whom even formidable left-wing critics have acknowledged as the 'most intelligent and significant German theoretician of the state' has made for the strangest bedfellows – philosophical, political and, not least, moral.[3] For instance, Schmitt was a prime theoretical opponent for many German liberals after 1945, just as much as his authoritarian solutions had been a temptation for German liberals despairing over mass democracy before 1933. Schmitt was present as an implied interlocutor in Hannah Arendt's work on revolutions, while his constitutional theory served Latin American lawyers justifying military coups during 'states of emergency' which had been declared in the face of supposed revolutionary threats. His thought was carried from Weimar across the Atlantic by Leo Strauss, Hans Morgenthau and Carl Joachim Friedrich, and spread in Iberia through Franco's and Salazar's legal theorists. Italian Marxists learnt as much from him as the twisted visionaries of the New European Right of the 1980s and 1990s. The student leaders of '68 – his 'dialectical epigones'[4] – avidly read Schmitt to feed their suspicion of liberal parliamentarism – and the conservatives who opposed them were ready to deploy the legal instruments that Schmitt had forged for the strong state during the 1920s and early 1930s. A Social Democrat influenced by Schmitt sat on the German Constitutional Court. In a seminal 1993 ruling on the Maastricht Treaty, a majority of that Court, at least partly inspired by Schmittian thought, declared that a democratic Europe needed a homogeneous European people first.[5]

This is a book about what precisely 'one of the most equivocal and notorious' modern intellectuals has meant for twentieth-century European political thought and cultural life – and why his thought has meant *so much* and *so many seemingly contradictory things* to *so many*.[6] Just why has it been so difficult to lay Schmitt's ghost to rest? In February 1920, a few weeks before his death, Max Weber, after a discussion with Oswald Spengler, told his students that 'the integrity of a scholar today . . . can be measured by how he positions himself vis-à-vis Nietzsche and Marx'. Something similar appears to have happened with Schmitt in the late twentieth century. The question 'What does Carl Schmitt mean for us?' or 'Why Schmitt?' has been posed numerous times without yielding a satisfactory answer.[7] Just why have his theories had such a polarizing effect, often prompting the observation that his claim that a distinction between friend and enemy was the essence of politics, however flawed in other respects, holds true for the reception of his own work? Why have no other thinkers – except perhaps Max Weber and Machiavelli – been associated with 'the demonic' so frequently? Was it simply because Schmitt was himself so prone to invoking devilish forces?

The significance for European thought of what is often called Schmitt's 'intellectual drama' is easily sketched. He lived for most of the twentieth century, and continued to write for almost seventy years, from the early 1910s to the late 1970s. During the 1920s, he was a central figure in the heated debates on the Weimar constitution and in Germany's battle against the Versailles Treaty. Schmitt also played an important role in efforts by conservative nationalists to transform the Weimar Republic into an authoritarian presidential regime in the early 1930s. In 1933, he switched his allegiance to the National Socialists and attempted to elaborate a theoretical framework for Nazi rule. Despite his outspoken antisemitism, he was attacked by the SS in 1936 on account of his Catholicism and past association with Jewish scholars. Subsequently, he retreated from domestic debates in favour of formulating an international law doctrine of 'great spaces', which served to legitimate Hitler's policies of conquest in the East. For this doctrine, among other things, the Americans sought to put him on trial in Nuremberg. After a number of interrogations, however, they eventually let him go.

When Schmitt returned from the internment camp to his provincial Westphalian hometown of Plettenberg in 1947, the man whom many regarded as the 'Crown Jurist of the Third Reich' seemed discredited forever. His fall from intellectual grace had been even more spectacular than Heidegger's and he was permanently banned from teaching in West Germany. Yet, Schmitt exercised a profound influence on post-war political thought. In the 'internal exile' of Plettenberg, he remained an *éminence grise*, paradoxically both absent and present in the public intellectual life of the Federal Republic, but subject to major controversy throughout.[8] As a more or less secret reception of his ideas unfolded, Schmitt himself remained actively involved in their promotion. He was everything but a 'living period piece, to all appearances an intellectual invalid from an antediluvian world'.[9] Rather, he continued to comment on matters from day-to-day public life in West Germany to the role of partisans in the global politics of the Cold War – comments eagerly received by many younger thinkers who were to play leading roles in the intellectual life of the Federal Republic.[10]

Many of these younger intellectuals were dissatisfied with the newly imported Anglo-American doctrines of liberal democracy and felt that Schmitt offered deeper insights into the true nature of politics. They shared Schmitt's view that 'the victor feels no intellectual curiosity' – and even the more left-leaning among them suspected that defeated right-wingers posed the sharper questions after the War.[11] Many of his pupils never tired in their efforts to secure his status as a contemporary 'classic' of political thought. Schmitt himself continued to have major shares in the interpretation industry of his ideas, an industry sustained not least by Schmitt's ability to both shock with his apodictic pronouncements in political realism, while at the same time remaining curiously elusive. His hermetic works and often equally cryptic self-commentary have not failed to produce a steadily growing oeuvre in Schmitt hermeneutics.

Schmitt's Legacy, Liberalism and the Struggle for Stability

Schmitt bequeathed to his heirs *and* to his enemies a set of preoccupations with particularly extreme kinds of political situations and a specific vocabulary for talking about the fate of the modern state in the age of mass democracy and industrial society. On the one hand, this vocabulary appeared thoroughly antiquated and shot through with deeply antimodern assumptions. On the other hand, for many it seemed to be far ahead of its time and contain sharp questions that pierced through liberal orthodoxies.

In particular – and not surprisingly – post-war thinkers across the political spectrum were preoccupied with questions of political stability and social cohesion. In the shadow of Weimar's failure, the preconditions of liberal democratic institutions had become a central concern – so much so that it is not an overstatement to say that the quest for political integration is the one overriding concern of post-war German political and legal thought. It is no accident that a legal theorist heavily influenced by Schmitt wrote what is arguably the most quoted sentence in post-war German political thought, namely: 'the liberal, secular state lives off preconditions which it cannot itself guarantee'.[12] It is also no accident that Ernst-Wolfgang Böckenförde's famous dictum appeared in an essay on the topic of secularization. There was a pervasive anxiety among Schmitt's students that the decline of religion left few sources of legitimacy for the modern, complex industrial state. This was one reason why the relationship between politics and theology, as well as the legitimacy of the modern age as such remained live issues for Schmittians.

Many post-war thinkers claimed that it was not only possible but also highly desirable to 'liberalize' Schmitt's thought. These 'adversarial successors' argued that the supposed 'Lenin of the bourgeoisie' could provide intellectual resources to make liberalism more sensitive to questions of social stability and democratic self-defence, thereby strengthening it against opponents who see it as a fair-weather ideology sustained by feeble compromises. In other words, not only could the profound antiliberal Schmitt be disarmed – the weapons he used in his general attack on liberal modernity could also be re-deployed in its defence.

This raises the question of what the prominent German political scientist Wilhelm Hennis once called the 'problem of the German view of the state', around which, after all, much of Schmittian thought revolved.[13] The ideal of a powerful, rational state standing above society and remaining immune from sectarian social interests constituted a benchmark not just for conservatives, but also for many liberals in the post-war period. In fact, one might say that since Hegel, in one way or another, the state – society distinction has been a kind of theoretical axis on which much German political thought has turned. Moreover, German political and legal thinkers have tended to invest the state with metaphysical foundations – the state was a matter of real substance and could not simply be reduced to its functions, let alone to the role as an agent of civil society. In the same vein, the 'German view of the state' was usually adopted from the heights of the executive. In many ways, Schmitt's theories reflected this view of the state – both in his initial effort to strengthen the state in the age of mass politics and in his subsequent search for substantial, legitimate forms of political community beyond the state. Consequently, those who sought to save, modernize or liberalize the German view of the state under the conditions of mass democracy and industrial society almost inevitably felt compelled to engage with the former 'Crown Jurist'.

Reading and Reversing Schmitt

The post-war period, then, saw a succession of inter-related debates in which the limits of liberalizing Schmitt were tested. In the second part of this book I examine these debates, asking, among other things, where various Schmitt pupils stopped short of drawing out the antiliberal implications of his thought. Did they succeed in addressing the problems in liberal democracy which Schmitt had highlighted? Or did adopting a Schmittian perspective on particular problems predetermine the answers, thus contaminating the reflections of liberal legal and political theorists with authoritarian elements?

Consequently, this is also a study in the complex metabolization of liberal and antiliberal political thought in a transition to democracy – and, in particular, the uses of antiliberal ideas, whether prophylactic, catalytic, constructive or even integrative in a liberal democracy. What I undertake here is in itself a historically inflected exercise in separation: what distinguishes legitimate critiques of liberalism from varieties of antiliberalism which are ultimately driven by a non-negotiable antimodernism? Where does one draw the lines between antiliberal arguments that have been adapted for liberal purposes, antiliberalism grounded in arguments and mere hatred of liberalism or bourgeois self-hatred – a feeling sometimes attributed to Schmitt himself?

This, then, is a study in the reception of Schmitt's work – or rather, a series of reception histories which revolve around particular problems and concepts which formed a central part of Schmitt's ambiguous legacy.[14] It is not another attempt to identify the essence of Schmitt's thought. In fact, there is no such essence, and, as Hannah Arendt once pointed out, the search for a singular, final key to thought is in itself deeply ideological.[15] The first part of this volume is not a definitive account of the first half of Schmitt's life, but an overview of Schmitt's career and the development of his tension-ridden and sometimes apparently contradictory oeuvre.

I then discuss what others made of Schmitt's legacy after 1945. This post-war story, however, necessarily includes Schmitt's own work and his self-interpretation after the War. It also has to be an international story, especially as Schmitt himself, in an attempt to escape the confines of West German intellectual life, conducted self-consciously European conversations and correspondences. After the War, many prominent right-wing lawyers and humanist intellectuals remained, or became, committed Europeanists. Just like Schmitt, they saw themselves as the guardians of an authentic European heritage that was being threatened by the two superpowers.

Converseley, many left-wing radicals in different parts of Europe felt repulsed (and sometimes secretly attracted) by Schmitt's supposedly supremely realist antiliberal theories. This was not a simple case of *les extrêmes (antilibéraux) se touchent*. Rather, as I shall argue in a number of chapters, it reflected the fact that European political thinkers after 1945 often addressed similar problems: the fate of the supposedly post-liberal state, and the welfare state in particular; the relationship between legality and legitimacy; and the question of what model of political *action* was appropriate on a continent overshadowed by a global polarization (and an apparent freezing of politics) between friends and enemies. The struggle for political and social stability after the twentieth century's Thirty Years War was a particular pan-European preoccupation.[16] Ultimately, however, many of these thinkers came up against an issue that was central to Schmitt's politics: the logic and potential limits of modern sovereignty – a problem that certainly transcended Schmitt's own times and his own theoretical efforts and one I shall return to in the third part of this study.

The secret (and sometimes not so secret) path of Schmitt's thought in the twentieth century was marked by dangerous liaisons and a succession of scandals – from Jürgen Habermas declaring that Schmitt was the 'legitimate son of Max Weber' in the early 1960s to the publication of Schmitt's post-war diaries in the early 1990s, which turned out to be profoundly antisemitic diatribes. The symbolism of the 'case of Carl Schmitt' raises important questions about the peculiar dynamics of German intellectual life. It also points to the peculiar politics of public-cum-academic scandal-making, ideological conversion as well as 'deconversion', theoretical appropriations and misapproproations, and, in particular, canonization and de-canonization. These are phenomena to which students of political thought – especially of liberalism – have often paid too little attention.

Writing about Schmitt and those writing about Schmitt poses particular interpretative challenges – mainly due to the *cauchemar de richesse* caused by the sheer volume of his writings and writings about him. He published for almost seventy years, intervened polemically in numerous ongoing political debates and had a strong tendency towards constructing myths around his own politics and personality.[17] Moreover, he employed what has been called a kind of philosophical 'double talk', shifting the meaning of concepts central to his theory and scattering allusions and false leads throughout his work.[18] In addition to a certain 'conceptual opportunism', he often made subtle changes to new editions of his books.[19] Schmitt, after all, was a lawyer – and, after the War, he was primarily a lawyer in his own case. These attempts at self-revision and self-mythologization form an integral part of the reception of this paradigmatic European right-wing intellectual's work and will be examined alongside the more theoretical engagement of post-war thinkers with Schmitt's legacy. Antiliberalism had and has its affective as well as its aesthetic elements – and a study of Schmitt in the post-war period is necessarily also a study in spitefulness and its attractions, as well as an examination of the peculiar *aesthetics* of anti-liberalism.

Between Politics and Aesthetics

What was it in Schmitt's theories that proved so seductive? Their sheer stringency, their conceptual innovation, or the mysterious sources behind their deceptive clarity? Or was it Schmitt's activity as a kind of political pamphleteer commenting on day-to-day politics, offering sharp antitheses to deal with concrete situations, strident calls for decisions and, in Ernst Jünger's famous phrase, 'mines which exploded silently' inside liberal orthodoxies?[20]

It was Schmitt as a *political* thinker, rather than as a legal thinker who proved attractive. His legal theory as such, while of great influence, is in fact often impressionistic and illogical. This is not to say that the Schmittian legal tool kit did not contain important instruments – some of which were used in the construction and interpretation of the Basic Law, that is, the West German constitution, after the War. What exercised Schmitt's contemporaries most, however, were his political theory and his politics – as well as his ability to make law into politics.

But there is also the aesthetic appeal of his writings. As nearly every observer has pointed out, Schmitt's supposed attractiveness has an aesthetic element, a fascination with Schmitt's so-called *Begriffsmagie* (magic of concepts), just as Schmitt's own fascination with politics had an aesthetic dimension.[21] First-time readers of the 'Gabriele d'Annunzio of public law' regularly report an experience resembling a revelation or even awakening in political realism that seems comparable to first opening *The Prince*. Schmitt supposedly 'made reality itself think'.[22] But he also announced 'the scandal of content in a scandalous manner', and even where analysis predominates, the tone of voice has the slightly dismissive accent of the superior intellectual idea which bypasses conventional views'.[23]

Schmitt is often said to impress with his supposed Weberian *Sachlichkeit*, a matter-of-factness and realism. In an interview with the Maoist radical Joachim Schickel, Schmitt himself claimed rather disingenuously that 'I have a particular method: to let the phenomena approach me, to wait a little and think from the subject matter, so to speak, not from preconceived criteria. You could call this phenomenological, but I do not like to engage in such general methodological preliminary questions'.[24] He undoubtedly had a 'passion for defining concepts',[25] originating in an aesthetic appreciation of 'form', and a style that has been called both *Blitzkrieg* and *Blitzlicht* (flash)-like.[26] However, when daylight returns after the flash, many interpreters have found Schmitt dazzling, rather than illuminating, detecting an apodictic style rather than clarity, and numerous contradictions even within a single work. Schmitt himself, quoting Goethe who in turn had quoted Hamann, pointed out that 'clarity is an appropriate distribution of light and shadow'.[27] Arguably, many of these shadows have yet to be explored, so that present-day readers of Schmitt may not only be dazzled, but can also be clear about where he leaves them in the dark.

As has often been pointed out, Schmitt's style seemed to oscillate between an objective, cold mode in which he uncovered the hard truths about politics on the one hand, and, on the other hand, an almost feverish expressionsm which aimed to identify the enemy and even to incite hatred. Schmitt, after all, was not just a lawyer and political theorist, but also a man of letters, penning books on Hamlet and expressionist poetry alongside legal treatises. Even in his academic writings, he freely mixed supposedly crystal-clear definitions and distinctions with images, metaphors and myths. If in doubt, he persistently seemed to opt for the arresting phrase over the analytical argument.

Yet, there was a method to Schmitt's stylistic magic, which turns out to be intimately related to his larger political beliefs. Schmitt was not simply a conceptual opportunist, who changed the meanings of his words to suit changing political circumstances. Rather, as in Edmund Burke's writings, style and thought were interdependent. Schmitt did not intend his work to be neutral analysis, which could be abstracted and systematized (a reason why so many logical reconstructions of his work have ended up empty-handed). Instead, his strategic deployment of concepts, metaphors and myths as lines of demarcation between friends and enemies was itself part of a larger *combat spirituel.* Language was to persuade and even to mobilize – its aesthetic quality was essential, not accidental.

Schmitt, Liberal Modernity and the History of the Present

In the final part of this book, I offer some reflections about Schmitt's most recent and, one might say, almost global renaissance. At a time when Left and Right remain confused about their respective identities – or deny the distinction altogether – it is perhaps no accident that Schmitt has also reappeared at the supposed cutting edge of political theory. Jacques Derrida has portrayed Schmitt as a besieged, terrified and insomniac intellectual 'watchman', driven by fear and lucidity to anticipate 'the storms and seismic movements that would wreak havoc with the historical field, the borders of concepts and countries', as well as 'the axiomatics of European law'.[28] Like many other theorists whom one would have expected to be hostile to Schmitt, Derrida has hinted that contemporary thought could benefit not only from understanding Schmitt's 'panic of a defensive', but also from comprehending the 'equivocations' of Schmitt's influence among the Right and the Left.[29] That equivocation itself has come to characterize many intellectuals who draw on Schmitt's ideas.

Not surprisingly, scattered fragments of Schmittian thought have been picked up by postmodern and poststructuralist political theorists preoccupied with questions of inclusion and exclusion.[30] These theorists are eager to marshal his concept of the political against a liberalism which they view as 'displacing' politics and stifling genuine pluralism in favour of the uncontested reign of the free market. Yet, it often remains unclear what the 'return of the political' these theorists desire would entail – popular mobilization, a sharpening of particular conflicts or merely a recognition of the limits of rational consensus-finding in existing democracies? The proliferation of engagements with 'the political' – that strange construction of a noun out of an adjective – seems to be directly proportional to the anxiety of living in a 'post-political' age – whatever that might mean.

Schmitt is also increasingly recognized by theorists in international relations who subscribe to what in American parlance is known as the 'realist' paradigm, in which states are assumed to pursue their own interests relentlessly and conflict constitutes the unchanging nature of international politics.[31] Yet, it is not so much the supposedly timeless insights of political realism as such which appeal in an age of increasing geopolitical uncertainty; rather, it is Schmitt's theses on the reconfiguration of political space after the era of the sovereign European nation-state. Schmitt, it has to be remembered, had early on come to the conclusion that the modern era of statehood had ended in the first half of the twentieth century. Partly in dialogue with thinkers like Alexandre Kojève and Raymond Aron, he had already attempted – in the 1940s and 1950s – to think beyond the nation-state, envisaging a 'new order of the Earth'.

Now, as the age of 'territoriality' wanes, and as patterns of organized violence are changing in complex ways both inside and across state borders, Schmitt's observations on political space seem to gain increasing relevance. This is particularly the case with those who yearn for a new 'episteme of separation', through which clear lines of political demarcation could be established – or re-established.[32] Not surprisingly, then, theorists who seek to embed the European Union in an adversarial structure with Islamic countries draw on Schmitt's ideas no less than Russians who want to regain the country's role as a 'gatherer of lands' inside a 'Eurasian bloc' defined against a US-led 'Atlantic Great Space'.[33]

Conservatism and Catastrophe

Studying the reception of Schmitt's thought can tell us much about the still largely uncharted topography of post-war European thought, and also about the 'history of the present'. But, I contend, such a study also holds more general lessons about the relationship between politics and morality under the particular circumstances of modernity. Schmitt, I claim, embodies a European political sensibility which is rather inadequately described with the concept of conservatism – 'radical conservatism' or 'reactionary modernism' come closer to the mark, but they still miss it. Schmitt had no illusions about re-enchanting the world or returning to an ideal past. But neither was he prepared simply to accept certain elements of modernity such as an unrestrained development of technology and the supposed rise of mass society.

What we are looking at is a mindset that could best be described with the term philosophical or anthropological conservatism – which might or might not be realized in particularly conservative positions, centred on gradual change, in actual politics.[34] This mindset is uncomfortable with the abstractions of liberalism and universalism, as well as any accounts of progress and increasing individual human liberation. It has an acute, but highly selective awareness of the history of the victims of liberal modernity, the exceptions and the non-identical. It distrusts a liberalism that only the successful appear to be able to afford.[35] It relentlessly seeks to unmask liberal universalist claims in the name of power politics and the concrete. It is a mindset that seeks to cut through the web of liberal procedures and indirect action which mediate every political claim and to end the endless liberal postponements of final decisions in favour of what is both the ultimate and the immediate. It cannot bear ambiguity, and, above all, it cannot bear the seeming subjugation of politics to ethics on the one hand and economics on the other. It denies that political argument could be mediated by morality – in fact, morality would only exacerbate the darker aspects of politics. In any case, modern ethics is – at best – merely a form of ironic value relativism. It cannot accept mere self-interest, which could be satisfied by the accumulation of goods and an exchange of mutual advantages, as a basis of the political universe. 'Irony and utility' – which Benjamin Constant saw as the main characteristics of liberal modernity – both have to be repudiated for the sake of the seriousness of a true grand politics which is beyond both calculation and conversation.[36]

If Max Weber was a liberal in despair, as is often claimed (rightly or, rather, wrongly), then Schmitt was a conservative in despair. The modern world meant an apparently irreversible loss of meaning and substance. Schmitt, a man of ambition and a self-declared 'intellectual adventurer', keen to achieve 'power over history', was not only willing, but eager to act politically. Consequently, he always sought 'access to those in power' (a problem which became a major theme in his post-war writings).[37] Thus he attempted to translate his conservative intuitions into political action. These translations, based on the hope that the political itself could become the carrier of meaning and substance, turned into what can only be called a series of moral (and political) catastrophes. A philosophical conservatism in despair, when put to the test of political practice, is prone to tip over into a kind of nihilism, rather than live with the supposed hypocrisies and indecisiveness of liberalism. Yet, this mentality which is predisposed towards direct action and decisionism is not just found on the Right. It has an element of what theorists inspired by the Frankfurt School have long referred to as *Ideologiekritik* – a critique that unmasks the power interests behind moral and political claims. In this respect it is fixated on its theoretical opponent, liberalism – after all, only liberalism is committed to a principle of public justification, whether through ethics or economics. Yet, these justifications constantly invite their own deconstruction – a game at which Schmitt became a master.

In the present, globalization proceeds under the twin banners of ethics and economics – global human rights and global free trade, without, as yet, proper global political structures. Such a constellation poses the permanent temptation to replay Schmitt's critique of a liberalism that is alternatively helpless or hypocritical. As humanitarianism and economic globalization spread, so will their shadow – the anti-moralism and anti-economism proposed in the name of a peculiar political morality which Schmitt embodied more fully than any other antiliberal in the twentieth century.

Part I
A German Public Lawyer in the Twentieth Century

Most conservatives come from the margins. Carl Schmitt was no exception. He was born in the Mosel region of Germany in 1888, the year Wilhelm II ascended the throne. Like Heidegger, he emerged from an intensely Catholic and petty bourgeois background. He grew up in the Sauerland region, a Protestant pocket in the largely Catholic Rhineland, which in turn was situated on the margins of an Empire whose public culture remained dominated by Protestantism and Prussianism. Schmitt was too young to have lived through the *Kulturkampf* – the political battle between Bismarck and the Catholic Church in the 1870s. However, even at the height of his power as a law professor in Berlin and foremost jurist of the Nazis he apparently felt himself to be an outsider in the capital.

In 1907 Schmitt briefly studied law in Berlin – the city which he later recognized was to become his fate – describing his first experiences there with these telling words:

> I was an obscure young man of modest origins . . . part neither of the governing elite nor of an opposition movement . . . that meant that, standing

wholly in the dark, I looked from the darkness into a brightly lit room . . . the strong repulsion which I experienced left me no comfort with my role. The feeling of sadness which filled me, increased my distance and evoked distrust and alienation in others. A governing elite senses anyone to be a heterogeneous element who does not find happiness in coming into contact with it, but shows himself saddened instead. . . It leaves him with the choice to adapt or remove himself. . . So I stayed outside.[1]

Much later, Schmitt, driven by immense ambition, would find suitable means of adaptation and enter the brightly lit room after all. Yet, despite all the self-stylization typical of his later writings, there was some truth in the fact that this uprooted conservative's inner distance provided him with a sharper image of the age – and sometimes made for complete distortions. Schmitt was a mirror and a medium of his time – but he was also a supreme manipulator, a myth-maker and a political activist. A deep desire to *act* and be at the forefront of historical developments went hand in hand with a strange passivity, which Schmitt himself and many contemporaries remarked upon, a stance that waited for historical developments and phenomena to approach and even to overwhelm the scholar.[2]

After the initial disappointments in Berlin, Schmitt continued his studies in the much more congenial Munich and the even more congenial Strasbourg, writing his first and second dissertations on problems of legal indeterminacy. Like a number of other scholars dissatisfied with the reigning orthodoxies of legal positivism, Schmitt was concerned about the relationship between statutes and the actual decisions of judges. He attacked liberal legalism, denying that the law could ever form a closed and unified set of norms. Instead, he emphasized an inevitably discretionary and therefore arbitrary element in every judicial decision.[3] He still thought that this fact would not have to lead to a chaotic unpredictability of the law – it was only that the criterion for a correct judicial decision had to be reduced to the assumption 'that another judge would have decided in the same way'. However, this call for a homogeneous judiciary was clearly not yet a satisfactory answer to the question Schmitt's legal antiformalism posed – a question that would haunt him for decades.

During the waning years of the Wilhelmine Empire and the beginning of the First World War, Schmitt lived a kind of double life as a jurist and expressionist *littérateur* – a semi-bohemian existence in Munich's most intensely intellectual coffee houses. Under a pseudonym, he published satirical books – or what he would later call 'Dada *avant-la-lettre*' – on Thomas Mann and other supposedly 'bourgeois writers'. He ridiculed the official culture of the Wilhelmine Empire – a somehow fake age, he felt, in which self-important cultural epigones were wearing a 'Goethe mask'.[4] Schmitt, whose post-war writings endlessly revolved around his own past and his public image, time and again expressed his deep distaste for the reigning 'cult of the self'. He had first detected this romantic cult in the age of Thomas Mann and Walther Rathenau. More importantly, such names stood for a progressive, metropolitan synthesis of liberalism, Protestantism and assimilated Jewish culture, which dominated Berlin's academic life and which had already alienated the provincial Catholic Schmitt.

Schmitt's personal life also remained driven by apparently romantic and anti-establishment visions. Just after the completion of his legal education, he married a woman he thought was a Serb aristocrat – but who turned out to be an Austrian con-woman with a dubious professional past. For a number of years he was to publish as Carl Schmitt-Dorotić. The divorce ensued in 1924, but the Church refused to annul the marriage. When Schmitt re-married in 1926, he was officially ex-communicated. Consequently, the man whose admiration for the Catholic Church as one of the highest achievements of Occidental rationalism and as capable of mediating and containing any conflict never wavered, would remain outside the Church until the death of his second wife in 1950.

Schmitt spent most of the First World War in the Bavarian Ministry of War censoring foreign propaganda, before he suddenly found himself in the middle of the civil war which broke out in Munich after anarchists had declared a council republic in April 1919. At one point, communist revolutionaries entered the office where Schmitt was working and shot an officer at the table next to his. It was in this year that the public lawyer, who had previously appeared to be almost apolitical, opted in favour of the state asserting itself against the revolutionary masses.

In 1919 Schmitt also published a book which seemed like a repudiation of his earlier half-romantic and half-bourgeois life. The treatise *Political Romanticism* attacked the Romantics for clinging to a cult of the self and, above all, for a lack of moral seriousness. Schmitt criticized the Romantics' search for the 'interesting', in which all aspects of the world became mere occasions for the romantic fantasy to work on. The Romantics, Schmitt charged, were unable to think truly politically, irrespective of their particular political allegiances. They never reached a decision, attempting instead to overcome philosophical contradictions and political conflict through a spurious search for what they called a 'higher third'. This 'higher third' was then used to establish a false unity instead of truly resolving an antithesis.

For Schmitt, even when the Romantics wrote ostensibly political treatises, they did not take politics seriously: politics was just another 'occasion' for romantic emotions to work themselves out. Romanticism denied the inexorable causality and consistency which characterized political reality. *Causa* was in fact the very opposite of *occasio*, and the remedy for Romanticism was a proper 'recherche de la Réalité'.[5] Most importantly, Schmitt directly opposed Romanticism to 'political action'. Its indeterminacy and its fake 'higher thirds' had to be cleared away if genuine political action was to be possible – and if the political was to emerge as a genuine carrier of meaning and substance.

Most of the Romantics whom Schmitt attacked had turned conservative (and, in many cases, Catholic) towards the end of their lives, subscribing to a view of state and society as great organisms. Schmitt repudiated such visions and thereby also the contemporary conservatism of those such as Othmar Spann, an Austrian social philosopher who advocated a recreation of quasi-medieval estates as part of an organic society. For Schmitt, a deep, but also dislocated conservative without any superficial sentimentalism, the post-war revolutions in Europe had destroyed any legitimacy based on the past, let alone dynastic or feudal traditions.

Yet, the critique of Romanticism was also a fundamental critique of bourgeois civilization. Schmitt's Romantics bore many of the traits of the modern liberal bourgeoisie, especially in their exalted individualism, and their propensity to postpone decisions through an endless conversation. Liberal modernity was not just about a loss of meaning and substance – rather, it was about the uncontrolled proliferation of seemingly contingent, ambiguous meanings which could only *occasionally* be connected. Schmitt, himself in many ways an archetypal Wilhelmine *Bürger* (despite all his bohemian leanings), for the first time displayed a strong antibourgeois affect in his political thought. He also espoused a strong political anti-aestheticism, despite his own obvious aesthetic temptations. Thus the book almost appeared to be an act of exorcism and, not surprisingly, appealed to other philosophically conservative critics of bourgeois civilization such as György Lukács, who authored a favourable review of *Political Romanticism*.[6] Schmitt characterized the era as a 'confused intermediate situation between form and lack of form', in which 'the classical', defined as the 'possibility of unambiguous, clear distinctions' had been dissolved and replaced by the romantic.[7] In such an era an aesthetic longing for form could unite individuals from across the practical political divides.

Roman Reassurances

In the aftermath of the Bavarian Civil War and in the face of the continuous instability of the Weimar Republic, which remained subject to right-wing violence and coups, Schmitt sought some political and theoretical reassurances in previous models of political order. His explorations ranged from ancient political thought through the idea of the Catholic Church as a political 'form' to the counter-revolutionary Catholic tradition of the nineteenth century. Not all these explorations were compatible – but from them a political vocabulary (and a tone and a political temperament) emerged which would determine much of Schmitt's later thinking.

While still in Munich, Schmitt hastily penned a sprawling book on dictatorship, in which he drew a fundamental distinction between commissarial and sovereign dictatorship.[8] Commissarial dictatorship, as in the classical Roman conception, dealt with exceptions and emergencies as the agents of the existing, legitimate powers. It was essentially about restoring a normal situation. Sovereign dictatorship, by contrast, was unlimited, and established a completely new order. At this stage, when the young Weimar Republic seemed under permanent threat from revolutionary violence and right-wing coups, Schmitt clearly favoured a commissarial concept of dictatorship – sovereign dictatorship, on the other hand, potentially embodied a Communist, revolutionary legitimacy.

Dictatorship was published in 1921, the year Schmitt received his first offer of a professorship at Greifswald on the Baltic Sea, one of the least prestigious German universities in a Protestant cultural backwater. In what was clearly a difficult time for Schmitt, he wrote, almost simultaneously, two books which dealt with the relationship between religion and political order. In *Roman Catholicism and Political Form*, he again defended the dignity of politics against what he saw as the all-pervasive modes of modern economic and technological thinking. Unlike instrumental and utilitarian types of thought, there always had to be a genuine idea behind the political. He also proposed that the Catholic Church, as what he called a *complexio oppositorum*, was truly capable of integrating contradictions and antitheses, unlike the Romantics' conception of a 'higher third'. It contained what Schmitt called a 'juristic rationality' superior to the instrumental and mechanistic rationality supposedly characteristic of the modern age. The Catholic Church also relied on a scholastic idea of representation, namely the representation of an idea, which shines through the representative, just like Christ appears through the Pope. Representation, according to Schmitt, had to be personal, and had to involve the re-presenting of substantive beliefs, ideals or even myths. It also meant representation before, rather than for the people. It was opposed to a notion of representation as mechanical reproduction of private interests, which he associated with the bourgeoisie and the liberal institution of parliament.

In *Political Theology*, initially part of a volume dedicated to the memory of Max Weber, whose seminars Schmitt had attended in Munich, he began his jurisprudential war against 'normativism'. The first battle was waged against the positivism associated with the neo-Kantian school and the Austrian jurist Hans Kelsen in particular. Schmitt played the personal political decision off against the abstract norms which Kelsen had argued were identical with the state. Where Kelsen had identified a basic norm as the ultimate ground of the legal order, Schmitt argued that 'like every other order, the legal order rests on a decision and not on a norm'. No norm as such could be sovereign, Schmitt charged. Moreover, one had to recognize (and re-affirm) the fact that the state confronted situations outside the norm: 'Sovereign', Schmitt claimed in what would become one of his most famous (or infamous) sentences, 'is he who decides on the state of exception'. The exception could not be subsumed under legal concepts and exposed the fact that all order was based on a decision. Norms only applied in a normal situation. Ultimately, it was the authority capable of coping with the exception which was at the heart of the legal order: with Hobbes, Schmitt affirmed that *auctoritas non veritas facit legem* – authority, not, truth, makes the laws.

Thus, Schmitt claimed, 'the exception can be more important than the rule', and insisted at the same time that the state of exception was not mere chaos. In what seemed like a rather romantic twist to the argument, Schmitt added, 'the exception is more interesting than the rule. The rule proves nothing; the exception proves everything. It confirms not only the rule, but also its existence, which derives only from the exception. In the exception, the power of real life breaks through the crust of a mechanism that has become torpid by repetition'. At this point, Schmitt essentially sought to found an authoritarian, unified state out of a normatively groundless decision, with an undivided sovereignty. By re-injecting the brute facts of sociology and power into Kelsen's pure theory of law, he also affirmed 'decisionism', namely the notion that it mattered not so much how and which decisions are made but that they are made at all. The state did not have to be right to create right.

Schmitt now also aligned himself with some of the theorists of the French and Spanish counter-revolutionary tradition of the first half of the nineteenth century. Joseph de Maistre, the Savoyard diplomat, Juan Donoso Cortés, Spanish reactionary and one-time ambassador to Berlin, and, to a lesser extent, the early nineteenth-century legitimist Louis de Bonald, became crucial figures for Schmitt in what was, after all, also an unstable post-revolutionary situation in the Weimar Republic. In Schmitt's reading, these thinkers had all lost hope in grounding post-revolutionary regimes in traditional monarchic legitimacy. Instead, they advocated a form of dictatorship based on decisionism, with de Maistre coming closest to making dictatorship a matter of pure despotism, as true sovereignty consisted of 'doing evil with impunity'. Donoso, faced with the revolutions of 1848, had famously claimed that 'it is a question of choosing between the dictatorship from below and dictatorship from above . . . In the last resort it is a question of choosing between the dictatorship of the dagger and that of the sabre: I choose that of the sabre because it is nobler'. For philosophical conservatives without a belief in tradition and harbouring apocalyptic visions of a liberal or socialist future, legitimacy was to be found in nothing but the effective possession of power. The desire to delay those apocalyptic futures entailed a paradoxical, activist conservatism that was unrestrained by the past.

At the same time, these thinkers had freely mixed politics and theology – or, more precisely, while they were also genuine Catholics, they instrumentalized religion to bolster authoritarian regimes. Schmitt did not openly share this view – at least in this book. Instead, in what he called a novel 'sociology of concepts', he held that all modern concepts were secularized theological concepts. The absolute monarch was a secularized version of an all-powerful God, the political state of exception was a secularized miracle, and the opposition of transcendental versus immanent corresponded to an antithesis of dynastic and democratic principles of legitimacy.

Schmitt managed to escape from Greifswald after only a year, and relocated to Bonn – a sleepy university town full of retired civil servants, but subject to different intellectual cross-currents, such as the French Catholic *Renouveau*. Schmitt's personal and professional situation, as well as the internal politics of the Republic, finally became more stable – at which point Schmitt chose to subvert the theory and practice of liberal democracy in a more radical fashion.

Taking Positions against Weimar, Geneva and Versailles

So far, Schmitt's works had been exercises on the borderline between the history of ideas and legal theory – but they had also been exercises in finding his own intellectual voice. By 1923, he had assembled a powerful arsenal of conceptual weapons against the Weimar Republic. Conceptual weaponry is indeed the right metaphor here: Schmitt himself claimed that concepts could only be understood if one knew whom they were aimed against.

In 1940, Schmitt would call a collection of his essays *Positions and Concepts in the Fight against Weimar-Geneva-Versailles 1923–1940*, referring to the Weimar Republic, the League of Nations and the Versailles Treaty. In many ways, this was an accurate summary of Schmitt's activities from 1923 onwards. Much of his thought revolved around the concept of *politische Einheit* – which in German refers both to political unity and the political unit which is the carrier of that unity. Most important here was the question of the fate of the state in a supposedly post-liberal era of mass democracy and industrial capitalism. What Schmitt called the 'European state form' appeared to be undergoing a profound crisis. In particular, the nineteenth-century distinction between state and society, which had been introduced by Hegel and had played a central role in liberal political thought, seemed to become blurred. In particular, society, in the form of a plurality of economic and other associations, appeared to have invaded the state.

The Weimar constitution was arguably the most democratic constitution in the world at the time, on account of its many provisions for plebiscites and direct elections. Yet it was, in one sense, also the outcome of an aborted civil war and a complete political stalemate.[9] The Weimar constitution lacked legitimacy for parties on both the far Right and the far Left. The Right resented it, because legitimacy could only have been grounded in tradition and, above all, the monarchy; for the Communist Left, which had been brutally crushed by the Social Democrats in 1919, only a revolution could have generated real legitimacy. The constitution also contained many unresolved questions, last-minute compromises and contradictory provisions – for instance, for the protection as well as for the socialization of private property – which became subject to intense party politics, bordering occasionally on a renewal of civil war. The positivism which had dominated German legal thought up until the First World War was simply not of much use in an intensely politicized situation. Furthermore, it was actively opposed by those on the Right who saw it as bolstering the new welfare state regime. Many legal thinkers on both the Left and the Right felt that law and politics could not be separated in the way the positivists believed and that a heavy dose of sociology or political science was necessary to make sense of the crises of the 1920s. The line between law and politics, then, was being smudged in both theory and practice.

A further distinction – between inside and outside – was also becoming blurred. Germany, subject to recurrent Allied occupations and demands for reparations, had lost its sovereignty as a European power. Schmitt witnessed the occupation of the Ruhr area by the French army in 1923 at first hand. His nationalist indignation over an indeterminate grey area of interstate relations that was neither proper war nor proper peace but gave all the advantages to the stronger powers became an impetus to attack the League of Nations and the Versailles Treaty. Subsequently, many of Schmitt's closest pupils would describe how Schmitt had opened their eyes about the true nature (and limits) of law during the occupation of the Rhineland. Ernst Rudolf Huber, for instance, wrote in 1940 that 'it had to be a Rhinelander who revealed the situation politically and academically in such a way that there could be no more masking'. Huber even speculated in the same letter that Schmitt's subsequent preference for 'concrete thinking' had emerged in the concrete situation of the Rhineland occupation.[10] Perhaps it was also at this point that his preoccupation with discerning the real enemy – and the link of that recognition to political action – began.

International law, in Schmitt's view, was being reshaped by the Western victors to suit their own purposes. Accordingly, the League of Nations was merely an instrument for pursuing political goals under the veneer of a hypocritical ethical universalism centred on principles such as self-determination. Selective demilitarization, financial coercion and all kinds of police measures that stopped just short of proper war served as the means for a spurious legal universalism. Time and again, Schmitt pointed to what he called the 'fraud of anonymity' – the fact that Britain, France and the United States were imposing a victors' justice from behind the veil of international law. 'Whoever says humanity, wants to deceive' – Proudhon's claim, frequently quoted by Schmitt, summed up his view. He argued that the great powers would never become subject to international law in the way that weak states were. Accordingly, the supposed neutrality of international law towards small and great powers alike was either ineffective or hypocritical.

In 1923, Schmitt also made his first systematic attempt to undermine liberal parliamentarism with what has been called an immanent 'deconstructive critique'.[11] In a treatise best – but awkwardly – translated as *The Intellectual-Historical Situation of Contemporary Parliamentarism*, Schmitt set out an ideal model of parliamentarism as it had supposedly existed in the nineteenth century. Then, a bourgeois elite had represented the population as a whole, engaging in open, rational discussion to arrive at policy choices and ensuring broad publicity of their activities. Schmitt contended that the conditions for publicity and discussion were no longer given in a parliament where highly disciplined parties and special interests dominated debates and where backroom negotiations had replaced open parliamentary exchanges. Thus, a homogeneous bourgeoisie could no longer effectively represent the state as a whole – and while parliament as an institution might still exist, parliamentarism as a political principle had lost its legitimacy in the age of industry and mass politics.

Schmitt was hardly a true supporter of the earlier, idealized version of parliamentarism. His story of decline was a means to play off the ideal against the real without even believing in the ideal. Schmitt, after all, never had faith in open discussion as such. Liberals, he held, would never arrive at a decision, but postpone it in a futile effort to dissolve all truly political dilemmas into questions of either economics or ethics. Economic questions, or so they hoped, could be subject to negotiation and compromise, while ethical questions could be resolved through rational discussion. Liberals, in other words, fell victim to the same illusions as the Romantics who believed that an 'eternal conversation' would dissolve oppositions in a spurious 'higher third'. Deconstruction, then, was to serve the purpose of political destruction.

Schmitt also drew a stark distinction between liberalism and democracy.

Parliamentarism was a *liberal* principle of representation – and therefore had nothing to do with democracy. Democracy, on the other hand, defined by Schmitt as the 'identity' of governors and governed, was a real political concept. Consequently, in line with Schmitt's later definition of the political as the distinction between friend and enemy, it had to contain an agonal element. He claimed that democracy was founded on equality and that 'the democratic concept of equality . . . like all real political concepts refers to the possibility of a distinction. Political democracy thus cannot rest on the sameness of all human beings, but on belonging to a distinct people. Belonging to a particular people can be determined by very different factors (conceptions of shared race, faith, shared fate and tradition)'.[12]

Schmitt defined democratic equality as internal substantive homogeneity, which pointed to and depended on some external 'other' which could be excluded, thereby establishing the identity of the demos. In Schmitt's words, 'democracy requires, therefore, first homogeneity and second – if the need arises – elimination or eradication of heterogeneity'.[13] The requirement of equality in the sense of homogeneity was essential and could not be fulfilled by what he dismissed as the liberal 'abstract, logical-arithmetical games' and 'indifferent equality'; rather, it depended on a 'substance of equality'. In the past, such 'substantial equality' had been found 'in certain physical and moral qualities, for example in civic virtue, in *arete*, the classical democracy of *vertus* (*vertu*)'.[14] Recently, however, the distinction between member and alien had become a national one due to the fact that 'since the nineteenth century, belonging consists above all in belonging to a certain nation, in national homogeneity'.[15] The content of the 'other' was historically contingent, that is, it depended on the construction of national identities in the nineteenth century. In theory, however, the 'heterogeneous' could also be slaves, as in Athenian democracy, or the colonized, as in the Age of Empire. What supposedly remained a constant of political reality, however, was that 'there has never been a democracy which has not known the concept of the alien and which realized the equality of all men'.[16] Thus, the substance of equality could change over time, as long as equality remained 'interesting and valuable politically', which it did as long as it had substance, 'and for that reason at least the possibility and the risk of inequality'.[17]

Schmitt was one of the first commentators in Germany to draw attention to Georges Sorel's philosophy of direct action, violence and the action-inducing myth of the general strike.[18] Schmitt spoke admiringly of Sorel's idea that 'out of true life-instincts come the great enthusiasm, the great moral decision and the great myth'.[19] He saw Sorel's irrationalist theory of 'unmediated concrete life' as an advance over 'intellectualist' Marxism and in sharp opposition to the liberal ideal of rational compromise. Schmitt stressed that 'the great psychological and historical significance of the theory of myths could not be denied'.[20] While agreeing with Sorel on the sheer power of myths to generate the enthusiasm and courage necessary for any great moral decision, Schmitt profoundly disagreed on the question of what actually constituted the most powerful myth. He acknowledged the impact of the Marxist myth of the bourgeois, but argued that the Russian Revolution had been a success precisely because Lenin had managed to transform the myth of the bourgeois into a nationalist Russian myth. In this indigenous myth, the bourgeois became first and foremost a Westerner oppressing the Russian peasants. Only the fusion of socialism and Slavism into a powerful myth had brought the Communists to power. This demonstrated that 'the energy of the national was greater than that of the myth of the class struggle'.[21] Powerful myths were myths of an existentially threatening 'other', who could be cast as constitutive enemy. This sense of heterogeneity, of 'otherness', which was needed to mobilize politically through a myth and which in turn would be strengthened through myths, was most powerful in the case of *national* difference. In Schmitt's words, what was needed was 'a sensitivity for difference as such; all that is moving today in the direction of national antagonisms, rather than class antagonisms'.[22]

Schmitt's concern that under the conditions of the twentieth-century welfare state and mass democracy, the bourgeoisie could no longer effectively unite and represent the nation, his conception of democracy as dictatorship and his belief in the power of national myth all came together in his admiration of Italian fascism. Here, as early as the mid-1920s, Schmitt saw the combination of nationalism and plebiscitary dictatorship realized. He claimed that the fascists, through the creation of a national myth, had increased the civic and national self-confidence of the Italian masses, thereby restoring the dignity of the state based on national unity.[23] The fascists had realized that 'the Italian people could preserve their concrete way of national being only with a showing of political will'.[24] Not least, the leadership's identification of the enemy as an existential threat as another 'way of national being' had restored national unity and reined in the pluralism that had supposedly undermined the state.

Thus, already in 1923, Schmitt had constructed a complete antithesis of liberalism and democracy, which was to remain one of the axioms of his political thought. Democracy effectively had to be conceived as a Ceasarist, plebiscitary dictatorship based on nationalism, as in Mussolini's Italy. Rule by acclamation in the public sphere, as a form of direct identification with the leader and not the private act of voting, was the distinguishing feature of democracy. Thus democracy and dictatorship could become not only perfectly compatible – the latter could constitute the most authentic expression of the former.

Containing Democracy: Schmitt's Constitutional Theory

The 'golden years' of the Weimar Republic lasted from 1924 to 1928, as corporatist compromise came to characterize domestic politics and a policy of peaceful change was successfully pursued by foreign minister Gustav Stresemann. Schmitt, despite his rapidly growing reputation in Bonn, decided to leave the provincial Rheinish town and accept a job at the less prestigious School of Business Administration in Berlin in 1928. On the surface, Schmitt's *Constitutional Theory* from the same year, his first (and last) sustained treatise in constitutional jurisprudence, also signified a rapprochement with the principles of liberal democracy. Yet, despite the fact that the book explicitly aimed to offer a constitutional, as opposed to a state theory, his ambition clearly ran towards a reconstituted unified theory of the state in an age when the state appeared to have lost its integrative and representative functions.

Schmitt drew a fundamental distinction between a properly political part of the Weimar constitution and a rule-of-law (or *Rechtsstaat*) related, liberal and therefore ultimately apolitical part. The political part recorded and elaborated the decision on the fundamental constitution, that is, a 'total decision' on the 'form of political existence' which the people had supposedly chosen. The apolitical part dealt with a separation (rather than constitution) of powers and individual rights, which merely protected citizens from politics and could not constitute a state (or a politics) by themselves.

With regard to the political part of the constitution, Schmitt essentially conceived of it as a nation's free – and normatively groundless – decision. The nation was not the same as the state, defined by Schmitt as 'the status of political unity'. The state preceded and in fact constituted a precondition of 'national awakening', as absolutist princes had formed the political unity as a framework of political existence for the 'coming to consciousness' of the nation.[25] The nation, however, had given the state a new content or 'substance', and also increased state power through constant and conscious national mobilization, since the *Volk* now identified with itself in its state.[26] Referring to Sieyes's writings on the popular sovereignty of the Third Estate, Schmitt argued that the Abbé's teachings of the creative *pouvoir constituant* presumed 'the conscious will of a people to political existence, that is, a nation'.[27] The paradigm case of this was of course the French Revolution, when 'a people, with full consciousness, took its destiny into its own hands and made a free decision about the type and form of its political existence'.[28]

The power of the nation was therefore essentially unlimited, precisely because it remained unconstituted and the political national will remained present besides and above the constitution. To change the constitution, it was sufficient that the 'substance' of the state, that is, the nation, in the immediacy of its sheer power, reasserted itself.[29] Constituted power, that is, the state, as powerful as it might have appeared externally, was therefore always dependent on the will of a 'substantial' nation as the *pouvoir constituant* and its latent capacity to disrupt everyday, constituted politics. Conversely, what Schmitt then called the absolute constitution could not simply be changed by the constituted powers. Schmitt vociferously opposed those who thought that Article 76 of the Weimar constitution allowed simple Reichstag majorities to change essential parts of the constitution in the same way it could fix the spoils of particular interest groups.

Furthermore, Schmitt posited as one of the axioms of his constitutional theory that there were only two political forms, namely representation and identity.[30] He initially indicated that national unity had democratic consequences understood as the identity between the rulers and the ruled.[31] The *Volk* which had achieved political unity would always be directly present, and consequently could not be represented.[32] Immediately, however, he relativized this notion, arguing that 'a complete, absolute identity of the *Volk* with itself as a political unity' was impossible.[33] No state could dispense with either representation or identity entirely.[34] Representation had an existential quality, however, and no 'arbitrary, low way of being' could be represented.[35] Therefore, in contrast to a group of people who just happened to live together, the nation was capable of representation because it signified a 'heightened, more intensive way of being'. This was based on the *Volk* being identical with itself and present in the public sphere, as well as capable of national will and consciousness, that is, the capacity to distinguish friend and enemy.[36] Governments were to represent the nation, making an invisible being publicly visible. Thus, the nation acquired a transcendental quality and had to be represented in the same manner that, according to Schmitt, the Church represented a transcendental reality.[37] Summing up his theory, he claimed that the state rested on the identity of the *Volk* as a political unit constituted through its national will to distinguish friend and enemy, and on the representation of this political unity through the government.[38]

Thus Schmitt had not only provided an original interpretation of liberal democratic constitutionalism; under the guise of discussing constitutionalism he had once more played liberalism off against a notion of democracy that had little to do with actual individual citizens exercising any kind of collective self-determination. Mass democracy was apparently affirmed, and yet immediately contained and made compatible with authoritarianism through the categories of representation and identity. Thus Schmitt had also provided what he now thought was a means of salvaging the political unity of a strong state in the age of mass politics. In the end, *Constitutional Theory* was a brilliant conservative effort in deconstructing and containing mass democracy.

A Mine that Explodes Silently

In the opening sentence of what was to become his most famous (or infamous) work – a typical Schmittian opening, one that generated more flashes than light–Schmitt claimed that 'the concept of the state presupposes the concept of the political'. The state, according to Schmitt's initial assessment in *The Concept of the Political*, had lost the monopoly of the political: the ability to determine friends and enemies. This was due mainly to the rise of what Schmitt called 'self-organizing society', which had taken over parts of the state as well as the streets in what looked like a potential civil war. He argued that 'the equation state = politics becomes erroneous and deceptive at exactly the moment when state and society penetrate each other'. With liberal democracy and the transition to the modern welfare state of the twentieth century, society occupied the state, but the state also came to invade and regulate almost all aspects of society. Schmitt termed this new constellation 'the quantitative total state' – a state in which potentially everything could become political, and everything subject to state regulation and intervention. But what precisely was the political? Schmitt offered a definition of the concept – or, rather, the criterion – of the political which was to haunt him for the rest of his life:

> The specific distinction to which political actions and motives can be reduced is that between friend and enemy . . . Insofar as it is not derived from other criteria, the antithesis of friend and enemy corresponds to the relatively independent criteria of other antitheses: good and evil in the moral sphere, beautiful and ugly in the aesthetic sphere, and so on. . . The distinction of friend and enemy denotes the utmost degree of intensity of a union or separation, of an association or dissociation. It can exist theoretically and practically, without having simultaneously to draw upon all those moral, aesthetic, economic, or other distinctions. The political enemy need not be morally evil or aesthetically ugly; he need not appear as an economic competitor, and it may even be advantageous to engage with him in business transactions. But he is, nevertheless, the other, the stranger; and it is sufficient for his nature that he is, in a specially intense way, existentially something different and alien, so that in the extreme case, conflicts with him are possible.[39]

Schmitt stressed that only the actual combatants could correctly recognize who the enemy was. Moreover, politics, by definition, was a matter of public, not private enemies. Schmitt claimed that 'an enemy exists only when, at least potentially, one fighting collectivity of people confronts a similar collectivity. The enemy is solely the public enemy, because everything that has a relationship to such a collectivity of people, particularly to a whole nation, becomes public by virtue of such a relationship'.[40]

Initially, then, the political was defined as an autonomous sphere of collective life. However, a few years later, when Schmitt had read the criticisms of Leo Strauss, he was to repudiate this view of the autonomy of the political. Strauss had argued that the conception of the autonomy of the political remained within the 'horizon of liberalism', since it was based on the idea of a differentiation of value spheres which, for instance, Max Weber had expounded. 'The political' as merely a distinct domain would remain caught in the same cultural logic. Therefore, Schmitt shifted to a definition of the political as purely a matter of *intensity*, so that any antithesis, if it was strong enough, could become political. Thus it was not the substance of enmity that mattered, but the intensity of an existential threat. The litmus test for the political nature of an opposition was essentially the danger of mortal combat and death. As Schmitt put it, 'the friend, enemy, and combat concepts receive their real meaning precisely because they refer to the real possibility of physical killing. War follows from enmity. War is the existential negation of the enemy'.

Here then was the link between the concept of the political, constitutional theory and state unity. State unity was constructed to a great degree through a decision on the enemy. Unless the state had lost the monopoly of the political, this meant an external enemy. If any internal polarization reached sufficient intensity to turn political, the state had a civil war on its hands – and effectively ceased to exist. As Schmitt's contemporaries already noted, this theory was based on circular reasoning, as the existential decision both established and presumed a political unity.

Nevertheless, *The Concept of the Political* was yet another ingenious attempt to reassert the distinction between state and society. It was directed against pluralists like Otto von Gierke in Germany, and Harold Laski and G. D. H. Cole in Britain, who treated the state as just one association among many. Schmitt reaffirmed the distinctiveness of the state by emphasizing the power to demand the sacrifice of an individual's life for the sake of preserving the political unit.

In this context, Schmitt also refined his critique of liberalism, which he now viewed as depoliticizing and politicizing at the same time. He claimed that 'in very systematic fashion liberal thought evades or ignores state and politics and moves instead in a typical always recurring polarity of two heterogeneous spheres, namely ethics and economics, intellect and trade, education and property'. But politics remained destiny, and liberalism's attempt at escaping the logic of the political was either self-deceptive (and therefore self-defeating) or hypocritical: liberalism would either destroy the political unit in question or it would assert political values against its enemies and therefore violate its own principles of neutrality. For Schmitt, humanitarianism and universalist international law were particularly glaring instances of liberalism's inconsistent wavering between impotence and immoderation.

Those opposed to Weimar soon realized that Schmitt had provided them with another supremely effective weapon in the battle against liberal democracy. Ernst Jünger, for instance, wrote to Schmitt that, today the rank of an intellect is determined by its approach to the question of armament. You have succeeded in a technical-military invention of a special kind: a mine that explodes silently. One watches how, magically, the wreckage caves in, and the destruction is done before anybody knows it. For myself, I feel particularly strengthened by your substantial food for thought.[41]

Jünger's reference to armament was not accidental. After all, much as Schmitt would later deny it, the distinction between friend and enemy had a primarily military dimension. Recognizing the real enemy was crucial for the capacity to engage in politics – and arming oneself adequately required unmasking the enemy, a revelatory experience that so many of Schmitt's students, especially of his pieces on international law, seem to have shared.

An appeal to clear distinctions between friends and enemies could not fail to be attractive in an age when clear oppositions and distinctions appeared to be dissolving entirely. Musil's General Stumm, for instance, necessarily had to founder in his vain effort 'to bring some order into the civilian mind' by putting together a 'Domesday Book of modern culture': 'After taking inventory of the Central European stock of ideas, he had not only discovered to his regret that it consisted of nothing but contradictions but also been amazed to find that these contradictions, on closer scrutiny, tended to merge into one another'.[42] Schmitt's silent mine was consciously planted in a culture that appeared to have lost all sense of proper oppositions and demarcations – a culture in which the enemy had become indeterminate, and in which indeterminacy had become the enemy.[43]

The mine's intended target was not least liberal modernity itself, with its futile attempts to mediate oppositions and neutralize conflict through irony and utility. After all, Schmitt wanted the *Concept of the Political* to be read in conjunction with his 1929 essay, 'The Age of Neutralizations and Depoliticizations'. In this piece, originally delivered as a lecture in Barcelona, Schmitt came as close as he ever did in his pre-war writings to an overarching historical interpretation of modernity' – although he pointed out that he did not want his paper to be understood as a philosophy of history.[44]

Schmitt claimed that modern Europe had moved through a number of stages in its attempt to 'neutralize' contentious and antagonistic 'central spheres' of human life. Europeans had first tried to 'neutralize' the religious central sphere in the sixteenth century, as it had given rise to endless theological disagreement and successive religious wars. Subsequently, they had sought to neutralize the 'metaphysical' sphere in the seventeenth century, the moral-humanitarian sphere in the eighteenth and the economic sphere in the nineteenth, before arriving at 'technology' as the latest hope for a 'neutral' sphere in the twentieth century.

However, the modern European quest for neutralization proved to be continuously frustrated: rather than neutralizing a sphere and abolishing enmity and political conflict for good, a new central sphere of conflict would open up somewhere else. Thus, a dialectic came to characterize the quest for neutrality. Every shift to a new central sphere only created a new battlefield, as novel and intense conflicts of people and interests emerged on the new, supposedly neutral ground. The political simply could not be expunged from the modern world – and its moralization or juridification would only exacerbate its inevitably evil aspects.

Into the Brightly Lit Room: The Outsider as Insider

As Weimar, burdened by the Great Depression and torn apart by the extreme Right and the extreme Left, was heading towards the political abyss, Schmitt began to network himself into the inner circles of power. He also became a popular speaker with major industrialists. Heinrich Brüning, the first Chancellor to govern without a majority in the parliament, but by presidential decree, had rebuffed Schmitt's attempts to act as an *éminence grise* in the corridors of power. The confidants of General Schleicher, Minister of Defence and a heavy influence on the octogenarian President Hindenburg, however, became increasingly interested in the lawyer from the School of Business Administration. Schmitt had started to advocate that the president, rather than the courts or parliament, act as what he called the 'guardian of the constitution' during times of crisis. Rather disingenuously, he called the president a neutral power, drawing on the conception of a *pouvoir neutre* which Benjamin Constant had elaborated for the French monarch in the early nineteenth century. The special legitimacy of the president was not constituted by legality, but through the will of the people who had directly elected him. Schmitt, reversing an earlier position, now advanced an argument according to which Article 48 of the Weimar constitution granted the president unlimited emergency powers. These would permit the president to combat what Schmitt saw as the danger of an unchecked party pluralism destroying an increasingly dysfunctional political unity.

Schmitt also sought to close down what he termed the 'equal chance' of parties opposed to the political system as a whole. He claimed that the state needed to defend itself against the danger of what he called a 'legal revolution'. Schmitt warned about a legal entry into government for parties which would then benefit from what he termed the 'political premium of power', that is, the use of governmental and legislative power to 'close the door of legality behind them'. Thus, Schmitt clearly saw the dangers of a democratic suicide. As an antidote, he advocated a strong leader, bolstered by a strong bureaucracy, who was to ban radical movements and govern by decree.[45] The 'quantitative total state', in which the self-organizing society permanently produced an excessive pluralism that undermined the state, had now effectively lost the monopoly of the political. In other words, it had lost the capacity to distinguish friends and enemies, to the parties and street movements fighting each other to the death. What needed to be re-established, Schmitt claimed, was the 'qualitative total state' – an essentially Hobbesian authoritarian solution.

As part of this authoritarian solution, Schmitt justified the so-called *Preußenschlag* [strike against Prussia] of July 1932, whereby the central government took over the administration of Prussia, which had been in the hands of democratic parties for the entire period of the Weimar Republic. By installing the Reich Chancellor as commissar, the government had sought to end what was seen as a fateful 'dualism' between Prussia and the Reich, but also to gain control of the Prussian police force in case of a civil war. Schmitt had not been involved in planning the strike, but he defended this measure in the most spectacular court case in modern German constitutional history, 'Prussia versus the Reich'. In October 1932 the Leipzig High Court decided that the actual suspension of the Prussian government had been unlawful, but that the Reich government also had the right to install a commissar. This judgement, interpreted by the government as a de facto victory, but experienced by Schmitt as a defeat, confirmed Schmitt's misgivings about the role of courts in guarding the constitution. Berlin now hosted three governments that could claim some legitimacy in deciding Prussia's fate. But Schmitt's ultimate question – *quis iudicabit*, who decides? – had not been answered.

Schmitt, now a 'star lawyer' of the Reich despite the defeat in Leipzig, was offered a professorship at the University of Cologne, after some hesitation by Cologne's mayor – Konrad Adenauer apparently judged Schmitt to be a 'difficult character'. At the same time, Schmit now frequently remarked in his diaries how 'proud' he was to be close to power. He was frantically preparing further authoritarian measures for Schleicher, who was to become Chancellor in December 1932. One plan was for the president not to accept 'negative majorities' in forming a vote of no confidence and thereby govern against a nominal majority; another was to declare a state of emergency and suspend elections for an indefinite time. However, by early 1933 Schleicher lost the trust of Hindenburg, who was always eager to be seen as being faithful to the constitution, without being stigmatized as a democrat – a position not that dissimilar from Schmitt's. When Hindenburg chose not to declare a 'constitutional democracy' – a euphemism for a de facto presidential dictatorship – by appointing Hitler on January 30th, the Nazis had succeeded in their legal march to a revolution. In his diaries, Schmitt, who had already lost touch with the inner circles of power at the beginning of the year, recorded severe depressions – and too much wine-drinking. His laconic judgement was that 'the old man had gone mad'.

Nevertheless, when on a trip to Rome in March of 1933 a call reached him to serve as Prussian Councillor of State, he was ready to accept immediately. Schmitt was to elaborate new legislation which was to complete the destruction of German federalism, the work he had begun in 1932. Heidegger also wrote him a note urging him to join the revolution, and Schmitt soon found himself at the centre of Nazi power, enjoying Göring's particular patronage. He finally returned to Berlin as a full professor at the University and as a member of the prestigious, albeit perfunctory, Prussian State Council – an institution designed by Göring to effect a fake marriage of Prussian tradition and Nazi revolution – which also included cultural luminaries such as Wilhelm Furtwängler.[46] Yet the fact that Schmitt had become a follower relatively late – as party member No. 2,098,860 – left him under suspicion of being an opportunist.

Schmitt did his best (or, rather, worst) to dispel such suspicions. In a number of articles in newspapers, he railed against the emigrants, claiming in 1933 that they 'had been spat out from Germany forever'. In the summer of 1934, he justified the murders of the 'Night of Long Knives', in which Nazi thugs killed not only the leaders of the SA, who threatened to become a centre of power rivalling Hitler and the army, but also Schleicher and his wife. Schmitt cynically claimed that 'the Führer protected the law', as the leader was automatically the highest judge of the land, for whose decisions there could be no appeal.[47]

Schmitt was not merely the willing legal executioner of pre-existing Nazi plans. He sought to elaborate his own constitutional framework for the new state, entitled *State-Movement-Volk*, in which he declared the old Hegelian notion of the state dead.[48] Instead of the strong state that had to defend itself against a self-organizing society, Schmitt now offered an unholy trinity of state, movement and people, which were to be united by the Führer. Homogeneity – *Gleichartigkeit* – was now replaced by *Artgleichheit*, that is, racial homogeneity among the people. The leader, as an almost mystical embodiment of the *Volksgemeinschaft*, expressed the popular will. Thus Schmitt could claim that 'law is the plan and the will of the leader'.

Schmitt retained some elements from his quasi-fascist vision of the 1920s, but radicalized it further. Under the influence of the French institutionalist Maurice Hauriou, he came to repudiate decisionism alongside positivism, now opting for what he called 'concrete order thinking'.[49] In fact, decisionism, he now proclaimed, could be as arbitrary and abstract as legal positivism and normativism. Real legitimacy was based on an already existing 'concrete order' of institutions, not on 'abstract legality'. Order and institutions supposedly preceded norms, and institutions also preceded and defined individuals.[50]

This new jurisprudence finally appeared to solve the problem of legal indeterminacy that Schmitt had already confronted in his dissertations. Racial homogeneity made judicial decisions determinate, as both judges and the people were part of an overall 'concrete order' preserved by the Führer. Thus, there was complete identification of the people with the leader through being of the same racial substance, and 'species sameness' became a substitute for the categories of identity and representation. Moreover, the leader was now a wholly *immanent* figure – a position which stands in stark contrast to the model of representation Schmitt had previously advocated with reference to the Catholic Church.

Yet, Schmitt was still salvaging statist elements for the new order – while other younger and more radical Nazi jurists sought to subordinate everything to the movement. They argued that any notion of the state, let alone the rule of law, even a National Socialist one, would contaminate the new order with traces of liberal constitutionalism. What neither Schmitt nor his competitors initially realized was that the Third Reich destroyed jurisprudence itself. Hitler hated intellectuals and he certainly did not want academic lawyers to constrain him in any way; nor did he want a constitution or a party programme to limit his actions.[51] As one Nazi functionary put it,

> just as the old state will not return, the old state theories will have no meaning. It is equally futile to write learned treatises on the nature of the new state; here the pens are scratching in vain, too. What the new state structure will look like in ten years, only one man knows, the Führer alone, and he will not let himself be influenced in his knowledge by scholars, be they ever so learned.[52]

Schmitt's former student Franz Neumann saw much more clearly that the 'Behemoth' of Nazi rule would soon turn into a 'non-state, a chaos, a situation of lawlessness'.[53] And what mattered in an increasingly 'polycratic' political system was less law than 'access to the incumbent of power', as Schmitt was to put it in a slim volume written during the 1950s.[54]

Schmitt was useful for a while, as his authority could help with the *Gleichschaltung* [coordination] of the German legal system and the legal profession – but 'leading the leader', as Schmitt had imagined he could, turned out to be an intellectual's hubris. Not only did the Nazis not need him – he was also participating in a regime that made the permanent exception the rule and, even by his own standards, exacerbated the problems of legal indeterminacy which had preoccupied him in the 1920s. His jubilant cry after the Nazi seizure of power that 'we are learning again how to distinguish' was self-deceptive. As he was only to recognize much later, National Socialism accelerated the fateful modern developments he deplored, rather than provide a model of political action to restrain them.

The Crown Jurist and his Fall

For now, Schmitt continued to accumulate offices and influence. He also unleashed his antisemitism, calling for the removal of books by Jewish authors from law libraries and for marking the Jewishness of legal scholars in all publications. At a 1936 conference in Berlin on 'German Jurisprudence in the Struggle against the Jewish Spirit' – the nadir in the history of German jurisprudence – Schmitt concluded his rabid antisemitic speech with Hitler's words from *Mein Kampf*: 'By fending off the Jew, I struggle for the work of the Lord.' This was no mere opportunistic ornamentation. The new 'German jurisprudence' based on 'species sameness' that Schmitt was elaborating was suffused with anti-universalism, anti-individualism and antisemitism through and through.[55]

Outside Germany, Schmitt was soon labelled the 'Crown Jurist' of the Third Reich by his former friend Waldemar Gurian, a Catholic intellectual who had emigrated to Switzerland and who would eventually teach at the University of Notre Dame. Aurel Kolnai dedicated large parts of his *War against the West* to Schmitt, portraying him as the most able defender of 'an unchecked sovereignty of group egoism and self-worship', with his friend/enemy distinction as the best example of the 'grammar of tribal subjectivism couched in a scientific phraseology'.[56] Jacques Maritain, who had once shared Schmitt's affinity with the fascist *Action Française*, saw Schmitt as one of 'the most intelligent theoreticians of National Socialism' who advocated a 'sovereignty of hatred' as the foundation of a 'pagan Empire'.[57] Karl Löwith, one of Heidegger's most brilliant students, offered one of the most devastating critiques when he charged Schmitt with 'Romantic occasionalism', arguing that Schmitt would always decide in favour of the decision (and thereby in favour of whoever happened to be in power) – irrespective of substantial convictions. In other words, try as he might to appear as a true Nazi – Schmitt was ultimately not only the kind of Romantic he himself had condemned, but a nihilist without any real beliefs whatsoever.

In fascist countries, Schmitt was also portrayed as the foremost proponent of a specifically National Socialist approach to law. In Italy, his texts appeared in the volume *Principles of National Socialism*. He enjoyed close contacts with Gaetano Mosca and Julius Evola, while the representatives of the official fascist philosophy of Hegelian 'Actualism' claimed that Schmitt's thought did not *go far enough* in a 'universal renewal of state and man'.[58] It was also the Italian fascists who claimed that Schmitt had lost a sense of Roman statehood and that his thought had moved too far in the direction of *Völkishness*. Nevertheless, Schmitt did eventually have the opportunity to meet Mussolini in 1936. During their conversation, Mussolini supposedly declared a number of times that 'the state is eternal, the party transient', which must have chimed with Schmitt's thinking.[59]

For all his international fascist fame and despite his loyal services to the Nazi regime, protection by Göring and ever more rabid antisemitism, Schmitt fell victim to internal Nazi and university intrigues in an increasingly factionalized political system. In 1936 the SS magazine *Schwarzes Korps* attacked him openly and polemically, playing on old suspicions about his Catholic background and former Jewish acquaintances. Eventually he was forced to resign from almost all his positions. Even so, the anti-Berliner Schmitt remained a professor at Berlin University and a Prussian State Councillor until the disappearance of Prussia itself.

After his resignations, he wrote a self-consciously esoteric book on Hobbes, *The Leviathan in the State Theory of Thomas Hobbes: Meaning and Failure of a Political Symbol*. On one level, it could be read as testimony to Schmitt's disillusionment with the total state, which he himself had advocated before 1933, and which now threatened to destroy him.[60] On another level, however, the book could be seen as ratifying the final end of the Hobbesian state as it had emerged in the sixteenth and seventeenth centuries. The state had offered protection in return for obedience – or so, according to Schmitt, went the axiom of the Hobbesian solution to the religious strife of the early modern period. This axiom had now also been violated by the National Socialists, who withdrew their protection from an obedient Schmitt.

However, Schmitt's *Leviathan* was hardly a veiled form of resistance alongside, for instance, Ernst Jünger's famous novel *On the Marble Cliffs*, as Schmitt's apologists later claimed. After all, the destruction of Leviathan had begun, so Schmitt argued, when the 'Jew Spinoza' found a liberal loophole in Hobbes's authoritarian construction. Once the state had conceded a private sphere to its citizens in which freedom of thought and religion were guaranteed, subversive Jewish lawyers could claim that the state had to serve individuals and their religious freedom. Eventually, the Leviathan was disembowelled by a moralizing and self-organizing society led by self-serving semites. Schmitt thus combined vile antisemitism with a melancholic retrospective on the state.

Escape towards Great Spaces

Taking leave of the state did not mean that there were no other authoritarian political forms left for Schmitt to advocate, as he tried to regain a position of intellectual leadership in the Third Reich. Towards the end of the 1930s, he turned his attention primarily to international affairs. He claimed that with the end of the state, a particular European interstate law, or what Schmitt called the *ius publicum Europaeum*, had also ended. This kind of international law, as a supposedly 'concrete order', had ensured limited war between sovereign states and its regular army combatants on the model of a duel.

The *ius publicum Europaeum* had come to be complemented by a law centred on the sea, elaborated by the sea-faring powers – above all, Britain.
These two kinds of international law were rooted in different forms of consciousness, which in turn produced different conceptions of space.[61] It was
also predicated on a Eurocentric world-view and the exploitable lands which
European powers could colonize, thus preventing war in Europe from ever
becoming a total war. Unrestrained warfare remained limited to the colonies and the as yet unconquered spaces of the globe.

Yet, as the 'open spaces' outside Europe had finally been filled by the end
of the nineteenth century and as the colonies became state territory of the
empires, the distinction between Europe and the colonies began to break
down. The *ius publicum Europaeum*, underpinned by a family of European
'kings, states and nations', had been dissolved into a fictitious international
law of heterogeneous states.[62] In other words, once the European family of
states had been extended globally, the system had effectively ceased to exist;
instead there was only a chaotic co-existence of incommensurable norms,
as there could be no international law at all without a common 'civilization'.[63]

In Schmitt's view, towards the end of the nineteenth century the US had
left behind its concrete, isolationist order centred on the Americas in favour
of an aggressive 'dollar diplomacy' and an unholy alliance with the universalism of the British Empire.[64] Consequently, it had now adopted an imperialist 'world ideology', which justified interventions anywhere in the name
of humanitarianism. This 'world ideology' hypocritically used universalist,
general concepts of international law to intervene in the service of its own
interests.[65] Because of the dispersed nature of the British Empire, he argued,
the defenders of the Empire resorted to universalism to further their own
interests, in particular the safety of the sea lanes. Freedom of the seas always
meant nothing more than freedom for the power that currently ruled the
seas.[66] This universalism, which in turn facilitated total war in the name of
a spurious 'humanity', was allied with a liberal individualism expressed in
the interwar treaties for the protection of minorities. Such treaties again
allowed for powers alien to a particular space to intervene in the politics of
that space without restraint.

The Western European powers, advancing hypocritical pacifist-human-
itarian goals, had also turned to a 'discriminating concept of war', which no
longer recognized the equal standing of a combatant state, but aimed at

its utter destruction.[67] The Treaty of Versailles sought to keep in place an impossible dualism between a global, hypocritically humanitarian international law, which ensured the continuing vitality of the British Empire, and a Balkanization of Europe into 'small states', both of which ignored the underlying development towards what Schmitt called 'great spaces'.[68]

Schmitt seemed to waver, however, between the suggestion that Versailles had been a ploy by the Western powers to keep Germany weak and contained, and the view that the order of Versailles had been objectively inappropriate to the new 'spatial dimensions' and economic structures of Europe.[69] In any case, it was necessary to reconceptualize international law as a concrete order and launch a frontal attack on Western universalist norms. This new international law was to replace the principle of the equality of sovereign states with a hierarchy of *Reiche*, or empires, based on race, space or ideology, while an archaic notion of Germanic 'faith' was substituted for fundamental principles like *pacta sunt servanda* (pacts must be respected). Schmitt himself did not use the biologistic category of *Lebensraum* [space for life] and belonged to the geopolitical, rather than racist strand of National Socialist theorizing on international law. Yet his anti-universalist and anti-normative thought could easily be filled with racist categories. Moreover, the whole idea of a jurisprudence focused on 'concrete' situations lent itself to political opportunism through its built-in vagueness and the flexibility to affirm any newly created order. Not surprisingly, then, Schmitt's conceptualization came directly to legitimise Hitler's policies of conquest.

Nazi Visions of World Order

Two weeks after the Third Reich had invaded what remained of Czechoslovakia after Munich created the 'Protectorate Bohemia and Moravia', and just four months before Hitler unleashed the Second World War, Schmitt unveiled a new theory of *Großräume* [great spaces] to supersede the system of nation-states.[70] At a time when the Third Reich had taken actions which could not possibly be justified in terms of a necessary revision to the Versailles Treaty or the protection of ethnic Germans in Eastern Europe, Schmitt, the 'foremost proponent of *Geojurisprudenz*', provided concepts and categories to legitimise Hitler's decisions.[71] His theory effectively gave the Third Reich free reign in the East, while claiming that the Western powers had no right to intervene in the 'great space' which the Nazis were establishing. Schmitt's theory made the invasion appear to be an appropriate contribution to a new world order, and was widely discussed in both the German and foreign press.[72]

Schmitt advised Hitler to declare a European Monroe Doctrine which would prohibit the intervention of 'powers alien to the European space'.[73] The great space as an 'order-inducing' legal principle would preserve the political, since it provided a new criterion of demarcation.[74] The empires at the core of each great space were based on a particular *Volk*, and the *Großraum* in general on homogeneity, just as the German federation in the nineteenth century had been based on national homogeneity.[75] For Schmitt, Eastern Europe, excluding the Jews, constituted such a homogeneous *Großraum*.[76]

Schmitt claimed that the concept of *Großraum* originated in the 'technological-economic-organizational sphere', where crucial developments had been taking place during a time when the state was weak.[77] This new notion of space was said to be 'dynamic' and 'qualitative' in contrast to a neutral-mathematical notion of space. According to Schmitt, such a new concept of space could not be grasped by either legal positivism or traditional theories of the balance of power and spheres of influence.[78]

Other National Socialist theorists of international law argued for the *Volk* as the exclusive organizing principle and basis of the *Großraum*. For Schmitt, however, *Volk* was 'too imprecise, too disorderly and undisciplined a concept'. It could not replace the traditional state in the way envisaged by some National Socialists. Simply relying on *Volk* meant to overlook the 'real achievement of order' by the state.[79] The concept of *Volk* on its own did not provide a sufficiently new principle to overcome the nineteenth-century idea of the nation-state and to create a new order.[80] Rather than relying on supposedly 'natural' racial and national characteristics for the 'new ordering of the Earth', Schmitt argued that the new central units of the international system, that is, the *Reiche*, needed 'a great measure of conscious discipline, increased organization and the capacity to create out of one's power what could only be created and secured with enormous resources of human understanding, namely a modern polity'.[81] The old states had ensured the order and discipline comparable to a duel, a war relationship between states of 'order to order'.[82] In short, the holist notion of *Volk* was insufficient as a new 'concept of order' to structure the international law envisaged by Schmitt, and in fact posed the perverse danger of 'a *völkischer* universalism'.[83]

Thus, Schmitt defended the *Reich* as a new conception in international law, which carried over the elements of order and discipline contained in the concept of the state. The *Reich*, unlike the state, also did justice to the supposedly new 'planetary consciousness' of space without destroying all demarcations in a universalist 'world law'.[84] Schmitt seems to have realized that the complete replacement of the 'formal state' by the organic *Volk* would also have entailed an end to the notion of 'limited wars' and the equality of combatant states which he had cherished in the old *ius publicum Europaeum*. In other words, the hierarchy of entirely racialized *Großräume*, which the more radical Nazi theorsts were proposing, would have destroyed the *ius in bello* as well. Nevertheless, Schmitt clung to the idea that the *Reich* was to supersede the colony-centred British and French Empires. Great spaces were supposed to secure peace through the flexible notion of 'soil' and a potentially neo-medieval organization of overlapping, but clearly hierarchical sovereignties.

While Schmitt's vision differed from the utopian plans of most of the Nazi legal scholars who wanted to annihilate international law and reconstruct it through a complete biologization of the social, it shared their underlying anti-universalist thrust.[85] Moreover, neither Schmitt nor any other Nazi ideologist ever elaborated on the legal relationships between different great spaces, other than the imperative to preserve their 'spatial purity'. Analysis stopped short with the regionalization and racialization of international law. In the end, as one contemporary observer put it, Schmittian geo-jurisprudence was 'neither law, nor geography, nor politics'. If anything, it was the 'projection of National Socialist power dreams and wishful spatial thinking into the sphere of jurisprudence'.[86]

As such power dreams began to be shattered, Schmitt still did his part for Nazi propaganda. In 1943 and 1944 he criss-crossed Europe from Lisbon to Bucharest to lecture to foreign lawyers and dignitaries as part of the Nazis' cultural policies.[87] Schmitt conferred with fellow intellectuals like Mircea Eliade, and was also received by 'Professor Antonescu', that is, Ion Antonescu, the dictator of Romania. Everywhere, he defended a vision of Europe asserting itself against Anglo-Saxon fake universalism in the West and Bolshevist nihilism in the East. Yet, he also subtly recast the political expression of his conservatism. In lectures on the 'The Historical Situation of European Jurisprudence', he now told a story about the emergence of a common European legal civilization as a 'concrete order'. This legal civilization was in danger of being destroyed by accelerated or 'motorized' legislation. Even worse was the increasing conflation between law on the one hand, and decrees and measures on the other. Schmitt called upon fellow lawyers in European countries to act as guardians of the common European legal heritage. In short, Schmitt reverted to a classically conservative account of politics and legal determinacy. It was inspired by the nineteenth century German lawyer Friedrich von Savigny and centred on notions of traditional legitimacy and gradual change. Under the impression of the cataclysmic failure of National Socialism, political conservatism – a position Schmitt had resisted up until now – became the default option for the philosophically conservative Schmitt.

Tales of the End

As the fortune of the War turned against Germany, Schmitt also escaped into eschatological and literally elemental ruminations. In what appeared to be a children's tale, told to his daughter Anima, Schmitt gave an account of world history based on the fundamental opposition between land and sea. Here hatred of hypocritical Anglo-American universalism was mixed with admiration of English courage to enter the open seas and found a rival world order.

For a while, Schmitt still had hopes for the possibility of creating a Nazi world order. He now referred to a 'concrete order' with the Greek word *nomos*. *Nomos*, he held, should not be translated as 'law', as is commonly the case. Rather, he claimed, it was related to the German verb *nehmen* – to take or grab. This relation, according to Schmitt, was not at all accidental, as all establishments of a concrete, lasting order began with an appropriation of land. The old *ius publicum Europaeum*, for instance, had been inseparable from imperialism. The new *nomos* of the twentieth century, expressing a rescaling of actual political spaces, had to be based on new powers appropriating land – as well as the air space which had become available with airfaring technology. Consequently, Schmitt could claim that

only in struggle can the new *nomos* arise. Many see in it only death and destruction. Some believe that they are experiencing the end of the world. In reality we are experiencing only the end of the former relationship between land and sea . . . Also in the cruel war of old and new powers, just measures arise and meaningful proportions form. Here, too, gods are and rule / Great is their measure.[88]

The last lines, drawn from the German poet Hölderlin, foreshadowed a final shift from elemental mythology to eschatology. After what appeared as decades of abstinence from political theology, Schmitt now suddenly put his trust in the *Katechon*, a figure mentioned in Paul's second epistle to the Thessalonians. There the *Katechon* appears as an anti-utopian force restraining the arrival of the Antichrist, ensuring a deferred eschatology. For Schmitt, one world united by nihilism and technology loomed ever larger, as the Nazis' attempt to create a new *nomos* and thereby a meaningful organization of political space was foundering in front of his eyes.

On the first day of February 1945, Carl Schmitt gave what was to become his last university lecture. Soon after he was drafted into the ragged ranks of the *Volkssturm*, Hitler's last army of the very young and the very old, to defend Berlin. On April 30th, he was arrested by the Red Army, only to be released after a few hours of interrogation. In August he was already writing a defence of the principle *nullum crimen, nulla poena sine lege* in preparation for defending businessmen like Friedrich Flick at the Nuremberg trials. In the autumn, he was arrested and interrogated by the Americans as a 'security threat', only to be released in autumn 1946, when he registered his profession in Berlin as a 'freelance scholar'. In March 1947, he was interned again as a 'possible defendant' at Nuremberg and interrogated by Robert Kempner and by Ossip K. Flechtheim, who formed part of Telford Taylor's staff at Nuremberg. In heated exchanges with Kempner, Schmitt portrayed himself as a mere scholar – and, occasionally, as an 'intellectual adventurer'. He finally returned to Plettenberg on May 21st 1947. Yet, as it happened, for the most disgraced jurist of the Third Reich, the intellectual adventure was far from over.

Part II
The Afterlife: The Uses and Abuses of Antiliberalism

Now, I'm sure you can see – I've made certain that the drawing shows this clearly – when looking at any set of ideas in action, that it draws its supplies of additional troops and intellectual matériel not only from its own depots but also from those of its opponents; you see how it keeps shifting positions and how it suddenly turns unaccountably against its own backup forces; you can see ideas constantly crossing over to the other side and back again, so that you will find them now in one line of battle, now in the other. In short, there's no way to draw up a decent plan of communications or line of demarcation or anything else, and the whole thing is – though I can't actually believe what I'm saying! – what any of our commanding officers would be bound to call one hell of a mess!

Robert Musil, *The Man without Qualities*

Masks and Mirrors

All deception is and remains self-deception.

Carl Schmitt, 1947

Nobody could possibly have predicted in 1947 that Carl Schmitt had a great part of his intellectual life still ahead of him. That year Schmitt returned from American internment to his hometown of Plettenberg, where he was to live for almost forty years, in what he called a 'world of greatest tension'.[1] Supposedly, he had been ready to emigrate to Argentina or stay in Spain after a series of lectures in 1944, but in retrospect he claimed that he could not 'live without his enemies'.[2] 'Internal exile' seemed preferable – except that the exile was partly due to his steadfast refusal to undergo a process of de-nazification. He was never to teach at a German university again.

After much heated internal debate, he was also refused admission to the German Association of Professors of Public Law, when it was refounded in 1949 – despite, or perhaps because of, the fact that, in many ways, the Association remained deeply conservative and was to be directed by a number of Schmitt's pupils. At the time there was a suspicion that by excluding the Crown Jurist of the Third Reich, many lesser jurists of the Third Reich could be included.[3]

Many of the public lawyers who had undergone de-nazification and dis-
tanced themselves from their brown past, remained undercover partisans of
extreme nationalism and authoritarianism. One of the most spectacular
cases was that of Schmitt's colleague Theodor Maunz. Maunz, who had distinguished himself under the Nazis with the argument that wars for a *Großraum* could not be unjust, had a stellar career in the Federal Republic.
One-time Bavarian culture minister, he also co-authored the standard commentary on the Basic Law, a work that was continued by the later Federal
President Roman Herzog. A few weeks after his death in 1993, it was discovered that under a pseudonym he had penned articles for the far-right
Deutsche National-Zeitung for decades.

Inevitably, Schmitt's 'case' became caught up in the politics of post-war
memory and *Vergangenheitsbewältigung* – the German effort to come to
terms with, or – literally – 'overcome' the past.[4] In a country that until
recently accorded enormous social respect to lawyers and public jurists, the
behaviour of the legal profession during the Third Reich remained taboo.[5]
Schmitt's public presence was either an embarrassment or a provocation –
while his defenders felt that attacks on Schmitt were a cheap way to prove
one's democratic credentials to the post-war powers that be. As Jacob Taubes
put it in no uncertain terms: 'every adjunct professor in political science has
to give a kick in the arse of Carl Schmitt, claiming that friend/enemy is not
the right category'.[6]

Nearly all articles by Schmitt, and in particular, the *Festschriften*, which
Schmitt's friend and students devoted to him, became subject to intense
controversy.[7] For decades, it was asked why one should waste one's time on
a jurist who lacked a 'moral minimum', and a sense for 'justice and decency'.[8]
Such claims were countered by two groupings of thinkers whom one might
distinguish as 'anti-moralizers' and 'modernizers'. The former sought to dissociate moral judgment from politics altogether and pointed to the timeless
insights into political realism which they believed Schmitt had offered. The
latter often conceded Schmitt's character flaws, but argued that elements of
his political theory could be updated and applied in the rapidly modernizing Federal Republic. In parallel to these tendencies, taking Schmitt's measure was often a form of apprenticeship for younger liberals who sought to
think seriously about dangers to the fledgling West German democracy.

Gradually, a peculiar dynamic developed in these controversies. Those
who argued that Schmitt was morally discredited to such an extent that all

his political and intellectual arguments should be dismissed had to contend with the counterclaim that such a policy was itself immoral. In the discussions on Schmitt, a logic of what one might call mutual moral unmasking was established, a logic which could also be found in larger (and more significant) debates about the past. This logic necessarily led to increasing polarization: Schmitt's opponents projected his opting for the Nazis back onto his earliest writings, while those eager to defend Schmitt were inclined to justify all his pre-Nazi writings as essentially democratic. As Bernhard Schlink once pointed out, 'it is not enough for Satan to be Satan; he must be a fallen angel'.[9]

The Invisible Counter-College: Resentment and Realism

Schmitt had claimed in front of Robert Kempner that he sought to retreat into the 'security of silence' after the cataclysmic mid-century events. Soon, however, the man who now called himself an 'outlaw' (using the English expression) re-established contact (and ongoing conversations) with friends and old colleagues.[10] These quickly formed an informal network to support Schmitt in the so-called 'Academia Moralis'. Throughout the 1950s they organized a series of semi-secret seminars and gatherings at which Schmitt could speak and meet other intellectuals. After much bureaucratic infighting, they also ensured that he received a state pension from 1952 onwards.[11]

Rather than retreat into silence, Schmitt in fact established a counter-public sphere; a conservative 'invisible college'. It found its intellectual coherence in a counter-canon centred on the works of the counter-revolutionaries Donoso Cortés and de Maistre, and their supposed political realism. This almost self-contained intellectual world defined itself against the 'licensed public sphere', that is, the media licensed by the Allies, which supposedly 'destroyed everything'. According to Schmitt, 'whoever dances on that stage, has already been judged . . . no matter what he actually says'.[12]

In the same vein, Schmitt only had contempt for all the major intellectual trends of the immediate post-war period, whether humanism, Europeanism, Christian personalism or neo-liberalism. The humanist calls for a 'return to Goethe' seemed to him anachronistic and ridiculous. Jacques Maritain, a one-time Schmitt ally who had moved from Catholic authoritarianism and an admiration of the *Action Française* to a humanist and personalist conception of democracy, had become *cauchemaritain*. In his diaries Schmitt also sneered at humanist liberals such as Karl Jaspers,

Theodor Heuss and Gustav Radbruch, whom he denounced as the intellectual 'pin-ups' of the post-war era.[13]

Above all, Schmitt seethed with resentment against the émigrés who had returned to Germany and were supposedly 'enjoying their revenge'. Hardly less contemptible were fellow radical right-wing intellectuals such as Heidegger, Jünger and the poet Gottfried Benn who had made a successful 'comeback' in the Federal Republic.[14] They were loathsome not only for their relentless public self-promotion, but also for their hypocrisy and, worst of all, their apparent inability to understand the true situation into which Europe had fallen. What left-wing critics were to deride as a restoration of pre-war traditions, was for Schmitt a mere 'salvaging of stranded objects' from the Wilhelmine era – which was true of Ernst Jünger no less than it was of Thomas Mann.[15] But then who was Schmitt himself in this world-historical morality play? It was a question he posed over and over in his public and private post-war writings. And it was a question to which he had many answers.

Solitude and Self-deception

Schmitt named his house in Plettenberg San Casciano – after the place where Machiavelli had retreated when the Medici banned him from the Florentine Republic. Schmitt consciously constructed this parallel with the author of *The Prince* – like Machiavelli himself, he thought, he was actually not a Machiavellian. As a proper Machiavellian he would have hidden the hard truths about politics and simply flattered the rulers. Time and again, he lamented that with his exposition of the friend–enemy relationship he seemed to have broken a profound taboo, and attracted the very moralized enmity which he had condemned.

There was a further allusion hidden here, however. San Casciano was the scholar whose students had stabbed him to death with their pens. Yet, Schmitt not only felt betrayed by his pupils, he was also intensely anxious about the dangers of self-deception. In his first post-war book, *Ex Captivitate Salus*, a mixture of essays and diaries from his time in the internment camp, Schmitt retreated deeply into the self, despite his general loathing for romantic introspection.

In his so-called 'wisdom of the cell', thrown back upon himself and his 'last reserves', even 'naked', Schmitt attempted to rethink the deepest presupposition of politics, namely enmity – and its flip side, identity.[16] He returned to the subject of modernity as such – Descartes's subject and the ego of Max Stirner, the nineteenth-century German philosopher of 'singularity'. Both, faced with situations of solitude, were anxious about self-deception, as, according to Schmitt, 'self-deception belongs to loneliness'.[17] Descartes, for fear of being deceived by a *spiritus malignus*, had put on a mask to fend off deceptions and thereby become *l'homme au masque*. The ego of 'poor Max', on the other hand, had armoured itself for a similar purpose – and yet, according to Schmitt, 'self-armouring' had in fact been the highest form of self-deception. The real enemy, as an 'objective power', could not be deceived in any case – but the deceived self, in its deceptive efforts at avoiding confrontation with the enemy, had delivered itself to the enemy completely.[18]

What role then was reserved for the enemy? Schmitt asked: 'whom can I recognize as my enemy at all?' And he answered:

> Obviously only the one who can put me into question. By recognizing him as my enemy I recognize that he can put me into question. And who can really put me into question? Only I myself. Or my brother. That's it. The other is my brother. The other turns out to be my brother, and the brother turns out to be the enemy. Adam and Eve had two sons, Cain and Abel. Thus begins the history of mankind. Thus looks the father of all things. That is the dialectical tension which keeps world history moving and world history has not yet come to an end.[19]

Thus, recognizing the dialectical 'splitting power of the ego', Schmitt suddenly seemed to be ready to put his image of the sovereign, self-sufficient and static self into question. The self was neither complete nor clearly delimited. Most importantly, the enemy now turned out to be personal, after all. Here, one of Theodor Däubler's verses supposedly provided a crucial insight. Däubler had written that

> *Der Feind ist unsere eigne Frage als Gestalt.*
> *Und er wird uns, wir ihn zum selben Ende hetzen.*

> The enemy is our own question embodied
> And he will hound us, and we will hound him to the same end.

In other words, it was based on this capacity to put each other radically into question on a personal basis that true enemies could recognize each other. This mutual dependence – rather than a mere mutual positing – also put into

question the strict demarcations which had characterized Schmitt's changing theories of *public* enmity. Consequently, Schmitt could now hold that
annihilation of the other would necessarily amount to self-annihilation.
Ultimately, Schmitt's anxiety about ambiguity and indeterminacy as the
signs of modernity appeared to make him retreat again from this more dynamic, dialectical and, to some extent, indeterminate account of hostile
brotherhood. In his diaries he returned to the long-held desire to banish indeterminacy:

> Franz Kafka could write a novel: the enemy. Then it would have become
> visible that the indeterminacy of the enemy creates anxiety [Angst] (there
> is no other kind of anxiety, and it is the nature of anxiety to sense an in-
> determinate enemy); against this, it is a matter for reason (and in this
> sense of high politics) to determine the enemy (which is also at the same
> time self-determination) and with this determination anxiety ceases and
> remains at most fear.[20]

The naked, vulnerable Schmitt who had been presented in the cell soon
returned to his old self, ready to take on those who put him into question.
Once again, *Distinguo ergo sum* became the proper foundation of both
political and personal identity: 'I think, therefore I have enemies; I have
enemies, therefore I am myself'. Perhaps self-preservation had required self-
armouring and therefore another self-deception. But perhaps self-pity had
been a deeper cause of self-deception than self-armouring. In any case:
Schmitt would remain nailed to his mask until the very end.[21]

The Real Enemy
The labyrinth of self-examination had ended in yet another hall of mirrors,
in which Schmitt recognized the faces not only of his outright enemies, but
also of his 'hostile brothers' and deceptive friends. All these perspectives
defined him at a moment when his self seemed to have become completely
unmoored, and cast adrift in world-historical currents. Yet, to avoid self-
deception, self-definition also came with straightforward identifications.
    Schmitt wished to be seen as a Tocqueville of the twentieth century who
had to witness Tocqueville's nineteenth-century predictions come true, as
the globe was being divided between the United States and the Soviet
Union. He cried out that 'today from West and East children and creatures

of the European spirit itself meet on our old and sacred soil'.[22] The old European elites – with Schmitt himself as a typical representative – were left helpless. He lamented that 'our old poor Europe has at all times been a field for invasions from all directions' and that whatever appeared to be left of the sovereignty of European nations was a sham.

Schmitt also drew a parallel between himself and Melville's *Benito Cereno*. To the naïve American Delano, the Spaniard appeared to be the captain of the slave ship *San Dominick* – in fact, the slaves had captured the vessel and forced Cereno, under the threat of death, to follow their commands, while pretending to outsiders that he was still in charge. Schmitt claimed that Cereno, whom Melville described as giving the impression of an 'invalid courtier', 'has become a symbol of the intellectuals in a mass-system'.[23] For Schmitt, the recent past had been characterized by 'the treason of the intellectuals', as Julien Benda's famous title indicated. But Schmitt understood this not as betrayal *by* the intellectuals *of* the masses, but *of* the intellectuals *by* the masses, that is, the slaves who had taken command of the ship of state.

Schmitt saw himself as the 'last conscious representative of the *ius publicum Europeaum*, its last professor and scholar in an existential sense'. He supposedly experienced 'its end in the way Benito Cereno experienced the journey of the pirate vessel'.[24] Against the ideologies which now animated the moral crusades of Anglo-American liberalism and Soviet Communism, Schmitt disingenuously defined himself as an observer and as a jurist caught between theology and technology. He had merely diagnosed the end of modern statehood – and, very much in vain, assumed the role of the defender of a morally neutral European statecraft capable of containing war. Yet, somehow, the diagnostician had been mistaken for a prophet. Not surprisingly, then, he came to claim that 'woe to the diagnosticians! The anger directed at Ernst Jünger's "Worker" and perhaps even more my "Concept of the Political" is the anger of the sanatorium director at the doctor who diagnoses a case of the plague!'[25]

If nothing else, this Olympian perspective on the *longue durée* of European modernity effected a moral flattening of the ideological landscape of the twentieth century. Like other compromised conservatives, above all Arnold Gehlen and Hans Freyer, Schmitt escaped into global politics and world history to make the 'German catastrophe' a minor episode in a much larger world-historical (and apocalyptical) narrative which was still unfolding.

Ultimately, for all their theoretical and sometimes psychological sophistication, Schmitt's post-apocalyptical reflections were self-exculpatory and self-pitying. He never made a single statement admitting his complicity in the crimes of the Third Reich, nor did he ever express any empathy for its victims. His diaries, which were apparently intended for posthumous (and self-exculpatory) publication, are characterized by a profound antisemitism, in which the Jew – and the assimilated Jew in particular – appears time and again as the real enemy throughout the ages. It was also here that the self-declared 'theologian of jurisprudence' dropped the mask of the innocent jurist left among the ruins of world history. Ultimately at stake was the 'real Catholic intensification (against the neutralizers, the aesthetic decadents, against the abortionists, corpse burners and pacifists. . .)'[26]

The assimilated Jew appeared as a sign of the ambiguity and indeterminacy that had come to characterize modernity more generally. Already, in 1929, Schmitt had registered the 'feeling about being deceived which one could detect everywhere since the nineteenth century'. Indeterminacy, as Schmitt had put in his supposedly Kafkaesque account of the dynamics of enmity quoted above, constituted the cause of anxiety – and required a decision about the real enemy, piercing through his masks and 'mimicry'. Ultimately, it seemed that behind the complex theorizing lay nothing but a politics of antimodern paranoia – a paranoia expressed most clearly, but also most clandestinely during the post-war period, in Schmitt's profound antisemitism.

An Epistolary Empire

In a letter to a Portuguese colleague, Schmitt described *Ex Captivitate Salus* as the 'intellectual cry of help by a legal scholar in today's global situation'.[27] Schmitt made sure the cry was heard in all corners of the old continent. He sent copies of what appeared to be his most intensely personal book to many major European intellectuals, from Emile Cioran (who claimed to have been deeply moved by it) to Norberto Bobbio, who praised its 'profound autobiographical "pathos"'.[28]

As Schmitt diagnosed the decline of Europe (and not just Germany), he also sought a self-consciously European conversation in a post-European age (the phrase is George Lichtheim's). The conversation revolved around Europe's fate in a world dominated by two powers which based their claims on what Schmitt saw as nihilist nineteenth-century ideologies. Schmitt single-handedly managed to create through correspondence what lavish conference and publication grants fail to establish today: a small-scale, but genuinely European public sphere, in which lines of communication extended from Franco's legal advisors to conservative Greek jurists, from the Italian Marxist Left to Welsh literary scholars.

Schmitt had always been a brilliant self-promoter, and he now consciously created a new network of promoters and pupils in Germany itself. Whatever means were necessary were used to leverage his deeply damaged reputation. The religious scholar Jacob Taubes has related how he had innocently written to Armin Mohler about how the Israeli Justice Minister, engaged in drafting a constitution for the new state, had asked for Schmitt's *Constitutional Theory* to be fetched by soldiers from the beleaguered library at Mount Scopus. At the time, Mohler happened to be Ernst Jünger's secretary and the letter quickly found its way to Schmitt who sent copies to all corners of Europe. The fact that 'the Jew Taubes' had writen this 'important document' clearly impressed many of those he corresponded with.[29] Such strategic forwarding was complemented by a judicious policy of dedications in what soon amounted to a virtual epistolary empire – an empire based on the doctrine that 'unfortunately there is no longer a public sphere and the most important is said in letters'.[30]

Schmitt considered letters an initiation or continuation of conversation by other means, and his talk soon covered all of West Germany and Western Europe. He kept his interlocutors in thrall by hinting at 'taboos' and *arcana* of all sorts, thereby establishing a secret society of the initiated, of which he retained ultimate control. The correspondence was also a means for suggesting clandestine metaphysical and historical correspondences, ideally suited for those who not only wanted to be educated by Schmitt, but also to be kept guessing. At the same time, he encouraged a morally charged historicization of his own oeuvre, selectively distributing documents relating to his career, and subtly encouraging interpretations of himself as the last defender of the *ius publicum Europaeum*.

Mostly, however, Schmitt sought to convey the impression that he was above it all. Like Heidegger, Benn and Jünger, he displayed a more or less disingenuous stance of distance or even resignation. Heidegger's *Gelassenheit*, Jünger's *desinvolture*, Gottfried Benn's 'static existence' and Schmitt's retreat into the self which he had exemplified in *Ex Captivitate Salus* were all seemingly quietist gestures of those who declared themselves publicly misunderstood and whose political intentions were now being misconstrued in a liberal witch-hunt.[31] Those philosophical conservatives who had once been eager to act in politics now centred their philosophies on notions of passivity or mere responsiveness to higher forces. Heidegger claimed that thinking was thanking, while Schmitt conceived of the task of individual human existence as 'giving a response', or *Antwort tun*. But such exalted and openly displayed stances of passivity allowed for an even more effective underground intellectual activity.

Stigma and Enigma

An increasing number of scholars made pilgrimages to 'San-Casciano-in-the-Sauerland'. Schmitt, a man of enormous courtesy, charm and even cordiality, knew how to capture the young and the impressionable for his counter-public sphere (he also had a great talent for playing them off against each other). According to Odo Marquard, however, Schmitt sought conversations with the young not least because 'he wanted to be present (and be present in the future) as the kind of person whom he would have liked to have been'.[32] He had a real anxiety to influence – and the fact remained for many of his admirers that Schmitt was not only exciting, but also excitable. All day-to-day developments seemed to hold deeper meanings – through his intuitive mind, 'like a motor running day and night', everything appeared to be 'interesting' and lead to further intriguing political-cum-cultural associations.[33]

Many of those who were now in their early and mid-twenties had returned from the battlefield or the prison camp disillusioned and prematurely aged. Soon to be labelled the 'sceptical generation' by the conservative sociologist Helmut Schleksy, they were wary of 'ideologies' and strong identifications, whether with the state or the nation.[34] As Roman Schnur, one of Schmitt's closest disciples claimed, they were 'a generation in the shadows who were rarely set by others on a certain path of life, who had to find their own way'.[35] A figure like the self-styled 'invalid of the global civil war', who had the time and the talent to intensively cultivate intelligent young followers, could play an unusually critical role in this situation. As an acerbic critic opposed to all that the Federal Republic stood for, he was also an inspiration for younger intellectuals who sought to form their own opinions or adopt a self-consciously nonconformist attitude. During a time when a premium was put on stability and 'no experiments' (as Konrad

Adenauer's famous election slogan ran), they were tempted by what Gott-fried Benn had once called 'dangerous and endangered thinking'.

If nothing else, in the confusion and intellectual instability of the 'global civil war', Schmitt offered the returnees from the War a historical and philo-sophical framework to make sense of the cataclysmic events in which they had been caught up. In the words of one of the ex-soldiers who fell victim to his spell, Schmitt seemed to offer nothing less than a 'rendezvous with the world spirit' – even for those who did not necessarily share the more directly political views of the man who, after all, called himself a 'partisan of the world spirit'.[36] Consequently, Schmitt adopted the role of *Doktorvater*, or mentor, of a number of younger intellectuals, and trusted adviser for a number of antiliberal publications. Few, however, acknowledged the man from Plettenberg (and Schmitt himself advised many not to do so, as it might damage their career prospects).

Schmitt's involvement with the Nazis became a 'stigma and enigma' – and for some the fascination with the enigma became stronger than the danger of the stigma.[37] Ultimately, however, the private intellectual universe, into which an increasing number of young intellectuals were drawn, was a world turned morally upside down. A curious transvaluation seemed to have occurred. The victims of National Socialism became the new persecutors, crimes against humanity were perpetrated on the Germans, and the Federal Republic was more totalitarian than the Third Reich. Students, alongside family and friends, were also drafted into performing poetry and private plays which drew on the symbols of this private universe and, frequently, re-enacted a self-serving version of Schmitt's life – as the victim who had been swallowed by the Leviathan and then spat out.[38] These pieces were printed and distributed to further an image of Schmitt as part of a *samiszdat* that was conservative *and* radical at the same time. This private mythology of a supposedly persecuted intellectual in turn challenged his young followers to find meaning behind the various masks and mirrors.

The steady stream of visitors did not only wash up acolytes at Schmitt's modest bungalow in Plettenberg, however. Rudolf Augstein, the editor of *Der Spiegel*, came to see Schmitt as much as did the leading Social Democrat Carlo Schmid. Once, Schmitt even encountered the Christian Democrat Chancellor, Helmut Kiesinger – a fact that the East German propaganda publication *Grey Book* made much of in its attempt to prove that the West German government was still controlled by old Nazis.[39] Some of these visitors sought genuine advice from Schmitt. Augstein, for instance, wanted Schmitt's opinion on a law suit which his magazine was pursuing before the Constitutional Court.

Eventually, Schmitt sought to claw his way back into the German public sphere. In the first years after the War, he published under a pseudonym, (partly to make money in economically desperate circumstances). Then he anonymously published a call for an amnesty after the supposed 'civil war' of the preceding years.[40] Schmitt was delighted every time he could smuggle some conservative contraband into the mainstream media.[41] In his diaries he noted that

> in Christ und Welt a beautiful column by me has been printed, with an ad for Nivea cream inserted. It's good that way. In Tsarist Russia the nihilists draped their bombs in flower bouquets. Why should I not frame my analogous concerns with Nivea cream? Or, conversely, appear as the frame for Nivea cream, in order not to irritate the persecutors?[42]

Finally, his name reappeared in prestigious journals and even in *Die Zeit* – what later became the liberal, Anglophile flagship of German journalism was then still subject to a major battle between nationalist and more liberal editors.[43] Eventually, the fiercely liberal Gerd Bucerius and Countess Dönhoff won the battle and put an end to Schmitt's presence in the pages of the weekly.[44] Still, no less than four books also appeared in 1950, and, as part of his initial 'escape into the public', Schmitt authored reviews and occasional pieces, gave a number of radio talks and republished much of his work from the 1920s. He also advised German industrialists on how to construct legal arguments against pending nationalizations.

Schmitt remained a figure both absent and present in the early Federal Republic. For the majority, he seemed to play the role of an evil *éminence grise* who served as a reminder about the past and the treason of German intellectuals (conservatives in particular). But for a significant minority, because of his outsider status he seemed to occupy a central point of magic attraction and hold the key to insights which were no longer politically welcome in West Germany. For instance, in a law journal in 1950, one writer argued that Schmitt had a 'strong, Lucifer-like mind, whose radiation could illuminate the spiritual situation of our age like a flash of lightning.'[45] Yet, what were these supposed illuminations?

In Search of Stability I: Schmittianism in German Constitutional Jurisprudence

> When I read the Basic Law, the amusement of an omniscient old man comes over me.
>
> Carl Schmitt, 1949

How could a liberal democratic constitution last in what appeared to be a profoundly illiberal society? Were there – or could there be – any real guarantees for a democratic West Germany after 1945, other than the ultimate sovereignty of the Allies? The anxiety that Bonn would become Weimar was, unsurprisingly, one of the deepest concerns behind much political and legal theorizing in the post-war period. It led to an incessant search for sources of stability and social cohesion, as well as for instruments of democratic self-defence. In fact, the 'master idea' in constructing the Federal Republic turned out to be stability, a concept that initially derived from technology and the natural sciences, and did not enter political language until the nineteenth century.[1]

Guarding the constitution became a preoccupation – even if views of who should do the guarding diverged widely between a strong president, the courts and even the unions. The issue seemed settled when the Constitutional Court emerged as the widely accepted occupant of this role after a number of landmark decisions in the late 1950s. In particular, the Court handed down a seminal judgement in the so-called Lüth case of 1958. There the judges defended the right to free speech of Hamburg's director of information, who had called for a boycott of the film *Immortal Lover* by Veit Harlan. Harlan had been popular with Goebbels and had made antisemitic films such as the infamous *Jud Süss*. The Court used the case to reinterpret basic rights, which had so far been understood exclusively in terms of defence mechanisms against the state, as principles which permeated the entire legal order.

Subsequently, the Constitutional Court, alongside the *Bundesbank*, became the most respected public institution of the Federal Republic. Critics, on the other hand, persisted in deploring the 'juridification' of German politics. Not the least of these critics was Carl Schmitt. After all, for Schmitt the guardian of the constitution had to be a *person*, ideally the head of the state. The power of the Constitutional Court, in contrast, posed the danger of a 'government by judges'. Schmitt eventually agreed with the famous formula: Bonn was not Weimar. Things were worse: Bonn was Karlsruhe (the seat of the Constitutional Court).[2]

Nevertheless, in general Schmitt lacked interest in the Federal Republic. He did write on the constitution occasionally (curiously, his first article on the subject appeared under a pseudonym in the magazine of German railwaymen).[3] Yet there was a certain logic to this lack of interest. The Federal Republic possessed neither full sovereignty nor political unity in Schmitt's sense – and therefore, in his eyes, could hardly be taken seriously as a proper state. What called itself a state was at best a functional mechanism without any genuine legitimacy.[4] Schmitt, as the self-styled diagnostician of the end of European statehood, did not wish to attend to what he perceived as the distasteful disembowelling of the Leviathan.

Not surprisingly, however, Schmitt's thought (and fate) loomed large for those who continued to doubt that liberal democracy could guarantee its own preconditions and who felt that courts could not and should not guard the constitution. In particular, the search for more or less secure guarantees took constitutional theorists into familiar territory where Schmitt had mapped out a strong executive as the most plausible guardian of the constitution. Even those who did not share this vision, however, tended to confront and test the new order with concepts and questions from Schmitt's Weimar oeuvre. The Schmitt sound, so to speak, turned out to be the *basso continuo*, and sometimes a sharply discordant note, in many post-war debates of legal theory and state law.

The Father of the Founding Fathers?

There is a long-standing debate on whether Schmitt could legitimately be called 'the father of the fathers of the constitution' of the Federal Republic.[5] After all, despite his lack of interest in the West German state as such, Schmitt suggested that his *Constitutional Theory* remained as relevant to the Federal Republic as to the Weimar Republic, when the book was reissued in the 1950s. Above all, he saw himself vindicated in a number of the basic characteristics of the constitution.[6]

One was Schmitt's seminal distinction between *Verfassung* [constitution] and *Verfassungsgesetz* [constitutional law].[7] The former referred to the very essence of the constitution, and in particular, in Schmittian parlance, its political form such as a democracy or a monarchy; the latter simply designated particular constitutional provisions. The constituting power, according to Schmitt, had made a fundamental decision in favour of a political form of existence – and this form had to be guarded and should not be changed by majorities, however large. Constitutional amendments and 'breaking through' the constitution as such [*Verfassungsdurchbruch*] had to be carefully distinguished.

On this account, the Weimar constitution had not only permitted amendments, but also revision – thereby allowing its own destruction. To avoid the possibility of a 'democratic suicide', the constitution of the Federal Republic included an article, the so-called eternity clause, closing off the possibility of abrogating the fundamental principles underlying a liberal-democratic order. In a Schmittian interpretation, the German people, by voting in large numbers in the first Federal election in 1949, had made an existential choice for democracy. The constituted powers could not simply then change the basics of the constitutional order. *Superlegality* – another concept which Schmitt had appropriated from Maurice Hauriou – stood above constitutional laws and protected the 'concrete political order'. In Schmitt's view, it referred to the legitimacy of the constitutional order – not to a higher form of legality which would then be ensured by the Constitutional Court.[8] For him, a representative person would have been a far more appropriate embodiment of such legitimacy.

However, even among Schmitt's followers there was disagreement over whether the Basic Law was the outcome of a basic decision. Ernst Forsthoff, one-time assistant of Schmitt and a highly influential professor of administrative law after the War, claimed that the constitution was the product of a situation, that is, the devastating circumstances of defeat, rather than a decision. As a consequence, the constitution continued to lack the kind of clarity and sharp definition of legitimacy that came with a proper decision.[9] According to Forsthoff, this lack of a decision in turn led to a general insecurity in constitutional matters and a fateful democratization of constitutional interpretations. Given the supposedly indecisive character of the constitution, all and sundry, from theologians to journalists, could compete in constitutional interpretations, Forsthoff complained.[10]

Werner Weber, a former doctoral student of Schmitt's, concurred that while in 1919 the German people had made a real decision, in the deliberations of the Parliamentary Council in Bonn no fundamental choices could be made.[11] Rarely, in fact, had a 'European-Occidental constitution' been created 'with so little publicity'. Moreover, the entire process of constitution-making had lacked 'political immediacy'. Yet, what often appeared to be arguments for more political participation and even direct democracy always turned into calls for more authority – whether for the bureaucracy or for a new *pouvoir neutre* to 'keep the state together'.[12]

Weber warned that in a misguided attempt to exorcise the demons of Weimar, the creators of the Federal Republic's constitution had simply defined away the state of exception and the need for a strong executive. He claimed that 'for sure, the enormous vital power of the political, which had not been avoided during Weimar, seems to have been outwitted in the Basic Law. But it will nevertheless break into Germany from inside and outside'.[13] The existential, uncontrollable quality of the political could only be kept in check by a strong executive. Yet, that quality was not only to be feared – it was also to be cherished and celebrated. From such a perspective, liberal constitutions would always be too weak and too strong simultaneously: too weak to contain the political and yet too strong to let the existential and therefore life-affirming quality of the political emerge fully.

Finally, there was the idea of a 'militant democracy' or *wehrhafte Demokratie* – a democracy capable of defending its political substance against its enemies. This concept had first been clearly defined in 1938 by the exiled German political scientist Karl Loewenstein, as one European country after the other was taken over by authoritarian movements using democratic means to disable democracy.[14] Loewenstein had argued that democracies were incapable of defending themselves against fascist movements if they continued to subscribe to 'democratic fundamentalism', 'legalistic blindness' and an 'exaggerated formalism of the rule of law'.[15] Since democracies could not compete with fascism in political 'emotionalism', they had to find political and legislative answers to anti-democratic forces, such as banning parties and militias, and restricting the rights to assembly and free speech.[16] As Loewenstein put it, 'fire should be fought with fire' through a new 'disciplined' or even 'authoritarian' democracy.[17]

In less extreme versions, this idea became highly influential in the Federal Republic, leading to the banning of both the Nazi Socialist Reich Party and the Communist Party in the 1950s, and the draconian measures against those guilty by (suspected) association with leftist terrorists in the 1970s.[18] An equal chance to gain power was denied to those who sought to use power for anti-democratic ends. And the task of defending the substance of the constitution mandated its defenders to clearly identify friends and enemies. Above all, unlike in Weimar, legality and legitimacy were to be reunited, as all such measures were supposed to be mandated by specific articles in the Basic Law. However, as many critics on both the Right and the Left eventually pointed out, such a substantial, antipositivist understanding of the constitution could have decidedly illiberal results. Those dissenting could be stigmatized as 'enemies of the constitution'. In fact, just as, according to Schmitt, those in power were in possession of a 'political premium', those in a position to offer the authoritative interpretation of the constitution would benefit from possessing the 'spirit of the constitution' and be able to cast out supposedly disloyal citizens.

Many of Schmitt's pupils criticized the tendency to treat the constitution as the real sovereign of the Federal Republic. Ernst-Wolfgang Böckenförde, a left-leaning Catholic and Social Democrat who would later sit on the Constitutional Court, emphasized that the constitution had to be preceded by – and remain based on – a state.[19] Any constitutional provisions relied on a pre-existing form of political unity, whether that of a people or inhering in a monarch. The constitution could shape and stabilize this unit – but a sovereign constitution, free-standing and somehow above the people (in the case of a democracy), was a normativist fiction. As Schmitt had taught all along, no norm applied itself, and as soon as deeper conflicts emerged within the constitutional state, the true sovereign would emerge. In other words, the vision of a material constitutional state as an attempt to extinguish sovereignty altogether was necessarily doomed to fail.

Such normativist fictions and reductions themselves constituted what Ernst Forsthoff was later to call 'introverted rule of law thinking' – a way of thinking about the constitution which simply explained away the hard questions about political unity and stability. The rule of law, or the *Rechtsstaat*, had always been thought of as the protective 'coat' around the state – with so many legal theorists attempting to diminish the role of the state, the coat would not remain standing without a body inside. However, like Böckenförde, Forsthoff held that conflicts endangering the political unit would expose introverted legalistic illusions for what they were.

Two Schools of Social Integration

Most schools of thought are initially imagined and polemically labelled by their opponents. This was the case with the so-called 'Schmitt school' of constitutional thought after 1945. Like all interesting schools, it was highly heterogeneous; indeed, it was not always clear what those who were initially identified with it had in common other than a personal admiration for Schmitt. However, as intellectual positions solidified during the early 1950s, it became clear that these jurists did share a tendency towards statism as well as decisionism, and a propensity for treating constitutional questions in existential terms. They also shared a sentiment of being outsiders, or even victims, in some of the debates in constitutional law. Within the Association of German Professors of Public Law, they were increasingly seen as a distinctive group – causing Gerhard Leibholz, a prominent liberal who had returned from exile in England, to perceive a 'National Socialist shadow faculty' of law.[20]

Members of the Schmitt school, consisting of both anti-moralizers and modernizers, mostly sought to update Schmittian ideas without losing, or even compromising, any of Schmitt's core positions. These theorists – for the most part Schmitt's pupils from the 1920s, fewer from the 1930s – had almost all internalized Schmitt's critique of liberal democracy. Almost all of them attacked the central role of the Constitutional Court, which, like Schmitt, they saw as the 'breeding ground of apocryphal acts of sovereignty'.[21] The dilemma they faced was that they could not openly advocate any authoritarian solutions to the threats of instability in general, or of a socialist takeover of the state in particular – and therefore often had to resort to rather ingenious redescriptions of Schmittian prescriptions. Nonetheless, there remained clear limits to such a redeployment of Schmitt's categories, as no fundamentally different political form seemed available after the *Reich* had foundered as a political order.

Those willing to think beyond Schmitt, however, broke new theoretical ground, when they attempted to come to terms with what to them appeared to be a structural change in the nature of statehood.[22] They agreed with Schmitt that the nineteenth-century rationalist state and the liberal rule of law, or *Rechtsstaat*, had passed into history. However, rather than adopting a stance of resignation, they forged new concepts, which in many cases served the attempt to restrain what they perceived as the development towards socialism or more democracy. In particular, these concepts were used to attack the de-formalization of law that these thinkers associated with the welfare state, or *Sozialstaat*.

Followers of Schmitt were hardly the only thinkers preoccupied with questions of stability and social cohesion. The single most important rival group of public jurists was the 'Smend School', members of which took the 'integration doctrine' of Rudolf Smend as their starting point. Smend had already formulated most of this doctrine in the 1920s, when it carried decidedly nationalist overtones.[23] At that time, Smend had essentially argued that political unity – one of Schmitt's central concepts – could not be considered as either existing or not existing, as Schmitt had regarded it. Rather than adopting such a static view, Smend claimed that social integration was a dynamic process which depended on the ethos and the experiences of individual citizens. Somewhat akin to Ernest Renan's famous conception of the nation as a daily plebiscite, Smend's antipositivist doctrine relied on shared values – although, rather than citizens consciously affirming certain values, integration was mostly 'unconscious' and resembled Hegel's 'cunning of reason' in that it seemed to take place behind individuals' backs.[24] Integration was thus not so much a matter of theoretical reflection, as of empirical observation. The process of integration had to be understood, rather than philosophically constructed.

During Weimar, Smend had an ambivalent relationship with democracy. He argued that democratic integration was best achieved through plebiscites and political symbols such as the national flag, but also through general pride in the political system. Citizens had to come together in an ever renewed 'total experience' of the state.[25] This experience had to be rooted in the values which emerged from a particular country's history. Culture and law came to be intimately connected, in particular through the ordering by

rank of values at the heart of the constitution. Thus, Smend's theory combined a de-formalization of law with an emphasis on everyday political
reality and cultural history – a combination which at one point made him
think that Italian fascism was best placed to achieve social integration in the
circumstances of mass democracy. Yet, after the War, Smend positioned
himself as one of the foremost defenders of liberal democracy, inspiring
many young Social Democratic lawyers who were to become leading constitutional theorists. In particular, he justified the prominent role of the
Constitutional Court on the basis that the Court's highly visible role added
to citizens' political education and overall experience of the state.[26]

Members of the Smend and Schmitt Schools battled vigorously, and
sometimes viciously, throughout the 1950s and 1960s, while Schmitt and
Smend themselves kept a polite distance, hardly ever missing the chance to
congratulate the other on a birthday with bland letters and postcards. The
pupils' battles in legal theory were fought over two issues in particular: the
role of values in holding the polity together and the relationship between
state and society; or more specifically, the relationship between the rule of
law and the welfare state.[27]

Resisting the 'Tyranny of Values'

One of the ironies of the post-war debate on constitutionalism and legal
theory was that decisionism *and* positivism were widely held to have facilitated the rise of the Third Reich – in other words, Schmitt *and* Hans Kelsen
became culprits in a jurisprudential morality play. Positivism in particular
was blamed for having left German jurists morally defenceless vis-à-vis a
regime which could claim that 'law is law' even for criminal acts.[28] Few
seemed to remember (or want to remember) that in the early 1930s Schmitt
had abandoned both positivism and decisionism in favour of 'concrete
order thinking'. Even fewer remembered that Nazi law in general was closer
to natural law thinking – albeit not in content – than positivism.[29]

As a result of this rejection of positivism there was a brief flowering of
natural law in legal thought, and, subsequently, a much more extended and
philosophically complex search for secure foundations to fortify the liberal-
democratic order. In particular, the 'material value-philosophy' of Max
Scheler and Nicolai Hartmann appeared as a non-religious alternative to
natural law thinking. Such material, Christian-inspired conceptions had
initially been behind the judgements of the Constitutional Court – a fact

not unrelated to the prominent role of the Church as one of the very few untainted public institutions in the immediate aftermath of the War. Increasingly, however, the Court interpreted basic rights and norms as being based on an objective order – and ranking – of values. The notion of an objective order of values, which affected all areas of law – including private law – had also been the crucial innovation in the Lüth case. This form of jurisprudence was often explicitly based on Smend's antipositivist communitarianism, and in particular the idea of social integration through a concrete symbolic ordering of values expressed in the constitution.

Schmitt vociferously opposed the philosophy of values and repeatedly condemned what, following Hartmann, he called the 'tyranny of values'.[30] According to Schmitt, value thinking, which originated in the economic sphere and only had a proper place in that sphere, contained its own inexorable logic. Every value, he argued, implied a counter value or opposite value – a value that was then literally de-valued. The importance of such judgements about value and 'un-value' would lead to a fateful moralization of politics as those who had no values, or held the opposite values of the 'correct' values, also had no value, and in the extreme case could be declared absolute enemies worthy only of annihilation. The logic of values, he claimed, carried an 'immanent aggressiveness'. It was not enough for values to be posited, their validity also had to be enforced.[31] In Schmitt's untranslatable German wordplay: *Setzung*, the positing of values, implied their *Durchsetzung*, their, if necessary, violent enforcement.[32] In any event, higher values permanently had to subordinate – or tyrannize – lower values. It was not surprising, then, that Schmitt could suggest in letters to his pupils that Hitler himself had subscribed to the philosophy of values.[33]

In relatively peaceful pluralist democracies, different interest groups would dress up their demands as values to make them commensurable in financial terms. In other words, value philosophy lent some spurious dignity to the conflicts in an industrial society which had overwhelmed the state and limited politics to distributive politics. Accordingly, thinking in terms of values – and their equivalence – was not only a failed attempt at rescuing morality in the face of the rise of the natural sciences and of nineteenth-century nihilism; it was also another chapter in the modern history of futile and counterproductive neutralizations and depoliticizations which Schmitt had first analyzed in 1929.

Some of Schmitt's most brilliant pupils seconded this attack on the philosophy of values. Böckenförde, for instance, argued that the idea of an 'empire of values' existing apart from human will was subject to all kinds of legitimate doubts – and even if the existence of such an empire was granted, it remained unclear how conflicts between different values were supposed to be resolved.[34] This problem was obviously exacerbated even further if no objective empire was said to exist, and instead it was held that all values were subjectively chosen. Ultimately, both natural law doctrines and the philosophy of values fell to the suspicion that its proponents extracted from nature and the empire of values precisely what they had initially put into them.

The opposition of Schmitt and his followers to the philosophy of value pointed to a paradoxical reversal. After 1945, Schmitt's enemies defended an understanding of the constitution as embodying values emanating from a particular culture. This understanding had, perhaps, more to do with Schmitt's concrete order thinking than the ostensibly liberal arguments that Schmitt's pupils – although not Schmitt himself – marshalled against the Smend School. It was not only Schmittians who could claim that the communitarian emphasis on values was unlikely to lead to a truly inclusive form of social integration, as values had no clear and uncontested ordering.

Values, left-wing critics also charged, were ultimately more like goods. And as with economic goods, there was always a temptation to trade them off against each other. Values led to a teleological or purposive approach to the constitution and required a permanent and in all likelihood subjective balancing of different goals by constitutional judges. Kantian opponents of 'value philosophy' argued that proper rights and norms, understood as unconditional precepts, could either be followed or not – they did not, generally, require an arbitration between different values and goals.[35] Yet, an essential difference remained between the different criticisms of 'value philosophy'. Where left-wing critics sought to rehabilitate democratic decisions about the law against a court's imposition of inherited values, Schmitt's followers opposed, above all, the increasing intrusion of the state into society through economic and social legislation based on values.

Ernst-Wolfgang Böckenförde, probably Schmitt's most creative post-war student, saw the people, rather than the Constitutional Court and its dedication to values, as the ultimate source of legitimacy and as the guardian of the constitution. Rather than putting his faith in a militant democracy and judicial decisions based on values, he sought to ensure stability through a politically homogeneous people and the 'moral substance' of individuals sharing values and practices. Böckenförde feared that a 'totalitarianism of the constitution' was lurking behind the conception of a militant democracy.[36] No constitutional provisions and no abstract insistence on values, he argued, could prevent the demise of the republic, once the necessary political homogeneity had been lost. Political homogeneity was ultimately identical with 'political culture' – or perhaps simply the nation. In other words, on some level Böckenförde and others agreed with Schmitt that the existence of a concrete order was decisive for political stability. Yet, they cleansed that concrete order of the notion of 'blood and soil', while retaining the philosophically conservative predilection for the concrete and the particular.

Salvaging Leviathan

The intellectual leader of the Schmitt School was Ernst Forsthoff, the most important conservative jurist of the 1950s and 1960s. Unlike Schmitt, Forsthoff was allowed to teach again after the War. He went on to have a distinguished public career, which included his (controversial) appointment as President of the Constitutional Court of Cyprus in 1960, as a neutral force in the Turkish–Greek conflict. He was frequently reminded of his infamous 1933 treatise, *The Total State*, and was subject to attacks from student activists in 1968 – although a while later, right-wing students also marched with torches in his favour, when he decided to take early retirement at the university of Heidelberg. Like Schmitt, Forsthoff retreated into a semi-private sphere of discussion circles, seminars and 'summer academies' which defined themselves against the intellectual life of the early Federal Republic. In fact, Forsthoff took a certain pride in being (or at least feeling like) an outsider in West Germany. In his Ebracher Seminars, which were attended by many young intellectuals who would become leading thinkers in fields as diverse as art history and philosophy, Schmitt's thought was a constant reference point – and Schmitt himself a frequent guest (when he was not there, postcards, which all attending signed, were sent to Plettenberg). It was also in Ebrach that Schmitt first delivered his thoughts on the tyranny of values, which he later dedicated to the 'Ebracher of 1959'.

What one might call the right wing of the Schmitt-inspired 'statist school' was united by a call to halt the erosion of 'stateness' that the Federal Republic was supposedly experiencing in the 1950s and 1960s. In his letters to Schmitt,

Forsthoff attributed more or less all political calamities to the fact that the Federal Republic was no longer a proper state, and only produced 'democratic mist', behind which a marshalling yard of special interest groups remained hidden.[37] According to Forsthoff, it became increasingly difficult to explain to students just what a state *was*.[38] For many members of the Schmitt School, 'stateness' translated into a view of the state as positioned clearly above society and the divergent and conflicting interests within that society. It also meant leadership by a strong elite, imbued with a sense of authority.

However, the diagnosis of society as such by the Schmitt School oscillated considerably. On the one hand, society had been homogenized into a 'mass', as all organic institutions, with the possible exception of the family, had been destroyed. As an antidote, Werner Weber, for instance, advocated the restoration of a strong bureaucracy, which could embody a new authority and resist the encroachments of organized interests.[39] Weber froze the moment of Schmitt's advocacy of a kind of bureaucratic-cum-charismatic authoritarianism from the late 1920s and early 1930s and resurrected the model for 1950s Germany. Weber argued that while there was not much sovereignty left in the Federal Republic, at least the administration could be salvaged from the ruins of statehood. Social cohesion was not to be provided through nationalism, as in Schmitt's late Weimar authoritarianism, but through a bureaucratic ethos of public service. This common good determined by the state was not only opposed to the particular interests of industrial associations and trade unions, but also to those of parties. Political and social integration, Forsthoff concurred, was accomplished through homogeneous administration, rather than constitutions, and a homogeneous administration required homogeneous legislation.[40]

Here the distrust of parties – and, by extension, parliament – so familiar from Weimar, extended directly into the 1950s. Consequently, an uneasy opposition emerged between the state, which monopolized the political, and the entirely subservient, depoliticized economy and society. Mass parties, and even non-economic associations in civil society, were not given any role in social or political integration, while their role in 'mediating' the people's will was subject to constant criticism.[41] However, this opposition was bound to be weakened, as parties moved ever further from their role as narrowly representing particular economic interests. The rise of the catch-all party (or people's party) made it difficult to argue that parties in parliament were fighting a thinly disguised civil war, and that only the state and the bureaucracy could integrate divergent interests. Where previously the parties had been seen as corrupting and dividing the general will of a homogeneous people, they were now increasingly integrated into the state and seen as quasi-constitutional organs. The Basic Law explicitly recognized them, while the Weimar constitution had not.

The Schmitt School, then, affirmed, but also adapted, many of Schmitt's Weimar positions, in particular the idea of the autonomy and the primacy of the political. Schmitt's theories were at least slightly modernized in the sense of a selective move from substance to function, as the substantial legitimacy of the nation was replaced with the functionalist ethos of the state's administration. While Weber's and Forsthoff's positions might often have seemed classically liberal, even libertarian, they fundamentally distrusted any free play of private economic interests in the market. Unlike neoliberals, they did not view the state as merely supplying a neutral legal framework which promoted competition and supplied a certain amount of social welfare. For them, it still represented an entity above the economy which forged a common will out of divergent interests. Ultimately, pluralism of any kind remained anathema to them.

In Search of Stability II: Industrial Society, Technocracy and the Extinction of Political Will

Nothing is more mistaken than to continue thinking in the categories of the Weimar era.

Ernst Forsthoff, 1971

Probably *the* central debate in constitutional theory of the 1950s and early 1960s revolved around the relationship between the rule of law and the social (or welfare) state, which the constitution mandated in one of its clauses. Ernst Forsthoff, one of the major protagonists of the debate, claimed that the principles of the *Rechtsstaat* [rule of law or, literally, state under the rule of law] and of the *Sozialstaat* [social or welfare state] were incompatible on the level of the constitution. The former, Forsthoff argued, was about guarantees, the latter concerned provisions. Thus, as the undeniable reality of the social welfare state had to be located *below* the constitution, Forsthoff disputed the direct legal effect of the constitutional principle of the *Sozialstaat*. As he frequently admonished the Germans, 'the constitution is no supermarket in which all wishes can be fulfilled'.[1]

Forsthoff was not an opponent of welfare provision as such, however. On the contrary, in the late 1930s he had identified the 'provision for existence' or *Daseinsvorsorge* – a term he had appropriated from Karl Jaspers – as an essential task for the state administration.[2] Forsthoff argued that the way individuals conducted their lives had changed fundamentally since the beginning of the nineteenth century. In particular, the 'effective space' in which human beings actually lived their lives had expanded enormously, but the 'life space' effectively controlled by individuals had steadily shrunk. Given the increased vulnerability of citizens, the modern 'social state' therefore necessarily had to be a state for provisions and redistribution. Consequently, 'modern man lived not only in the state, but also off the state'.[3]

This supposed fact exposed the individual to total state domination, if the state chose to exploit the social dependency of its citizens. Forsthoff, therefore, argued that the 'social functions' of the state could only be 'servicing' and had to be kept separate from power. However, Forsthoff also warned that the state was being invaded and instrumentalized by associations pursuing their own social and economic interests. Parliament, as Schmitt had claimed all along, was no longer a site of rational deliberation and decision-making. An embodiment of 'neutral' statehood, which could be above sectarian interests and therefore claim 'authority and dignity' for the state, was no longer available, as the president and the professional bureaucracy had been decisively weakened.[4]

Nevertheless, even if these elements could be restored an element of disquiet would remain. Forsthoff claimed that

> even the well-constituted social state will always be a subtle and to a high degree an artificial construction, which one will view with a conservative shudder, when one realizes its manifold immanent dangers resulting from the interlocking of social function and power . . . It is a life form of modern peoples, created with much art and subtlety, a surrogate of genuine popular order [*Volksordnung*].[5]

Such genuine *Volksordnung* would consist in returning a measure of controlled 'life-space' to individuals – in this regard Forsthoff specifically mentioned social programmes for veterans and expellees. In fact, to the degree that such an order could be realized, the social state would become 'superfluous'.[6] In the meantime, conservatives could affirm the social state, 'with the will to overcome it'. Such overcoming would only be effected by 'policies which combined a realistic view of matters with a concrete image of the measure of man and human order, which, in a time of organization, the artificial and the manipulated retained a sense of the genuine, the intact and the integral'.[7]

It was not an accident that Forsthoff concluded his essay with one of Carl Schmitt's favourite quotations: '*ab integro nascitur ordo*'. Behind the concerns about legal indeterminacy and a blurring of the separation of powers lurked a desire to regain an 'integral' form of politics – the ideal of a strong, dignified state represented by a president and professional civil servants standing above a homogeneous society. Such a concrete order was clearly more organic and natural than the 'artificial constructions' of the post-war period. Their affirmation, then, appeared like a world-historical holding operation, rather than any genuine turn away from nineteenth-century ideals of state and society.

Forsthoff's prime adversary in the *Sozialstaat*-controversy was Wolfgang Abendroth, the only openly socialist professor of political science in West Germany at the time. Abendroth hoped that a transformation of West Germany could be accomplished from within the framework of the Basic Law – according to him, the constitution left the 'legal road to socialism' wide open.[8] Abendroth was also the supervisor of Jürgen Habermas's *Habilitation*, his second doctorate, which all German academics are required to submit. As it turned out, Habermas himself drew extensively on Schmitt, Forsthoff and Weber for his second doctorate. In *The Structural Transformation of the Public Sphere*, he adopted Schmitt's stylized narrative of the decline of both parliament and the public sphere, and used Forsthoff's diagnosis of an increasingly blurred line between state and society to bolster his thesis about the decline of the bourgeois public sphere.[9] Habermas more or less directly adopted Schmitt's claim that in early liberalism, rational discussion had indeed been the guiding principle of parliaments and that in the course of the nineteenth and twentieth centuries, open parliamentary debate had been replaced by back-room dealings between interest groups. An increasingly monopolized capitalism and media manipulation had all undermined the possibility of discussing public policy in a rational and transparent manner.

Perhaps this shows a peculiarity of German political thought. The post-war advocates of liberal democracy were profoundly influenced by an anti-positivist and, to some extent, anti-pluralist and antiliberal doctrine, namely, Smend's theory of social integration. In contrast, it was radical Weimar conservatives and former National Socialists who adopted what appeared to be a liberal or even 'libertarian' position in the post-war period. Yet, their defence of the separation of state and society always ended in the state enveloping or even overwhelming society. Conversely, many liberals and Social Democrats, again inspired by Smend, felt compelled to advocate the mutual penetration of state and society. Sceptics on the Right and critics further on the Left, could then easily charge them with advocating a 're-feudalization' of society, as well as promoting the fragmentation and de-formalization of law. Like Habermas, they could easily detect signs of a new corporate order of privileges and an erosion of the uniform rule of law. Such a feudal fusion of state and society would make it ever more difficult for the subjects of law to find the legal order general and predictable – let alone see themselves as the actual democratic authors of the law.

Arguably, this polarization constitutes one of the tragedies of German political thought – the fact that potentially liberal positions like the advo-cacy of a separation between state, Church and society were adopted by de facto conservatives who always ultimately made the state overwhelm soci-ety. Liberals, in turn, were prone to put their trust almost exclusively in strong, perhaps even slightly authoritarian institutions in defence of dem-ocracy. Critics of these views then seemed to feel compelled to adopt a posi-tion which, paradoxically, collapsed liberalism into authoritarianism, and to cast doubt on ideals central to liberalism, such as the rule of law, simply because they were advocated by Schmitt's heirs.

Cold-eyed Conservatism

Apart from recycling, or to some extent rethinking, some of Schmitt's con-stitutional positions from the early 1930s, there was another, altogether dif-ferent route that some of Schmitt's pupils (and other conservatives) began to take in the mid- to late 1960s. It led away from the supposed cadaver of Leviathan and ended with the birth of a rather different social body that supposedly could fulfil the former functions of Leviathan. This body was the highly interdependent industrial society of mid-century Europe. Rather than being in permanent need of a strong state, as previous thinkers had held, it was now argued that such a society could in fact stabilize itself. After all, as the concept of stability initially derived from the sphere of technology, why not trust in technology and the modern economy to deliver stability reliably? As the success of the Federal Republic in modernizing – without necessarily developing a consciousness of its own modernity – became more and more obvious, some of Schmitt's pupils began to think again.

It was once more Forsthoff who, rather than continuing simply to re-deploy Schmitt's categories in the way Weber had after the War, increasingly recognized a structural and qualitative change in statehood. This diagnosis was prompted by the apparent stabiliziation of the Federal Republic in the 1960s. Industrialization, Forsthoff now claimed, had gone hand in hand with the increasing 'disciplining' of those taking part in the process.[10] As Forsthoff put it, 'the hard core of the social whole is no longer the state, but industrial society, and this hard core is characterized by the notions of full employment and increase of the GNP'.[11] Now the state had a minor, complementary function to industrial society, gaining legitimacy not through representing the social whole on a higher plane, but through extensive redistribution and social services.

Above all, industrial society required *Daseinsvorsorge*. The 'provision for existence', according to Forsthoff, had a depoliticizing effect. For the state, however, it held both negative and positive consequences. It increased the state's political impotence, but it also anchored the state more firmly in the 'vital sphere of the population', as long as it managed to deliver the services it promised.[12] Consequently, the state also effectively lost its inner sovereignty, as it had no choice but to provide *Daseinsvorsorge*. This in turn was dependent on the continuity of what Forsthoff called 'technical realisation' – the ever more rapid development of technology over which the state also had no sovereignty.

Forsthoff, while clearly impressed with the apparent stability offered by industrial society, did recognize some of the costs. In particular, industrial society lacked the immediate transparency for individuals which the state had supposedly possessed. It therefore inevitably increased individuals' psychological insecurity. Yet there remained no alternative: industrial society was the only resource which could provide the Federal Republic with some permanence.[13] The amalgamation of state and industrial society was also to be welcomed, not least because Forsthoff was confident that industrial society would respond ferociously if it were challenged. Such challenges would, however, become extremely rare, as industrial society could fortify the very normal functioning on which it depended and 'seal itself off' from disruptions – as supposedly evidenced by the French *événements* of May 1968, which, according to Forsthoff, had had absolutely no consequences.[14]

Another conservative sociologist, Helmut Schelsky, theorized what he called the 'technical state', in which democracy had become an empty shell altogether – as the authority of function would finally replace the authority of majority decisions. According to Schelsky, 'modern technology is not in need of legitimacy; one "governs" with it, because it functions and as long as it functions optimally'.[15] Rather than lamenting the end of statehood, these theorists diagnosed a structural change in statehood – and immediately gave this diagnosis a decidedly anti-democratic twist.

Emphasizing the apparently inexorable imperatives of industrial society and technology was a way for post-war conservatives to demand the complete submission of the individual to large-scale socio-economic imperatives. After the failure of fascism as a project of collective self-transformation through a united political will, these thinkers had become disillusioned with politics – and history – altogether. Subscribing to technocratic imperatives, however, allowed them to hold on to some of the basic intuitions behind their negative philosophical anthropology – the view that human beings were weak as well as dangerous, and consequently had to be kept in check by larger, impersonal forces. Now, however, they did not have to base their arguments about political action on such views directly.

Philosophical conservatism would no longer be expressed in radical political action in the name of anti-universalism, anti-individualism or a pessimistic philosophical anthropology – rather, conservatives cast a cold eye on post-war modernization and decreed that political action be frozen altogether. Politics as such was relegated to the pre-modern. Technocracy was about expunging political will or political decisions from politics altogether. Political will had to be replaced by a willingness to do what experts had singled out as the correct course of action.

Planning and Progress

Joseph Kaiser, who had attended lectures by Schmitt during the last years of the War and who became a professor of law at Freiburg in the 1950s, attempted a fusion of technocratic arguments and Schmittian concepts. He stayed in very close contact with Schmitt, asking for advice in making sense of apparently conflicting political and legal developments after 1945. After a stay at the University of Michigan, where he studied American pluralism and the role of pressure groups in US democracy, he put forward a theory of the 'representation of organized interests'.[16] He immediately drew criticism from Forsthoff and other members of the Schmitt School. According to Schmitt and his pupils, private social and economic interests were incapable of proper representation – although in fact Kaiser had concurred that 'the representation of political unity can fundamentally only be realized inside the substantial sameness of the nation and through institutions'.[17] However, he also wrote that the 'pluralism of interests in modern society is fundamentally incapable of being represented through a national institution'.[18]

Subsequently, however, Kaiser shifted away from the topic of pressure groups and began emphasizing *planning* as one of the major characteristics of the age. Planning was defined by 'systematization, rationality and science'.[19] For Kaiser, planning was fascinating, not least because existence [*Dasein*] itself could become increased, as it planned itself 'into the darkness of the future' with 'decisiveness, energy and success'.[20] Kaiser was also confident that planners, in mapping a whole range of possible long-term futures, would not easily submit to the tyranny of shifting values, as they were accustomed to value change in history.[21] Moreover, as a plan always involved the 'appropriation' of a particular area of human life, it also constituted a rational *nomos*. However, Kaiser called upon the planners not to conceive of the plan as an entirely rational construction or as a potential instrument for the manipulation of human beings.[22] Rather, their task was to find an already existing *nomos* – or the measure of man and a particular matter that was to become subject to planning.[23]

Kaiser, in line with other members of the Schmitt School, detected a steady weakening of state power in the twentieth century. He eventually followed his mentor in diagnosing the emergence of great spaces, as part of a historical development towards ever larger units. Kaiser claimed that there was a particular *nomos* comprising the elements of democracy, growth and the economy, which could already be observed in classical Athens.[24] This was also a model for the post-war era, when spatial *nomoi* had been complemented by functional *nomoi* centred on economic growth. Great spaces could now be controlled in a collegial manner, if a number of states became 'institutionally integrated'.[25] This was clearly the case with the European Community, whose *nomos* was apparently the same as that of the Athenian empire. Thus, Kaiser could conclude that 'the *nomos* of growth is planning'.[26] He was confident that this process could be completely controlled and steered by bureaucrats.

Kaiser made Schmitt's concepts compatible with a 'high modernist' vocabulary centred on 'self-confidence about scientific and technical progress, the expansion of production, the growing satisfaction of human needs, the mastery of nature (including human nature) and, above all, the rational design of social order'.[27] Such high modernist belief in planning and technology even went so far as a hope for the 'end of all crises' in politics.[28] Was this undertaking, in particular the combination of planning with existential categories, not inherently contradictory? As it turned out, the picture was more complex than a simple contrast between philosophical conservatism and a Promethean belief in planning. Schmitt himself wrote in 1970 that 'there is nothing more aggressive than the industrial progress constantly propelled by science. That is aggressiveness in an immense form'.[29] In such a situation, Schmitt continued, planning was in fact a form of conservation. The question remained nonetheless how to combine the compulsion for progress with order and stability. In the end, he had to confess that he did not know 'where in such a system, which wants progress, there is space for *conservatism*'.[30] Planning, then, was in fact a means of restraining progress. And there was space for a certain kind of conservatism – one not only shorn of calls for radical political action, but also one that, in contrast to Forsthoff and Schelsky, actually attempted to re-assert some measure of human control over technology.

In any event, Kaiser himself was eventually in a position to put his ideas about planning, informed by Schmittian existentialism, into practice. He became not only a consultant for the European Economic Community, but also for numerous countries around the globe, African ones in particular. Advising the governments of Mauritania, Mali and Senegal, Kaiser projected the emergence of a new African 'great space'. He also witnessed the unfolding of a number of coups in Africa. Time and again, Kaiser wrote to Schmitt on the stationery of the world's great hotels to confirm the importance of 'access to power'. Apparently, what could be learnt in the capitals of developing countries had been known in San Casciano all along. More important, however, turned out to be the lesson that technocracy was not only *not* apolitical – the technocrat, if anything, was even more dependent on understanding the machinations of power. The rule of technology still depended on the techniques of the rulers.

Empty Boxes: The Formed Society

A different technocratic vision came close to being directly implemented through governments in the mid-1960s. Then the young political theorist – and Schmitt disciple – Rüdiger Altmann formulated his conception of the *formierte Gesellschaft*, which could (awkwardly) be translated as formed, aligned or, perhaps, disciplined society. Altmann, often seen as the 'coldest of Schmitt's pupils', argued that traditional criticism of a pluralism of interests left conservatives theoretically helpless. It had to be superseded by the recognition that pluralism was in effect central to the functioning of modern industrial society; integration and pluralism had become 'complementary concepts'.[31] Different interests would no longer give rise to the kind of social conflict that could tip over into a civil war, but had to be politically recognized and channelled so that they would form part of a harmonious whole. In short, the legal constitution and the functions of the economy had to be completely integrated.

This process was helped by the fact that the formed society increasingly recognized its own uniformity, as modernization had eroded diverse traditions and ways of life. Moreover, after the chaotic experiences of the Third Reich, the formation of post-war pluralism had already been conducted in a highly disciplined manner – the same discipline which had impressed Forsthoff. Now, however, an uncontrolled growth of organized interests could endanger the prime tasks of any government: guaranteeing economic development and distributing the national product. For this reason, the government, Altmann claimed, had to assume the authority it had been granted in the constitution, if the Federal Republic was not to remain a 'democracy in a wheelchair'.[32] According to Altmann, the government in a redistributive state had (and had to have) more authority than previous forms of parliamentary government.[33]

Altmann had conceded much to post-war developments, only to end on a classic Schmittian call for strong government. Mostly, his social vision amounted to a sophisticated rationalization (in both senses) of the status quo from above, a disciplining of the participants in the economic process,[34] and, of course, a taming of the unions in particular. The Christian Democratic Chancellor Ludwig Erhard initially endorsed this idea at the CDU party conference in 1965.[35] He soon dropped it, however, amidst criticism of the ostensible authoritarian overtones of the notion of a 'formed society', with some critics going so far as seeing it as a 'new, more closely knit *Volksgemeinschaft*' – the Nazi term for a racially homogeneous community.[36] For others, it was merely 'a mixture of nostalgia, feudalism and lack of imagination'.[37] But there were also increasing doubts about what the slogan 'formed society' could really stand for at all, so much so that it became the subject of satires and cartoons. One cartoon showed the Chancellor stacking a number of boxes with *formierte Gesellschaft* printed on them, and exclaiming: "Really pretty boxes; now we only have to think practically what should be inside them!"[38]

Altmann was quick to revise his vision: the state, he conceded in 1967, had now been dissolved into its functions, and society had finally defeated the *deus mortalis*. The state now resembled a neutered tomcat that was growing fat in the absence of its libido.[39] Yet, despite ever-increasing pluralism, Altmann had not quite given up his hope that some kind of political will and political authority might still be formed, except that he recognised that a total society weakened the willingness of the individual to participate politically. Such a society, Altmann argued, 'weakens the energies to which it appeals. It uses up the substance it cannot reproduce'.[40]

Thus, Altmann finally honed in on the prime question (and anxiety) of post-war political thought: was the political order slowly consuming the preconditions of its own stability? Here Altmann was clearly torn. On the one hand, he admired the discipline of industrial society and accepted the importance of pluralism and regulated conflict in ensuring social integration. On the other hand, there was the lingering suspicion that social integration, as well as the prevention of major crises, required strong authority. For Altmann, just as for Forsthoff, the post-war order was problematic for individual citizens, who were said to experience increasing insecurity or apathy – although only Altmann clearly granted them a liberal 'right to distance'.

Ultimately, Altmann could do nothing but cast a cold eye on developments which more sympathetic observers might simply have seen as signs of social and cultural liberalization. He offered diagnosis after diagnosis of the decline of the state and its representative functions, while never being quite sure whether what appeared to be an ersatz 'idea of the state' could in fact perform this function.

In the Name of the Political

There were also more theoretical criticisms of technocracy. One of the fiercest critics turned out to be the young German philosopher Hermann Lübbe – a Social Democrat *and* an avid reader of Schmitt. In an essay entitled 'The Political Theory of Technocracy' (published in 1962, appropriately enough, in the first issue of a new periodical ominously called *Der Staat*) Lübbe argued that technocratic thinking was ultimately an illusion.[41] Technocracy could not abolish politics, no matter how much it 'depoliticizes the state, drags it into society and deliberalizes society in the process'. On the contrary, technocratic government would become particularly vulnerable to sudden bouts of ideological fervour.

Lübbe had taken a clear lesson from his more or less clandestine post-war teacher that technology could never be politically neutral and that no proper *political* form could emerge from the mere functions of the economy and technology.[42] The political could not be expunged but only obscured, and 'the will to prosperity' was not really a political will by itself – a point made against the likes of Harold Wilson who had claimed that 'socialism, as

I understand it, means applying a sense of purpose to our national life', only to continue that 'purpose means technical skill'.[43]

As Lübbe put it at the end of his essay, the technocratic system 'is the system of silence about everything about which different opinions are possible. It educates to be silent'. Lübbe thus mixed a central Schmittian insight – that even the supposed objective imperatives of technology cannot yield genuine political neutrality – with a more liberal demand to debate different political options. One had to preserve room for political (and democratic) manoeuvre instead of completely aligning or disciplining industrial society according to economic and technological criteria.

Schmitt's students and pupils were deeply split on the question of what has sometimes too quickly been called 'technocratic conservatism'. They almost uniformly insisted that the state and political will continued to play a role, and that thinking otherwise was an illusion. They clearly did not share the conservative view that technocratic necessities could be entirely divorced from political will – in fact, political will was still responsible for the ways in which technology affected and constrained industrial societies. Yet, political will in a prescriptive sense could come in various shapes and not all of them were liberal or democratic. Moreover, Schmitt's followers split on the ability of industrial society to provide stability. Forsthoff was clearly most optimistic, whereas Altmann merely claimed that 'industrial society had made the most out of the ruin of the state', since 'mass prosperity had made the state as a shell as comfortable as central heating makes an old castle'.[44] Nevertheless, Schmitt's students all agreed that a proper state and a proper form of representing society as a whole could not be reconstructed. The title of Altmann's collection of essays was most apt in this regard: *Taking leave of the State*.

Thus, these thinkers, like Schmitt himself, remained sensitive to the changing cultural contexts of political thought – and they understood that while the structures of the state and industrial society appeared to remain intact, these were merely the ruins left behind after the cultural earthquakes of the post-war decades. Forsthoff's seemingly self-satisfied pronouncement that 'events' could not affect industrial society was more like an anxious whistling in the theoretical dark – prompted by the realization that even technocratic conservatism could not be a brake on large-scale socioeconomic and cultural change.

Visions of Global Order: Schmitt, Aron and the Civil Servant of the World Spirit

verborgen bleibt der liebe gott
die ganze welt wird melting pot

Carl Schmitt, 1957

S chmitt had begun to formulate his vision of a world order of great spaces in the early 1940s, but only published his magnum opus on the topic, *The Nomos of the Earth*, in 1950. Obviously, parts of what had still seamlessly fitted into his vision for a Nazi-dominated great space among other empires with global reach had to be revised to become palatable in the post-war period. Yet *Nomos of the Earth* was to remain the touchstone for all his post-war reflections – not least because it allowed him to shift the level of discussion away from the German past and domestic politics to more lofty world-historical and even mythical ruminations. When a number of his admirers sought to publish a collection of his political writings in the early 1970s, he insisted that they start with *Nomos* and include only post-war writings – as if his earlier, more open antiliberalism had not remained the foundation on which his post-war vision of global order was erected.

With his reflections on the decline of territoriality and the end of the European state system, Schmitt was thoroughly in tune with the post-war cultural pessimism of thinkers such as Arnold Toynbee. During this apparently 'post-European age' many intellectuals sought to engage Schmitt in an essentially European conversation about the new global politics which had led to what Schmitt often termed 'Europe's dethronement'.[1] While for almost all European intellectuals this conversation was a form of compensation for the very real loss of European political power, it especially served Schmitt's purpose of dissolving the Nazi era in world-historical reflections.

Location, Law and Order

In what is probably his most idiosyncratic book, Schmitt argued on many different levels. He frequently mixed traditional historical and legal analysis with his private mythology of the Earth, dubious etymological claims and barely hidden resentments towards the victors of the Second World War. Yet, through it all ran an argument against the dangers of global unification under the auspices of the Anglo-American powers based on commerce and control of the seas.

Schmitt began with myth, namely with the startling claim that the Earth was the mother of law and that the great *Ur*-acts of law-creation had all taken place on a particular soil: 'the occupation of land, the foundation of cities as well as the foundation of colonies'.[2] The occupation of land was the most fundamental of these acts. The 'appropriation of land', or 'taking of land', as Schmitt literally called it, established a clear outside and inside. This line in turn could become the basis for distinctions such as public and private law as well as political domination and private property.[3] Appropriating land, therefore, constituted the beginning of a concrete order, but it was also the only way of 'putting down roots in the realm of meaning in history'.[4] Localisation, or *Ortung*, order, or *Ordnung*, and meaning became inextricably connected – while the separation of *Ortung* and *Ordnung* would, necessarily, not only cause (literal)dislocation, but also political and moral disorientation.[5] Utopianism – understood as the absence of *topos* or *Ortung* and therefore as the absence of the concrete unity of measure, order and law – would also have to be a form of nihilism. The proper conjunction of place, law and order, Schmitt termed *nomos*.[6]

Schmitt chose an unorthodox interpretation of the ancient Greek word to avoid what he saw as the positivist connotations of the German word *Gesetz*, which appeared to imply a notion of human positing (of law). Nevertheless, for all its mythical and etymological baggage, the notion of *nomos* was not by itself necessarily a mysticism of the soil – after all, a *nomos* was a human creation, a measure willed by those capable of establishing effective distinctions between inside and outside.

Schmitt then moved on to a brief world history centred on the notion of *Nomos* – the succession of concrete orders from the ancient *polis* to the medieval republics and finally to the creation of the state and the *ius publicum Europaeum* in the sixteenth century. This last creation, Schmitt argued, had been dependent on the discovery of the New World. The major powers, according to Schmitt, could only manage to contain warfare on the European continent because the rest of the globe remained available for unrestrained warfare. Schmitt once more celebrated a form of war – modelled on the duel, which supposedly neither discriminated against nor morally defamed the enemy – as a unique and humane achievement. In this scheme, the silencing of the theologians had led to a humanization of warfare, as the *justa causa* had been replaced by the *justus hostis*. This particular Eurocentric *Nomos*, according to Schmitt, had preserved peace inside the various strong states and minimized cruelty in inter-state relations. Yet this – in Schmitt's eyes extraordinary – creation of Occidental rationalism crucially depended on the availability of a space outside Europe which could be freely exploited and fought over outside of the law. The culturally homogeneous system of sovereign European states presupposed an outside, 'uncivilized' space open to conquest and colonization. The exceptions to the 'normality' of the system – privateers, for instance – had to be located on the outside, in a 'wild', lawless zone. Only then could a plurality of European sovereigns be in turn sovereign over the globe, in what was a fundamentally asymmetric world order.

According to Schmitt, the civilizing achievement of what Vattel had called 'la guerre en forme' was destroyed with the rise of England as a maritime power. England, significantly also the first industrial society, now made the sea the basis of a new global order. Where other European powers appropriated ever more land, England appropriated the sea.[7] England's emerging supremacy was based on the indirect exercise of power through commerce and credits. Yet it was also based on the direct exercise of power in naval warfare, which, according to Schmitt, by its nature could not be contained. A sea-based system was nothing less than unnatural, as, Schmitt claimed, 'the sea is alien to man and hostile. It is not a living space [*Lebensraum*] of man.'[8]

Eventually, Anglo-American imperialism – under the cover of a new universalist legal vocabulary – destroyed the old *ius publicum Europeaum* and reintroduced a discriminating concept of enmity centred on the notion of the just war. Britain, the United States and their allies were erecting a new world order which was not properly 'grounded' and therefore lacked clear lines and demarcations. Schmitt held that a 'loosening of the order centred on the nation-state without a clear organisation of great spaces or even a world organisation' could only produce 'smudged spaces' and 'pseudo fronts'.[9] The clearest sign of this smudging and the resultant ambiguity was the fact that both England and the United States appeared to be simultaneously both in and apart from Europe. Schmitt was indignant that 'America' now claimed to embody the 'true Europe' as the 'stronghold of law and liberty'. As he put it, 'the old Europe, like old Asia and old Africa, was put on the side as the past. Old and new. . .are here not only measures of condemnation, but also of distribution, of *Ordnung* and *Ortung*'.[10]

Moreover, as Schmitt had already noted in his diary in 1947, the traditional state had meant sovereignty capable of a decision to end civil war. However, global domination meant almost the opposite. It amounted to a 'combination of war according to international law and civil war'.[11] The new world order clearly failed to externalize the exception – instead internalizing a potential permanent state of exception. It also broke the link between order and location, the only guarantee of meaning in world politics. *Nomos* was replaced by nihilism.

Schmitt advocated a proper 'pluriversum' of great spaces which also remained the proper repository for 'agonalism', that is, a concept of enmity that did not imply the annihilation of the enemy. Compared to the Anglo-American 'ethical-moral conception of enmity', agonalism and its non-discriminating treatment of the enemy fared much better – even from a moral point of view, according to Schmitt.[12]

Schmitt claimed that even if Britain and the United States somehow succeeded in establishing a proper world order, an order without plurality would also mean the end of the political. Here, Schmitt wavered between finding such a situation completely inconceivable and finding it merely deeply undesirable. Soon he was to come across an utterly un-American and un-English figure who proposed a highly sophisticated philosophical account of precisely what he feared most.

Kojève's Comedy

In 1967, a year before his death, Alexandre Kojève travelled from Beijing to address the students rebelling in West Berlin. The main advice of the philosopher-turned-*éminence grise* of the French civil service consisted in the instruction to learn Greek. On this occasion, he mentioned to Jacob Taubes, with characteristic nonchalance, that he was planning to visit Carl Schmitt. In response to Taubes's surprise, Kojève claimed that Schmitt was 'the only one with whom it was worth talking' in Germany.[13] In one sense, it was not surprising that Kojève and Schmitt would sooner or later correspond and meet. Kojève – like Schmitt a highly cultivated man – not only knew how to capture ideas, but also the minds of fellow intellectuals, who would be turned into life-long disciples. Like Schmitt, he fascinated others by constructing myths around his past and his own personality.[14] As in Schmitt's case, there always remained traces of the bohemian character Kojève had been in his youth, before he opted for life in academia and, ultimately, for putting his services at the disposal of the French state. And like Schmitt, Kojève had something about him that led some to compare him to the Grand Inquisitor, even to Mephistopheles – while others saw in him a mixture of Dostoevsky's Ivan Karamazov and Stavrogin from the *Devils*.[15]

Twenty years before his first encounter with Schmitt, Kojève had begun to change French philosophical life almost single-handedly through his seminars on Hegel's *Phenomenology of Spirit*, which he held in the *École pratique des hautes études*. He convinced a whole generation of intellectuals that 'it is possible that the future of the world, and therefore the meaning and direction of the present and the significance of the past, depends in the final analysis on the way in which we interpret Hegelian texts today'.[16] That generation came to be known as the 'generation of the three H's' – thanks to Kojève, one of the three H's happened to be Hegel (Heidegger and Husserl being the other two).[17]

Kojève had hardly been predestined for this role. He was born Alexander Kojevnikov in Moscow in 1902, into a cosmopolitan bourgeois family – the artist Vassily Kandinsky was his uncle. Despite the fact that he was arrested for racketeering by the Cheka in 1918, he became an ardent supporter of the Russian Revolution – the only reason he left for the West was that Moscow University denied him entry in 1919 because of his bourgeois background. Kojève ended up in Heidelberg, where he led the life of a gentleman scholar, a highly sophisticated amateur dilettante who happened to know more than the professionals in subjects ranging from Sanskrit to Russian philosophy. Eventually, this Russian dandy wrote a dissertation with Karl Jaspers, before moving to Paris to squander his considerable wealth on a luxurious life with his young Russian wife. All this ended in 1930, after Kojève lost most of his money in the stock market crash, where he had imprudently bought shares of the cheesemaker *La vache qui rit*. Consequently, he had to find employment as a librarian and settle in a modest suburb of the French capital. From then on, he would meet students and visitors only in cafes, appearing to his admirers like a 'man without qualities'.[18]

From 1933 to 1939, every Monday at 5.30 in the afternoon, Kojève offered his seminar on Hegel – a seminar located very much on the periphery of prestigious French university life, but attended by, among others, Raymond Aron, Georges Bataille, André Breton, Jacques Lacan and Maurice Merleau-Ponty. However, Kojève, never became a regular French professor. Instead, after the War, he embarked on a career as a bureaucrat for the French government. He was helped by Robert Marjolin, who had attended Kojève's seminar. Marjolin had also been de Gaulle's economic adviser in London and after the War became a high-ranking administrator for trade in the French Economic Ministry. He enabled Kojève to join a group of high-minded technocrats working for European economic unification. As a young bureaucrat, the later French prime minister Raymond Barre described Kojève as an 'excellent negotiator for France', and even as the 'terror of other trade delegations', who, nevertheless, seemed to retain a considerable inner distance from his tough-minded diplomacy. One of his mottos, according to Barre, was: 'life is a comedy – but we have to act seriously in it'.[19]

Sometimes Kojève's own philosophy appeared like a comedy – although the stakes were deadly serious throughout.[20] Following Hegel, he argued that history would come to an end when all bloody revolutions and battles for prestige and recognition had been played out. In the meantime, the dialectic of master and slave, in which the former took away the autonomy of the latter without actually killing him, would repeat itself again and again. For Kojève, unlike for Hegel, history was exclusively the 'history of the working slave'. Unlike the master, who remained frozen in his victory with nobody to give him proper recognition, the slave desired 'change, transcendence, transformation, "education"'. The slave would thus drive technological progress and acquire an increasingly refined understanding of the world – while the master, having attained humanity through risking death in his struggle for recognition, would, in all other respects, remain on the level of animal existence. At the end of this largely impersonal process the opposition between master and slave, however, would be overcome. It was at this point that a 'universal homogeneous state' would emerge, in which all human needs were satisfied. There would no longer be any opposition, nor anything external to the state. Such a state would see the reign of the 'Sunday of life', as Kojève's friend, the writer Raymond Queneau, put it in a novel with the same title. It was the vision of universal peace in which the political had vanished alongside all more profound human passions – politics had been replaced by free-wheeling play among 'happy men'. But such happy men were not only Nietzschean 'last men' – they were no longer properly men at all. As Kojève wrote,

in point of fact, the end of human Time, or History – that is, the definitive annihilation of Man properly speaking, or of the free and historical Individual – means quite simply the cessation of Action in the full sense of the term. Practically, this means the disappearance of wars and bloody revolutions. And also the disappearance of Philosophy; for since Man himself no longer changes essentially, there is no longer any reason to change (true) principles which are at the basis of his understanding of the world and of himself. But all the rest can be preserved indefinitely; art, love, play, etc.; in short everything that makes man happy.[21]

Globalizing Politics and Globalizing Play

Schmitt first took notice of Kojève in the early 1950s, and in due course contacted him in the middle of the decade, yet again casting his net for fellow intellectuals to take part in his European counter-public sphere. He persuaded Kojève to give a talk in front of the 'Rhein-Ruhr Club' in Düsseldorf, which invited speakers ranging from the banker Hermann Josef Abs to the editor of the news magazine *Der Spiegel*, Rudolf Augstein, and Hannah Arendt. On 16 January 1957, Kojève held forth in front of major industrialists on 'Colonialism from a European perspective' – an event that, as Schmitt wrote to Ernst Jünger, was attended by at least 'twenty first-rate people' from among his 'young friends'.[22]

Schmitt and Kojève turned out to be friendly philosophical adversaries, who could easily find a common, sometimes excessively polite language. Yet, this language hid the fact that their visions of the world were in almost all aspects diametrically opposed. When he first contacted Kojève, Schmitt had just written his essay on 'Appropriation – Distribution – Production', in which he argued that this three-step approach characterized the history of the world under the sign of *nomos*.[23] Kojève immediately countered that there had been no genuine land 'appropriation' since Napoleon. In fact, he admitted that Hegel had been even more right than he had initially thought.[24] He confessed to Schmitt that in his pre-war seminars he had always thought 'Stalin' when he read Napoleon, and that he had hoped Stalin would turn out to be an 'industrialized Napoleon' to whom Kojève himself would play Hegel. Only now had he realized that Stalin (and Hitler) had meant nothing new – world historically speaking. The Second World War had also 'brought nothing essentially new. And the First had only been an intermezzo anyway'.[25]

For Kojève, Napoleon had attempted to sublate (*aufheben*) the state in favour of society through a 'total war'. Yet the Anglo-Saxons had long been able to do the same without war, and the entire world was now moving in the direction of a similar stateless peace. Kojève agreed with Schmitt that there was no authentic statehood left – administration had replaced proper government, and police work substituted for politics. The global dominance of the Americans only hastened this trend, as they had never known the meaning of 'war, politics and state'.[26] The Soviet Union, however, still remained a step ahead in this development. In Russia the government had been completely and officially replaced by administration – and, Kojève contended, nothing would change fundamentally in the West either if governments and parliaments were abolished. If the West remained capitalist and nationalist, the Soviet Union was likely to conquer it – if it ceased to be so, the West would be in a better position to resolve the seeming global dualism in its favour.

Either way, one day the world would be uniformly administered, because the world already had a unity of purpose – living peacefully and living prosperously (and, one might add, living playfully, in the way Kojève had outlined the brave new world depicted in his lectures on Hegel). In fact, for Kojève, Molotov's cowboy hat was 'a symbol of the future'.[27] 'After ten to twenty years', he claimed, 'even a non-Hegelian will notice that East and West not only *want* the same (apparently since Napoleon), but are also *doing* the same'.[28] The universal homogeneous state, then, was no proper state at all in the Schmittian sense, but simply a global mechanism for the universal satisfaction of human needs – a world-wide 'Sunday of life' indeed. In Kojève's account, this state would emerge through a gradual process of transnational constitutionalization, that is, a homogenization of private and public law, and, ultimately a 'judicial union' based on a common conception of justice. The rule of law could only be fully realized in the universal homogeneous state, in which, politics, understood as potentially deadly conflict between states, would no longer subordinate law in moments of exception. Thus, the full realization of the *Rechtsstaat* required the abolition of the nation-state.[29]

Schmitt, who also felt that he had all 'exempt papers of the world spirit', agreed that the state, the mortal god as it had been known in Europe since early modern times, was indeed dead. It had become, and here Schmitt used the term Ernst Forsthoff had coined in the 1930s, a mere provider of *Daseinsvorsorge*.[30] But he disagreed with Kojève's point that the Cold War dualism was a prologue to the proper unity of the world. Instead, it was a phase between the age of European states and a new era of great spaces. The globe, Schmitt claimed, was not yet a unit for economic and technological planning – and he 'left it open whether it ever could be'. In other words, Schmitt cast doubt on the very notion of globalized modernity, that Kojève, the self-declared 'Marxist of the Right', painted.[31] Great spaces would – and *should* – constitute a new plurality of *magni homines*: political entities comparable to 'great men', who could experience meaningful – and non-moralized – enmity among each other. Only such enmity would then also yield what Schmitt called a 'capacity for history', or *Geschichtsfähigkeit*.[32]

Yet Kojève kept disagreeing with Schmitt. The political itself, he argued, would vanish, once and for all. His criterion of the political was not the possibility of enmity as such, but the possibility of battling for prestige. After all claims for recognition had been satisfied, enmity itself had been overcome and preserved at the same time in the act of recognition. Enmity was merely one moment in the Hegelian dialectic – not the perennial element constitutive of political (and sometimes, it seemed, personal) identity which it appeared to be for Schmitt. Conflict might not disappear at any point soon – but at one point meaningful conflict could be brought to an end once and for all, as no rational political alternatives to the world state could be constructed.

For Schmitt, such a final resolution or synthesis was simply unavailable. A system in which all meaningful opposition – and therefore all moral substance – was dissolved, a system, in other words, that no longer required a 'sophisticated moral decision', had to be anathema for the philosophical conservative Schmitt. No wonder then that he anxiously inquired of Kojève whether there could be an enemy at all in Hegel, 'given that he, the enemy, is either a necessary transitional stage of the negation, or else void and without essence?'[33] Kojève's answer was placid and predictable: 'As always, yes and no. Yes – insofar and so long as there is struggle for recognition, that is, history. World history is the history of enmity between men . . . No – insofar and as soon as history . . . is "sublated" in absolute knowledge'.[34] Kojève did not concede any essential human need for struggle or enmity. There was only a need for recognition – a need that could be rationally satisfied in the universal homogeneous state.

For Schmitt, Kojève's vision could ultimately be nothing but a dystopia. It meant not only the end of the political – it also meant the end of any moral seriousness and any notion of transcendence. Kojève's world was one of complete immanence – a wholly man-made artefact in which the 'seamless functioning' of technology combined with an aesthetic and romantic play with the merely interesting.

Kojève did not necessarily disagree with any of these evaluations – he simply appeared to view the end of history with equanimity.[35] Following his encounter with Schmitt, he went even further afield – geographically and philosophically. After a trip of 'philosophical tourism' to Japan in 1959, he decided that Japanese society presented yet another world-historical option, one that could be superior even to the American (or the Soviet) way of life.[36] The Japanese, Kojève now contended, had invented a snobbism for the masses, or what Kojève called 'democratic snobbism'. This meant a mixture of superficial democratisation and Americanization, which had resulted from Japan's reluctant opening to the West, and the fundamental continuity of home-grown traditions. In particular, a thoroughly depoliticized samurai tradition could provide the elite with an aesthetic re-enactment of meaningful traditions, or play, without disturbing the seamless functioning of modern technology and bureaucracy. Schmitt, in an article on Rousseau in 1962, eventually conceded that 'in the welfare state, in the society of consumption, with its automation and abundance, a philosophy of play seems to be timely, or rather, a philosophy of leisure time. But the player is not a world-historical figure'.[37] For Schmitt, only the partisan – or *guerilla* fighter – was a world-historical figure in the post-war world, a claim to which I shall return in a later chapter.

Kojève was not the only intellectual – and not even the only dandy – who put forward a vision of the world state in the late 1950s. Ernst Jünger, one of Schmitt's 'hostile brothers', also offered a slim volume on *Der Weltstaat*, in which he argued that the world state was born out of the spirit of technological innovation – in particular a general *accelerando*, a further 'acceleration of modernity'.[38] Like Schmitt and Kojève, he contended that '. . . old pictures fade away, old meanings become empty of the historical state and its claims. That is the reason why war becomes suspicious, its limits questionable. What enters now explodes its norms'.[39] But Jünger was clearly mindful of his old friend Schmitt when he claimed that

the planetary order has been accomplished already, both in terms of type and furnishing. All that is missing is its recognition, its declaration. It would be thinkable through a spontaneous act . . .or also forced through convincing facts. Always, poetry, the poets have to go first. The further expansion of great spaces into a global order, the world states into the one world state, or, rather, the world empire, is connected to the concern that now this perfection will exact its cost in terms of freedom of the will. Especially for this reason, there are many who advocate a world divided into three or more parts.[40]

In other words, *everybody* in this 'post-European debate' on global order agreed that meaning arose from tension, or, more precisely, from struggle – only Kojève had resigned himself to the cessation of both at the level of deadly intensity. Schmitt, on the other hand, thought that struggle could and *should* be preserved. Jünger was even looking for a cosmic antithesis, as the world state would shift the borders to outer space, while Schmitt desperately clung to his vision of earthly great spaces.

There was another – indirect – contribution to this debate which clarified what was at stake between Schmitt and Kojève. Leo Strauss, in a 1948 letter to the 'civil servant of the world spirit', claimed that 'no one has made the case for modern thought in our time as brilliantly as you'.[41] Yet he also politely begged to differ with Kojève's image of the universal homogeneous state. Strauss claimed that 'the fact that great deeds are impossible in the End-State, can lead precisely the best to a nihilistic denial of the End-State'.[42] Such a state, he suspected, would also turn out to be a tyranny. Moreover, universality and homogeneity, he argued, would never satisfy human beings. Strauss then advanced his own – somewhat paradoxical – view that only wisdom would satisfy and that consequently wisdom had to be 'popularized'.[43] Irrespective of that, Strauss concluded that Kojève offered a vision of nihilist, rather than liberal, modernity – and that liberals and antiliberals had reason to object to his peculiar Hegelianism. Such nihilism – and particularly the impossibility of great politics between *magni homines* – was precisely what horrified Schmitt.

In the late 1950s, the prospect of a world state, or, perhaps more accurately, world society, not only caused anxieties for Schmitt, but also for thinkers as different as Jünger and Strauss. The suspicion of universal empire that runs so deep in Western political thought did not only affect those who associated the end of history and politics with a loss of meaning and substance. Even philosophical liberals could argue that the joke in Kojève's comedy would be at humanity's expense. After all, the world state would imply the end of genuine moral conflict – and therefore the end of genuine moral autonomy.[44]

Yet, the choice was not simply between politics and play. After all, Kojève could only claim that the universal and homogeneous state would spell the end of politics because ultimately he had adopted Schmitt's definition of the political. Politics as non-deadly disagreement could of course continue – but there were no longer any alternative models to satisfy the human need for recognition. In Kojève's account, any action provoking deadly conflict would become a matter for the police, rather than politics.

Aron versus Schmitt: Reclaiming the Autonomy of Politics

A liberal thinker on international relations stood between Schmitt and Kojève. Raymond Aron had not only read Schmitt's *Nomos* 'with profit', as he claimed in a letter to Schmitt in 1954,[45] In fact he had also attended Kojève's seminars in the 1930s, and had been asked by Kojève for a final summing-up and commentary at the very last session of the seminar in 1939.[46] After the War, Kojève also kept sending Aron copies of his memos for the French government (in fact, Schmitt, most preoccupied with power, was the only interlocutor who had none. He dedicated his book on the problem of 'access to power' to Kojève with the words: 'whoever has no power needs sweets').[47]

Aron had no doubt been fascinated by Kojève's vision, but his thinking had also evolved in such a manner that he had to see both Kojève and his

German adversary as making *political* misjudgments. The man who called himself an engaged spectator grappling with questions of political choice and conscience could only view Kojève and Schmitt as *disengaged* spectators. Both their visions, in different ways, left no room for individual political responsibility.[48] Kojève could only cast a disengaged ironic glance at world history – even if he himself turned out to be a crafty actor in the international politics of post-war Europe. Schmitt, on the other hand, hoped for the recovery of genuine historical agency on the part of great spaces – and, presumably, the great statesmen whose 'great politics' would generate or regenerate the meaning that would be lost for good with Kojève's end of history.

Many of Aron's central observations and judgements were ostensibly similar to what Schmitt had to say on international law and politics, with both men united in what Schmitt had called 'la recherche de la réalité'. In fact, while he was always careful to keep his distance from Schmitt and apparently met Schmitt only once, Aron had great respect for the German savant in the tradition of Max Weber. He was also instrumental in having his works published in French. According to Aron, as a 'man of high culture' Schmitt could not have been a 'Hitlerian' and had not joined the Nazi party (here the usually well-informed Aron had it wrong).[49] While he still refused to contribute to a Festschrift for Schmitt in the late 1960s, he later allowed the editors of another *liber amicorum* to include a reference to Aron's 'best wishes' for Schmitt on his ninetieth birthday in the preface.[50] It is also clear from Aron's exchanges with his student Julien Freund, who often acted as a go-between for the two men, that Aron was anxious to know what Schmitt really thought of his work.[51]

For Aron, international relations were likely to remain driven by what he called the forces of 'Power, Glory and Ideas'.[52] They were also likely to remain irreducibly political and morally complex. This was not because politics and morality were polar opposites, so that any mixture of the two would lead to the catastrophes which Schmitt foresaw. Rather, morality was deeply woven into the fabric of political life – alongside numerous other threads. He shared Schmitt's view that international and domestic politics were becoming increasingly intertwined and ideological. But he was also concerned to bring out the crucial differences in their perspectives.

In 1963, Aron wrote a long letter to Schmitt, in which he put his finger on the essential ambiguity – and perhaps even hypocrisy – of Schmitt's position. With his customary 'icy clarity',[53] he suggested that one had to ask oneself whether Schmitt's thought was not 'pulled in two directions simultaneously. On the one hand, the conflicts between men are existential . . . and essentially violent, and not susceptible to arbitrage. . .'. But 'on the other hand', he continued,

> you keep a nostalgia for the public European law where the state establishes internal peace, solely determining the external enemy . . . But even in terms of your own philosophy, European public law was nothing but and could have been nothing but an admirable, but precarious work of art. To use my language, the European system had to be homogeneous . . . These sociological conditions require a conjunction rare and transitory.[54]

In other words, what Schmitt wanted was neither consistent with his own existentialist-cum-religious demands on politics, nor could it actually be engineered in any manner.[55] International relations remained a realm of historical contingency in which responsible political action required working with the constellations at hand. It also required working with the moral demands which had made their way into public international discourse. A return to duelling and chivalry, which remained Schmitt's (and Jünger's) ideal for international politics, could only be quixotic – and politically dangerous.

More importantly, Aron, for all his 'admiration of the grand jurist', left no doubt that he felt Schmitt's account of the *ius publicum Europeaum* and the degeneration of international politics in the twentieth century to be deeply disingenuous.[56] Proper distinctions had to be drawn between 'biologically absolute enmity (the Jews for the Hitlerians)', 'politically absolute enmity (Carthage for Cato)' and 'ideologically absolute enmity (Lenin's doctrine)'.[57] In his book on Clausewitz he was to point out more bluntly that only 'Ludendorff-Hitler' gave,

> a precise meaning to what Carl Schmitt calls 'absolute hostility' – what neither the authors of the Versailles Treaty nor the Marxist-Leninists nor the Western victors of the Second World War have done. Ludendorff and Hitler posited the racial community as the subject of history and the enemies of this community as transhistorical enemies of the German

people, even of all peoples. This hostility, and this only, deserves the term 'absolute', because it logically leads to massacre or to genocide.[58]

On a conceptual plane, Aron also rejected the connection Schmitt had made between absolute war, in Clausewitz's sense, and the 'criminalization of war'.[59] And on an ideological level, Aron distinguished between a hostility based on racism, which necessarily had to become absolute, and Communist class warfare. The latter had not been any less extreme or cruel than biologist aggression, but 'for those who seek to "save the concepts" there remains a difference between a philosophy whose logic *is* monstrous and that which lends itself to a monstrous interpretation'.[60] Aron had seen through the tendentious readings of international law which Schmitt offered. And, following Schmitt's injunction to analyze which concrete enemy particular concepts were directed against, the Frenchman had identified Schmitt's real targets – and therefore also his blind spots – 'Ludendorff-Hitler'. Schmitt never responded to Aron's criticisms. He simply kept restating his role as a 'realist' and a 'polemiologist' [sic!].

Aron was no less concerned than Schmitt about the fragility and potential frailties of liberal polities – after all, he had witnessed the last years of the Weimar Republic as a visiting student in Germany from 1930 to 1933.[61] But he understood where to draw the line between genuine worries about the amount of order necessary to render liberalism viable and a fixation on the past which could suddenly flip over into existentialism or apocalyptic, definitive solutions to political predicaments. More clearly than many others, he saw the counter-revolutionary and counter-Enlightenment temperament at work in Schmitt's writings. Aron claimed that 'la finalité de la politique est l'amitié' to reassure Julien Freund, who felt caught between his two masters, Aron and Schmitt.[62] He made the claim in response to a letter by Freund, in which his student had realized that if one gave priority to enmity, rather than friendship, it became 'quasi impossible' to resolve the problem of the '*finalité de la politique*'.[63] Against Kojève – and other liberals, such as Friedrich von Hayek – Aron pointed out that 'as long as there are wars, belonging to a political order will be equivalent to discriminating between friends and enemies'.[64] But what might have appeared as a purely Schmittian statement was a fact, not a value. In his messages to Schmitt, Aron denied the existential import of the political. He also stressed that the world-historical clock could not be turned back. Once moral claims had become part of world politics, one could not simply revert to a demoralized system of great spaces.

The Logic and the Limits of Liberal Internationalism

Kojève and Aron, for all the 'tragic realism' that has sometimes been attributed to Aron, and the authoritarian tendencies associated with Kojève, were *philosophical* liberals. They held on to a firm belief in universalism and human equality.[65] Aron, more so than Kojève, or even Schmitt, made the idea of 'antinomy' basic to his political thought. Yet what has been called his 'moderate Machiavellianism' was tailored to allow for liberal political action in the circumstances of modernity, circumstances which very often made for plain contradictions between philosophical and practical political liberalism. Kojève, on the other hand, was confident that the end of History would allow for a responsible, and yet playful role of counsellor to the Prince.

The disturbing fact remains, however, that Schmitt's analysis of the *ius publicum Europaeum*, may have uncovered a certain logic at the heart of liberal political modernity. Much of this analysis – like his account of the principles and the evolution of parliamentarism – had been stylized, selective or just plain inaccurate. In particular, it was, broadly speaking, the theologians who emphasized moral constraints on state action, whereas their opponents, the humanists, advocated a large degree of state autonomy and allowed pre-emptive strikes out of fear.[66] A common moral fabric among European political actors was torn apart by the *silete Theologi!* which Schmitt supposedly cherished. Instead, self-assertion and self-empowerment came to characterize the international realm, in which an analogy of modern individuals and *magni homines* was played out. The international arena turned into a 'laboratory for testing liberal political ideas'.[67]

Yet, if the *ius publicum Europaeum* was at least partly a liberal invention, then the fact that it depended on free spaces for conquest and colonization is all the more unsettling. Max Weber, when despairing about the future of freedom under conditions of 'high capitalism', had already mentioned as one of the preconditions of the emergence of modern liberty 'overseas expansion'. He went on to claim that 'in the armies of Cromwell, in the French constituent assembly, in our whole economic life even today this breeze from across the ocean is felt . . . but there is no new continent at our disposal'.[68]

Schmitt, as a philosophical conservative, played philosophical liberalism off against the practical political liberalism that expressed itself as a kind of competitive individualism in the international realm. Schmitt, in the name of morality, in fact, sought to retain the old liberal *ius publicum Europaeum* – and restrain philosophical liberalism at the practical political level. This moral restraining had two reasons: one was that the old duelling did provide existential meaning and satisfactions; the other that a fully liberal international order would not only be unstable, but also cause more violence than a system of *Großräume*. Even if an order of *Großräume* did not emerge, Schmitt felt that a seemingly uniform world would require a freely available and contestable outside to be stable. It was only logical, then, that he could occasionally imagine a *Weltraumnahme*, an appropriation of outer space, instead of a *Landnahme*, in case the United States came to exercise global domination.[69]

The question remained whether a world without a political outside or an internal frontier was even thinkable politically. Would the fact that the ideals of philosophical liberalism seemed to be at least partially realized at the domestic level, but contrasted with an apparently illiberal world at the practical international level be a matter remedied with the end of History? Or was this not merely a matter of practical inconsistency or hypocrisy, but rather an indication of deep complicity? Kojève alone gave a clear answer: only a transnational and even 'transpolitical' realization of the rule of law would be consistent with philosophical liberalism – and with human nature. But the question would continue to haunt Schmitt's disciples and detractors, all the way to contemporary debates on globalization.

Schmitt and his Historians: Philosophies of History, the Global Civil War – and Stranded Objects

A historical truth is true only once.

Carl Schmitt, *Gespräch über den Neuen Raum*, 1955

I n the early 1950s, Schmitt spent long periods in Heidelberg, where his wife was receiving special treatment for cancer. In the old university town Schmitt already had a number of secret admirers who set themselves against what was later to be called 'the spirit of Heidelberg' – a liberal spirit associated with figures such as Karl Jaspers and Alfred Weber, the brother of Max.[1] Immediately after the War, many observers – and not least the occupying powers – had hoped that Heidelberg would become a central source of academic and moral renewal in Germany.[2] In particular, there was the hope that German nationalism would be transformed into a kind of European humanism – as already represented by Jaspers and Weber. The atmosphere was intellectually charged – and, at least according to Jaspers, 'it was as if in Heidelberg humanity itself was at stake'.[3]

As the antithesis of the Heidelberg spirit which liberals longed for, Schmitt became 'omnipresent' in the conversations of three young students. Nicolaus Sombart, the son of the famous political economist Werner Sombart, Reinhart Koselleck and Hanno Kesting heatedly debated Schmitt's ideas – although 'curiously', as Sombart put it half a century later, they never discussed his Nazi past.[4] 'That Carl Schmitt kept silent', Sombart understood in retrospect, 'was normal. What was not normal was that we accepted his silence and thereby justified it. That was undoubtedly how he wanted it. Someone who is not asked cannot owe an answer.'[5]

Instead of 'interrogating Carl Schmitt as a prominent witness of contemporary history', the three, to varying degrees, became fascinated with – and fixated upon – Schmitt's idiosyncratic interpretation of modern European history.[6] They also came personally to consult the 'man from Plettenberg' on their different academic projects. Schmitt knew how to present himself as an omniscient old sage who calmly observed the unfolding of history without much interest in how things would turn out.[7] Such wisdom was particularly welcome for a generation which, in Sombart's judgment, felt like stranded objects left behind by the last convulsions in world history. They were desperately searching for 'meaning in history' – all of which seemed to have been washed away.[8] As Kesting put it in a letter to Schmitt, he admired the 'secret Principe in the invisible empire of German intellectuality' not only as a scholar and teacher – but also as 'a figure and as a historical problem – as the personified riddle of historicity'.[9] Schmitt's secret, according to Kesting, was perhaps ultimately the *arcanum* of historical and political action as such.

All three students complemented the instruction they received from Weber and Hans-Georg Gadamer with Schmitt's radical conservative counter-canon of, above all, de Bonald, Donoso Cortés and de Maistre. Kesting, for instance, affirmed that as a truly vanquished historical figure, the Savoyard reactionary de Maistre had understood the French Revolution and the logic of liberal modernity much more profoundly than the liberals who thought the Terror a mere historical accident. Kesting in particular took Schmitt's post-war works on the search for a global order as his inspiration and was deeply impressed by Alexandre Kojève's lecture at the Rhein-Ruhr Club in 1957.[10] Sombart even made a pilgrimage to Paris and was granted a long audience by Kojève at his offices in the shadow of the Eiffel Tower.[11] All three shared a plan to found a journal entitled 'Archive for Global Civil War and Spatial Order'. According to Sombart, the journal's editorial offices were to be located inside a restaurant, to be opened in Heidelberg under the name of 'Dr Kesting's and Dr Sombart's potato waffle catacomb'. An alternative, according to a letter from Kesting to Schmitt, was for Sombart to try to subvert the highly respectable journal *Neue Rundschau* by removing authors such as Thomas Mann and making it de facto into the *Archiv.*[12]

Eventually, Koselleck and Kesting wrote complementary, and to some extent overlapping, dissertations on the pernicious effects of philosophies of history and the moralization of modern politics that supposedly went along with them.[13] For both of them, not just the history of humanity was at stake in Heidelberg – the concept of history itself had to be contested and saved. Koselleck had the courage to put Schmitt's name in the acknowledgements; Kesting did not. These books were enthusiastically reviewed by an anonymous writer in the journal *The Historical-Political Book*. This reviewer happened to be none other than Schmitt himself.[14] Another rising academic star felt less sanguine, but was prepared to concede that 'at least now we know through his pupils what Carl Schmitt is thinking these days'.[15] Jürgen Habermas, who was a friend of Kesting, could easily see that the two were working directly against the very interpretation of the Enlightenment he was developing at the time.

The Deception of the Enlightenment

Both Koselleck and Kesting took as their starting point the success of the Hobbesian absolutist state in overcoming the religious civil wars through comprehensive acts of neutralization and pacification. Yet, as Schmitt had argued in his book on the Leviathan, it was in the space of the private sphere, which the Hobbesian state had separated from politics, that philosophers began to formulate what initially appeared to be entirely apolitical thoughts. Yet what began in the clubs, lodges and *societés de pensées* as apparently apolitical moral philosophy eventually amounted to a direct challenge to a state which failed to fulfil certain moral demands.

Koselleck's book *Critique and Crisis*, which has rightly been called the 'most successful dissertation by a German academic in the humanities of the twentieth century', came closest to being a direct elaboration of Schmitt's 1938 *Leviathan*.[16] Yet Koselleck, a significantly subtler thinker than Kesting – or Schmitt for that matter – probed much more deeply into the moral psychology of the *philosophes* and their radical separation between politics and morality.

Koselleck claimed that the protagonists of the Enlightenment had suffered from the twin evils of hypocrisy and self-deception. In their moral opposition to the absolutist state, they had never admitted their own desire to govern in the name of the new morality. In fact, some of the *philosophes* even deceived *themselves* about the claim to power that they were mounting for seemingly apolitical reasons. They were acting *indirectly* from within the moral inner space which the Hobbesian state had left to the individual and they now sought to abolish the state altogether. This cover-up of the cover-up infinitely radicalized the politics of the Enlightenment and led directly to the crisis which then unfolded as a bloody civil war. The strict dualism between politics and morality, which was the Enlightenment's sharpest weapon, was in fact not a dualism, but a dialectic: morality turned out to be the most potent political claim. 'To be apolitical was the *politicum* of the Enlightenment' – and this *politicum*, the *politicum* of morality, also remained the Enlightenment's most deeply hidden secret.[17] No wonder Koselleck had initially intended to call his study *The Dialectic of the Enlightenment* – until he realized that the title already existed.

Hypocrisy was a charge which Schmitt had already brought against liberalism – the fact that speaking in the name of humanity and morality was either politically impotent or a particularly perfidious exercise of power. Schmitt had also extensively dealt with the perennial threat of self-deception in politics in the pages of *Ex Captivitate Salus*. Koselleck now put the two together. Genuine self-deception was a permanent risk in politics – and, in particular, those speaking in the name of humanity and morality should examine their real motives.

According to Koselleck the *philosophes* had misunderstood the autonomy of the political, the nature of power and – above all – themselves. In his historical analysis, the moral opposition to the absolutist state did not and could not admit its own claims as political, because it would have lost a major part of its legitimacy. Irresponsible critique had necessarily led to crisis, as a morality without a proper state as its opponent had to discover that morality, when in power, could not govern. The revolutionaries in turn were furnished with moral certainty by philosophies of history which seemed to allow them to plan the future – a totally moral future. But in the end a totally moralized politics only produced terror and a total state, in which the sovereignty of actual individuals was hidden behind the façade of a supposedly anonymous government by morality. This amounted to the same as a utopian government – which also meant government by terror and ideology, the two prime characteristics that Hannah Arendt had famously attributed to totalitarianism.

From Philosophies of History to Global Civil War

Where Koselleck let off, Kesting continued. He complemented this tableau of the dialectic of the Enlightenment by drawing a direct line from philosophies of history as part of the pernicious legacy of the Enlightenment to the global civil wars of the mid-twentieth century. Like Koselleck, he focused on the *sociétés de pensées* and other associations in the emerging public sphere, and claimed that these were the historical agents of Enlightenment, and both the carriers and the addressees of philosophies of history.[18] From the very start, the philosophy of history had not been merely critical, but particularly aggressive.[19] Like the various moral philosophies on which Koselleck had focused, the philosophy of history led to a 'consciousness of crisis', which became oblivious to the essential connection between protection and obedience established by the pacifying absolutist state.[20] Under cover of seemingly pure moral argument, civil war became thinkable again, as the enemies of a morally unified humanity had to be treated not merely as enemies, but as criminals to be put *hors la loi*.[21]

Kesting claimed that the philosophy of history had been the decisive factor behind the outbreak of the French Revolution. The inherently utopian and moralizing character of the philosophy of history also accounted for the terror and the aggressiveness of the Revolution. Its humanitarian concepts would not only lead to a complete discrimination and defamation of the supposed enemies of the Revolution – they also required the construction of the first modern 'total state' to combat them.[22] The one-party state of the Jacobins was mandated by a world-historical exception – a final and excessively violent moment of transition in which the tyrants, the enemies of the Revolution and therefore the enemies of humanity, would be vanquished by whatever means necessary.[23]

Once philosophies of history had entered European intellectual life as a whole with the French Revolution, history – in the singular – had become omnipresent, while the present had become completely historical.[24] Even the enemies of the Revolution (and subsequent revolutions driven by different utopias) could not help thinking 'historically' and trying to explain events through some deeper pattern or meaning hidden in history. What followed was a permanent state of crisis – defined by Kesting as a general 'entanglement, a Gordian knot of revolution, civil war, terror and counterterror, the paradoxical unity of progress and regression, of civilization and barbarism, of Enlightenment and obscurantism, of enthusiasm for liberty and horror, of sublime humanitarianism and animal frenzies for blood'.[25] All of this could apparently be summed up by 'unity as process' or, even more concisely, 'dialectic'.

Kesting also linked philosophies of history to the other themes that pre-occupied Schmitt's pupils in the post-war period. In particular, his almost completely unexamined starting point was that philosophies of history were forms of secularized eschatology – a view shared by Koselleck. Here he followed the lead of Karl Löwith, whose influential *Meaning in History* had been published in 1949 and had been translated into German by none other than Kesting himself, after Carl Schmitt had recommended him for the job.[26] Much as in Schmitt's thought, this secularization thesis was a means of denying the legitimacy of the modern liberal age as one of permanent crisis due to the Promethean self-empowerment of a deluded humanity. The greatest illusion of progress, and therefore of the philosophy of history, was the notion that somehow history in the singular could be moulded or steered by mere humans.[27] This discrediting of human agency in history seamlessly led to a critique of planning and post-war *planisme*. According to Kesting, the *philosophes* had been the first technocrats, since they foolishly believed in the *plannability* of history. Planning became conceptually asso-ciated with the ideological 'complex of philosophies of history, moralism and democratism', with its 'enormous power of discriminating and defam-ing the political adversary'.[28] Kesting, like all those criticizing philosophies of history and planning in the post-war period, was also aiming at Marxism, even if not every writer made the connection explicit.

Liberal Modernity and International Law

Essentially, Koselleck and Kesting had painted a picture of modern Euro-pean history as Schmitt would have seen it, had he wanted to fix his gaze on the dialectic of the Enlightenment from his philosophically conservative vantage point. Yet, there remained a conspicuous blank space in this tableau: the effects of the Enlightenment and the French Revolution on inter-national relations and the *ius publicum Europaeum*. The painting was com-pleted by yet another of Schmitt's young pupils; Roman Schnur had already discovered Schmitt's writings in the late 1940s, and subsequently became instrumental in establishing contact between Schmitt and Kojève.[29] In 'The Idea of World Peace and Global Civil War 1791/92', dating from 1963, he praised Koselleck's and Kesting's theses as having paved the way for a deeper understanding of the French Revolutionaries' thought on international law.[30]

Once again, the *sociétés de pensée* came under scrutiny. Once again, they were indicted for having constructed the utopia of a world resembling nothing but a giant *société de pensée*, in which the *philosophes* and *littérateurs* would not so much govern as permanently proclaim the truth.[31] Schnur focused on the ideas of Cloots and Brissot and detected in their political thinking a fanatical striving for universalism and political unity of the *genre humain*. In the eyes of Cloots, Schnur claimed, the political unity of a world state would supersede the spurious unity and universalism of the old *complexio oppositorum*, the Catholic Church.[32]

There were, however, subtle differences between Schnur's account and the parallel analyses of Koselleck and Kesting. Schnur did not see the outcome of the Revolution as preordained – there had been a possibility of avoiding the European, and subsequently global, civil war if the French and their European adversaries could have agreed on a common constitutional norm. They could have accepted liberal constitutionalism in their own countries and the principles of constitutional monarchy as a basis for a common European constitutional standard. Instead, they elevated themselves to the position of humanity's guardian of the constitution, thereby obliging themselves to make war on any country deviating from their constitutional standards.[33]

The result was once more the attempt to abolish politics *per se* – the French Revolution could be read as, above all, an attack on politics.[34] What followed, however, was not the end of politics, but, in Schnur's eyes, a crueller and less calculable version of it, in which 'the other' of the revolutionaries became an aggressor qua being the other.[35] The more that revolutionary aggression was unleashed on Europe, the more elusive the 'end of politics' became. This in turn led to a fateful spiral of violence, in which utopian thinking sought historical clarity and certainty through a flight forward into a final war or 'crusade of universal liberty', in the words of Brissot.[36] Wars were to be enlightened – but they were also to be enlightening, as they clearly marked and vanquished the world-historical enemy.

This kind of war, in Schnur's view, was the precursor of the wars of annihilation of the twentieth century. It became legitimate to destroy human beings as carriers of certain ideas – and, in nothing less than a footnote, Schnur drew a connection between the utopianism of Cloots and the Holocaust. He also linked his critique of the French Revolution with another crisis identified by Schmitt's followers: the philosophy of value, which produced a permanent political crisis due to the fact that values did not yield determinate guidelines for politics. When the proponents of values attempted to *make* them more determinate, they became more aggressive – as in the case of the ultimate value of 'perpetual peace' against which no other argument (or value) could claim validity and which therefore lent legitimacy to the final crusade of the Enlightenment.[37]

Again, Schnur deviated from the account laid out by Koselleck and Kesting. His condemnation of the French Revolution was driven less by a principled opposition to the Promethean project of modernity, as against its supposed rationalist excesses. He did not diagnose modernity *in toto* as producing a permanent crisis, which would necessarily require a drastic decision about life and death, as the Greek *krinein* would imply. Drawing on Michael Oakshott, as well as Hegel's critique of the 'abstract self-consciousness' of the French revolutionaries, Schnur identified a liberal democracy tempered by tradition and a national 'ethical life' as the default option of a liberal modernity shorn of its utopian ambitions. Kesting, in contrast, construed an opposition between a utopian rationalism propounded by both parties in the current global civil war on the one hand, and another, initially undefined option that could save Europe from the United States and the Soviet Union on the other. In his first book, he dealt with National Socialism and fascism not as instances of philosophies of history – but as movements that had missed the crucial hour for saving European nations from being mere satellites of the superpowers.

The Secret of Critique: Three Trajectories

Koselleck, Kesting, Sombart and Schnur all engaged in virtuoso play with Schmittian concepts and categories. They provided theories of history which selectively substantiated – and only rarely contested – the general resentment towards liberal modernity that the seemingly disinterested 'old man from Plettenberg' exuded. Subsequently, however, the paths of the four disciples diverged decisively, most conspicuously in the case of the three Heidelberg friends, whom Sombart later compared to Mephisto, Faust and Wagner, Faust's diligent, if uninspired student. The supposedly Mephistophelian Kesting followed Schmitt's lead most closely. Unlike Koselleck who steadily moved away from Schmitt's condemnation of modernity (while continuing to make use of Schmittian concepts and categories), Kesting increasingly fell under Schmitt's spell – and, in addition, adopted Schmitt's spitefulness.[38] In the face of rebelling students in the late 1960s, he openly pointed to Franco's Spain, and in particular Salazar's Portugal, as models for other European states.[39]

Koselleck seemed to suggest in subsequent writings that prudential reformism, with Prussia in the first half of the nineteenth century as the most prominent example, could serve to solve the aporias of the Enlightenment.[40] Like Schmitt, Koselleck remained suspect of the 'acceleration' that characterized modernity as a whole, and centred an entire theory of modern history on the increasingly sharp disjunction between the realm of experience and the realm of expectation. Modernity permanently threatened the realm of human experience itself and destabilized the categories of historical experience. And yet any attempt to control and plan the future would only exacerbate the problems of the present. In modern times, humans also had to let go of any hope of learning from history – the idea of history as *magistra vitae*. It remained unclear, however, what political prescriptions or even what forms of political action under the circumstances of modernity, if any, followed from these aporias. Philosophical conservatism remained politically paralyzed – or, as was the case with many of Koselleck's positions on current political questions – turned to a prudential practical liberalism. A very moderate version of the Schmittian role of *restrainer* remained as a default option – but without the apocalyptic elements which had inevitably accompanied Schmitt's perspective on history.[41]

Sombart, the self-styled Faust, left academia altogether and worked for the Council of Europe in Strasbourg for thirty years. But he could not escape his fascination with Carl Schmitt. He eventually devoted a thick monograph to the former master, in which he psychoanalyzed Schmitt as a typical example of the 'Wilhelmine man' – and then sold off his entire Schmitt-related library.[42] Schmitt's political theory, it turned out, had, at the deepest level, been driven by a fear of the feminine – the implication being that antiliberalism was a *psychological* state. The further implication, which Sombart was to draw out in later works, was that either one was liberal or one was not – there was no philosophical, or even practical, cure for antiliberalism.

Apart from such enduring fixations, what legacy did the encounter with Schmitt's view of history leave? For one, a historically substantiated critique of the moralization of politics. If nothing else, Koselleck, Kesting and Schnur thought they had uncovered an inner logic of why morality was unfit to govern. They also held that philosophies of history, like morality, contained an inner dynamic which, since it failed to understand power, had to resort to increasing (and ultimately unlimited) violence. Did it follow from this that politics simply had to be left to the politicians – and that participation by those not practiced in the art of ruling could only lead to a moral over-burdening of government?

Of course, the critiques of critique put forward by Koselleck, Kesting and Schnur were themselves informed by a moral point of view – and yet that point of view remained unarticulated.[43] Any claim about the political future seemed to be in danger of falling victim to the charge of teleology as well as of hypocrisy. In that sense, the stance of the three Schmitt students repeated what they accused the *philosophes* of – but in a conservative vein. The secret of the critique of the Enlightenment was a philosophical conservatism that (at least initially) did not turn into a *politicum* and seemed to remain on a purely moral and historical level; the stranded objects were left behind in a 'world-historical no man's land', to use Sombart's expression. As the trajectories of the two historians and the jurist showed, philosophical conservatism could be articulated in politically very different ways. The only common prescription remained to *politicize* moral questions – where the Left supposedly moralized political questions.[44] Perhaps then the secret of history that Schmitt 'embodied' was ultimately just this: politics and morality could never be substituted for each other. They could not even be completely disentangled. Only very careful individual moral and political judgement could do justice to their changing entanglements.

Historical Existence and the European Civil War

In Germany, the interpretation of a 'pathogenesis' of modernity through the entry of the masses into politics and the moralization of public life had already been advanced by many older historians in the immediate post-war period. But it had now found detailed and sophisticated historical scholarship to support it – and, down to Ernst Nolte in the 1980s, it was to remain influential as a broad historical narrative among those who sought to pit the West against the Communists as the prime carriers of a philosophy of history.[45] In such a picture, the essential moral differences between authoritarian nationalist and democratic countries would become blurred once the united front against Bolshevism had been accepted. In the immediate post-war period, one of Schmitt's closest pupils had claimed that the totalitarian-ism of the East had to be resisted with a totalitarianism of the West – which should not dissipate its energies with liberal hesitations or be distracted by trifles such as de-nazification.[46] The concept of the global civil war could have – but did not necessitate – an authoritarian and exculpatory connota-tion.

However, there remained fundamental differences between Schmitt's view and the interpretations advanced by Nolte, arguably Germany's most controversial post-war historian. Nolte's most contentious claim – that Na-tional Socialism was a reaction to and in some sense even a copy of Soviet Communism – did not amount to a world-historical indictment of moder-nity. Nolte acknowledged Kesting and Schnur in his most heatedly debated work on the 'European civil war'. Yet the book was less a critique of the po-litically disastrous consequences of critique than an analysis of what Nolte called the 'overshooting' of ideologies – which were in turn based on overly strong emotions in politics, rather than morality tout court. Nolte's protag-onists, from Lenin to Hitler, were not victims of self-deception, let alone progressives who deluded themselves with promises of self-empowerment – rather, they were driven by extreme states of fear and hatred. In that sense, Nolte had recourse to a much more traditional conception of civil war – a Hobbesian one animated by fear and quasi-religious fervour. While his world-historical tableau relativized National Socialism, it did not indict the Enlightenment, nor did it portray Germany as a victim in quite the way that Schmitt's pupils had done in the 1950s.

Schmitt also posed a further, and perhaps more lasting challenge to his-torians – one that Nolte was to answer in his magnum opus on 'historical ex-istence'. The question was how history related to the political itself. Were they identical? In other words, did history only start with politics, and should history then be understood primarily as the history of conflict? Nolte himself had been one of the first historians who had asked, in the early 1960s, whether the experience of fascism might not have revealed the deep-est ground or source of politics itself.[47]

Towards the end of the 1990s, he offered his own 'historical anthro-pology', which included a 'scheme of historical existence' to determine what was to count as pre-history, history proper and an age of *posthistoire*, which might already have been reached.[48] The scheme in turn contained a number of elements which were not connected logically, but which seemed to emerge from an examination of world history itself. Among elements such as religion, the economic and sexuality, there were also war and peace. Nolte claimed that

> war – one has to say with and against Carl Schmitt – is the collective state of emergency, just as the immediate proximity of death is the individual state of emergency, while everyday existence means life without the state of emergency and therefore possibly a deficient life. Only war is an unconditional friend–enemy relationship, and the corresponding definition of politics is only permissible in a situation of civil war – a situation in which Carl Schmitt found himself, rather than having created it through his definition.[49]

In other words, Schmitt really was *the* political theorist of the age of European and global civil war. Moreover, while history could not be reduced to warfare, war was an essential element of proper historical existence.[50] Even more significantly, the end of war would also constitute the end of some of the highest (and most extreme) human possibilities. Therefore, those intent on abolishing warfare had to ask themselves what might replace war to bring out these possibilities, or whether the loss of an element of what it means to be human simply had to be mourned. Nolte, then, agreed with Schmitt and Kojève that on some level a world without political division and self-division was a world without moral seriousness. Thus, it would not only mark the end of history, but also the end of humanity. Given that he criticized a world dominated by what he called a hedonistic 'liberism' – an extreme and unopposed form of liberalism – he also clearly stood with Schmitt against Kojève.[51]

Melancholy Modernism: The Ritter School

Much of post-war German philosophy could be mapped between two cities that became associated with highly influential schools. Frankfurt was of course the home of Critical Theory.[1] The other school was based in the provincial city of Münster, located in the deeply Catholic part of Northrhine-Westphalia. Münster was the home of what came to be known as the Ritter School, named after its founder, the philosopher Joachim Ritter. It was also the university where Hans Blumenberg, one of Schmitt's most formidable challengers on the topic of secularization, later taught.

Ritter had not set out to found a school. True enough, as became clearer in retrospect, a set of common concerns emerged among his most gifted students. Initially, however, Ritter had sought to provide a common intellectual home, the legendary *Collegium Philosophicum*, which started in 1947. In the German tradition of exclusive private (but free) – *privatissimum et gratis* – study groups, this was an informal gathering of promising young students from different disciplines. Initially they met in a shack, an unsentimental, functional and, above all, provisional building, symbolic of the post-war situation and post-war sentiments. As Ritter claimed in a letter to Schmitt ten years later, he felt that 'small personal circles, like islands of personal continuity, are important for the further existence of *Geist* [intellect]'.[2]

From the mid-1950s to the mid-1960s, Ernst Tugendhat was to write later, 'Ritter's circle was probably the liveliest in Germany'.[3] Ritter had gathered a number of brilliant young men, who shared an interest in renewing practical philosophy, while paying particular attention to the historical preconditions and potential historical sources of such a renewal.[4] Ritter permanently stressed the need to connect philosophy to politics and theology, and, in the spirit of Hegel, to make philosophy understand its own times.[5] According to the accounts of former members, the *Collegium* cultivated an open conversation, in which only 'gestures of unmasking' and extreme positions claiming 'nothing but' were unwelcome.[6] Ritter himself, who would not reveal his own position very clearly, apparently embodied a spirit of *complexio oppositorum*.

Most of Ritter's students had fought in the War, experienced the collapse and radical break of 1945 and been left with an acute awareness of historical contingency. Many of them also adopted a self-consciously sceptical, pragmatic and anti-utopian attitude. One of the basic injunctions was that philosophical prescriptions simply had to be practicable under circumstances of complex historical contingency and in the face of the fragility of political institutions. *Ars longa, vita brevis* became an often-repeated sentiment in the works of Ritter's most prominent pupils, alongside the more general Hegelian thought that the rational could already be found in the real.[7] Most importantly perhaps, Hegel's concern with political stabilization resonated with members of the School.[8]

Ritter had started his philosophical career – at an early point of which he was an assistant to Ernst Cassirer – with considerable sympathies for Communism.[9] In 1937, however, he joined the Nazi Party, but did not take part in the War. After 1945, he propounded an innovative version of Hegelianism which understood Hegelianism as a form of modernism and even as a kind of liberalism. In his short, but seminal book *Hegel and the French Revolution*, Ritter presented Hegel as a philosopher who had celebrated freedom and, more particularly, the modern principle of free subjectivity as the main achievements of the French Revolution. This marked an important difference with some of Schmitt's students, in jurisprudence and history in particular. Intellectuals such as Koselleck, Kesting and Schnur had interpreted the French Revolution as the prelude to the global civil war of the twentieth

century, which had left no positive philosophical legacy whatsoever. Ritter
and his pupils not only recognized such a legacy – they also understood that
there was no return to the old ideals of the *ius publicum Europaeum* and the
limited rationality of the absolutist state. Modernity was an essential precondition of free subjectivity – and retreating from such free subjectivity was
undesirable and perhaps even impossible. This might have been a grudging
acceptance of liberal modernity. Yet it was an acceptance nonetheless.

Ritter had also taken from Hegel's 'Philosophy of Revolution' the lesson
that modernity was inevitably characterized by divisions. Division – or *Entzweiung* – was a particularly important precondition for 'freedom of subjectivity'.[10] Modernity was divided against itself and any hope for a simple
reconciliation was thoroughly utopian – all that could be achieved was to
perceive an ultimate unity in division and to see certain parts of modernity
as complementary.[11] Philosophy was charged with effecting a 'reconciliation
of the Occidental origins' of contemporary life with 'the future determined
by modern civilization'.[12] In addition, the humanities, or *Geisteswissenschaften*, could provide considerable comfort and compensation in the face
of the increasing disorientation caused by rapid technological and socio-
economic developments.[13]

Schmitt had been in touch with a number of Ritter's students from Münster's law department, in particular Ernst-Wolfgang Böckenförde, who
came from a town close to Plettenberg and had first met Schmitt in 1953.
Schmitt was eventually invited to give a talk to the *Collegium* in 1957. This
occasion was also to serve as a test-case for whether Schmitt could still in-
spire interesting debates in political theory among a much younger audience.[14] In fact, the day (and especially the evening) with Schmitt turned out
to be a great success. After the presentations, Odo Marquard delivered a
'fundamental cantata for a solo voice with choir and mixed feelings to celebrate the tenth anniversary of the *Collegium Philosophicum* in Münster'.
Subsequently, Schmitt had one of his poems fetched from his hotel room.
The text he delivered – 'The Sub-Stance and the Sub-Ject' – could not have
been more fitting for his audience. After all, what preoccupied Ritter and his
students most, was the tension between modern subjectivity and the historical substances off which subjects inevitably lived.

While Schmitt's visits to Münster remained rare and his correspondence
with Ritter rather sporadic and overly polite, Schmitt's thought left a deep
impression on some of Ritter's pupils. They made it their task to work on a

set of identifiably Schmittian problems – and to take a hard look at liberalism in the mirror of its enemy. Most importantly, they tried to liberalize parts of his thought in the service of making liberal democracy more robust and better equipped to deal with antiliberal challenges. Questions about the limits of liberalism in recognizing and dealing with the enemy, however, also became questions about the limits of liberalizing Schmitt.

It was Böckenförde who systematically undertook this task, drawing on both Schmitt's and Ritter's thought, but also on the doctrines of Hermann Heller, a prominent Social Democrat legal theorist during the Weimar Republic.[15] Böckenförde, following Ritter, claimed that it was representative democracy which did justice to division, or *Entzweiung*, as a fundamental character of modernity and which offered the opportunity for a 'positive-productive dealing with division'.[16] Böckenförde also insisted – against many fellow Social Democrats – that the division between state and society enabled modern freedom. Political will-formation and political rule in representative democracies were organized in such a way as to accept the division into private human being or *homme* on the one hand and citizen or *citoyen* on the other, as well as the Rousseauvian division into 'general will' and 'will of all'. The representatives, as public figures, would then serve to articulate the real self of the citizens and could formulate questions or options for the electorate. Rather than having to produce the general will immediately from the people, representatives, responsive to the wishes of citizens, could mediate between the electorate and the general interest.[17] A dynamic and dialectic process of question and response, or of 'the action of the few and the approbation or reprobation of the many', would thus unfold between the representatives and the electorate.[18]

Böckenförde re-calibrated the relationship which Schmitt had sketched out between identity and representation in a liberal democracy, denying any possibility of direct democracy, but finding a way to ensure both democratic responsiveness and individual freedom on the basis of modern division. As in Schmitt's thought, representation was still seen as a particular achievement, rather than the mere reproduction of already existing interests – but representation was *not* a 'depiction of . . .an invisible being'.[19]

Böckenförde eventually went on to attempt to liberalize Schmitt's concept of the political, arguing that the political had to be understood as an 'aggregate'.[20] The identification of the enemy was only an extreme situation – normally, politics inside the state should not reach the level of enmity, whereas in international relations enmity was also only a *possibility*. But sovereignty, which was of course indispensable for the state, implied the potential necessity to identify and fight enemies. Not surprisingly, Schmitt's more radical conservative followers charged Böckenförde with having 'pulled the teeth out' of Schmitt's constitutional theory and made it fit for the domestic uses of the Federal Republic, whose raison d'être was mere '"inner peace"'.[21] But in reality, the Ritter school advocated not so much a political philosophy of pacification as one of peaceful pluralism. For them, philosophy – and the state – had to become the guardian of modern *Entzweiung*. As Odo Marquard was to put it much later, Ritter's teaching would serve as a 'philosophy of non-identity': 'that is less than the starry-eyed idealists demand; it is more than the Cassandras fear: the modern – that is, bourgeois – world is not Heaven on Earth and not Hell on Earth, but the Earth on Earth'.[22]

Odo Marquard and the Sceptical Turn in German Philosophy: Conservatism as Compensation

Reasonable is he who avoids the state of exception.

Odo Marquard

One of Joachim Ritter's students was to become what one might call the Federal Republic's foremost philosophical anti-philosopher. Like the more clearly Schmittian thinkers Koselleck and Kesting, Odo Marquard sought to hold Enlightenment philosophies of history responsible for the cataclysms of the twentieth century. Unlike them he also attempted to formulate a new brand of liberal conservative scepticism, which was radically different from the technocratic conservatism of the 1950s and 1960s. Moreover, unlike Koselleck and Kesting, he did not hasten to the antiliberal conclusion that anything short of a Hobbesian state would lead to a violent and ultimately terroristic self-emancipation of society.

  Much later, Marquard admitted that he had originally identified with philosophies of history – only to become progressively disenchanted by them. He claimed that they had served as promises of innerworldly salvation in a country characterized by a lack of liberal reality. Simply put, the Germans had expected too much from philosophy and too little from themselves.[23] Philosophies of history were nothing but myths of enlightenment, or myths of emancipation in a context where the Enlightenment had never quite succeeded. And in the allusive, somewhat resigned fashion characteristic of his prose, he demanded: 'Philosophers of history have interpreted the world differently; what matters is to spare it'.[24]

Instead of following the lines of argument laid down by Schmitt, Marquard reconstructed yet another history of the Enlightenment itself. Theodicy, he claimed, had failed by the middle of the eighteenth century – Leibniz's justification of this world as the best of all possible worlds simply no longer rang true – and consequently, God was put on trial for the imperfections of his creation. Yet – paradoxically – one way to salvage God from these flaws was to declare God's non-existence. After all, non-existence was the best proof of innocence. Instead, then, man was made into the creator of his own history. And since history was already understood to be an endless trial, man immediately became a defendant. From then on, human beings were under immense pressure to justify themselves – primarily their actions, but ultimately even their own existence. Alongside God, grace had disappeared from the mental universe and left a merciless, ideological and ultimately total 'super-tribunalization' of human reality.[25]

To escape from this enormous pressure for public justification, to evade the permanent accusations supposedly produced by philosophies of history, the thinkers of the eighteenth century threw open a number of intellectual emergency exits: the aesthetic, as art became by definition free from the need for justification; travels; unspoilt nature, into which the Romantics could escape; and even madness. It was not only the irreducibly particular which provided relief: even universal human rights relieved individuals from justifying an existence that now became ipso facto protected. Consequently, human beings turned into escape artists – or experts in compensating for the enormous moral pressures exercised by the Enlightenment.

Yet, there was also a more sinister exit. One way to escape the 'tribunalization' characteristic of the modern world was to become part of the tribunal oneself. Just as theodicy was ultimately made consistent through the negation of God, philosophies of history were made consistent through the negation of the individual human being. The adherents of philosophies of history, Marquard argued, could only absolve themselves by setting themselves as absolute judges and thereby making absolute enemies.[26]

Marquard brought together the critique of the Enlightenment initially formulated by Schmitt and subsequently elaborated by Koselleck and Kesting, with the kind of philosophical anthropology originated by Johann Gottfried Herder and radicalized in the twentieth century by Arnold

Gehlen. Where the Schmittian view charged the proponents of the Enlightenment with philosophical hubris and political irresponsibility, Gehlen
described human beings as characterized by insufficiencies. Unlike animals,
their instincts were not sufficient in determining a clear response to their
environment. This indeterminacy had to be compensated for through
strong institutions and traditions which provided both orientation and
limits to human action. Yet, while both Schmitt and Gehlen had drawn
starkly authoritarian conclusions from their analyses, Marquard somehow
added two negatives and ended with a (cautious) positive. He claimed that
modern man was best described as *homo compensator* – as a being defined
by the forms of compensation he chose and by his specific responses to the
disenchantment brought about by scientific and technological progress.[27]
Like his teacher Ritter, Marquard took modern disenchantment for granted
– but he claimed that one had to be completely conscious of the compensation offered by selective re-enchantments. Whatever masqueraded as being
untouched by modernity was only of interest to the moderns because of
modernity itself – such as supposedly 'pure nature' and 'pure art'.

Apart from that, the disenchantment with the other main modern legacy,
the various philosophies of history, led to a thorough scepticism – a scepticism at least nominally weary of becoming another dogmatism itself. Like
Schmitt, Gehlen and Ritter – and consistent with any conservatism – Marquard stressed the essential and ineradicable weakness of human beings
and, above all, their finitude. No life was ever long enough for an individual
to rationally question and justify all beliefs. Politically, this scepticism translated into a presumption in favour of the tried and the tested. Traditions
were simply not in need of justification, as they provided a form of relief, a
sense of orientation in an increasingly complex world. Consequently, those
advocating change had to carry the burden of proof. In this context, the example of the Enlightenment and its supposed political irresponsibility was
again assimilated to the crimes (in particular the Nazi crimes) of the twentieth century.

However, tradition was not to be understood as unified and definitive.
Marquard claimed that the conditions of humaneness in the modern world
were pluralism and a division of powers – not only politically, but also philosophically. The modern self was divided against itself and, as for Ritter, that
was a good thing. Modern life served many different gods. And a kind of
polytheism was the only guarantee of liberty, of not being constantly hauled

in front of one of the world-historical tribunals set up by the philosophers of history.

Given this spirit of scaling back political expectations, it was not surprising that Marquard also sought to formulate a new notion of the *Bürger* – a German word not adequately translated as either 'citizen' or 'bourgeois', since originally it reflected both. However, for the most part it came to have the negative connotations of bourgeois, and Marquard sought to find a concept that reunited *citoyen* and bourgeois.[28] He argued for an unsentimental *Bürgerlichkeit* which accepted the heritage of the Enlightenment and modernity, even defended them, but without any ultimate trust in its values and certainly without any trust in further emancipation.

Marquard advocated a 'traditionalism of modernity', a conservative liberalism, or perhaps one might say: a liberalism prepared to settle for less, which therefore effectively left everything as it was. It involved a highly self-conscious affirmation of disenchantment, which was hiding a deeper sense of lost values, a melancholy not just about human beings' deficiencies, but also about the fact that these deficiencies would never be fully and finally relieved. It was no accident that Marquard adopted the motto '*tristesse oblige*' for his philosophical work.

Younger conservatives, not surprisingly, could not rest content with this vision (or lack thereof). As they pointed out, Marquard offered *Biedermeier* – a cosy, harmless philistinism – with a high level of philosophical sophistication, a kind of conformist 'feel-good' scepticism.[29] Ultimately, it was a form of what Henning Ritter, the son of Marquard's teacher, called an 'Ersatz-conservatism'.[30] Not only did it make compensation central to its thought – it was itself a form of compensation, a substitute for a true belief in traditions, or what, from Schmitt's perspective, would have been a properly political response to human beings' defects. Yet, arguably, Marquard's conservative liberalism was a particularly attractive option in a country whose national traditions had been put profoundly in doubt and which had an excess of experience of historical contingency.

Marquard's thought retained a conservative philosophical anthropology, but included enlightened answers to the problems thrown up by this anthropology. He made liberty central to his anti-philosophy – liberty understood as a form of relief and non-interference – while eliminating the principle of *public justification* from his liberalism. This peculiar philosophical mixture was perhaps only possible in post-war West Germany.

Marquard had journeyed some way with Schmitt and Gehlen, especially in his explorations of the past. Ultimately, however, he took a path less travelled – that of an ironic, disenchanted and thoroughly sceptical liberalism which affirmed modernity without expecting much from it. This liberalism had no precedents in Germany, but, arguably, a pedigree in the French moralists and Jacob Burckhardt. It was more likely to lead forward to postmodernism than back to Schmitt's world.

Hermann Lübbe and the Logic of Liberal Decisionism

. . .simply for political–pragmatic reasons it is advisable not to make an enemy of truths, because the enemy is advocating them. On the contrary, one should try to woo them away from him. A theory gains that freedom precisely because it does not obey the logic of the political unconditionally.

Hermann Lübbe

Herman Lübbe has been one of the philosophers most present in the German public sphere – perhaps, leaving aside Jürgen Habermas, *the* philosopher most present in the public sphere.[31] Not only has he commented on an astonishing range of topics, while continuously emphasizing the limited uses of philosophy in dealing with day-to-day political challenges – he also has had a way of being *au courant* that is again only matched by Habermas. His friend Marquard quoted another prominent philosopher as saying: 'Hermann Lübbe always arrives a day earlier – even if one is on the same plane with him'.[32]

Lübbe is also one of the few German philosophers who combined academic work with a brief career in the public bureaucracy. Lübbe, a member of the Social Democratic Party since the early 1950s, served as state secretary for education in Northrhine-Westphalia from 1966 to 1969 and then as state secretary to the minister-president of the *Land* from 1969 until 1970. Deeply disillusioned with Social Democratic efforts to reform the education system, however, Lübbe left government to take up a philosophy chair in Zürich in 1971.

Lübbe's unusual skills of sharply delineating concepts such as decision and technocracy, while putting day-to-day issues into larger political, historical and even theological contexts, were clearly honed during his apprenticeship in the Ritter School. Like Marquard, he adopted from Ritter the notion of compensation, arguing that tradition and conventions become

more important as modernization accelerates, not less. Again, like Marquard, he is a 'traditionalist of modernity' who cannot imagine going back
on the Enlightenment – but who also claims that the burden of proof is
always necessarily on those who advocate change. Perhaps it would be un-
fair to speak of him as a proponent of 'arrested modernity'. Like Marquard,
one might call him the spokesman of a 'therapeutic conservatism', a conservatism that understands the painful divisions, discontinuities and losses of
meaning associated with modernity and seeks to alleviate them, without
any hope for a final and proper reconciliation. Yet, the main lesson he took
from Ritter was that modernity remained necessarily the ground of freedom – a ground that had to be protected against modernity itself.

Lübbe has never hidden his long-standing project of selectively appropriating Schmitt's thought in order to strengthen liberal democracy. In the
1950s and 1960s, he felt that one could 'relate to Schmitt's work in an eclectic
manner, according to the rule that everything had to be evaluated and the
good elements had to be kept'.[33] In particular, he sought to formulate a version of 'liberal decisionism', which preserved Schmitt's theoretical insights,
but reversed his political preferences. He conceded that the 'term had been
compromised', but sought to salvage the concept of decision as an indispensable element of modern democratic theory. Rather than decisionism
necessarily leading to authoritarianism, Lübbe held that a properly qualified
and carefully hedged decisionism could bolster a 'militant' liberal democracy – in other words, a liberal democracy capable of defending itself against
its enemies.

Lübbe took as his philosophical starting point the common assumption
that the modern world is thoroughly disenchanted, and characterized by a
large plurality of incompatible and even incommensurable values, none of
which can be finally justified. After the 'death of God' and the decline of the
power of tradition, there simply are no secure foundations for choosing one
way of life or one world view over another. Once this has been recognized,
there remains the need to decide how to live and how to act on a day-to-day
basis. Even without secure moral and philosophical foundations, one has to
be able to cope with modern life somehow – especially modern political life.
The latter is particularly characterized by the fact that decisions often have
to be made under conditions where time is short. *Ars longa, vita brevis* – the
unofficial motto of the Ritter School – made another appearance here.[34]
Given these constraints – and given the sheer contingency of modern moral

life – according to Lübbe, it is necessary to decide in favour of decisions by procedure, as opposed to decisions based on claims to truth or superior moral understanding. Democratic decision-making has the advantage of relieving all those concerned with decision-making of the need to appeal to ultimate values and truths. Such appeals would necessarily raise the stakes of the democratic game and, in extreme circumstances, make a common life impossible after final decisions on crucial questions. According to Lübbe, the will of the majority has to take precedence over truth. Put differently, legitimacy based on legality, or commonly agreed procedures, has to supersede a 'pure legitimacy' staked upon claims to the truth or insights into the course of world history. These kinds of legitimacy, according to Lübbe, relate to each other like normal political life to the state of exception, or like institutionally regulated political will-formation to revolutionary will-formation.[35]

Lübbe opposed his vision to Jürgen Habermas's theory of communicative rationality, and the 'ideal speech situation' in particular. He argued that Habermas espoused a form of political romanticism. Habermas, according to Lübbe, completely overburdened modern politics – and political discourse in particular – with moral expectations. No rationality – and no inherent move towards consensus – could be extracted from language itself. In fact, if there were a presumption in favour of the truth of a political majority, those in the minority would feel doubly outcast and quite likely lose their stake in the political game altogether. Apart from this anti-normative normative point, Lübbe also drew on his experience in bureaucratic decision-making to claim that Habermas's theories could not take account of the radically different – and contingent – contexts of real decision-making procedures.[36]

Thus Lübbe felt he had preserved Schmitt's (and, in some way, Hobbes's) central insight that *auctoritas, non veritas facit legem* (authority, not truth makes law). The modern secular and procedurally neutral state had taken the (religious and moral) truth out of politics – and thereby relieved all decisions of a religiously or morally decisive character. At the same time, the secular state, with its fundamental decision in favour of a religiously neutral political order, had made space for the emergence of modern citizens with their free subjectivity – the very process which Schmitt had deplored in his book on the Leviathan. Schmitt, according to Lübbe, 'had described the genesis of liberalism in a plausible manner; the only thing left to do was to affirm this genesis. . .'.[37] And what had to be affirmed was the 'political will to peace' over the 'political will to truth'.[38]

Like Schmitt, Lübbe warned of the dangers of what he called political moralism. Instead of relying on the 'force of the better argument', participants in modern political debates should recognize the contingency of their own identities – which could not be measured against one proper standard of 'emancipation' – and the contingency of the outcomes of these debates themselves. Claims to truth – and claims about individual moral standing – had to be taken out of politics altogether. A proper morality for taking part in a discourse required abstaining from moralizing, that is, moral attacks *ad hominem*. Given the sheer complexity, even opaqueness, of modern political conditions, personality is the least important element – and yet, it is always tempting to reduce the flaws of modern politics to one's political opponent's supposed personal moral defects.

Lübbe, then, argued for what one might call a 'de-moralization' (including a secularization) of political debate and political decision-making. These processes should not be animated by a search for consensus among a 'community of civic inquirers', as Habermas wished. Instead, they should be underpinned by an acute consciousness of the contingency (and brevity) of political and individual life, and a sense of the sheer fragility of political order. Like Marquard, Lübbe repeatedly returned to the theme of the hard-won stability that is endangered by expecting too much from politics, as well as a general sense of urgency: life is short, political problems are complex, but decisions are necessary. Given these facts, he claimed, a decision can be rational, even if there are no rational foundations for taking one decision rather than another. Practical reason can underpin decisionism without providing any firm guidelines about which particular decisions to take. In this context it was also helpful to recognize that parliamentary committees and administrative offices were not seminar rooms.

Decisionism along Lübbean lines, then, was primarily a second-best strategy of coping, or, put differently, compensation. Paradoxically, it seemed that every situation in which it was necessary to decide was a small state of exception – but that decisionism as a strategy for justifying a liberal political order was deployed in order to *avoid* the real political state of exception. As with Marquard, the criterion of reasonableness was not consent, but coping as best as one could with the constraints imposed by the shortage of time, the complexity of political challenges and the fact that secure moral and religious foundations are no longer available under modern conditions. This also explains why for Marquard and Lübbe a belief in tradition and decisionism could go together, even after traditions had become questionable: both were strategies of coping or compensation. The fact that both were seen instrumentally – that is, that there were no intrinsic justifications for traditions and decisions – raised the problem every conservative who accepts the diagnosis of the modern world as disenchanted has to face.

Did Lübbe succeed in his justification of liberal decisionism? On the face of it, liberal decisionism remains a contradiction in terms. It is plausible to conceive a democratic decisionism, that is, a theory according to which the people remain completely at liberty to change the political order without having to appeal to ultimate moral, religious or philosophical foundations. In fact, those on the Left who share Lübbe's dissatisfaction with Habermas's theory, have often called for – and sometimes made tentative steps in the direction of – such a form of decisionism.

Yet, this is a fundamentally different question from *liberal* decisionism. At issue is not the fact that in political life sooner or later one has to take decisions – an utterly trivial point, which followers of Habermas would hardly deny – but the principle of public justification, or accountability. The problem decisionism is supposed to solve is that of political order – or, as Lübbe puts it, decisionism is a function of self-preservation. Liberals can live with the fact that a political order is initially founded on a decision for peace over particular religious or moral doctrines. Yet they would claim that the continuous existence of such an order has to be publicly justified by an appeal to particular values, including perhaps that of peace, but above all, that of liberty. Decisionism pure and simple is no doubt one answer to the problem that modernity is characterized by fundamental disagreements about the good (or right) life. To the minds of liberals, however, it will not be a stable one unless it is permanently justified in some manner or other. The antiliberal assumption that order justifies itself is mistaken, because, from a liberal point of view, an unjustified order will be *less* stable. This does not mean that one has to appeal to ultimate values and truths – an appeal to political values such as stability and peace might be enough. It is this distinction, however, which is erased in the argument for decisionism put forward by Lübbe and others. Eliding that distinction leads to a false choice between an essentially premodern politics based on substantial, ultimate truths on the one hand, and a supposedly neutral politics founded on nothing but pure decisions on the other. One does not have to follow Habermas's theory in any meaningful way to concede that ultimately the basic institutions of a society have to be justified to those affected by them – a point where liberalism and democratic thought, *pace* Schmitt, *do* meet.

To recognize the groundlessness of modern political and moral life is one thing – to distance oneself from the need for legitimation altogether is another. Decisionism can be divorced from the diagnosis of modernity as riven by deep disagreements. Decisionism remains illiberal per se – not because it is supposed to solve the problem of order, which, after all, liberals have to solve as well, but because it does not even admit the problem of public justification. 'Liberal decisionism' is meaningless unless it means that certain decisions ultimately become justified with regard to liberal values – but then it has moved so far away from what Schmitt, Donos Cortés and others understood by the term that it ceases to make any real contribution to liberal thought.

Liberal decisionism is born out of a melancholy about the loss of a world of fixed values and true foundations. Rather than admitting the contingency of our values – which makes them values no less – and remaining committed to a principle of public justification on which one cannot go back, it settles on an unstable mixture of liberal preferences and illiberal means. Ultimately, decisionism, through its internal logic, is bound to end with the affirmation of order for order's sake. Rather than a genuine form of political thought, it becomes a political sociology of self-preservation.[39]

Robert Spaemann's Counter-Revolution

The Christian commandment of love does not prohibit having enemies. It prohibits hating them.

Robert Spaemann[40]

The pupils of the Hegelian Ritter all followed Hegel's dictum that 'philosophy too is *its own time comprehended in its thoughts*'. Like Lübbe and Marquard, Robert Spaemann felt compelled to formulate an account of modernity itself, claiming that 'today philosophy explicitly or implicitly has to be a theory of modernity'. But it had to be thought in conjunction with an account of how to remedy modernity's deficiencies.[41] Modernity, in Spaemann's view, sought to legitimize itself completely through modern criteria – that is, through itself.[42] Against such self-legitimation and the total claims which the Enlightenment supposedly made on human beings and on nature, Spaemann, like Schmitt, started from a, broadly speaking, counter-revolutionary perspective. Yet his justification for finding intellectual resources among the thinkers of the Catholic Counter-Enlightenment was radically different from Schmitt's. For Spaemann, these French reactionaries were already a step ahead of the Enlightenment – both temporally and intellectually – and could understand modernity better than the eighteenth-century promoters of the Enlightenment themselves.

It was rather telling, however, that Spaemann cast aside Schmitt's masters de Maistre and Donos Cortés. Instead, he wrote his dissertation on Louis de Bonald, commonly known as the 'father of traditionalism', who, at least according to Isaiah Berlin, had been 'deservedly forgotten'.[43] According to Spaemann, Bonald had formulated a genuine and substantial conception of legitimacy. Against 'universalist legality', Bonald had set a notion of sovereignty resting on a general will embodying the principles of natural law and, ultimately, the will of God.[44] A truly substantial and truthful reason was therefore the real and legitimate sovereign – a view that contrasted sharply with de Maistre's claim that sovereignty amounted to being able to do evil with impunity. According to Spaemann, despite the fact that de Maistre had vested sovereignty in the Pope, rather than the monarch, de Bonald's conception of legitimate monarchy was much closer to authentic Christianity. It retained a substantial Christian content.

Here, almost in passing, Spaemann disqualified decisionism – or the recourse to a sovereign power without substantial content – as just another form of 'universalist neutralization'.[45] In other words, despite their ostensibly reactionary politics, thinkers like de Maistre, Donoso Cortés and, by implication, Schmitt, had remained caught in the dynamics of modernity as an 'age of neutralizations and depoliticizations'. Yet, even de Bonald himself could not free himself entirely from the modern conditions under which he was inevitably living and thinking. De Bonald had defined politics as primarily concerned with the 'preservation of man' through the 'preservation of society'. At least according to Spaemann, self-preservation – or functionalism, which regarded everything in terms of the function it served for self-preservation – was the prime concern imposed by liberal modernity itself. It, above all, had to be re-examined. Such a view of modernity as sacrificing everything to self-preservation and instrumental reason was not uncommon. As Spaemann later admitted, this view had not only been influenced by Ritter's lectures and the *Summa Theologica,* but also by a book published by an obscure publisher in Amsterdam which he had bought accidentally in 1949 called *The Dialectic of the Enlightenment.* But he felt that even Horkheimer and Adorno remained caught in modern prejudices and therefore ended in an uncontrolled back-and-forth between utopianism and fatalism.[46] It seemed that the moderns could not even understand themselves – a fact which made it all the more difficult to preserve modern achievements against the total claims of modernity itself.

If a genuine restoration, as the example of the relatively mild Counter-Enlightenment figure de Bonald showed, was neither desirable nor possible, and if modern philosophy could not understand modernity – how was one to comprehend one's time and derive appropriate ethical prescriptions from such comprehension? Spaemann's answer was a conception of philosophy as *remembrance.* Ultimately, Spaemann argued, philosophy had to comprehend modernity by remembering its preconditions and conceiving of it teleologically as the unfolding of a truth about human beings which modernity had not posited itself. Philosophy, as a form of remembrance, also called for the protection of modern achievements against modernity itself and its potentially uncontrolled expansion of total claims on human beings and on nature. Freedom for instance, was a particularly modern achievement, but it was also an indispensable part of the good life in general, as freedom was grounded in a truth about human nature. At the same time, from such a perspective, the modern tendencies to make progress and the domination of nature into absolute values, the homogenization of experience and the universalization of natural scientific thinking, could be effectively criticized.[47]

What did this mean for contemporary politics? Against the philosophy of value which, like Schmitt, he saw as a specifically modern form of relativism that could flip over into a form of positivism, Spaemann sought a rehabilitation of natural law thinking as well as a teleological concept of nature. For Spaemann, a harmony between natural law and the basic principles of a political system were a *precondition* for successful political action.[48] Freedom that ignored its natural preconditions was either an illusion or would turn self-destructive. Thus, Spaemann's thought could also incorporate ecological concerns into a philosophy that was to be integral, substantial and particular.

Spaemann grounded some of these beliefs in his own experience: Growing up in the 1930s and 1940s, he had understood National Socialism as 'radical-emancipatory' and as part and parcel of modernity. Resources to resist the promise of the 'radically new' and a remodelling of human nature could be found in Catholicism and its doctrine of original sin. As Spaemann put it in an interview, 'the pathos of breaking with civilization, the pathos of emancipation from it' was alien for a Catholic.[49] Therefore, National Socialism had already created a 'counter-revolutionary' impulse in the young man.[50]

Spaemann thus parted ways with Schmitt politically at an early stage – but he kept some of Schmitt's insights and arguments in the ideological baggage which he was to carry around on his further intellectual path. Most importantly, like Lübbe and Marquard, he tried to unmask representatives of the Left – and the student Left in particular – by pointing to the inevitability of the political. But unlike Lübbe and Marquard, who remained concerned about values such as self-preservation and the importance of compensation under modern conditions, Spaemann departed much more radically from modern assumptions. He opposed the specifically modern search for functional equivalents to provide modern men and women with relief and stability. For Spaemann, objective necessities and subjective beliefs had to be reunited. It was not enough to point to remnants of religious convictions and fading traditions as (diminishing) functional equivalents for more holistic worldviews which had provided orientation and stability for the pre-moderns. On this account, he felt, even Ritter had been too optimistic about the potential of religion and tradition for compensating modern pathologies.

Instead, Spaemann advocated the return to a fully-fledged Christian and Aristotelian vision of the world which far surpassed even Schmitt's attempts at political theology, without giving up on essential modern liberal achievements. It very much remained open to question, however, to what extent Spaemann's prescriptions could appeal outside a broadly Christian worldview. Schmitt's concerns about the inevitability of the political, the modern hubris of human self-empowerment and self-legitimation, no doubt informed Spaemann's outlook – and like Schmitt, he had no illusions about the political opportunism of the Catholic Church and the impossibility of anything resembling a theocracy.[51] But he demonstrated that a critique of modernity could take a counter-revolutionary shape *without* opting for an apocalyptical Counter-Enlightenment ideology (*á la* de Maistre) on the one hand or the adaptation of a Christian heritage to the functional requirements of modernity (*á la* de Bonald) on the other.

Don Carlos in Iberia: The 'New States' and the Integrity of Old Europe

Never forget that my personal enemies are also the enemies of Spain. This is a coincidence which elevates my private situation into the sphere of the objective spirit.

Schmitt in a letter to Francisco Javier Conde, 15 April 1950[1]

'Iam a Catholic not only according to my religion, but also according to my historical origin, and, if I may say so, according to my race', Carl Schmitt claimed in 1948.[2] In 1936 he had already advertised himself to the national Bolshevik Ernst Niekisch as 'a Roman according to origin, tradition and law'.[3] Schmitt's love affair with Latin cultures, or *latinidad*, as expressions of Catholicism went furthest in his relationship to Spain and, to a lesser extent, Italy and Portugal. From the early 1920s onwards, Schmitt had continuously found affinities with Juan Donoso Cortés's theologized politics of dictatorship – and for the rest of his life he returned to the Spanish counter-revolutionary as a source of political-cum-theological inspiration. In fact, he would ultimately be celebrated in Spain itself for having popularized and even 'universalized' Donoso Cortés's doctrines.[4]

Schmitt's love for Spanish thought and culture was reciprocated. From the late 1920s, Spanish political and legal theorists had eagerly read his works – and, in turn, Francoist Spain provided what Schmitt perceived as an intellectual refuge and a theoretical sounding board during the post-war period.

After all, as the German Schmitt aficionado Günter Maschke put it, Spanish thinkers knew 'what a civil war and what an Empire were' – and thus, supposedly, had a deeper appreciation of the disgraced German jurist.[5] Schmitt even became a kind of intellectual celebrity, receiving the recognition he felt he was being denied in his home country. Leading politicians such as Manuel Fraga Iribarne, Franco's Information and Tourism minister and later ambassador to London, would call him their 'buen amigo y maestro'.[6] Newspapers would carry stories about Schmitt and his family under titles such as 'Herlich Wilkommen Herr Professor[sic]' on his frequent visits to Galicia, where his daughter had married a law professor (and, according to some observers, a 'second-rank Spanish fascist').[7] Spain was a source of nourishment, intellectually, spiritually – and even literally, as Spanish catedráticos kept sending food to Schmitt in the immediate post-war years.

Political Theology in Practice
Eugenio d'Ors was one of the first intellectuals to comment extensively on Schmitt's grand theory of modernity, 'The Age of Neutralizations and Depoliticizations', which, Schmitt had initially delivered as a lecture in Barcelona in 1929.[8] His son, the Spanish traditionalist Alvaro d'Ors, took up a number of Schmittian themes and continued his father's work by providing lengthy commentaries on Schmitt's oeuvre, although he also frequently took him to task for his idiosyncratic Catholicism. Alvaro d'Ors arranged extensive lecture tours and travelled with Schmitt and his family through Spain and Portugal. Spanish was the language into which more of Schmitt's books were translated than any other, as well as some by the younger Germans influenced by him – most prominently perhaps Critique and Crisis, which appeared with the publishing house of Opus Dei, presumably as a manual on how to avoid Enlightenment critique turning into a regime crisis. Many translations were done by Schmitt's daughter, who had settled in Santiago de Compostela and frequently visited the family of Franciso Javier Conde, arguably the political theorist of Franquismo alongside Luis Legaz y Lacambra. Conde had studied with Schmitt in the 1930s and was lecturing in Berlin when the Civil War began. He eventually became director of the Instituto de Estudios Políticos, founded in 1939 as the first of its type in Spain and for a long time a 'think tank' or 'intellectual task force for the Falange'.[9] The Institute made 'Don Carlos' an honorary member in 1963.[10]
These dubious honours were not undeserved. Institutionalism along the

lines of Maurice Hauriou's doctrines, Kelsenian normativism and Schmitt's thought were the dominant strands of legal theory in twentieth-century Spain – before, during and after the Franco regime.[11] Even in the thought of individual legal theorists, these influences became intertwined. Legaz y Lacambra, for instance, had studied in Germany and became acquainted with Kelsen and the Social Democrat Hermann Heller.[12] Like Conde, he had supported the Republican Constitution of 1931, before converting to 'national syndicalism' and Schmittianism. Schmitt's right-wing readers would not always agree with his prescriptions – but all learnt lessons from his antiliberalism. They often faithfully reproduced his arguments against liberalism in general and parliamentarism in particular.[13] This was facilitated by the fact that the 1931 constitution of Spain's Second Republic had been heavily influenced by the Weimar Constitution.

Like fascist intellectuals in Italy, however, many authoritarian thinkers also found Schmitt's work – which they interpreted as either an instance of narrow nationalism or a kind of existentialist fascism – deeply flawed. Eugenio d'Ors, Schmitt's very first critic in the Second Republic, advocated a 'cultural revolution' and a new Spanish empire. Such a vision became opposed to what he saw as the relativism and naturalism of liberalism and socialism, but also nationalism and fascism.[14] Spain had a universal mission founded on its Catholicism – not a limited nationalist or racialist project. Even Conde, Schmitt's closest ally in Spain, also implicitly criticised Schmitt for the existentialist elements in his thought. He argued that the focus on intensity in Schmitt's definition of the concept of the political was a form of 'psychologizing'.[15] Enrique Gómez-Arboleya condemned the friend–enemy conception as ultimately 'biological-irrational' and indeterminate.

For these thinkers there was too much existentialism and too much decisionism in Schmitt's thought from the 1920s. Precisely because Franco's power was based on such shaky claims to legitimacy and because they were essentially defending a coup d'état, Spanish readers of Schmitt sought to go further in grounding the legitimacy of the new regime in supposedly eternal laws and values. In particular, they described the Spanish Civil War as the restoration of the 'authentic and immortal Spain', based on the values of 'unity, hierarchy and order'. Conde and Legaz y Lacambra pointed to the existence of a kind of 'basic' or 'essential' norm of order which already contained the truths of Catholicism and national unity.[16] The 'New State' had to be embedded in a particular, concrete Christian order. Any suspicion of a decisionist *creatio ex nihilo* had to be avoided – which is precisely why the visionaries of the *Estado Nuevo* sought a kind of *creatio a Deo*.[17] Thus, the Caudillo *por la gracia de Dios* also became the guardian of Spain's 'substantial' constitution – and his actions could be justified in the name of a 'super-legality' based on a national-Catholic legitimacy.[18]

Despite criticisms of Schmitt's supposed relativism, his Spanish interlocutors also learned a few more 'constructive' lessons from his anti-liberalism.[19] The ideas underlying 'national syndicalism' had more than an accidental affinity with what Schmitt had attempted to prescribe for the Führer after 1933. The division into state (or *Iglesia-Estado*), movement (or single party) and nation, all three united and led by the Caudillo, was a direct reflection of Schmitt's construction of a Nazi political doctrine around state, movement and people. The principle of *Caudillaje* essentially corresponded to the Nazi *Führerprinzip*. Yet, this was not a secular trinity, and it was not designed to save the state from the movement, as had been the case with Schmitt. As in Schmitt's construction, however, a strong conception of homogeneity held all three elements together. Yet where Schmitt had stressed racial homogeneity in Nazi Germany, the Spanish theorists relied on the conception of a Catholic, organic nation. As in Schmitt's theory, the nation in its mythical, even mystical, unity would only become visible through a proper representative – who would of course be, once more, none other than the Caudillo himself.

Arguably, Franco's Catholic authoritarianism put into practice what Schmitt ideally would have wanted in the early 1930s. The kind of 'clerico-fascism' or 'semi-fascism' practised in Spain and, to a much lesser extent, in Portugal meant that fascist political movements were consciously demobilized. They were kept in check by the army and the Church – and Schmitt was never a man of movements – while the state remained closely allied with the Church.[20] 'Latin fascism', was essentially fascism without a fascist movement.[21] It was a fundamentally statist, but also static ideology – unlike National Socialism, there was no dynamic, revolutionary element in the *Estado Novo*, which partly explained its longevity in contrast to fascist Italy and Nazi Germany.[22]

Like Schmitt, some theorists of *franquismo* declared that the political was the total – that under a new regime of 'theocratic totalitarianism' all aspects of human life were subject to political intervention in the interest of theological goals, above all, the salvation of the citizens' souls.[23] A religious (and nationalist morality) was superimposed on the legal order and led to a complete de-formalization of law. Where supreme theological and nationalist principles were supposed to reign, discretion for the sake of dictatorship was the outcome. Francoist thought was a confluence of home-grown reactionary Catholicism, espoused, above all, by Donoso Cortés (who was very much read through a Schmittian lens), and imported Schmittian Nazi ideology – which, to some extent, simply meant the re-importation of reactionary thought minus Catholicism.

Spanish political reality and Schmittian political thought corresponded in more than one way – in a certain sense, it was political theology in practice.[24] Like Schmitt's political theology, it was based on a decision *ex nihilo*, a violent act by a *pouvoir constituant* that sought to destroy doubts about its legitimacy through the construction of more or less fake 'substances', 'eternal laws' and 'immortal values'. No wonder, then, that after 1945 Schmitt found a personal and *intellectual* refuge in Spain – even if the Franco regime was now eager to deny the obviously fascist elements in its past, and was gradually liberalizing, especially after the late 1950s.

Yet, in a certain sense, even Schmitt's post-war agenda was parallel to the regime's attempt to redescribe itself as a type of 'organic democracy'. Increasingly, its theorists held that the fateful secularization brought about by modernity had led to the sacralization of the national community and the state, as in Germany under Hitler and Italy under Mussolini. The totalitarian state had had to rely on national (and pagan) myths for total mass mobilization, while leaders such as Salazar would remain opposed to 'pagan caesarism' and a state without juridical or moral limits. The Spanish and Portuguese states, then, supposedly presented the possibility of a third way of 'organic democracy' between relativist liberal democracy and the totalitarian and therefore necessarily pagan state.[25]

For Schmitt, the Iberian states had preserved their integrity throughout – and, as one of his favourite quotations went, *ab integro nascitur ordo* (from wholeness arises order)[26]. In this regard, he was particularly close to the movement of 'integral restoration', a group of thinkers associated with the journal *Arbor* and, in many cases, with Opus Dei. These intellectuals opposed fascism as well as liberalism in the name of militant Catholicism and Spanish traditionalism.[27] More concretely, the twin evils of Sovietization and Americanization were to be avoided through a corporatist, authoritarian 'monarchy of social reform'.[28]

Like these Spanish 'integralists' Schmitt put his hope into a renewal of
Europe from its periphery, against American and Soviet 'nihilism'. Essentially, he inverted José Ortega y Gasset's notion that 'Spain is the problem,
Europe is the solution', which expressed the feelings the liberal Spanish intel-
ligentsia harboured about Spain's peripheral and underdeveloped position
from the late nineteenth century onwards.[29] The 'existential crisis of Europe', Schmitt thought, might be overcome through the spiritual resources of
Iberian Catholicism – or what he saw as the authentic humanitarianism of
what Donoso Cortés had called 'Catholic civilization'.[30] Once more his
views chimed perfectly with Francoist self-presentation – or rather, propaganda – abroad. For instance, according to an English-language pamphlet
by Fraga Iribarne, then still a law professor at Madrid, 'Spain is an aged
trunk with manifold historical branches. Sometimes it looks as if the ivy
that wreathes it were choking it, but the sap still flows green within. A deep
sense of morality and virtue or courage still exists in the heart of the Spanish people, whose right will prevail at home and abroad'.[31]

Somewhat more concretely, the Spanish Civil War had extraordinary
significance in the global civil war which Schmitt and his post-war pupils
analysed or prophesied.[32] All 'non-Communist countries' should be indebted to Spain on account of its 'national war of liberation', Schmitt
claimed.[33] The implication was obviously that Western states were well advised to opt for forms of Francosim, if they wanted to prevent a Communist
take-over.

Authoritarian Options after the 'End of all Security'

It is not surprising that Schmitt encouraged and to some extent directly
guided the writings of West German right-wing thinkers who advocated
more authoritarian forms of government. For instance, he advised the journalist Winfried Martini almost line by line on his publications, which were
highly critical of liberal democracy. Martini argued that the liberal West
had turned 'soft' – its politicians and citizens were unable to confront the
deadly threat posed by their enemy in the East. After the supposed 'end of all
security' their inability to face this challenge was, in some cases, even
hidden from themselves. Here the Schmittian theme of self-deception came
to be projected onto the West as a whole. Martini argued that liberal
democracies needed to have more authoritarian forms of rule to ensure
their citizens' sense of security. Like Hanno Kesting, he advocated a system

modelled on Salazar's *Estado Novo* to remedy liberal democracy's short-comings.[34]

The more or less open advocacy of a practical political theology in authoritarian shape by Schmitt's pupils fitted well with 1950s West German conservatism. Like Schmitt, many conservatives undertook a 'flight into religion' which allowed them to present themselves in vague terms as having been opposed to National Socialism, without actually having to accept any of the positions of Nazism's ideological enemies, whether liberalism or Communism. For the most part, conservative intellectuals rallied around the concept of *Abendland* (Occident).[35] They advanced European Christian values against the Communist threat from the East, against the immediate past and, more subtly, against American culture – or lack thereof.[36] They also blamed secularization and the ideologies it had supposedly spawned to fill the vacant place of religion, for the catastrophes of the twentieth century. A new elite was then called upon to lead a Christian, and primarily Catholic *renovatio*, which would tame the twin threats of technology and 'the masses'.[37]

Theorists of the Occident, and Christian conservatives more generally could find a common platform to oppose cultural life in West Germany, without having to offer a real political alternative to democracy or the Western Alliance. Proponents of the *Abendland* who sought to rebuild the Holy Roman Empire (at least in spirit) could express a relatively subtle anti-Americanism which did not directly call into question the Federal Republic's military integration with the West. Most importantly, however, the *Abendland* allowed Conservative Revolutionaries to switch from a radical activism of the 1920s to a resigned cultural pessimism, which retained central features of their earlier world view. Philosophical conservatism was saved, but shorn of more or less all practical implications.

Perhaps the most important exception to this trend was Armin Mohler. A Swiss national who had volunteered for the *Waffen SS* during the War (he was refused, and went to work in Berlin instead), Mohler became a central figure of post-war West German conservatism – as well as its prime chronicler. He started his career as Ernst Jünger's private secretary in the 1950s, worked as a foreign correspondent for *Die Zeit* and other papers in Paris and eventually became head of the influential Siemens Foundation – remaining a close associate of Schmitt throughout.

For Mohler, the retreat to a conservatism which actually conserved constituted a regression in comparison to the Conservative Revolution of the

1920s, when conservatives had gone on the attack and actively sought to reshape modernity in line with their nationalist and authoritarian beliefs. Under the 'shock' of 1945, Mohler charged, conservatives had become preservers of the status quo again, driven by resentment, rather than resisting liberal modernity. Mohler then put down an ideological benchmark for a conservatism which actually resisted and reversed liberal modernity. With his study on the Conservative Revolution from 1950, he wrote contemporary history with the aim of salvaging a politically untainted, and yet activist conservatism which had made its peace with technology and other features of the modern world, but not with liberal democracy.[38] He sent another signal about what he hoped would be a new intellectual front by uniting contributions from Schmitt, Benn and Heidegger in the Festschrift he edited for Ernst Jünger.

Mohler sought to shift German conservatism away from the *Gärtnerkonservatismus* [garden conservatism], the preserving conservatism he associated with *Abendland* and Adenauer. He gathered theoretical ammunition from Jünger and Schmitt, and subsequently in Paris, where he witnessed the rise of de Gaulle and the beginnings of the Fifth Republic.[39] He argued that the Germans should develop their own brand of Gaullism, nationalist, neutralist and authoritarian. He had in mind the Bavarian minister-president Franz Josef Strauß – for whom he wrote speeches – as a potential German equivalent of the General.

Mohler continuously chided the Germans for being afraid of 'politics', 'history' and 'power'.[40] This demand to engage with 'power' and 'history' went hand in hand with the call for drawing a thick line under the past, and for ending the externally imposed *Vergangenheitsbewältigung* (coming to terms with the past), which supposedly kept the Germans from taking their fate into their own hands. As was to be the case with so many conservative demands for a *Schlußstrich* – a thick line under the past, Mohler played off the *pays réel* against the intellectuals, public against published opinion.[41] Schmitt and the semi-secret world of San Casciano, by implication, stood for the *pays réel*.

Lessons in Antiliberalism

During the 1950s and early 1960s, Mohler had kept in close contact with Plettenberg, and in 1966 dedicated one of his books to Schmitt, 'from someone who admits that he has learnt from him'.[42] Clearly, he sought to send a signal that a 'German Gaullism', a German nationalist and statist conservatism which actively reshaped the domestic and foreign policies of the Federal Republic, had to learn its lessons from Schmitt. Mohler also deployed Schmittian conceptual weaponry against the normative political science by now dominant in the Federal Republic when claiming that '... "power" is precisely the rest of reality, which "cannot be solved" [rationally]'. He linked this liberal-democratic failure to recognize the plain facts of power to the failure of liberals to engage with the 'exception' and the 'emergency'.[43] 'Reality' and contingency would always exceed liberal attempts to contain conflict in politics.

Speaking in the name of 'political reality' and 'realism' became a favourite rhetorical strategy for Mohler and other conservatives inspired by Schmitt. Mohler thought that conservatism could be reinvigorated because political reality itself showed the limits of liberal institutionalism and left-wing thought. Rather than return to nostalgic notions of the *Abendland* or accommodating Rheinland Catholic conservatism, he and his followers sought to forge a new ideological consensus out of Schmittian legacies and cold, technocratic conservatism. The latter, after all, also took a self-consciously 'realist' and cold-eyed stance. Gehlen and Schelsky, but also the natural scientists Konrad Lorenz and Irenäus Eibl-Eibesfeldt, were to be the new conservative icons. Where once conservatives fought in the name of traditional values against the march of modern science, they were now supposed to fight against progressive values in the name of science.[44] The Left, on the other hand, had now become as romantic as the conservatives had once been, as they sought to escape from industrial society. Mohler, instead of returning to 'nature', now explicitly affirmed the world's 'artificiality', and put forward Ernst Jünger's concept of an 'organic construction' as the essence of a conservative programme. Only then could the radical gesture of the Conservative Revolutionaries be recovered, and conservatives could begin to establish conditions which were worth preserving.[45]

Mohler was hopeful that the authoritarian presidentialism which Schmitt had advocated during Weimar could still be revived by re-establishing sovereignty and the power of the state in a moment of emergency – very much like de Gaulle had established a new order in the face of the Algerian crisis in 1958. Schmitt recognized the importance of the crisis in his *Theory of the Partisan* – although, unlike Mohler, he seems not have put such emphasis on the revival of presidentialism.[46] In fact, Schmitt increasingly resigned

himself to the all-pervasive dominance of bureaucracy and its modus oper-
andi of legality, which was no longer subject to any true political leadership.[47] The opposition between legality and legitimacy had now effectively
disappeared. Possessing the means of legality was sufficient for legitimate
government. The reason Hitler and de Gaulle had come to power, Schmitt
argued, was that they had used legality for their own purposes, not that they
had any higher claim on legitimacy. 'Rationality' was actually the same as
legality, and any substantive considerations seemed impotent in the face of
a state which had become like a giant machine; 'legitimacy' had become a
'helpless word'.[48] In that sense, Schmitt diverged from his self-declared
pupil's adulation of science and technology, and his hope for new forms of
authoritarianism – at least as far as Europe's larger countries were concerned. Hope, if anything, had to be directed to Europe's periphery where
legitimacy and integrity had been preserved, and where intellectuals still
understood that it was more important to create the right theory of the state
than to produce 'the best combustion engines'.[49]

Europe's Benito Cereno

As in Schmitt's ambiguous view of the partisan, which I will discuss in the
next chapter, there was a hidden advantage for countries in being underdeveloped. The fact that Spain and Portugal had resisted the modernization
and materialism characteristic of Western Europe after 1945, and the 'acceleration' of the modern age in general, was simply another way of saying that
these states had preserved the primacy of the political – and, in particular,
the primacy of the political will of a dictator.[50] Converseley, industrialisa-
tion had sapped the spiritual strength and weakened the existential resolute-
ness of Europe, making her into a Hamlet, or, worse still: a Benito Cereno.[51]
Like the captain and 'invalid courtier', Europe as such had been kidnapped
by slaves – yet, like Cereno, Europe's leaders had to keep pretending that they
were still in charge of its destiny. Melville's pragmatic captain Delano of
course signified nothing but the naivety of the Americans on the world-historical stage, who were unable to recognize the European tragedy which – in
Schmitt's eyes – they had brought about.

Not only Europe – but also Schmitt himself – was symbolised by Benito
Cereno. His destiny, he implied in none too subtle language, was that of
the old Europe. Lamenting the decline of the European spirit was a high-
minded way of talking about the impotence and confusion of European

elites. As the old Euro-centric worldview (and its corresponding politics and legal system) had imploded, Schmitt ever more frequently fixed his gaze on the periphery for rescue from the clutches of those who were now in charge of world affairs, but who remained mere slaves, both intellectually and technologically. These impostors had to be expunged from Schmitt's distant vision of a restored Christian West – a vision which seemed to include the figure of a Grand Inquisitor embodied by none other than Carl Schmitt.[52]

The Partisan in the Landscape of Treason: Schmitt's Theory of Guerilla Warfare – and its Partisans

> The old chivalry is dead . . . wars are conducted by technicians.
>
> Ernst Jünger, 1949

In a reception history rich in ironies, one of the most ironic historical twists was that, in 1970, a Berlin-based German Maoist could claim that Carl Schmitt had been the 'only person who was competent to say something about the topic' of partisans and irregular combatants.[1] Joachim Schickel's comment was hardly an individual ideological aberration. Schmitt's writings on the partisan contributed much to his secret and sometimes not so secret renaissance among the radical student Left, which I discuss in a later section.

The figure of the partisan allowed Schmitt to reiterate his theses about the end of modern European statehood and the international legal system of the *ius publicum Europaeum*, while at the same time reinserting the possibility of the political into what threatened to become Kojève's universal homogeneous state. The partisan not only relied on space as a precious resource against occupying armies, his violent actions also created a fracture in the modern, homogeneous political space dominated by what Schmitt saw as nihilistic ideologies.

Yet, there was no simple way in which the *guerilla* could be said to have redeemed the political. Schmitt's fear of ambiguity and betrayal was also projected onto the partisan as a quintessentially Cold War figure – namely, as a potential agent, a saboteur and, importantly, a seemingly conservative political type who could suddenly be turned into a revolutionary committed to absolute enmity. In the end, Schmitt relinquished his hope that the partisan could revive a meaningful notion of enmity – bureaucratic, industrial society, which functioned according to the standards of legality, necessarily proved stronger than the popular nationalist legitimacy any partisan could claim for himself.

Partisanship and Personality

Schmitt had become particularly interested in the partisan and his relation to the political in the early 1960s. His thinking had taken off from a book by the journalist Rolf Schroers, a liberal and a somewhat tragic figure in the intellectual history of post-war West Germany.[2] In 1961, Schroers had authored an extensive treatise on the partisan as a 'contribution to political anthropology'.[3] A self-consciously contrarian figure, he had previously written a book on T. E. Lawrence and edited a number of unsuccessful intellectual magazines. He first met Schmitt in 1955 and subsequently tried to persuade him to write a book on Hitler – an attempt which Schmitt countered with the argument that the 'stupid reactions with which one had aborted *Ex Captivitate Salus*' had relieved him of any further obligations in this respect.[4]

Although Schroers' book predated Schmitt's small volume on the *Theory of the Partisan* by two years, it had a clearly distinguishable Schmittian flavour. In fact, Schroers claimed in a letter that his book could not have been written without Schmitt – then going even further to reveal that Schmitt had been the intended audience for the work all along.[5] Schroers made the partisan a last incarnation of autonomy in a world that was increasingly regulated by bureaucracy and technology. More specifically, the partisan was the type of truly authentic personality who felt his identity acutely threatened, it not damaged, by a foreign occupation, even if there was no direct threat to life and limb.[6] He was driven by a feeling for *Heimat* – and therefore differed fundamentally from the revolutionary who was fighting for a different future, instead of a personally experienced past. Despite his desire to defend the law and way of life associated with a particular territory, the struggle of the partisan could easily be instrumentalized by what

Schroers called 'interested third parties'. These were primarily states that were using the partisan for their own purposes inspired by Realpolitik or, more likely, ideology. According to Schroers, ideological instrumentalization, often accomplished by the 'agents' acting on behalf of interested third parties, could only bring about the 'moral death' of the partisan.[7] Essentially, Schroers accepted the pessimistic diagnosis of the post-war world put forward by thinkers like Gehlen and Hans Freyer who had dramatically reduced the scope of action for the individual in the face of a globe subject to comprehensive state planning and technocracy. Yet, where Gehlen and Freyer advocated resignation in the face of such a 'second nature', Schroers discovered a reserve of individual will and resistance in the *guerilla* fighter. For the liberal Schroers the figure of the partisan had an ultimately *moral* character. It was the last refuge of an independent personality in the face of a society – and a kind of warfare – which had become completely constrained by impersonal imperatives.

Since the partisan confronted a machine-like state run by technocratic functionaries, his counter-terror against occupation forces and an imposed alien order amounted to nothing less than existential acts of authenticity – and therefore possessed a kind of 'illegal legitimacy'.[8] This liberal partisan, however, also contrasted with the figure of the revolutionary guerilla, who – despite ostensible similarities – was just another kind of functionary fighting for a pre-determined ideological programme. Schroers' partisan precisely did *not* have a party. Thus, the partisan was in the first instance a romantic figure. But he was also in all likelihood destined to be a victim of an age of ideologies and a new kind of global technocratic warfare which left no space for authentic individual struggle.

Partisans of Tradition and Partisans of Revolution
In two lectures delivered in Pamplona and Zaragoza in the spring of 1962, Carl Schmitt adopted a surprising number of arguments and themes which Schroers had laid out. In his slim volume on *The Theory of the Partisan*, first published in 1963, however, he also related the partisan much more systematically to his concept of the political – in fact calling his book an 'intermediate remark on the concept of the political'.[9]

Even more than Schroers with his emphasis of *Heimat*, Schmitt tied the concept of the partisan to the notion of territory – thereby also indirectly distinguishing him from the figure of the terrorist.[10] Partisans – or guerillas – fought primarily for the control of territory. Apart from what he called his 'telluric' character, Schmitt also stressed the guerila's irregularity and the heightened intensity of his political engagement as essential attributes. Schmitt conceded that the partisans' goals could be fused with other ideologies such as socialism, but nationalism or a mutation thereof was their ideological essence. Despite the fact that they were illegitimate bearers of arms, they were potentially an army and a state in the making. They did not wish to gain any kind of universality, nor could they.

Schmitt, then, argued that the authentic partisan necessarily had an autochthonous and perhaps even conservative character. To support this image of the ideal-typical partisan as a peasant, Schmitt reconstructed a historical genealogy of the figure of the partisan. According to this analysis, it was no accident that guerilla warfare had originated among the deeply reactionary priests and peasants under Napoleonic occupation in early nineteenth-century Spain. The partisan was a proper representative of the people, and the opposition of occupation army against *Volk* constituted the original friend–enemy distinction for partisan warfare.

The *guerilla* was in almost all cases an uneducated 'poor devil' who fought a hopeless fight for his *patria chica* without support from the nobility, the high clergy and the bourgeoisie, all of whom were *afrancesados* – sympathizing with the French occupiers on account of class and culture.[11] In the same vein, Schmitt described the Tyrol uprising in 1809 and the Russian partisan war of 1812 as elemental, autochthonous movements of the poor and the uneducated. They were inspired by a traditional Catholic or Orthodox religiosity, which had not been touched by the philosophical spirit of revolutionary France.[12] In that sense, authentic partisan warfare was tied to underdevelopment or even a self-conscious resistance to modernity.

However underdeveloped his social and economic background, the partisan had at least one political advantage. He instinctively knew the concrete enemy – the liberal bourgeoisie of both developed and underdeveloped countries did not. Moreover, while the partisan did not create the state of exception, he could learn to move in what the occupation forces appeared to have made a permanent state of exception already. At the same time Schmitt stressed that, against the backdrop of larger developments on the chess-board of European politics, the partisan was mere 'irregular cannon fodder in global conflicts'.[13] Supposedly 'great' interstate politics could simply swallow the peasant struggling for his soil.

Yet, there was already an ambiguity in the figure of the partisan at the birth of guerilla warfare. After all – and this at first appeared to be a major contradiction – Schmitt also wanted to argue that the partisan was a quint-essentially modern figure. He had only entered the world-historical stage with the rise of the masses and the beginnings of popular warfare. The age of total mobilization, in which the contained warfare between states mod-elled on a chivalric duel was left behind, also saw the emergence of particu-larly intense conflicts – and particularly cruel conflicts, which had first been depicted by Goya's paintings of the Spanish guerilla campaigns.

In this scheme, the rise of the partisan was just another element in the disintegration of the *ius publicum Europeaum*. Partisans, of course, did not engage in public, regulated open warfare; one of the characteristics of the guerilla fighter was that he did not display (or choose) a single identity as soldier or civilian.[14] Moreover, international law found it difficult to deal with the figure of the partisan, as he had turned away from the 'conventional enmity of tamed and limited warfare'.[15] Instead, he had opted for 'a differ-ent, real enmity', characterized by 'terror and counterterror' which would 'escalate up to the point of complete annihilation'.[16] Ultimately the partisan appeared as a paradoxical figure from the very beginning: he was a tradi-tionalist who could only have emerged under modern conditions – and, al-though desperately trying to turn back the clock in his part of the world, was actually hastening the decline of conventional European inter-state law.

According to Schmitt, a spark then flew North from the Spanish guerilla war and set Prussian minds under Napoleonic occupation on fire. Clause-witz formulated a theory of the partisan *in nuce*, while Kleist, with his *Her-mannschlacht*, wrote what Schmitt considered the 'greatest partisan poetry of all times'.[17] It was in Berlin under the eyes of the French occupiers that the partisan received a proper philosophical 'accreditation' as a 'new figure of the world spirit' by Clausewitz and Fichte – who had also written on Machi-avelli as a great theorist of national resistance. Unlike in Spain, where the ed-ucated classes failed to connect with the guerillas, those imbued with Prussian *Bildung* went so far as to formulate the first theories of popular up-risings, or 'the nation in arms', against foreign occupation.

Such theorizing about guerilla warfare also marked the beginning of a new alliance of the partisan with philosophy, an alliance which was sub-sequently solidified by Lenin. Lenin made the partisan into a professional revolutionary who viewed the class enemy as an absolute enemy. According to Schmitt, this fusion of partisanship and absolute enmity marked a further step in the destruction of the Eurocentric world Napoleon had supposedly sought to rescue and which the Congress of Vienna had attempted to restore. Stalin then perfected this combination by harnessing the energies of the essentially defensive partisan devoted to his *Heimat*, while also drawing on the aggressiveness of the ruthless professional revolutionary. It was Mao, however, who fully implemented this combination. He consistently relied on the telluric character of the partisan by recruiting his fighters among the Chinese peasants, and finally united resistance with revolution.

It seemed, then, that Schmitt simply could not make up his mind about the partisan. On the one hand, the partisan appeared as an authentic carrier of the political after the end of the era of the European nation-state. When the partisan confronted a situation in which his own state had been vanquished by a foreign power, he was immediately able to make an effective distinction between real friends and real enemies. His life was no longer mediated by a regular politics – and therefore distinctions between private and public would break down in the face of the sheer seriousness of partisan warfare.

Here the partisan was essentially a reincarnation of the romantic figure of the hero – a selfless individual who left his individuality behind in the service of the national collective. In the debate with Kojève, it had been clear that the modern state put an end to heroism, as the hero became criminalized and cast completely outside *civil* society and the system of regulated and contained interstate warfare. Now the figure of the partisan, precariously perched on the line between criminality and real legitimacy, could appear as a newly heroic figure resisting a world dominated by technology and a uniform administration devoted to the satisfaction of individual interests.

The partisan pushed the site of authentic politics to the periphery of the Cold War. Here Schmitt arguably exemplified a deeply hidden affinity between philosophical conservatism and anti-colonialism.[18] The romanticism of the earth and the primacy of particularity combined with an idealization of the 'underdeveloped countries' as the last resource to resist the universal homogeneous state. The fusion of order and locale, or *Ordnung und Ortung*, that the partisan exemplified was also the last source of political legitimacy.

The revolutionary partisan also clearly marked another decisive stage in the destruction of the supposedly humane form of European interstate conflict. By definition, the partisan was a totalitarian figure – existentially and totally absorbed in his struggle. Therefore, according to Schmitt, he could also be totally usurped by parties, which were the only truly totalitarian organizations. Parties, as quintessentially modern inventions, and the quintessentially modern 'motorization' and acceleration of politics, combined to effect a total mobilization of the partisan. At the same time, this could mean a complete loss of legitimacy, as the infinitely mobile partisan literally lost touch with the territorial ground and therefore his *only* form of legitimacy.

Yet, there were also internal conceptual difficulties with Schmitt's analysis. What accounted for the difference between the real and the absolute enemy except for a link to one's territory? Schmitt might have claimed that only territory would impose some limit on war, but he had already conceded that partisan warfare created a new kind of political space. It was no longer the open plain or the open sea which served as the spatial basis of the old wars modelled on duels between gentlemen, but a space with unsuspected depths in which regular soldiers would be trapped. It was unclear why Communist ideology could not also aid in the determination of the real enemy – unless Schmitt sought to disqualify class as an element in enmity altogether. This, however, was hardly credible, given that he did not agree with Kojève's expectation of a world of 'last men' united in peace and prosperity.

Schmitt's study, like virtually all his works, was ultimately more suggestive than systematic – 'the object [of inquiry] remains hidden in the mist', as one reviewer put it.[19] This was due, in part, to the fact that Schmitt's own ambiguities about politics in the post-war world came to be reflected in his portrayal of the partisan. Schmitt's partisan was essentially a romantic, traditional figure linked to the land and, in particular, the woods, very much like Ernst Jünger's *Waldgänger* – literally someone who wanders into the forest. The *Waldgänger*, more akin to Schroers' partisan in this regard, was also a figure of permanent, but indirect resistance against the modern administrative and disciplinary apparatus. According to Jünger, the *Waldgänger* was 'the concrete individual who acts in a concrete situation. He does not need theories, no laws worked out by party jurists, to know what is right. He descends to the sources of ethics which have not yet been channelled into institutions'.[20] Opposed to this figure of essentially conservative resistance stood the motorized and de-localized partisan who could strike anywhere in the name of absolute enmity based on an absolute, abstract ideology.

Partly these were Schmitt's own confusions. As Raymond Aron pointed out in a scathing critique which sought to draw clear lines between Schmitt's analysis and his own reading of Clausewitz in the 'planetary age', Schmitt had failed to draw rigorous distinctions between the levels of policy, tactics and law.[21] But partly these confusions had to do with the fact that the 'classical concepts' of the *ius publicum Europaeum* could no longer do justice to the complexities of world politics at the height of the Cold War. A new *nomos*, and therefore a new vocabulary for international law, had yet to develop in an age, when, in Aron's words, war had become a 'chameleon'. In the meantime Schmitt and his followers were left either confused or speechless in the face of global conflict and the excessively messy re-ordering of political space. In the year of the Cuban Missile Crisis, Schmitt hardly had anything to say about the atom bomb – except that it made notions of order and locale even more complex than they had been at the beginning of the Second World War.[22]

However, he also vaguely understood that the Cold War had created an entirely new 'landscape of treason', an expression Schmitt adopted from the influential journalist and writer Margret Boveri, with whom he corresponded occasionally in the 1950s.[23] This was not least a new *theoretical* landscape characterized, according to Schmitt, by the 'open collisions and hidden collusion' of multiple legitimacies.[24] Schmitt chose the plural of legitimacy consciously, arguing that in such a world, even 'deep and desperate enmities' could no longer create clear demarcations, as the shifting allegiances of Clausewitz demonstrated.[25] In the face of apparently multiple political meanings, myriads of criss-crossing allegiances and affinities as well as dimly perceived new political structures, old conceptual boundaries had, necessarily, become blurred – and the *Gestalt* of the partisan had itself become deeply ambiguous. Rather than casting political actors such as the pirate and the buccaneer outside a de-moralized *ius publicum Europaeum*, profoundly ideological figures such as the subversive, the agent and the traitor became integral to the ideologized anatagonism of the Cold War.[26]

Schmitt had hoped that partisans of tradition might be capable of disrupting the apparently seamless legalistic workings of the universal homogeneous state – thereby perhaps establishing a meaningful conception of enmity before a new system of great spaces could emerge. Instead, the partisan turned out to be less than politically reliable. Treason was nothing but another expression for a changing of friends and enemies, and the partisan himself could not be clearly identified as the friend or enemy of Schmitt's politics. Irrespective of actual ideological allegiances, he could be turned into a spy or a saboteur, that is, a mere technician in the Cold War – or he could resurrect a heroic form of political action and therefore be a genuine carrier of the political. The fact that the diagnosis remained blurred was a result of the fact that the figure itself appeared to be oscillating.

Ultimately, Schmitt drew the consequences from the fact that the partisan would be unlikely to disrupt the new post-war world order in any decisive manner. He concluded that the telluric legitimacy of the partisan was simply not enough to overcome the legality of the post-war state, or rather what he saw as the remnants of the state amidst industrial society. The clearest example for Schmitt was the failure of the French general Raoul Salan, leader of the illegal *Organisation d'Armée Secrète* (OAS), to defend French Algeria by carrying the methods of the Algerian war into the French metropolis.[27] The coup of the renegade parts of the French army failed. The legitimacy they claimed for defending the *pieds noirs* and for honouring the nation against a state which had supposedly betrayed its own citizens counted for nothing in a trial at the end of which they were declared mere traitors. French republican legality, according to Schmitt, remained the only legitimacy for members of a French army – and therefore the irregularity of Salan and his co-conspirators became not only a form of illegality, but also a form of illegitimacy.[28]

Schmitt had always held that the institutional and the political could part company. For a short time, the partisan in his struggle against imposed foreign institutions appeared to be a genuine carrier of the political. Yet, legality proved stronger than legitimacy. In a world run according to technocratic imperatives and the ideal of seamless functioning, the partisan was likely to disappear again 'like a dead dog from the Autobahn'.[29] In this sense, the *Theory of the Partisan* was a resigned restatement – rather than an intermediate remark – on the concept of the political. It left the nostalgic Schmitt with nothing but the insertion of a hidden homage to Salan and the OAS.[30]

Left-wing partisans, Right-wing partisans

The suggestive and deeply ambiguous nature of Schmitt's diagnosis facilitated its influence on the Left considerably. A generation for whom Che

Guevara became a global hero could make use of the romantic elements of Schmitt's thought on the partisan as well as his essential optimism about telluric anticolonial struggles. However, the Left's interest in Schmitt's theory of the partisan seemed to be based on a misunderstanding encouraged by Schmitt's tendency to group revolutionary and traditional, telluric partisans together. The Left was interested in the guerila fighting for a revolutionary ideology, whereas Schmitt had sided with the partisan defending his concrete, traditional order against the acceleration and loss of roots brought about by modern developments. Both, however, were essentially antibourgeois, antiliberal and, above all, *romantic* figures – and therefore enabled a short-circuiting of at least some extreme left and right positions.

In fact Schmitt paved the way for some leftists to become nationalists, before switching to a fully-fledged right-wing conservative stance altogether. The student radical Günter Maschke, for instance, began his intellectual career as a member of the legendary *Subversive Aktion*, the German quasi-branch of the Situationist International, and as an ardent admirer of Fidel Castro.[31] A draft-dodger with an international arrest warrant hanging over him, he fled first to Austria, where he became the 'Dutschke of Vienna'. He was lauded by Theodor Adorno as a 'boy of genius', while Dutschke himself paid him the dubious compliment of calling him 'Maschkiavelli'.[32] Psychologically, Maschke later claimed, he and his fellow revolutionaries lived in the inter-war period, under the sign of an approaching civil war. They even paraded with old machine guns and had the 'girls' dress up as field nurses.[33] Under pressure from both the German and Austrian authorities, he gained political asylum in Cuba at the end of the 1960s. It took a year and a half for Maschke to become thoroughly disillusioned with the *maximo líder* – and then deported on account of 'counter-revolutionary activities'.[34] He later claimed that he had taken part in one of the many assassination attempts on Castro.

Subsequently, he veered sharply to the right – an ideological turn facilitated by the fact that he had already imported much Schmittian analysis of the partisan into his theories on guerila warfare.[35] In his writings on the guerila, Maschke fused Schmitt's account of the character and the origins of the partisan with Koselleck's and Kesting's theses about the emergence of a European civil war and absolute enmity after the French Revolution.[36] In such a picture, the Napoleonic armies battling the Spanish guerila were armies of bourgeois subjects. The soldiers acted as carriers of the

Enlightenment, whose humanitarianism introduced an absolute and discriminating concept of enmity into Europe. Yet, Maschke still disagreed with Schmitt about the chances of a return to an age of warfare contained through and between states. He thought such a return entirely unrealistic and claimed that Schmitt was wise enough to know that the material, the political and ideological preconditions for a renaissance of this type of warfare, were missing.[37]

Maschke himself rationalized his change of allegiance by appealing to the fact that he had remained faithful to his original antiliberal – and anticapitalist – leanings. Rather than dealing with his 'Arthur Koestler complex' by becoming a militant liberal, Maschke retained some continuity with his communist youth.[38] Subsequently, he became a fervent supporter of Schmitt, whom he frequently visited in Plettenberg and who, each time, 'put him to bed like a father'.[39] An autodidact, he made it his life's work to promote Schmitt's thought and to re-issue and painstakingly edit his *oeuvre*, following up obscure references in the master's writings and editing the work of thinkers who inspired Schmitt, most prominently Donoso Cortés, whom he also translated into German.[40] He wrote regularly for the *Frankfurter Allgemeine Zeitung* up until the mid-1980s, when his Schmitt-obituary outraged liberal and conservative opinion alike and provoked a flood of letters to the editors.[41] Throughout, he portrayed his mentor as a 'Hobbes of the twentieth century' who had desperately searched for political order in an age of aggressive global ideologies – particularly Communism. In short, Maschke perfectly exemplified a reversal of antiliberalism of the Left into antiliberalism of the Right. Both remained grounded in a deep philosophical and anthropological conservatism as well as a decisionist disposition.

As time went on, Schmitt's theory of the partisan seemed to become more relevant than it had been at the end of the 1960s, when the revolutionary, 'accelerating' partisan whom Schmitt opposed was on the rise. In the 1980s, conservative, counter-revolutionary partisans like the Nicaraguan *Contras* and the Afghan *Mujahedeens* reasserted themselves.[42] It seemed plausible that the participation of partisans in a global civil war was not part of their nature, but a world-historical aberration. In retrospect, Schmitt's picture, for all its inconsistencies and moral distortions, seems largely confirmed for much of the twentieth century, when guerilla warfare became closely associated with world revolution, both in the eyes of Communist strategists and Western hawks.[43] The slogan that revolutionary warfare equalled 'partisan warfare plus political propaganda' turned out to be a poor description of the actual conflicts played out at the periphery of the Cold War.[44] If there have been any constants in guerilla warfare, it has been an element of nationalism or sometimes agrarian populism – and the fact that guerillas have been much more likely to succeed against foreign occupiers than native incumbents.[45]

Nevertheless, while Joachim Schickel had been right to point to Schmitt as one of the few thinkers who seriously engaged with the topic of partisans in post-war Germany, he was not the 'realist' admirers made him out to be. Schmitt was adamant that his thinking was unlikely to be fitted into the theories of other realist thinkers:

> A word from the Bible assures us that God can rouse children of Abraham from dead stones. We believe it. But we also know from experience that the world spirit creates ever new monstrous forces and power, which know how to control partisans faithful to their homeland from a world-political centre and how to incorporate honest, lonely thinkers into the programmes of their mass media. There will not be a lack of realists, for whom an interested third party is much more interesting than the poor partisan or the honest thinker himself.[46]

There remained an essential difference between the romanticism of Jünger and, to some extent, Schmitt on the one hand, and a more sober assessment of national liberation movements on the other.[47] Schmitt realized that such irregular movements had to become associated with some kind of regularity – whether that of a king in exile, the nation or other entities which could serve as sources of genuine legitimacy to prevent the partisan from becoming a mere criminal. His and Jünger's celebration of the partisan was about the importance of the guerilla as an instance of existential political seriousness – not a real question of legitimation. The real opponent of Schmitt's partisan was not an army but the spectre of Kojève's pure *player* or fake samurai as a world-historical figure. In that sense, the theory of the partisan was not ultimately about 'saving the concepts' – and therefore lacked a certain seriousness itself.[48]

Dangerous Labyrinths: Political Theology and the Legitimacy of the Liberal Age

Nemo contra deum nisi deus ipse
Goethe

Nemo contra Deum nisi plures Dei.
Odo Marquard

Gods can play; but God is serious.
Jean Paul

For Carl Schmitt, political theology was always nothing less than a matter of life and death. Despite his lamentations about jurists like himself being caught between theology and technology after the War, it was in theology that the personal and the political met for Schmitt. For the rest of his life, he always – wrongly – claimed to have invented the term 'political theology' and he defended it, as a research programme and, less openly, as a peculiar political programme.[1] It was not surprising, then, that the penultimate chapter in Schmitt's own post-war intellectual life included a return to what he once called the 'dangerous labyrinth of "political theology"' – the very topic on which he had first written for the Festschrift dedicated to Max Weber in 1922.[2] In many ways, *Political Theology II: The Legend of the Finishing-Off of Political Theology*, published when Schmitt was eighty-two, constituted his theoretical-cum-theological last will and testament.

This was not a mere message in a bottle, much as Schmitt might have stylized himself as a lonely sage. A wide-ranging debate about political theology unfolded at the end of the 1960s and in the first half of the 1970s.

Much of this debate has to be seen in the context of the aftermath of the Second Vatican Council and the rise of liberation theology as well as so-called 'theologies of revolution'. Behind it stood the question to what extent Christian belief called for direct social and political engagement on behalf of individuals. Connected to this was a concern about how many degrees of separation there should be between politics and religion under modern circumstances, and whether liberal politics could survive in a non-religious society. This in turn raised the question whether religion should be instrumentalized for purposes of political stability – a question on which the pupils of the Ritter School had much to say, in particular Hermann Lübbe and Robert Spaemann.

A set of even more profound questions was at stake in the dispute between Schmitt and Hans Blumenberg, who, like Joachim Ritter, was a professor of philosophy at Münster University: to what extent was the modern age legitimate at all, if it was conceived of as a derivative from pre-modern thought and religion? Was secularization not a synonym for illegitimacy? If the modern age could not generate or guarantee its own legitimacy, was one not thrown back on the paradox of the moderns (and liberals in particular) living off preconditions which they cannot possibly maintain or renew? Böckenförde's already classic question was now transposed to a world-historical level.

The Last Word on Political Theology

Schmitt himself made it unmistakably clear that his last book was about settling scores. In a footnote, he compared writing it to removing an arrow which had stuck in his flesh for almost forty years. The arrow in question was a thesis which the theologian Erik Peterson, who, partly under Schmitt's influence, had converted from Protestantism to Catholicism, had advanced in an essay on *Monotheism as a Political Problem* in 1935.[3] In this short book of around a hundred pages, Peterson had aimed at proving nothing less than the 'theological impossibility of political theology'. To that end, he had analyzed the rise of a political theology of monotheism as a Hellenistic reconstruction of Jewish beliefs. Peterson had argued that the combination of the principles of monotheism and monarchy with the Roman Empire and the idea of a universal peace under Roman auspices had been a conscious attempt to reconcile and even mutually reinforce Christianity and the *Imperium Romanum*. In such a vision, Christ turned into a Roman citizen or *civis Romanus* and monotheism into an imperial ideology or *Reichs-politik*, as Peterson had put it.[4]

According to Peterson, orthodox trinitarianism and, in particular, the teachings of Augustine, dealt a fatal blow to this kind of theology. The trinity simply could not be projected onto actually existing political systems, in the way that monotheism could be instrumentalized for legitimating monarchies. Peterson concluded that only Jews and pagans could have political theologies at all – whereas the peculiar trinitarian nature of Christianity had 'finished off' political theology for Jesus's followers. Peterson thus managed to combine anti-Judaism with a not so subtle warning to his old friend Schmitt about the dangers of dabbling in politics under pseudo-theological auspices.[5]

Despite the fact that Peterson mentioned Schmitt only in the final footnote of his book, Schmitt was apparently haunted by this frontal challenge and the man behind it. Marianne Kesting – Hanno's sister – relates how Schmitt suffered a heart attack when she told him some details about Peterson's life one day in January 1972 – so that Schmitt's housekeeper had to admonish her not to bring up the topic again.[6] Schmitt spoke of *Political Theology II* as a 'cathartic effort'.[7] The anti-Peterson polemic was plainly intended as a cure of some sort.

In what, in a letter to Ernst Jünger, he referred to as a 'desperately hermetic piece of writing',[8] Schmitt set out to argue that political theology had not been 'finished off' at all. One by one he took his opponents to task for misinterpreting arcane and intricate details of Church history. Most importantly, however, he homed in on the conclusions of his long-dead former friend Peterson. A clean separation of politics and theology was only possible as long as both were represented in distinct legal institutions – the state and the Church. Augustine's doctrine of the two cities would always be confronted with the arch-Schmittian question: *who decides?* Thus, at least during times of crisis (and therefore times of blurred separations), political theology was inevitable. Peterson's political neutralisation of theology had failed – but, like all neutralisations, it had had a political function. Consequently, Peterson's attempt at 'finishing off' political theology had been a double failure.

Moreover, Schmitt claimed that the trinity *itself* could be political. With reference to Goethe's famous dictum *nemo contra deum nisi deus ipse* (nothing against God except a God), but scant theological or historical evidence, Schmitt projected a dualism of a God of creation and a God of redemption into the trinity. In other words, he resorted to a form of Gnosticism in order to prove that even the trinity, the prime piece of evidence in the trial to end all political theology, could be politicized. Enmity could not be expunged from the world – ultimately, it was God-given. Therefore, all theology and all of reality could be political. Anybody claiming to have de-theologized politics was merely a theologian of the anti-theological.[9] Once more, the political had become total – and the concept of political theology a supremely versatile and dangerous polemical weapon.

Blumenberg's Challenge: Modernity Redeemed

Schmitt's other major opponent in the debate on the possibility of political theology was Hans Blumenberg – one of the most significant post-war German philosophers. Blumenberg, one might say, specialized in imploding *idées reçues* about modernity. As part of this effort, he had explicitly criticized Schmitt in his first larger work, the famous *Legitimacy of the Modern Age*.[10] In this rich and sprawling book, Blumenberg was concerned to disprove the idea that the modern world had come about in a process of secularization. For Blumenberg, secularization constituted a 'category of historical injustice'. It denied the legitimacy of the modern age, which was made to seem derivative and somehow inferior.

The task Blumenberg set himself was to show that there were no real transformations of religious into worldly concepts in the areas where advocates of the secularization thesis saw them. Focusing on Karl Löwith's famous thesis that Christian eschatology had become secularized as the modern notion of progress (the very thesis which Kesting and other Schmitt pupils had taken up in their attack on modernity), Blumenberg sought to demonstrate with great erudition that such a transposition was impossible. As the end of the world failed to arrive, eschatology had indeed thrown up problems for early Christians – but the worldly answers they found for these problems were *not* a secularization of eschatology.

Blumenberg did not seek to deny that there had been continuity in some of the concerns and questions of the premoderns and the moderns. Premodern systems of thought such as Scholasticism, however, had also produced questions which these systems themselves were incapable of answering. Modernity, Blumenberg boldly claimed, was really *better* in the sense that it was capable of supplying precisely these answers.[11] Even where there appeared to be ostensible similarities between Christian thematics and modern thought, this was not a matter of secularization, but of what Blumenberg called a 'reoccupation' of positions left vacant. Modern thinkers had sought to provide answers in areas of particular significance which had initially been mapped out by theologians and which were now 'reoccupied' by the moderns.

Specifically, Blumenberg argued that at one point medieval men had faced the challenge of what he termed 'theological absolutism'. Theological absolutism referred to the belief in an incomprehensible, absolutely sovereign God, a notion which Blumenberg identified with medieval nominalism. Such a God could change the world arbitrarily at any moment. Two consequences followed: such an apparently contingent world lacked all order and intelligibility, and such a God understood as *potentia absoluta* also appeared to be a hidden God – a *deus absconditus*.

This conception precipitated a situation of profound 'metaphysical insecurity' and an existential insecurity with regard to a ruthless nature that seemed hostile to man. It was in such a situation, where human beings seemed entirely thrown back upon themselves, that the modern notion of 'human self-empowerment' arose. Human self-empowerment included the idea of self-preservation, but also referred to a conscious effort rationally to control and dominate nature. This effort in turn depended on a rehabilitation of 'theoretical curiosity', which had still been 'discriminated' as a vice by Augustine.

Blumenberg's narrative, or 'phenomenology', of epochal shifts went directly against Schmitt's research programme of secularization as a sociology of conceptual change.[12] Schmitt had advanced a systematic and a historical concept of secularization. Yet, contrary to what Hermann Lübbe would argue some years later, 'secularization' was not a mere research program – Schmitt's systematic and structural approach was shot through with normative and religious assumptions.[13]

Blumenberg launched a broad attack on both the sociological and the normative claims that Schmitt made about secularization. He argued that 'the sentence "all significant concepts of modern state theory are secularized theological concepts" has not become more credible since it was first uttered in 1922, as one has learnt to doubt whether this "modernity" has ever been modern. . .'.[14] Blumenberg substantiated his doubt by offering a different account of modern politics – or rather a politics that temporally coincided with modernity, but actually contained many elements which could not be called fully modern. In particular, he argued that 'theological absolutism had provided an "experimental demonstration" of the fact that it was humanly unbearable through the political effects of religious pluralism'.[15] The resulting religious civil wars had then made it necessary to transfer the friend–enemy relationship between 'absolute religious factions' from inside the state to the international arena of 'integrating nation-states'. According to Blumenberg, this containment of absolute domestic enmity through the projection of enmity into international affairs had marked the 'historically specific picture of modernity'.[16]

In the twentieth century this picture would necessarily have to be revised, given entirely new levels of violence in international affairs. Just as the domestic plurality of religions had had to be contained by the absolutist state, three hundred years later a new international system would have to be found to control violence – at least in Europe. Blumenberg clearly hoped that a new – or rather, a properly modern – historical stage could be reached in which one would no longer believe that 'the decision between Good and Evil is immanent in history' and 'that every political act takes part in this decision'.[17] In the same vein, the suggestion of 'the state of exception as the normal state of the political' might finally lose its credibility – and instead the 'technique' of the political might come closer to the 'type of great administrations', instead of resembling 'the arrows of Zeus and the decrees of Predestination'.[18]

What Schmitt had admired and defended as an achievement of occidental rationalism – the *ius publicum Europaeum* – was not properly modern at all, but neither was it a theological residue of a process of secularization. It was essentially an unresolved problem within modernity itself, left by the claims of theological absolutism, some of whose attributes had been transferred to the absolute state. Schmittian politics were the result of a failed modern 'reoccupation' of pre-modern questions. Thus Blumenberg threw down a double challenge to Schmitt – questioning both his 'sociology of concepts' and the substantial political concepts Schmitt defended.

Schmitt's Parody: Process-Progress and the Persistence of Political Theology

Schmitt took up the double challenge and extensively responded to Blumenberg in the afterword of *Political Theology II*, which was part polemic and

part parody. What he had to do according to his own strategy was establish
that Blumenberg was somehow a political theologian – and that even modernity could not expunge enmity, and therefore political theology, from the
world.

Schmitt first attacked Blumenberg for cunningly having appropriated
the concept of legitimacy – when predictable and rationalistic legality was
obviously the functional mode of modernity, while legitimacy had always
been associated with the familiar and the inherited.[19] Under modern conditions, Schmitt argued, those claiming legitimacy were always intent on
empowering themselves.[20] At the same time, Schmitt charged, Blumenberg
sought to refuse any real need for justification. The modern age simply
justified itself – just like human curiosity and the desire for the new as such,
which had been completely unleashed in modernity. But, according to
Schmitt, this kind of immanence or even 'autism', polemically directed
against any theological transcendence, could only be described in the language of the philosophy of value – the very philosophy which Schmitt had
declared as one of his prime intellectual targets after 1945. The new, or what
Paul Valéry once called néomanie, had become a value in itself. But all
values, according to Schmitt's long-held beliefs, automatically negated their
opposites – such as the old – in a particularly aggressive way. Therefore, enmity could not be expunged even from a de-theologized world.[21]

Schmitt, shifting tactics, then went on to resort to his oldest polemical weapon: satire. In the way he had once parodied Thomas Mann in the
1910s, he now caricatured a completely de-theologized, de-politicized, de-
juridified, de-ideologized, de-historicized world – a tabula rasa which de-
tabularizes itself and disappears. He painted a picture of a completely
immanent world, governed by a 'process-progress' driven by insatiable
human curiosity. As Schmitt put it,

> the process-progress produces not only itself and the New Man, but also
> the conditions of possibility of its own renewals of the new; this means
> the opposite of a creation out of nothingness, which is the creation of
> nothingness as the condition of possibility of the self-creation of an
> always new reality.[22]

This complete nihilism of a world in which function had been completely
substituted for substance, a world that permanently deconstructed itself,

was Schmitt's last word on – and for – political theology. This world, Schmitt charged in no uncertain terms, would be one of utmost aggressiveness. And, on any account, whether political, moral or theological, a world of proper and properly recognized enmity was preferable to such a dystopia.

For all his attempts to substitute parody for argument, Schmitt had put his finger on an important point. Blumenberg *had* been concerned to show that modernity made the notions of self-empowerment and self-preservation central to human life – and was justified in doing so by the demands which the pre-modern age had failed to meet.[23] Modernity was legitimate not only by virtue of its own criteria, but also by criteria employed during the Middle Ages. The very notion which Robert Spaemann criticized as central to modernity – self-preservation – Blumenberg invested with legitimacy.

In response to Schmitt's attack, Blumenberg toned down his emphasis on self-empowerment, shifting from self-empowerment to the weaker 'self-assertion' – a rather significant concession and an apparent loss of self-confidence by the proponent of the modern age. In fact, Blumenberg was haunted by Schmitt's criticism, explaining at one point to Schmitt how eager he was to understand the 'logic of our difference'.[24] In a letter he alerted his adversary to the changes which he had made to the second edition of *Legitimacy of the Modern Age*, admitting that 'none of the comments on my book have enervated me as much as yours to go beyond what has been achieved. . .'.[25] He also conceded that he had made Schmitt's position much too harmless by reducing his thought to the category of secularization. He now understood that they were interested in similar phenomena, but approached them with different questions: Blumenberg asked 'how can this preserve itself?', whereas Schmitt took an answer to be satisfying if it responded to the question 'What is the extreme state?'[26]

However, Blumenberg went on to charge Schmitt with pursuing a 'theological' or 'theologized' politics. 'Theology as a political ideology', he claimed, performed the same authoritarian function it had served for counter-revolutionaries like de Bonald and de Maistre: it bolstered the worldly power of an absolute monarch. Political theology was really a matter of deploying a mobile army of metaphors in order to appropriate legitimacy for what had already lost legitimacy. As Blumenberg put it, the 'quasi-divine person of the sovereign has legitimacy and must have it . . . because . . . he . . . first has to constitute or reconstitute it'.[27] Thus, the political theologian was a truly Machiavellian figure, who could cover his decisionism and his drive for power by appealing to the authority of the past and origins, and whose metaphors saved him from the 'cynicism of an openly "theological politics"'.[28] In short, political theology masked a political mythology which in turn was a resource for modern power politics. The secularization thesis was a convenient way of 'finding' legitimacy for a person proclaiming positive law in a decisionist manner, when otherwise legitimacy would have had to be invented.[29]

As his onetime university colleague Odo Marquard pointed out, Blumenberg told a story about human beings' struggle to gain relief from the absolute.[30] They protected themselves from the theological absolutism of an all-powerful God by unleashing the modern cultures of self-assertion, self-preservation and scientific curiosity. An absolute and immediate reality – including a religious reality of this sort – had essentially been unliveable. Ultimately, angst and defensive inertia (or *Beharrung*) were behind humanity's reluctant steps towards modernity – not a Promethean desire for self-empowerment.[31] It was this defensive liberal modernity that was threatened by Schmitt's account of personal, sovereign self-assertion draped in ostensibly pre-modern clothes of legitimacy.

Marquard might have projected some of his own concerns about compensation onto Blumenberg's oeuvre. He was right to point to Blumenberg's stress on the pathos of distance, and to the self-sufficiency which humans sought to claim against the overwhelming pressures of religion in order to achieve some inner-worldly stability and contentment. The typical post-war concerns with stability, compensation and relief came head to head with Schmitt's insistence that there were limits to all of these. According to Schmitt, modernity would not only fail to achieve its goals, but also have distinctly perverse effects which could never be compensated.

Blumenberg, however, tried to side-step the question of the depletion of moral resources under modern conditions altogether. In his account, there were no substances in history which could be consumed or transformed, as the proponents of the secularization thesis claimed. There were only functions and 'reoccupations'. Secularization and similar categories were not only categories of historical illegitimacy – they were themselves historically illegitimate.

Through Schmitt's criticisms, Blumenberg was pushed into a position where he had to affirm precisely that which, to Schmitt, was modern hubris.[32] He also had to defend Goethe's dictum as an instance of poly-theism, rather than following Schmitt's Gnostic reading. Polytheism – as opposed to the deadly dualism (and enmity) between a creator god and a redemptive god, or enmity between father and son – was supposed to serve as a means of separating and limiting powers that could be deployed against theological absolutism. It was supposed to bolster modern liberal pluralism, in which interests could be balanced and negotiated, and enmity – even be-tween gods – was moderated. Many gods had many powers. Consequently, polytheism yielded a division of powers in which god kept god in check. This was the mythical 'Ur-scheme' of what Blumenberg, in a virtually un-translatable phrase, called the *Entängstigung* of human beings – broadly speaking, their relief from fear.[33] Thus, a properly modern politics – as op-posed to the quasi-theological or even fake theological politics centred on the state of exception advocated by Schmitt – was about mechanisms for reducing angst.

For critics on the Right and the Left, such a vision appeared to be yet an-other form of liberal complacency, in which theological fragments served to legitimate liberal notions of progress and pluralism. In the mirror of polit-ical theology, liberal modernity appeared morally emaciated, as it left every-thing as it was. Schmitt and liberals like Blumenberg and Marquard – who had supposedly settled down comfortably into a 'liberal restoration' – ap-peared united in a front against a revolutionary political theology.[34] Such a theology shared with Schmitt's Gnostic dualism the absolute division into the new and the old as well as the emancipated and the oppressive. The cre-ation of an unjust world and redemption had to be separated, just as in Schmitt's reading of Goethe's dictum. From both a radical or even mes-sianic left-wing perspective, as well as from the vantage point of Schmitt's antimodernism, Blumenberg's liberal modernity settled for too little. As one critic warned, those who merely sought self-preservation, would not even achieve that minimal goal. The self, after all, 'could only preserve itself by seeking to preserve humanity as a whole'.[35]

Limiting Political Theology: Liberalism and the Modern Uses of Religion

Many of those who learnt from Schmitt in the post-war period felt com-pelled to take a position on political theology. Broadly speaking, Schmitt's students followed him in finishing off Peterson's thesis about the finishing

off of political theology, while at the same time attempting to limit the political claims of political theology. Saving the concept was supposed to be
combined with its liberalization, privatization or even neutralization. Thus,
with Schmitt, the inevitability of political theology could be affirmed, without granting that political theology had to make total claims on matters political.

The simplest route to achieve this goal was taken by Hermann Lübbe. He
stressed the continued relevance and usefulness of political theology as a research programme concerned with structural analogies between the theological and the jurisprudential as well as political spheres. There could be no
full emancipation of the moderns from religion – and there could be all
kinds of different political theologies based on different analogies, including a 'political theology of the bourgeois'.[36] Apart from that, he argued that
religion as such retained a separate function as an effective form of coping
with contingency – which immediately raised the question of functional
equivalents.[37]

On the one hand, Lübbe made political theology into a matter of metaphor, on the other, he prescribed religion as part of the general programme
of modern compensations. Here, Spaemann and others countered that subjective beliefs and objective necessities had to coincide.[38] Moreover, once
coping with contingency and compensation became central concerns, polytheism might become preferable – not least in relieving the moderns from
the potential for fanaticism. Thus, an advocacy of polytheism became Odo
Marquard's contribution to the debate.[39] In accordance with Blumenberg,
what Marquard called 'an enlightened political polytheism' appeared as
a potential political theology of liberal pluralism. In this context, Marquard explicitly affirmed the Schmittian account of modernity as an age of
neutralizations and depoliticizations – and, like Lübbe, he claimed that
Schmitt's evaluation of this process could simply be reversed from negative
to positive. Importantly, however, he posed the question of whether neutralization was in itself sufficient to cope with the problems of political
theology. While his own answer ultimately remained elusive, an alliance between proponents of neutrality and advocates of an enlightened poly-
theistic political theology appeared to be one legitimate response.[40]

Böckenförde, in a somewhat more subtle approach, drew seminal distinctions between three different meanings of political theology, after he
had once more affirmed Schmitt's refutation of Peterson's thesis.[41] First, he

claimed, there was juridical political theology, that is, a sociology of concepts that had been transferred from theology to law and the state. Second, there was institutional political theology which dealt with the relationship of ecclesiastical and political power. Such a political theology remained inevitable under modern conditions, as the relationship between Church and state necessarily continued to be renegotiated. Finally, there was a form of ethically motivated political theology which constituted an appeal for direct political action. Böckenförde went on to claim that the last two categories of political theology would never allow for final separations. Tensions would remain between Church and state, religious and secular, as well as individual Christian political engagement and civic obligations. This would even be the case where the state guaranteed religious freedom and where the Churches accepted a clear state–church separation.

The last claim plainly relied on Schmitt's definition of the political, as reinterpreted by Böckenförde. All issues – including theological ones, which necessarily touched on many areas of human life – could enter the force field of the political, as long as the relevant relations or polarizations between different groups of human beings became sufficiently intense in their association or disassociation. Theology would not have a constant political import, but as long as the existence of human beings was determined by the *res mixtae*, the mixture of religious and worldly matters, political theology could never be finished off, as the political itself could never be finished off.[42]

Yet, Böckenförde – partly in his capacity as a member of the Ritter School – also offered a larger reading of the role of religion in modern political life. He affirmed that the European state continued to retain a Christian ethical substance as one of the preconditions of liberalism – a substance which might or might not be slowly consumed. According to Böckenförde, it was important that this ethical substance at least be recognized and preserved – while not in any way interfering with individual conscience. Yet, it remained unclear how these two demands could ultimately be reconciled, unless public and perhaps even political cultures more narrowly defined remained imbued with Christianity. After all, Böckenförde, in an article groundbreaking and controversial for a young Catholic in Adenauer's 1950s West Germany, had already insisted that the Church should not engage in party politics.[43]

The answer might have been that individual citizens had to remain conscious of the fact that only the separation of state, Church and society had enabled the emergence of modern freedom and subjectivity. Christianity thus retained the status Hegel had assigned to it as a 'religion of freedom'. A liberal Christianity was by no means unproblematic in the modern world – but it was also not a sheer impossibility, as Schmitt had thought. It was potentially the kind of uneasy compromise that Schmitt, in his mode as a proponent of apocalyptical antimodernism, could not tolerate. However, Schmitt had provided the notion of *restraining* – and arguably it was the imperative to restrain which emerged most clearly from Böckenförde's thought. This imperative was rooted in genuine religious conviction – not functional concerns for stability, as with Lübbe.

Finally, there was a more ambitious attempt at liberalizing political theology. Robert Spaemann, in a radio broadcast in 1969, argued that no concrete political maxims could be derived from Christian eschatology.[44] Eschatology simply was not unambiguous in its meaning. Moreover, political action in the modern world simply did not need religious motivations or theological foundations. Most importantly, he claimed that the eschatological character of Christianity made it either apolitical or liberal – with even an antitotalitarian affinity to the rule of law.

All efforts to limit the claims of political theology, however, themselves remained limited in their applicability. Böckenförde's ethical state was clearly an exclusively European affair. Lübbe's research programme and his pairing down of religion as a 'praxis of coping with contingency' left the question unresolved of how to deal with religious energies which could not be channelled into private functional equivalents of therapy. Marquard's playful suggestions about polytheism only seemed to confirm that liberalism could deal with political theology as long as religious passions have already become no more than postmodern lifestyle choices. Only Spaemann's very brief sketch of an affinity between eschatology and the rule of law pointed towards a more general prescription. It allowed Christians to engage in political action without charging such action with eschatological meanings, while at the same time translating the inevitable uncertainties associated with eschatological expectations into a respect for a broadly liberal framework that was neutral vis-à-vis different religious experiences. It remained the only direct answer to an understanding of political theology as necessarily entailing an unquestioning political obedience to powers transcending worldly politics. It was therefore also the only real contestation of Schmitt's testament.

Dangerous Liaisons: Schmitt, the New Left and the Limits of Liberalism

I am a Marxist *in so far* as I have traced the economic concepts of Marxism to their political end; I am *not* a Marxist, because I have recognized the economic surplus as a purely political surplus on the proletarian side as well.

Carl Schmitt, 1979

The 1960s and 1970s were neither the first nor the last time that the Left became intensely interested in Carl Schmitt.[1] In the 1920s, thinkers like Lukács and Benjamin had entertained more or less dangerous intellectual liaisons with Schmitt, and, as I shall discuss in Part III, a post-Marxist Left was to rediscover Schmitt in the 1990s. However, it was arguably with the New Left, especially in Germany and Italy, that Schmitt had most effect on the Left as a broad intellectual and *political* movement – even if his influence was clandestine in the German case and short-lived and marginal in the case of Italy's *Marxisti Schmittiani*.

This was not a simple case of *les extrêmes se touchent*. In Germany, Schmitt became a 'hot tip' among the Left, because his dissociation of liberalism and democracy and the anti-parliamentarianism which followed from this dissociation, appealed to the extra-parliamentary opposition. In one sense, this appeal was hardly surprising, given that the distinction between liberalism and democracy was, if anything, originally a Marxist one. In Italy, however, Schmitt's concept of the political proved appealing in a context where Italian Marxism of the traditional historicist and idealist variety seemed increasingly implausible. It was also a time when society had become dangerously polarized. More broadly speaking, the coincidence of the end of the post-war Social Democratic consensus and the desire of the New Left to repoliticize what seemed like self-satisfied bourgeois societies opened a space for Schmittian thought. Suddenly, what had appeared to many as a conclusive liberalization of the major West European countries seemed under threat – while the students felt that they had reached the limits of a liberalism which only tolerated 'enlightenment as long as it remains without consequences for the whole'.[2]

The extremes were attracted to Schmitt – and Schmitt remained attracted to the extremes. He was clearly flattered by the attention some of the New Left theoreticians paid him. In a discussion with his disciple Rüdiger Altmann and Jens Litten, an ex-student leader, he even repudiated his pupil Armin Mohler's conservatism as essentially outdated – with the implication that the New Left had at least managed to shake up an ossified political system, something which Mohlerian conservatism had been incapable of doing.[3] He probably found the anti-bourgeois and anti-Establishment gestures of the '68ers appealing also: after all, in his own way he was as much an opponent and an outsider of the 'liberal-democratic Establishment' as the demonstrators on the streets of Frankfurt and West Berlin.[4]

Schmitt's desperate hope for a resurgence of friend–enemy relations against the technocratic universalism of both the United States and the Soviet Union seemed to make him put faith in any radical movement – even the student Left. In 1970, he wrote to Ernst Jünger that a 'general insecurity' seemed to be caused by the diffuse feeling of an incalculable 'turn' approaching, 'very different from the turn of 1945'.[5] It seemed that substance might be restored to politics, if a radicalized Left could recreate real enmity. Such a polarization would also lead representatives of the state back to Schmitt's thought on emergency powers – especially once parts of the student rebellion had become radicalized as terrorism.

Paradoxically then, in the late 1960s and 1970s, Schmitt appeared on both sides of the political divide – and the more that German politics became polarized, the higher his standing rose. Schmitt could be unmasked as the fascist face of bourgeois capitalism, and yet be championed as an 'unmasker' himself who had seen through the sham of liberal parliamentarianism.[6] His ideology *and* his critique of ideology, or *Ideologiekritik*, both provoked passionate responses on the Left.

The Critique of Parliamentarianism

To understand why parts of the '68 Left could feel an affinity with Schmitt's theories at all, one needs to appreciate the deep suspicion of liberal parliamentarism that ran through their theorizing. The most sophisticated critique of liberal parliamentarism was put forward by Johannes Agnoli, who was arguably *the* political thinker of the German 1968. He was born Giovanni Agnoli in Valle di Cadore in 1925. A life-long contrarian, he had become a fascist in his teens and even a volunteer for the Wehrmacht – apparently as a form of protest. After three years as a British prisoner of war in Egypt, he studied in Tübingen and Berlin, writing his second doctorate on Italian fascism. However, where Mussolini had moved from the extreme left to fascism, the ex-fascist Agnoli became a leading theoretician for the extra-parliamentary Left.

Yet, in many ways, his theory merely mirrored that of Schmitt's pupil Rüdiger Altmann. Altmann had praised the potential of pluralism for the purpose of social integration in the absence of a major external enemy, while warning that pluralism should always be tightly contained.[7] Agnoli identified precisely this strategy as the latest 'transformation' of bourgeois democracy, whose aim was to render actual democracy impossible. Agnoli started his theory from the premise that the 'bourgeois state' and capitalism were inextricably linked.[8] Under the conditions of capitalism no genuine or 'radical' democracy could ever be realized. The 'bourgeois state' systematically contained 'the political', that is, the room for political manoeuvre, by limiting popular sovereignty and the autonomous articulation of the population's desires. However, rather than reverting to fascism – a failed strategy for controlling and diverting the mass desire for political self-determination – the bourgeois state under the conditions of 'organized capitalism' transformed the existing institutions of parliamentary democracy. This happened in such a way as to make revolutionary change impossible without having to resort to open oppression. In short, this transformation of democracy meant a 'modernization of the state in the sense of an adjustment to the new forms of collective life (the so-called "mass society") as well as an improvement in the sense of a modernization of the means of domination.'[9]

The need for modernization was caused by 'technical-economic progress', but also driven by the 'unified interests of the dominating groups'.[10] These 'dominating groups' had a collective interest in defusing democracy as a potential means of what Harold Laski had called 'revolution by consent' and what Jakob Burckhardt had referred to as a potential 'permanent revolution'.[11] Parliamentary democracy was, after all, not the most secure guarantee for capitalism. It was by its very nature ambivalent. Parliament could, in theory, accurately reflect the basic social antagonism in society. Thus, parliament might be capable of overcoming it through majority decisions and serve as a springboard to socialism. Alternatively, it could be a highly effective means of preventing open terror by keeping up the façade of a pseudo-democracy to repress the popular will.[12]

Agnoli claimed that parliament and a plurality of parties were essential in transforming democracy into a more effective means of domination. The kind of 'unification' or political uniformity which the fascist state could only impose by one-party rule was now achieved through what was called 'aligned pluralism'. Society had not overcome the basic dualism (and antagonism) between capitalists and workers, but the pluralism on display in parliament veiled this fact most effectively. Through the negotiations between different parties and 'social partners' such as employers' associations and unions, social peace and the illusion of democratic participation for the masses could be maintained. Individuals would only see the 'republic of the market' – not the 'despotism of the factory'.[13]

The twist to Agnoli's theory, then, was that parliamentarism constituted the most effective way of keeping the masses away from actual power. Only one pole of the basic socio-economic opposition was represented in parliament, as the socialist parties had become integrated into the 'oligarchy'. Also, all parties had effectively evolved into 'cartel parties', which had fused with the state. In short, representation in parliament was the best means of repression.

In addition, the institution of parliament had become thoroughly corrupted. What Hans Kelsen had called 'the fiction of representation' ensured that it was not the people, but the state that was represented in parliament.[14] Legislative and executive power became fused, and parliament served as a transmission belt between the oligarchy and the people. Borrowing heavily from the elitist theorists Michels and Ostrogorski, Agnoli argued that not only had parties become oligarchic, but parliament itself had developed an oligarchic structure. Publicity and public reasoning, the characteristics of nineteenth-century liberalism, had been replaced by a 'representation' which did not in fact reproduce, but repressed the fundamental social antagonism.

Rational deliberation could never address actual social conflict, because conflict remained hidden from view – although rational deliberation had become impossible in an oligarchic parliament in any case.

Throughout this transformation the official ideology of democracy was left intact – the only semantic change was that languages of humanism and technocratic necessities were supposed to supplant the language of class struggle among the workers' representatives. Parties no longer knew workers and capitalists – only human beings as such. They no longer implemented platforms, they only observed economic and technological constraints. What a conservative politician had called 'the abolition of the proletariat' only meant that class consciousness could be eroded through increasing mass consumption and other 'grand attempts at collective corruption'.[15] Class and other social cleavages were erased imperceptibly, and the language of humanism effaced socio-economic difference. Thus, citizens were turned into consumers, and class consciousness was replaced by a mystified 'civic consciousness' – or what the Germans ominously call *Staatsbürgerbewußtsein*.[16]

As soon as the workers came to believe that 'the state is us', or to embrace the liberal illusion that the state stood above society as a neutral arbiter, the bourgeoisie had succeeded in defusing the ambivalent potential of parliamentarism. Ideologically tying the people to political institutions (and restricting their institutional imagination) was much more effective – and less dangerous – than open terror. Legality (through the 'constitutionalizing function' of parliament) thereby produced legitimacy. Yet, while the means were humane and peaceful, the end of social integration was not. The priority of the means over the end was simply another bourgeois ruse and prevented the masses from perceiving the priority of real emancipation over pseudo-democratic procedures.[17] Bread and circuses *were* more inhumane than violent revolution, and in any case, Agnoli argued, perpetual social peace inside the state was preserved not for humane reasons, but because it proved necessary for continuous capitalist expansion.

Under a democratic veneer the state would then extend its rule over any part of society and declare a state of emergency wherever it saw fit.[18] The 'emergency state' was the necessary continuation and even 'crowning' of the welfare state, and could be justified by the claim that emergency measures were necessary to preserve the 'general welfare'.[19] The state had a vital interest in repressing social conflict, and therefore had to extend its reign continuously – in fact, the line separating state and society, administration and economy, became increasingly blurred.[20] Such a situation, however, already meant a de facto 'permanent state of exception'. Consequently, there was no reason to stay within the limits of 'bourgeois legality', as bourgeois legality had already been abolished. The recurrent breach of the constitution, it seemed, had itself become part of the real constitution of the 'emergency state'.

In short, then, the state had been transformed into an authoritarian one without any outward change – and parliament remained essential in legitimating this situation. Just as Vilfredo Pareto, the 'Marx of the bourgeoisie', had advised Mussolini to keep parliament as an 'ornament' while transforming the Italian state into a fascist one, so the West German elite was engaged in a particularly perfidious game of anti-democratic deception.[21]

Thus arose what in retrospect appears like a full-fledged antiliberal antiparliamentarism, reminiscent indeed of the contempt Georges Sorel had for the socialists in parliament who only furthered their own interests.[22] Like Sorel, Agnoli and his followers believed that left-wing parties had effectively abandoned the workers and become, in Léon Blum's famous phrase, the 'loyal stewards' of the bourgeoisie. They had become more invested in social control and the satisfaction of economic wants than in any genuine transformation of society.

Like Schmitt (and, to some extent, like Habermas), Agnoli and his followers believed that in the nineteenth century, the notables in parliament had been devoted to open and rational discussion, and that there had indeed once been free political competition (albeit restricted to a narrow franchise).[23] Like Schmitt (and Habermas), they told a story of decline in which parliament had become a site of backroom dealings, in which powerful social interests brokered secret, undemocratic agreements. In other words, like Schmitt and Habermas, Agnoli and his followers diagnosed a 'refeudalization' of representation: representation had become representation before, rather than for the people. Elections did not present a choice, and parliament did not represent the actual complexity of society. Schmitt and Agnoli shared a roughly Rousseauvean definition of democracy.[24] They also, to varying degrees, clung to an 'ideal of resemblance', in which the representatives should resemble the represented as much as possible – even though Agnoli did not hold that such a homogeneity would necessarily produce a proper defence of the workers' interests.[25]

Agnoli went further than either Schmitt or Habermas in claiming that representation had actually become repression. Whereas Schmitt had prophesied the necessary disintegration of parliamentarism and the return of a sovereign decision-maker, Agnoli saw a steady state of manipulation and repression through parliamentarism, against which one had to intervene politically. It would not even be sufficient, if the representatives came to resemble the represented – they had to represent the repressed pole of the social antagonism, and, crucially, the *real* interests of the workers. Behind Agnoli's theory operated a rather traditional Marxist theory of ideology, in which the reproduction of bourgeois society required the persistence of false beliefs. A diagnosis of a crisis of representation could lead in many different theoretical (and practical) directions – and neither dictatorship nor direct action necessarily followed as remedies.

What, according to Agnoli, *was* the remedy for this situation? The answers to this question remained not only vague, but often contradictory. On the one hand, Agnoli hinted that societies which had not completely disintegrated were essentially beyond reform. On the other hand, he argued in line with Kant's 'Perpetual Peace' that international peace slightly increased the chances of 'liberation'.[26] The Berlin-based student leader Bernd Rabehl agreed that with the erection of the Berlin Wall, the GDR had come to be seen as less of a threat, and that the weakening of anticommunist ideology had been a vital precondition of the rise of the student movement.[27] But then again, the presence of Communist parties in some Western European countries also might alleviate a few of the problems posed by the 'transformation of democracy'. Ultimately, however, the process seemed essentially unstoppable within the current parameters of legality.[28] Clearly, then, the bourgeois state had to be abolished, including the institutions of parliamentarism which were controlled by the oligarchy. Yet, Agnoli insisted that this had to be brought about through a 'peaceful revolutionary process' – without much further specification how such a process might take place.[29]

Agnoli and his fellow theorists never wavered in making two assumptions, namely that liberalism had brought about fascism and could do so again anytime, and that advanced capitalist societies had reached an age of abundance in which the abolition of 'irrational domination' had in practice become possible.[30] A further background belief held that 'post-facist' liberalism had learnt its lesson in manipulating the masses to such an extent that the transformation of democracy actually appeared to be in their interest.

For the proponents of this view, there had to be a genuine 'change of political form' – any integration into existing institutions was condemned to failure, and only a complete political break could be counted as an adequate answer to the covert transformation of democracy.[31] Nevertheless, there remained a fundamental question of precisely who the agents of this change were supposed to be – who should be the carriers of the political. Agnoli and the student leaders never found a satisfactory answer to this question. German workers, as the obvious agents of change, seemed to remain unaware of its necessity. Yet a revolutionary subject that does not recognize that it is a revolutionary subject, is no revolutionary subject at all.[32] Fascism had caused a practical and theoretical caesura for the workers' movement, and there were no clear theoretical (let alone practical) guidelines for reconstructing a proper class consciousness.[33]

At the same time, Marxist theory seemed to prohibit the students and their leaders from seeing themselves as simply students. Rather arbitrarily, they began to search for other potential revolutionary subjects. At various points, it was prisoners, racial minorities, schoolchildren, and for some, the students themselves.[34] The more sober leaders of the movement, however, recognized that the students would not do as a revolutionary subject and sought to '*practically* problematize' the 'traditional theories of the workers' movement' – without much success.[35] Agnoli's theory, while highly influential among radicals, provided few specific guidelines on how to halt the 'involution' of democracy. If anything, it made the students dismiss the promises of 'more democracy' made by the Social Democratic government elected in 1969.[36] Taking Agnoli's ideas a step further, the more radicalized students would revert to old Communist arguments about the Social Democrats as 'social fascists' who were already integrated into the system. While of little direct impact, Agnoli's ideas helped set in motion an increasingly self-sustaining radicalization among the activists, who became more and more immune to the *real* transformations of West German democracy. Instead, they drifted into a political and ethical netherworld of direct action and, ultimately, terrorism.

Not surprisingly, Agnoli and others came to see the passivity of the proletariat as the 'most tragic aspect' of the 'German '68'.[37] A mobilized proletariat would have been the obvious agent for changing the 'political form'. Yet at the time, one of the fateful ideas of some student leaders was that the workers would only understand the language of violence.[38] While there had indeed been a few defectors from the proletariat to the rebelling bourgeoisie (to reverse an old Marxist dictum), such figures remained few and far between, and, in some cases, resorted to terror. The real tragedy was not one of the proletariat, but of a theory that had imbibed Schmitt's lessons about the failings of parliamentarism without finding a real foothold in society or identifying a proper carrier of the political.

Schmitt and Class Hatred: The *Marxisti Schmittiani*

The situation in Italy was ostensibly similar to that in Germany. A very forceful New Left emerged in the course of the 1960s, after the official representative of Marxist thought, the Communist Party (PCI), had made its peace with parliamentary democracy in 1956. At the same time, Marxist thinkers became disenchanted with the idea of a more or less automatic triumph of the working class preceded by a concentration of capital and proletarian pauperization.[39] In particular, what they saw happening in the factories of Northern Italy presented an entirely different picture: the workers, many of them peasants just arrived from the South, were confronted with completely new technologies. These technologies, according to Galvano della Volpe and other Marxist theorists, created a new psychological situation, which also called for new 'revolutionary instruments'.[40] Italian Marxism, however, had become highly philosophical. Inspired by the ideological figurehead of post-war Communism, Antonio Gramsci, Marxist theorists had become fixated on the idea of building a revolutionary culture before taking revolutionary action. They seemed to provide no real revolutionary instruments whatsoever.

Thinkers around the journal *Quaderni rossi*, who had previously supported the reformist course of the PCI, began to call for a radical break by building 'socialist self-administration' on the capitalist sites of production. Creating such a limited *dualismo del potere* [dualism of power] was the first step in the direction of conquering political power altogether.[41] Political organization had to start in the factories – to oppose what in the eyes of one of the leading theorists of the *Quaderni rossi*, Mario Tronti, amounted to de facto 'self-administration' and even direct democracy for the capitalists only. What mattered was that they were in charge of the factories – not who had a majority in parliament in distant Rome.[42] The workers had to oppose the economic developments furthered by new technologies (and steered by the capitalists) by *political* means. Tronti in particular called for a *primacy* of the political. Instead of concentrating on large-scale developments in history and economics, and instead of acting as philosophical party intellectuals, Marxist theorists had to start with the *concrete* situation of the workers. They also had to ask themselves how to create the conditions of possibility to effect a *concrete* political decision in favour of class struggle on the part of the workers. Class struggle in turn would have to be cashed out as a *guerra totale* – a total war against the capitalists.

What followed from all this talk about the concrete for concrete politics remained rather vague, however. Tronti advocated what he called an 'organization of anarchy', workers' autonomy and the self-conscious stoking of class hatred, as well as a continuous struggle – the famous formula of *lotta continua*. But, as with the German New Left, it was unclear which form of political organization was appropriate for such a struggle under fundamentally changed conditions of capitalist production. By the early 1970s, Tronti and his comrades were still seeking to add new theoretical weapons to their arsenal in order to make these slogans more meaningful and coherent. It was at this point that Schmitt's thought entered the ideological universe of the Italian Left.

At a seminar on the relationship between politics and economics, organized by Norberto Bobbio at the University of Turin in early December 1972, Tronti presented a paper about the 'autonomy of the political'.[43] There he reneged on the idea of a revolutionary break on the level of the economy, and in the factories in particular. The socio-economic situation, nationally and internationally, was simply too 'complex' for that. Instead, one had to combat directly the irrationality of the political action undertaken by the capitalists. Rather than creating a dual power on the level of the factory, *dualismo di potere* had to be instituted directly at the highest political level – the state.[44] This meant that workers should refuse outright to be integrated into the capitalist sham democracy.

This new emphasis on the primacy of the political and a struggle at state level was the precondition for a reception of Schmitt's thought among what came to be known as the *Marxisti Schmittiani* – a derogatory label initially applied by liberals to Tronti and his followers.[45] These thinkers did not deny Schmitt's right-wing politics and even to some extent agreed with previous Italian Schmitt-interpreters that his fascist theories had been intended to save the capitalist state. But Tronti insisted that the person Schmitt and his intentions were irrelevant – what mattered was his acute criticism of liberalism and parliamentary democracy.[46] Tronti pointed out that Schmitt's friend–enemy distinction could be mapped onto a new understanding of class antagonism and called for Schmitt's thinking to be radicalized even further by making the capitalists not just the real, but the absolute enemy.[47] To that end, any existing political and economic crisis also had to be radicalized in the direction of a real state of exception. What Schmitt had criticized in Lenin and other Marxist thinkers – in particular, the conception of absolute enmity – was now enthusiastically taken up by theorists like Tronti. Schmitt, apparently, had understood the Marxist-Leninist thinkers better than they had understood themselves.

Thus, Schmittian elements became part of a thoroughgoing 'Marxist critique of Marxism' which sought to take leave of the economic and historical categories that had been central to post-war Italian thought, and put a practical theory of power squarely at the centre of revolutionary theorizing. This theoretical move was like a leap of faith. Rather than analyzing the concrete situation of the workers – as in much conservative thought, the concrete was always stressed and never seen concretely – and instead of realistically gauging the balance of power in 1970s Italy, thinkers like Tronti engaged in a purely imaginary political leap – or perhaps flight – forward. Schmitt's idea that ultimately politics would not be based on norms, economics or history but on human decision proved sufficiently liberating and exhilarating to sustain such a flight. The Schmittian Left, it seemed, was hoping for a momentary state of exception as one might pray for a miracle. Political economy had been replaced by a left-wing political theology.

After the 'long autumn' of strikes and general unrest, the Schmittian moment in Marxist thought proved rather short-lived, however. While a new friend-enemy constellation along the lines of the *Marxisti Schmittiani* had some uses in simplifying an increasingly complex and shifting political situation, Marxist thinkers themselves soon realized that they had created *terribles simplifications*. If nothing else, the time simply was not ripe for a final and decisive friend–enemy confrontation, and consequently the Italian Left increasingly turned back towards its old theoretical patron saint Gramsci, whose works continued to suggest a strategy of gradually building 'cultural hegemony'.[48]

It is no accident that Schmitt's thought became influential for the German and Italian Left. In both countries, political thinkers across the ideological spectrum remained very much fixated on the state, albeit for different reasons. In Germany, the student leaders were working against – but in a sense also with – a strong state tradition. Yet, the New Left's theorists never truly answered the question of how to organize against the state, the endlessly debated *Organisationsfrage*. Partly as a consequence, the New Left split into numerous sectarian movements, which could agree neither on common friends nor even on common enemies. In such a situation, it was tempting to imagine a homogeneous carrier of the political, that is, a unified group clearly defined by it opposition to capitalism. Schmitt's theoretical template, centred on a homogeneous *Volk* as the carrier of the political in the circumstances of mass democracy, could then be taken up by those who wished for a homogeneous *class* as the carrier of the political.

In Italy, on the other hand, with its weak state tradition and strong civil society, theorists imagined that a wholly autonomous political realm could be built against the state. Nowhere else were Communist and socialist theorists as adamant about abolishing the state altogether and resisting any form of political representation.[49] Many of the Italians influenced by Schmitt put their faith in a constituent power outside the state, in the creation of a new public realm, which sometimes they came to call 'Republic'. Against the values imposed by capitalism, workers would use this autonomous realm to engage in acts of 'self-valorization' as well as acts of refusal. Moreover, it was not only Italy's parliamentary system which was strongly polarized – the post-war republic had also inherited a polarized tradition of political thought. Extreme idealism, best exemplified by the Hegelian Benedetto Croce, stood opposed to an extreme realism, best exemplified, of course, by Machiavelli, but famously continued by Pareto and Mosca. In the post-war period, this tension was played out in political thought as a polarization between Schmitt, the (supposed) ultimate realist, on the one hand, and Hans Kelsen, the (supposed) ultimate idealist, on the other.[50]

Finally, the Italian Left retained strong nationalist and anti-American elements (which also explains why the Italian Left and Right, and the *Nuova Destra* in particular, could become interested in Schmitt at the same time). Political unity, one of Schmitt's master themes, could not fail to fascinate in a political context where both Left and Right suffered from what they viewed as a national unification achieved under liberal hegemony – albeit a unification that remained incomplete even after almost a century and a half.

Terror, States of Emergency and Liberal Secessions

. . .the whole post-fascist period is one of clear and present danger . . . I maintain
that our society is in such an emergency situation, and that it has become the
normal state of affairs.

Herbert Marcuse, 1965

C arl Schmitt had virtually nothing to say on terrorism, except in connection with the partisan – in fact, it is doubtful whether he would
have recognized the category of terrorism (as opposed to terror) as
anything other than a morally asymmetric concept to name and at the same
time discriminate an enemy. Nevertheless, as one of the consequences of
terrorism in both Germany and Italy during the 1970s was political polarization, friend–enemy thinking came to contaminate not only the political
approaches of confirmed Schmittians, but also of those who saw the state as
a 'political unity' seriously under threat.

With extreme political polarization the limits of liberalism also appeared
to have been reached. No common ground – and no *modus vivendi* –
seemed to exist between the state and its enemies. Schmitt had claimed that
liberalism could not hold a state together in the face of a determined challenge unless it betrayed its own ideals. The goals of political unity and the
liberal rule of law would always pull in opposite directions. To some extent,
the European terrorism of the 1970s put this claim to the test.[1]

Many among both those who sought to fend off what was often called an 'attack on the heart of the state' and those undertaking the attack were groping for a concept of enmity which would give them a moral advantage, while discrediting their enemy. Among the former, a number of both philosophical conservatives and liberal conservatives influenced by Schmitt apparently lost their nerve. Industrial society, it now seemed, was not impervious to 'events', after all. Moreover, this was clearly a moment for Schmittian modernizers and anti-moralizers. In particular, a number of Ritter pupils subsumed the terrorists (and sometimes the Left more widely) under the label 'political moralism'. They turned from Hegel back to Hobbes, substituting a call for the strong state in place of the call for a more mediated politics. Most disturbingly, perhaps, there was an almost gleeful celebration of the emergency (and liberals' supposed failure to respond to it) among a number of Schmitt's closer pupils. Once again, the exception proved to be more 'interesting' than the rule – and was perceived, it seemed, not least as an aesthetic phenomenon.

Losing Nerve

'Drawing a clear line between ourselves and the enemy' – this slogan was at the heart of the 'concept of the urban guerilla' which the German Red Army Faction (RAF) declared in 1970.[2] A deadly dualism between the people and the state ran through all manifestos and 'confessions' of the RAF. This dualism, which took on an almost mythical character, served to reduce social complexity and mobilize action against the enemy. The state was characterized as always already fascist, ready to reveal its true face if properly provoked. The theorists of the group were determined to maintain this strict dualism at any price – only the capitalist-cum-fascist elites and they themselves could be recognized as political actors, with the 'people' or the 'masses' cast in a somewhat paradoxical role as passive, but also ultimately decisive. Depending on the particular theory adopted by rival RAF leaders, either the workers in Germany or the inhabitants of the Third World were viewed as the prime 'interested third party' in the struggle against the state.[3]

Like most terrorists, members of the RAF did not see themselves as aggressors. The capitalists and their servant, the state, were moving in the direction of a 'militarization of class conflict' – and therefore the urban guerilla was merely responding, or, put differently, engaging in preventive action. Consequently, compromise with those who had revealed themselves as 'enemies of the people' was inadmissible. According to a RAF pamphlet, the enemies of the people feared nothing as much as being called the enemies of the people.[4] Recognizing the real enemy and unmasking him in front of 'the people' was the *sine qua non* for this strategy.

Later, as the terrorists came to focus almost exclusively on themselves, that is, the liberation of those already caught and imprisoned, the RAF's defence lawyers made it their goal to have their clients recognized as lawful prisoners of war under the Geneva Convention. In other words, they sought recognition of the terrorists as proper *hostis* or internal enemies. With that recognition, the state would have conceded the interpretation that a civil war was raging in the Federal Republic – and that the government was making war on its own citizens. In a Schmittian analysis, political unity would have been lost and the state ceased to be the sole carrier of the political.

During the so-called 'German autumn' of 1977, politicians faced the simultaneous kidnapping of Hans-Martin Schleyer, the president of the employers' association, and the hijacking of a Lufthansa aeroplane in Somalia. In this extraordinary situation, they seemed to come close to losing their nerve and erasing the boundaries between normal parliamentary politics and declaring a state of emergency. In secret meetings between key government and opposition leaders in 1977, some politicians were even said to have raised the possibility of taking terrorist prisoners as 'counter-hostages' who could be shot in turn.[5] Such measures would not only have recognized the terrorists as equal combatants – they also would have implied a moral equivalence between the state and the terrorists. Yet, there were many voices – for instance that of the highly respected historian Golo Mann, son of Thomas – who were already describing the West German situation as a case of civil war.[6]

Ultimately, the government of Chancellor Helmut Schmidt – whom Schmitt is said to have admired – resisted these temptations and continued officially to treat the members of the RAF as criminals. Nevertheless, the treatment of RAF prisoners, and new legislation hastily adopted in response to terrorist acts, made it plain that the 'Baader-Meinhof Gang' was no ordinary gang. The government did not overstep the limits of legality. Arguably, however, it repeatedly overstepped the limits of liberal legality, as it extended its reach for supposed 'sympathizers' of the RAF and other 'enemies of the constitution'.[7] Pacification, the task Schmitt had assigned the state internally, came to take precedence over a more prudential (but also more self-confident) approach. West Germany revealed itself not as a latently fascist regime, but as an insecure democracy with a liberal deficit, haunted by the mistakes of Weimar – or perhaps mistakes projected onto Weimar.

Legality and Legitimacy Revisited

In this situation, the philosophy of value underwent a major renaissance, as politicians and legal theorists staked their defence of the state on the values embodied in the 'free democratic basic order', as the standard phrase went. Those with left-wing sympathies had to prove their allegiance to these values, instead of simply following the rules laid down by liberal legality. Left-wing critics – often made sensitive to the drawbacks of value philosophy by their readings of Schmitt – charged that a new and essentially undemocratic 'superlegality' or 'superconstitution' had gained supremacy in the Federal Republic.[8] Here the 'ghost' of Schmitt appeared as the real inspiration behind the Basic Law – the eerie right-wing double of his namesake Carlo Schmid, one of the most important Social Democratic framers of the Basic Law.

According to Ulrich K. Preuß, probably the Left's most important and insightful reader of Schmitt in the 1960s and 1970s, the Constitutional Court had developed the notion of a 'free democratic basic order' as a substantial 'value decision'. This 'militant' decision took precedence over positive norms laid down in the actual constitution and de facto relativized them.[9] Essentially, a two-level constitution had come to characterize the Federal Republic: the militant and existential decision for the free democratic basic order on the one hand and the positive Basic Law on the other. However, according to Preuß, this 'existentialization' of the constitution was limited to those parts dealing with freedom – which meant the protection of 'possessive individualism' and the actual pre-conditions of bourgeois existence.[10] For Preuß, this 'existentialization' was not merely borne of the bourgeois 'angst' in front of a potential Communist take-over in 1949, the moment of the constitutional founding. It was, more importantly, a response to the very real threat of structural changes in the capitalist character of West German society.[11]

Preuß, then, adopted parts of the Schmittian critique of the philosophy of value which had come to underpin the decisions of the Constitutional Court – but Schmitt was also said to have articulated the very real split into legitimacy and legality characteristic of a defensive bourgeois state. A number of left-wing legal theorists held that Schmitt's hour would always come, as bourgeois legality proved insufficient to uphold the current distribution of power – or, rather, as the rule of law could be used by legislatures to enact social demands. The Schmittian answer, so the argument went, was an executive no longer democratically controlled, an executive that would rule by measures and make use of de-formalized law to preserve a 'free society', that is, a capitalist society, guaranteed by a strong state. In other words, once the rule of law had ceased protecting private property, it would be sacrificed for a regime characterized by the permanent state of exception.

Theorists of the Left adopted an interpretation of National Socialism as a form of fascism which had been the last resort of capitalism – a truth which they took Schmitt to be articulating quite openly with his logic of the emergency state.[12] Consequently, 1933 and beyond had marked a consistent continuation of the bourgeois rule of law or *Rechtsstaat* in a moment of crisis. And Schmitt, by preserving private property as the apparent core concept of liberalism, was revealed to have been a liberal – albeit of the authoritarian variety – all along.[13] As the 'theorist of the counter-revolution', he had also revealed the 'latent dictatorship in the bourgeois state'.[14]

Subsequently, the claim about the continuity between Schmitt's fascist theories and actual West German constitutional jurisprudence was relativized and eventually abandoned by many theorists of the Left. More important in the long run was the rehabilitation of the rule of law, and even positivism, which left-wing legal thinkers had undertaken via their peculiar interpretation of Schmitt. The formalism of the rule of law was affirmed as a potentially progressive force – while material legal theories were associated with the status quo. In that sense, the critical engagement with Schmitt was an important step in the liberalization of the Left.

The Emergency between Politics and Aesthetics: Taking the Serious Case Seriously

Apart from the extensive debate about the basic values embodied in the constitution, there was much discussion about states of emergency and states of exception – in which some of Schmitt's pupils took the lead.[15] After the experiences with Article 48 of the Weimar Constitution, the framers of the Basic Law had purposely left out any general clauses concerning states of emergency. It was only in the late 1950s and 1960s that the Christian Democrats began presenting proposals to introduce special emergency powers into the Basic Law – proposals which were repeatedly rejected by the Social

Democrats. Only with the formation of the Grand Coalition that included both CDU and SPD did the government finally have a sufficiently large majority for constitutional change.

The fight against these powers drove much of the early student opposition, but also involved demonstrations by large numbers of concerned ordinary citizens. The danger of the forces of conservatism eroding democracy by legal means also sensitized many left-wing thinkers, who had previously been focused mainly on the economy, to the autonomy of the political. Above all, however, the debate on emergency legislation provided precisely the kind of intellectual framework in which Schmittian concepts could be deployed. Not surprisingly, then, the major proponents of the Schmitt School vocally favoured the introduction of legislation for emergency powers – which was eventually passed in 1968.

Ernst-Wolfgang Böckenförde offered what was probably the most creative reworking of Schmitt's thoughts on emergency powers.[16] He argued that, in general, the possibility of the state of exception tended to be repressed in a liberal democracy. However, attempts to regulate the state of exception in advance would only lead to a corruption of the normal state of affairs. Instead, there should be a clear separation between normal law and extraordinary measures, just as Schmitt had advocated. Also, there had to be a division between an institution declaring the state of exception and the *political* agency taking measures to deal with the actual emergency itself. Any executive measures should then be subject to review by a court charged with meting out specifically *political* justice.

Böckenförde stressed the inevitably political dimension of the state of exception – and the fact that any attempt to foresee and legally regulate the state of exception would be more likely to lead to illiberal results than a clear, pre-determined separation between laws and measures. Paradoxically, for Böckenförde liberals should not make room within the law for the state of exception; it could never be completely foreseen or contained in any event. Instead, they should recognize the potentially illiberal nature of the exercise of emergency powers and make it subject to extensive review by institutions specifically designed for such review. The problems of politics, in short, had to be solved politically, rather than being addressed through a further juridification of politics. What remained an unquestioned assumption, however, was the idea that *only* a strong state could deal with situations characterized by increasing social and political polarization.

For many other followers of Schmitt the Federal Republic remained an incarnation of the 'denial of the emergency'. They charged liberalism with a general blindness for its enemies and claimed that the 'repression of the exception' had the opposite effects of those intended. In the late 1970s, they saw democracy under threat not only from a supposedly increasing number of internal enemies, but also from the growing power of the Soviet Union. Old anxieties resurfaced that a liberal state would not recognize these dangers in time and then would hesitate to defend the basic political unity because of the catalogue of rights that citizens could claim against the state.[17]

The supposed weakness of liberal democracies remained that they seemed unable to properly identify the real enemy. The widespread attitude of seeing the Soviet Union as essentially 'defensive' only betrayed liberals' lack of realism and decisiveness in the face of a clear external threat. This was the supposed 'disease of liberal democracies'.[18] Given these weaknesses, argued nationalist conservative Hans-Dietrich Sander, 'one has the dark sentiment that one day everything will blow up . . .'[19] And a proper response to these threats required nothing less than a 'radical break with the kind of politics which after 1945 veiled the real scene'.[20]

Yet, such rhetoric of foreboding and emergencies to come ultimately remained just that: rhetoric. As had happened a number of times in post-war political thought centred around Schmitt, such supposed realism really hid right-wing resentment and ultimately resulted only in a rallying around symbols – not least right-wing symbols like Carl Schmitt himself. The emergency – the *Ernstfall*, literally, the 'serious case' – retained an aesthetic dimension. Ironically, it was Schmitt who complained on the occasion of a major symposium on the *Ernstfall* that the opposite concept of 'the serious case' was not 'normality' – but *play*.[21] Ultimately, it seemed, the preoccupation with 'the serious case' was itself apolitical, if not downright romantic.[22]

While some theorists – most notably Böckenförde – attempted to revise legal provisions in light of emergency situations, many others remained content with noting a certain perverse satisfaction about the supposed weaknesses which the liberal state had finally revealed. The 'introverted state of the rule of law' simply left the politicians 'in the icy cold of the political', with no means to defend a constitution supposedly characterized by the 'trauma of the emergency'.[23] Much of what might have passed as 'realism' at first sight contained a thinly disguised longing for the return of great – that

is, exceptional – politics. The return of the repressed was not merely diagnosed. It was celebrated.

Liberal Secessions

The terror and political turmoil of the 1970s also had an effect on those who
had made it their project to formulate a chastened liberalism in response to
Schmitt's challenges. While philosophical conservatives sometimes erupted
in a not so hidden celebration of the state of emergency, these philosophical
liberals came to redefine their practical political prescriptions in conservative terms. They renewed their (functionalist) faith in traditional morality
and religion as guaranteeing social stability – while 'political moralism', as
supposedly espoused by terrorists and extreme left-wing radicals, was criticized in the name of an often hidden morality centred on existing institutions and prudential political action.

Most important in this respect were a number of Ritter School members.
Many of these intellectuals had been close to left-wing Catholicism or the
SPD in the 1950s and 1960s. Some, like Lübbe, even served in the reform-
oriented SPD administrations of the late 1960s and 1970s. Yet, by the mid-
1970s, most of those who had first met in the *Collegium Philosophicum* in the
1950s, had become what critics – and eventually they themselves – called
'neo-conservatives'. They were uniformly opposed to the education policies
which the Social Democrats were pursuing. Instead, they defended the importance of the traditional humanities and religious education against what
they saw as increasingly technocratic curricula aimed at a spurious, empty
form of emancipation. Most advocated a form of what came to be called
Modernisierungstraditionalismus, or 'traditionalism of modernity' – with
Spaemann, the most religious thinker in this group, being the most sceptical and reluctant proponent. For the sake of stability, all efforts to cut
human beings loose from traditions and from religious sentiments were to
be avoided. At the same time the liberal achievements of the Federal Republic up until the 1970s had to be preserved.

Members of the Ritter School now drew on the more conservative aspects
of Hegelianism, and not least the idea that the 'rational is the real', while at
the same time losing faith in the once vaunted self-stabilizing capacities of
industrial society. Like many of Schmitt's pupils, they sought to contain critique. In turn, the supposed self-empowerment of the terrorists through
universalist morality could be criticized by affirming the morality already

embodied in liberal institutions and procedures – except that often enough a now generalized suspicion of the hypocrisy of the Enlightenment came to blur this distinction.[24] The apparent presuppositions of liberal democracy – traditional morality and capitalism, to put it crudely – were not supposed to be questioned. Rather than hypocrisy leading to crisis, this time crisis led to hypocrisy, and questioning – and explanation – simply had to stop somewhere.

The pupils of the Ritter School then turned into what has been called 'liberal secessionists', who seceded from a Social Democratic Party that appeared to be moving steadily to the left.[25] They saw themselves as the authentic liberals, or at least as realistic liberals who recognized both the achievements and the limits of liberal modernity. Yet, what they thought was still chastened liberalism sometimes, but by no means in all cases, tipped over into outright practical conservatism. Philosophically, most members of the School remained liberals – but their functionalism and concern with stability now apparently dictated conservative political prescriptions.

The Double State and the Last Word on Legality

Arguably, Italy came closer to actual civil war than any other Western European democracy in the 1970s. There, the polarization into a left-wing bloc on the one hand and the traditional Christian Democratic governing party, flanked by neo-fascist groups on the other, really seemed to take the state to the point of losing what Schmitt had called political unity. More so even than in Germany, the state saw itself engaged in a direct confrontation with a group, the Red Brigades, which viewed itself, at least initially, as engaged in a defensive or preventive antifascist struggle.[26]

The 'strategy of tension' and the 'black terror', undertaken by extreme right-wing political groups (with some help from the state), attempted to exacerbate this polarization further – with the distant goal of a coup d'état to defend democracy, since clearly democracy could not defend itself.[27] The advocates of this strategy had essentially declared the Communists 'internal enemies' and, at least in a rudimentary fashion, were engaged in erecting a parallel or 'dual state'.[28] As with so many right-wing thinkers in post-war Europe, an authoritarian-bureaucratic presidential system, a kind of radicalized Gaullism, also remained their ideal.

The Communist leader Enrico Berlinguer had already learnt a bitter lesson from the coup against Salvador Allende in 1973. Through the Historic Compromise with the Christian Democrats he sought the broadest possible democratic consensus to defend the Second Republic.[29] Eventually, Italy managed to avoid the kind of radical breaking of a stalemate which had happened, for instance, in Austria in the inter-war period. In fact, the Italian Communists became the defenders of democratic legality, even the 'shield of the constitution' – but shielding a corrupt state exacted its own costs through significant electoral losses.

With the decision by Eurocommunists such as Berlinguer and the Spanish Communist leader Santiago Carillo in favour of a 'legal revolution', the syndicalist hopes of Tronti and others were finally disappointed.[30] Rather than engage in violent revolutionary activity, Berlinguer and Carillo sought a parliamentary road to power – and to the revolutionary transformation of the state. Carl Schmitt was an avid reader of Eurocommunist theories – and of Carillo's writings in particular – during the 1970s. In what turned out to be his last publication, Schmitt noted a new respect for the state by 'professional revolutionaries' such as Carillo.[31] Rather than sharing Schmitt's diagnosis of the death of the state, and rather than wishing for such a death, for Eurocommunist theorists the state was 'more necessary and more alive than ever', as it was the 'carrier of legality' and therefore capable of performing the 'miracle of a peaceful revolution'. The revolution would 'legitimate the state in exchange for the favour of a legal state-revolution'.[32]

Thus, Schmitt repeated his diagnosis – already familiar from his writings on the partisan – that the state's legitimacy had effectively been emptied out and been replaced by rationalist legality. Legality was the mode of functioning for the bureaucracy – whether that of the state or private industry. Schmitt now warned that Communist revolutionaries might have learnt the lessons of Mussolini and Hitler and would use the 'premium of the legal possession of power' – primarily the bureaucracy – to transform the state completely.[33] Legality, according to Schmitt, could become an 'inescapable mode of revolutionary change'.[34]

Ultimately, legal revolution remained either a spectre or a matter of wishful thinking, depending on one's position. Yet this did not mean that the 1970s had no consequences. The Italian 'years of lead' left a sinister legacy, especially emergency and other kinds of illiberal legislation.[35] They also left a legacy of questions about what Gianfranco Miglio was to call 'the gigantic explosion of conflictuality' in the 1970s and what in Italy came to be known as

Contestazione.[36] Increasingly, political thinkers – liberal and conservative – asked whether Western democracies, with their seemingly excessively powerful parliaments, interest groups and extra-parliamentary oppositions, could still be governed at all. Clearly, the 'end of all crises' had failed to materialize.

There ensued a heated debate in the 1970s which had more than a slightly Schmittian resonance and in which many of Schmitt's pupils became involved. Political thinkers across the continent were preoccupied with the threat of 'ungovernability' – the idea that the state was in the grip of so many interest groups that it had effectively lost any independent room for manoeuvre.[37] In particular, the ever increasing claims of ever more interest groups were said to have led to ever higher fiscal deficits. As in Schmitt's diagnosis of the Weimar Republic as a quantitative total state, the state had become both all-pervasive and powerless at the same time. Planning and the faith in technocracy had exacerbated this problem, but at the root this was a case of 'over-politicization'. In the eyes of most neo-conservative and neo-liberal critics, the autonomy of civil society and the economy had to be restored and the state had to retreat to the position of a strong umpire.[38]

However, what might have seemed like a simple regression to an earlier model of separating state and society hid a larger and more long-term development. On the one hand, there was what appeared to critics to be a large-scale democratic demobilization, or at least a decisive weakening of mass politics; on the other, a thorough disillusionment with the technocratic faith in sheer plannability. Gradually, the high modernist vocabulary for talking about the state and its relationship to society came to an end.[39] At the same time, however, another structural transformation in European statehood already appeared to be under way – a transformation that also had much to do with what were variously analyzed as processes of pluralization, individualization, de-industrialization and de-territorialization.

The End of Enmity

Did Schmitt's diagnosis – and warning – about legal revolutions signal that he finally sought to locate the real enemy in Communism, rather than in liberalism? Schmitt's question was not so much about the future of the state – he merely re-affirmed his opinion that the era of statehood was at an end – but the supposed 'arcanum of a legal world revolution'. Schmitt, returning to one of his preoccupations from the early 1920s, claimed that Communist revolutions had taken place in nation-state frameworks, even if the Russian Revolution had made a global impact. A proper world revolution – with a global constituent power – was hard to conceive practically, but not conceptually impossible. It would require a global or 'species' patriotism, and, Schmitt hinted, it would also require a new political theology. Such a political theology would have to replace what Schmitt now revealed had been Sieyes's political theology all along: the projection of Spinoza's theological-political contrast between *natura-naturans* and *natura-naturata* onto the politics of *pouvoir constituant* and *pouvoirs constitués*.[40] But, for Schmitt, the 'esoteric of such an intensive political-theological reflection' was 'severe' and could no longer be expected from 'today's humanity'.[41]

What then was left for such a humanity, still supposedly bent on empowering itself through technological progress and the 'grabbing of industry'?[42] Nationalism as an ideological force seemed exhausted. Schmitt explained the failure of Nazism with the fact that 'revanchist' nationalism – and the struggle against Versailles – had been the backbone of the 'Hitler movement'. Once the First World War had been re-fought – and won – by 1940, the Nazis failed to meet the challenge of taking power in an industrial great space. Now, a pattern seemed to have emerged with three great spaces – the United States, the Soviet Union and China. There was another 'block-free' space, in which substitute wars and interventions by superpowers took place – just as much as the open spaces beyond the *ius publicum Europaeum* had once served as a stage for the conflicts between European empires.

Schmitt also cast a melancholic eye on Europe's failure in this political triversum. Even 'a many "good Europeans" expect the political unity of Europe only as a side-product (not to say: waste-product) of the global political unity of our planet', he lamented.[43] Schmitt thought that European political unity would require a European constitutional assembly, which in turn would presuppose a European patriotism. According to Schmitt, that was 'at least imaginable, if England does no longer want to be an island'.[44]

For now, however, the world remained a pluriversum – albeit one lacking in true forms of legitimacy. The unity of the world was conceptually thinkable – but it would only be achieved at a price. 'Global patriotism', after all, implied the identification of some other. 'Humanity as a whole and as such', Schmitt claimed, 'has no enemy on this planet'. 'Humanity' was an 'asymmetric counter-concept' – a term coined by Koselleck – which implied that the enemy necessarily had to be cast out as 'inhuman' and annihilated.[45]

A 'patriotism of humanity' would thus fall victim to all the charges Schmitt had already brought against liberal universalism in the 1920s.

Schmitt's last published words, however, were not so much a summary of his warning against a world unified and without enemies. They were about power:

> The final result one has to fear [from a patriotism of humanity] reminds one of the word of a dying ruler, which had already been invented in the nineteenth century. Asked by his spiritual advisor on his deathbed 'Do you forgive your enemies?', he replied with a clean conscience: 'I have no enemies; I have killed them all'.

The Death (and Strange Rebirth) of Carl Schmitt

Carl Schmitt will suffer the fate of Machiavelli and Thomas Hobbes not to be recognized for centuries.

Helmut Schelsky, 1983

C arl Schmitt died on Easter Monday 1985, at the age of 96. His last years had been extremely difficult, especially after the death of his only daughter in 1983. Old age – and the image of the sage – were marred by bouts of paranoia, in particular the fear that SS hordes were hunting him outside his house. The massive correspondence, however, continued and brought occasional consolations. Ernst Jünger, for instance, in 1983 offered the thought that 'one outlives one's friends, but also one's persecutors'.[1]

According to Rüdiger Altmann, some of the anxieties expressed forty years before in *Ex Captivitate Salus* had apparently come true: 'He was a morally broken man', Altmann claimed. 'In the end he was a failed man, because he was no longer able to find his identity. He could no longer answer the question "Who am I?"'.[2] On the other hand, his wish, also expressed in *Ex Captivitate Salus*, to be laid to rest in the Sauerland, in the same cemetery as his parents, was fulfilled. Schmitt received a proper Church burial, with Wolfgang Böckenförde, the brother of Ernst-Wolfgang Böckenförde, as minister.

Schmitt died at a time when conservatism (and neo-conservatism) seemed to be on the rise in West Germany, and when the memory of Nazism was particularly contested. It was in this context that Schmitt's critics prominently restated their arguments against the 'Crown Jurist'. A liberal like Kurt Sontheimer repeated his criticism of Schmitt in an obituary in *Die Zeit*, arguing that 'whoever cares about liberal democracy, does not need Carl Schmitt'.[3] Dolf Sternberger, the doyen of West German political science, recapitulated 'Carl Schmitt's errors'.[4] Habermas made a pre-emptive strike against a broader Schmitt reception in the English-speaking world by arguing that Schmitt's gravest mistake (and the one fatefully repeated by the New Left) was separating liberalism and democracy. Habermas's own attempts in the 1980s and 1990s to reconcile democracy and the rule of law were in part meant to solve a problem for those on the Left tempted by this strict Schmittian antithesis.[5]

At the same time, a smallish scandal erupted when the British scholar Ellen Kennedy claimed that Habermas and other members of the Frankfurt School had appropriated Schmitt's arguments against liberal democracy.[6] In many ways, however, the controversy was much ado about nothing. There could be no doubt that in the late 1950s and early 1960s, Habermas had drawn on Schmitt's thought, alongside Gehlen's, Forsthoff's and Schelsky's.[7] There was also no doubt that Habermas, at that time, regarded Schmitt as a formidable opponent who had seen through the logic of parliamentarism and correctly diagnosed its decline. There could, finally, be little doubt that Habermas was always a democrat first, and a liberal second. It is one of Habermas's strengths, however, to reflect critically on his own previous stances, and to incorporate new theoretical positions, as well as synthesize older ones. In 1986, he wrote of how his generation had been under the influence of figures like Schmitt, Heidegger and Freyer 'during the long phase of latency until the late 1950s'.[8]

The intensity of the debate indicated that Schmitt's legacy was going to remain controversial for years to come. Tainting others with the Schmittian brush – or painting oneself a Schmittian – remained enormously powerful gestures in German intellectual life. In short, a logic of mutual, polemical unmasking persisted: Schmitt, the great unmasker, could in turn be unmasked – but the unmaskers themselves could be unmasked in turn. The prime examples of this logic were the repeated efforts to prove some close proximity between Habermas and Schmitt, in particular the argument that at least Habermas's practical politics operated with a strict friend–enemy distinction.

German legal thinkers, however, remained strangely silent at the time, leaving it to Schmitt's right-wing disciple Maschke to counter the negative press on the master.[9] Günter Maschke published an unapologetically apologetic obituary in the *Frankfurter Allgemeine Zeitung*, in which he interpreted Schmitt's works between 1933 and 1945 as 'parodies' of National Socialist jargon, portraying Schmitt as a distant, ironic observer of the Third Reich.[10]

Schmitt's friends and supporters kept a relatively low profile at the time of his death. Instead, they organized what was often seen as a 'family gathering with some distant relatives of dubious loyalty' at a 1986 conference in Speyer, where Arnold Gehlen had once taught and Schmitt's pupil Helmut Quaritsch was a leading professor.[11] The meeting, the first conference ever devoted to Schmitt's work, assembled personal friends and scholars who had clearly been influenced by Schmitt. Beyond much (revealing and sometimes consciously misleading) reminiscing among the 'disciples at the grave', it also initiated the effort to make Schmitt into a 'classic', a claim presented most forcefully by the neo-nationalist conservative Bernhard Willms.[12] This meeting opened the floodgates. Even those who profoundly disagreed with the disciples assembled in Speyer now indirectly promoted Schmitt as a major thinker. Academia, after all, thrives on revisionism.

Publicity and Postmodern Politics

Around the same time both friends and enemies began to publish more reflective pieces asking 'what really remained of Schmitt' – a question that inevitably (and perhaps unfortunately) became bound up with wider contemporary debates about postmodernism and the supposed 'exhaustion of modernity'.[13] Some of Schmitt's allies asked whether his concept of the political retained its validity under drastically changed historical circumstances. Here, even friends conceded that perhaps a sociologically more complex approach had to succeed Schmitt's deceptively simple distinctions.

The highly influential sociologist Helmut Schelsky, who always acknowledged Hobbes and Schmitt as his true intellectual masters, had already sought to bring the concept of the political *empirically* up to date in a 1983 article.[14] He claimed that every definition of the political emerged from a particular historical experience. The historical development which affected the concept of the political most, however, was not the deployment of the atomic bomb or the process of decolonization. It was the rise of the global electronic media, what Schelsky called the 'global unity' of the media.

The media, he claimed, had created a wholly new dimension of power, which had rendered Schmitt's 'crystal-clear' definition of the political too 'abstract' under current circumstances.[15] According to Schelsky, it was the Nazis who began this fundamental transformation. Their propaganda machine had changed the Germans from a people centred on a common national consciousness into a 'media-directed unit of opinion'. Subsequently, even in the Federal Republic and other Western countries, the nominally democratic 'popular will' had become a 'publicity-directed opinion-will' which was determined by access to the means of 'media domination'. The political had to be understood as gaining power through publicity.

This novel constellation also created a new type of politician. This type, on the one hand, had to engage in the traditional liberal tasks of negotiation and compromise, but on the other, had to play the game of publicity and sell any policy outcome as a 'victory'. Consequently, rational argument in the public sphere became severely limited. Public discussion, for the most part, turned into a matter of trading half-lies, and the political was denigrated to a 'published half-truth'.[16] Political decisions also became dependent on success in swaying public opinion. Ultimately, what Schelsky called a 'publicity election fraud' had come to characterize the political in *both* East and West.

Schelsky's diagnosis no doubt reflected some of the old technocratic distrust of public discussion and the German conservative aversion to the shallowness of the public sphere. Moreover, the clean separation into two 'levels of reality' – one in which reason ruled and one where public perceptions derailed the only rational course of action – was itself a technocratic and antidemocratic fiction. Yet, clearly Schelsky, a conservative capable of casting a cold eye over the current political landscape, had a point in diagnosing the rise of 'media democracy' – even if he exaggerated some of its effects.

Schelsky's remedy – state regulation – turned out to be the same statist answer which Schmitt had given in the early 1930s, when he first recognized the enormous power wielded by those with effective control of the media. In particular, Schelsky sought to ban TV cameras from parliamentary committees and plenary sessions. Political alternatives were somehow supposed to be presented directly to the voters. The old conservative distrust of mediation – whether by the public sphere, parties, or intellectuals – clearly shone through these recommendations.

Self-declared Schmittians were still able to diagnose some of the problems of legitimation that arose in a media democracy. They realized that the dangers posed to a liberal politics were not the existential conflicts of a civil war, but postmodern populism and socio-economic short-termism. But they could only conceptualize these problems as a challenge to sovereignty, from which more or less illiberal remedies had to be deduced.

A Different Modernity: Contingency, Complexity and the Denigration of Politics

The theory of Carl Schmitt does indeed not convince me. I think that good policies combine a maximum capacity for being realized with the creation of a minimum number of enemies.

Niklas Luhmann

Schelsky's was ultimately only a minor amendment to Schmitt's thought from within the Schmitt School. A much more profound challenge came from the social theorist Niklas Luhmann. Despite being the German thinker most concerned with distinctions and differentiations in the modern world since Weber, Luhmann hardly ever mentioned Schmitt in his vast oeuvre. For a thinker as fond of paradoxes and allusions as Luhmann, this in itself meant very little. Luhmann, after all, exhibited two characteristics most unusual for a German professor: irony and independence. He was at least somewhat autonomous, because he had not always been part of the German university system, with its quasi-feudal dependencies and rigid demarcations between different schools of thought. He had started out as an administrator in the state bureaucracy of Lower Saxony, became bored with his work, won a stipend to study at Harvard and went to work with Talcott Parsons. Only relatively late in life did he become a professor, writing his doctorate and second doctorate in record time and then producing a massive oeuvre running to tens of thousands of pages.

Luhmann came out of the same school of sociology as Schelsky, and, like the students of the Ritter School (some of whom he was also close to), he sought nothing but a theory of modernity as such. For 'modernity's most meticulous theorist', modernity was characterized, above all, by an increasing differentiation of society into systems and subsystems.[17] These systems – for example the state, the economy, the legal system and the universities – were said to fulfil particular social functions. A system is essentially any stable social practice, or organized pattern of behaviour, where it is possible to locate the difference between what belongs to the system and what does not.

Systems, in Luhmann's conception, seek to survive and retain their autonomy in complex environments. They do so by filtering out the information from the environment which is relevant to the maintenance of the system, ignoring the rest as noise. Meaning is a matter of selection, and based on this selection, the system permanently produces internal decisions. This is what Luhmann called a reduction of complexity, and this was what systems – and decisions – primarily do: they reduce the complexity of the environment to fit their needs.

A basic intuition behind this social functionalism was familiar from German philosophical anthropology: human beings are too weak and lack the instincts to cope with a complex world. Institutions, or, in Luhmann's parlance, systems, need to compensate for human beings' limited capacities by 'reducing complexity'.

Systems seek to stabilize themselves over time by operating according to a particular code, and by working through a particular medium, which, in turn, stabilizes the expectations of those inside the system. A code in the sphere of the economy, for instance, is to 'have versus not to have', with the medium being money. In science the code is constituted by the opposition 'true versus untrue'. Politics, finally, exhibits the code of government versus opposition, with power being the medium. These codes are essentially binary procedures, which enable the system to process and assimilate information from the environment and to remain autonomous.

What were the actual implications for politics in this scheme? For Luhmann politics was just another system, not a steering mechanism for the whole of society, standing above or surrounding all other systems. It was just one system among many others in a 'society without a top and without a centre'.[18] Any expectation that politics could steer society as a whole was illusory, although admittedly encouraged by outdated political semantics. To speak of 'sovereignty' as located in the government today was to fall victim to an anachronistic language. Power is located in the political system, but it is essentially self-reflexive – it does not affect the rest of society. As Luhman put it, 'the political system can now be construed as a self-regulating . . . system of power-application, in which power is applied to power and is subject to the application of power'.

The state administration, as a self-referential system, had its own logic and was not necessarily responsive to its environment. Society and politics were not connected by normative expectations, or by a social contract. There was no 'society' at all, but only numerous interacting systems with their own codes, held together by the communication between systems. Any notion of individual action might be a useful fiction – and Luhmann did not deny that such fictions were useful – but they could not serve as scientific descriptions of social reality.

Luhmann also rejected any notion that the differentiation of modern society could constitute a source of disorder or alienation. Any expectation that modern societies required consensus or normative social integration was, in Luhmann's view, misplaced. Political languages – whether of socialism, nationalism or any other ideology – did not 'hold society together'. The 'unity' of society was nothing but the mutual autonomy of the different systems.

In the same vein, Luhmann saw the value of democracy only in that democracy was the best response to an increasingly complex society. But it did not give power to 'the people', as an outdated eighteenth-century Enlightenment language suggested. There is no centre anymore, and there is no rule by particular people or the people as a whole. Citizens are, Luhmann claimed, ruled not by persons, but by codes – and the best possible situation is one in which these codes remain distinct and check each other from usurping their respective system.

Much of this fitted perfectly with the West European politics of the 1970s and 1980s; and Luhmann was an active participant in the discussions about 'ungovernability' and the overburdening of the state. In his view, more decision-making power should have been transferred to the bureaucracy and its planning elites. The bureaucracy, he claimed, was particularly well suited to detecting and solving social problems before they led to large-scale social mobilization and demands on the highest level of the executive.

Luhmann's theory, in its mixture of Western technocratic and home-grown conservative elements, could perhaps only have been devised in the Federal Republic. In a unique fashion, it combined the social functionalism espoused by Talcott Parsons with the negative philosophical anthropology of Gehlen (and, to a certain extent, Marquard and other philosophers of the sceptical generation). It also took leave of the German fixation on the state by decentring it from any account of society and refuting any notion of the state as transcendent. And yet, it remained profoundly indebted to German statism by assuming that politics was nothing but the political system, that is, the state. Political action was simply declared unavailable for *any* collective self-transformation of society.

Luhmann's theory brought to an end the long journey from a political thought based on substances and essences to a social theory based on mere functions. It also accomplished the proper de-moralization of politics, which many of Schmitt's students had made their project, as Luhmann affirmed the autonomy of politics against those 'drunk with morality'. Finally, it completed the long search for stability with a proposal in which systems stabilizing themselves created a contingent, but nevertheless stable order which did not in any sense depend on right origins for its legitimacy. Here the everyday level of stability under conditions of complexity was the real, surprising exception. Normality turned out to be the true miracle.

Thus, Luhmann could affirm that 'the true sovereign is the one who prevents the state of exception from ever materializing'.[19] Correspondingly, the question about the presuppositions of liberal democracy – which had haunted post-war political thought for decades – was rendered irrelevant. There was no necessary past and no necessary real outside, whether religion or civic patriotism or any other supposed source of social cohesion, for social systems – only self-contained, continuous and contingent communication. The instability – and danger – associated with a traditional negative philosophical anthropology could be left out of the theory. Just as mere human beings in general could be left out of the theory.

Luhmann offered a theory of modernity entirely based on distinctions, self-divisions and exclusions – with different codes governing different spheres, in the same way as Schmitt had initially described it in *The Concept of the Political* half a century earlier. Politics, *pace* Schmitt's revisions to his initial concept, turned out to be just another sphere of life – and not a general matter of intensity. The primary code of politics – government and opposition – presumed a common political space and procedures, which ensured legitimacy through correct procedures. There was no alternative to the code of government and opposition, and the concept of the political decision – as a decision about something that in principle could not be decided (otherwise it would not have been a decision, but merely a matter of recognizing the right course of action) remained a paradox.

Luhmann circumvented Schmitt's challenges by devising a theory that, in certain respects, appeared to be located in dangerous proximity to Schmitt – and that, in one sense, with its emphasis on mere functioning and

mere procedures could not have been more alien to Schmitt.[20] Schmitt
might have recognized the trust in strong administrations – but not the lack
of legitimacy and any notion of the political as a carrier of meaning. No
wonder, then, that Luhmann's theory was derided as the 'latest attack on the
state from the sphere of society' and even called the 'completion of nihilism
in theories of the state'.[21]

In a way, Luhmann dealt with Schmitt's questions by explaining the questions away. It was more difficult, however, to explain away the exclusions of
one's theory. What was to happen to those who did not want to be governed
by the code of government and opposition – those who sought to engage in
politics without fitting into the system? Luhmann, with admirable frank-
ness, once identified those completely outside and excluded as being the
new 'barbarians'.[22] I shall return to these barbarians – and the self-confessed
blind spots of a technocratic liberalism – in the last part of the book. First, I
shall briefly open what, at least for now, is the last chapter of Schmitt's reception in Germany itself.

Schmitt's Theologization

The German reception of Schmitt was to take a different turn altogether
from the canonization promoted by Schmitt's friends in public law, when
Heinrich Meier published his brilliant 1988 study of the implicit dialogue
between Schmitt and Leo Strauss.[23] Meier, the head of the Siemens Foundation, which Armin Mohler had once directed, was not the first to draw
attention to Schmitt's political theology. He was, however, the first, through
painstaking philological research, to read Schmitt as a political theologian
with conviction. Suddenly it seemed that a key to Schmitt's private mytho-
logical world had been provided – and the door stood wide open for a whole
new generation of researchers to rummage through the *arcana* which
Schmitt had left behind in his books and diaries.

Increasing interest in Schmitt could partly be explained through a basic
sociology of knowledge: a vast field of research had suddenly opened, which
fitted perfectly with the more historical approach in German political philosophy. It also fitted a system in which the accumulation of detail and
proficiency in historical craftsmanship were rated above sweeping new narratives – let alone controversial arguments against other academics better
positioned in a system still very much characterized by personal dependencies and quasi-feudal practices.

None of this is to deny that the majority of German Schmitt scholars made interesting, sometimes even brilliant contributions to the understanding of Schmitt, his motivations and the roots of his thought in relation to other thinkers in the nineteenth and twentieth century. Schmitt studies not only became 'theologized', but also 'personalized'. While some scholars, Bernd Rüthers in particular, continued an effort to situate Schmitt in the Third Reich and therefore contribute to the German legal profession's attempts to 'come to terms with the past', a majority of scholars began to treat Schmitt as an individual, rather than a 'case'.[24] To the extent that Schmitt was seen in context, the emphasis was clearly on Schmitt as great universal European intellectual and man of letters, rather than as a political or legal theorist in any narrow sense. Such interpretative moves all worked against what Bernhard Schlink sought when he demanded that Schmitt should be recognized for the banality of his evil.[25] The call to 'decanonize' Schmitt for intellectual, rather than moral, reasons went largely unheard.

Directly or indirectly, Schmitt was treated as a classic, who merited careful decoding. One could go so far as to claim that Schmitt's trap had finally sprung shut. The self-mythologization he had put so much effort into, paid off after his death. Schmitt's hermetic, self-consciously myth-making approach led to ever more hermeneutics – the kind of hermeneutics in which the German approach to the history of political thought and theory excels. Even those who sought to provide the final key to Schmitt's oeuvre and thereby end the debate and declare a final *damnatio memoriae* only made it more controversial and prolonged the debate.[26]

In 1994, Meier, by now the undisputed *spiritus rector* of the theological camp, continued his line of inquiry, reemphasizing his ambition to penetrate the 'centre of Schmitt's thought', and finding it, over and over again, in the theological.[27] He sought to cut through received opinions about the purity of Schmitt's concept of the political and agonal amorality. He argued that Schmitt's work was in fact based on a substantial moral conviction, namely a peculiar Christian faith, and directed against the modern notion of human self-empowerment.

On this reading, political enmity was not a matter of the agonal endowing life with meaning in a Godless world, as in Nietzsche and Jünger. Instead enmity was God-given and endowed life with the moral seriousness of a choice for or against God. Within this Schmittian logic, the Antichrist might take many disguises, but political theology could safely identify him in anybody who tried to abolish enmity for good. Since the choice of enemies was ultimately one between Satan and God, the political, grounded in the theological necessarily had to become totalized. This 'totalization of the political' had a double meaning: not only could *anything*, that is, any opposition, turn political, as soon as two assembled to treat a third as an enemy, but the political as theological also called on human beings in their totality, demanding one's entire being for the wager on salvation. Given these premises, Meier argued, Schmitt's focus always had to be on the emergency and the exception as the moment of an existential choice between God and Satan.

Meier, in contrast to Schmitt's own distinction between *inimicus* and *hostis* in *The Concept of the Political*, detached the political from larger communities such as state or *Volk*, arguing that Schmitt ultimately took an individualistic moral perspective.[28] This conflation of larger communities and individuals rested on the fact that Meier drew on Schmitt's entire *oeuvre*, including his diaries, and mixed the personal and the academic. While he convincingly showed how Schmitt's theological underpinning led to a totalization of the political, Meier himself chose a totalization of the theological and a 'substantialization' of Schmitt's often highly personal theories in his interpretative strategy. Meier only managed to present such a consistent core of Schmitt's *Weltanschauung*, because he assembled a collage of quotes drawn from divergent sources ranging across Schmitt's publishing career.

Subsequently, it was often assumed that the theological interpretation dealt a fatal blow to Schmitt's potential status as a modern political classic – and that doubting the theological interpretation implied exculpatory tendencies.[29] The proponents of the 'theological thesis' could certainly make a claim for the continuity in Schmitt's thought and therefore weaken the notion of a radical break (to which his apologists clung). Meier, however, also confirmed Schmitt's status as a classic. Substantially, he never referred to any contemporaries of Schmitt except Strauss, instead putting Schmitt as a towering political classic into dialogue with Augustine, Rousseau and Plato. This also revealed another aspect of Meier's overall purpose. As the title referring to a distinction between political theology and political philosophy indicated, he also sought to make the larger claim that political theology stood in an unbridgeable opposition to political philosophy. The former, Meier argued, rests on an unexamined and unexaminable faith, while it is only the latter which examined the social and political context in which philosophy becomes possible. In engaging with political theology and its ultimate basis in revelation, political philosophy could gain deeper insights into its own tasks and its distinctiveness. Thus, Meier asserted, the deepest lesson that Schmitt's theories held was a contribution to the self-clarification of political philosophy, and the insight that *inter auctoritatem et philosophiam nihil est medium* (there is nothing between authority and philosophy). In that sense, the case of Carl Schmitt, rather than being historicized, was universalized as a morality tale about the limits of political theology.

Ultimately, however, Meier himself lapsed into the kind of double talk, allusiveness, and high-minded esoteric tone so typical of Strauss and, to a lesser extent, Schmitt. Schmitt as a genuine *political* thinker disappeared completely. Where he had once been the fascist face of bourgeois capitalism, he now became the fascist face of political theology. Only that fascism disappeared from the picture altogether – after all, if Schmitt's political thought was simply an outgrowth of a bizarre private crypto-Catholic mythology, it was also less of a challenge to modern liberalism. Schmitt became not so much reprehensible, as irrelevant.

Schmitt's followers were sceptical of the primacy of the theological, but not because it was contrary to any apologetic tendencies. The Catholic character of Schmitt's writings was hardly news for them; after all, Mohler had pointed out in the 1950s that Schmitt was a 'Christian with his whole being'.[30] They accepted that Schmitt's motivations might have been theological, but they also sought to dissociate his legal and political writings from his private motivations. To which the anti-Schmittians could correctly reply that Schmitt himself had always pointed out that political theories could not be separated from metaphysics and, ultimately, theology.

On the one hand, the dissociation attempted by Schmittians served to leave Schmitt's political thought untainted by his profound antimodernism. On the other hand, it then became more difficult to excuse his thought with a private mythology. Moreover, the Schmittians continued their effort at canonization, with Böckenförde claiming in 1997 that Schmitt was now 'on the way to becoming a classic'.[31] Schmitt's Catholicism also helped, retroactively, to build a bridge between Schmitt and the Rhineland Catholicism which had dominated the early Federal Republic and which had become one of the main social pillars of post-war democracy.[32] In short, the connection between denying the theological interpretation and apologetics was far from self-evident. At the same time, every fervent reassertion of the 'theology thesis' seemed to be caught in a performative contradiction: if Schmitt was *only* an obscurantist theologian, why was it so important to have yet another treatise on him?

Schmitt scholarship became increasingly specialized and dissociated from actual politics. Where Lübbe, Böckenförde and others had once played a wider role as public intellectuals, the new generation of proponents and opponents of the 'theology thesis' did not engage with wider political or legal questions. Thought on Schmitt was safely contained within the universities. Yet Schmittian thought was not.

Integral Europe and the Rise of the European New Right(s)

> …in the main the question is how light or heavy we are, the problem of our 'specific gravity'. One has to be *very light* to drive one's will to knowledge into such a distance and, as it were, beyond one's time, to create for oneself eyes to survey millennia and, moreover, clear skies in these eyes. One must have liberated oneself from much that oppresses, inhibits, holds down, and makes heavy precisely us Europeans today.
>
> *Nietzsche*, The Gay Science, § 380

> Personally, I understand myself first as a European, then as a 'Norman', and then as a Frenchman.
>
> Alain de Benoist

'Integrity' was one of Carl Schmitt's keywords. For him, integrity was inextricably linked to the concept of order – various versions of Vergil's *ab integro nascitur ordo* were among the most quoted in his oeuvre. In a rather different – but not altogether different – sense, the combination of order and integrity also came to be at the heart of the various New Right movements which arose in Europe during the 1970s and especially the 1980s. These movements replaced the fascist primacy of the political with a primacy of the cultural. Where fascist parties in the first part of the twentieth century had sought to capture the state and dominate society for the sake of a national rebirth, these movements placed an emphasis on first reshaping a society's self-image. They took what they called a 'metapolitical' path and emphasized the imperative to preserve cultural particularity – of particular societies, but, more importantly, of Europe as a whole. They self-consciously sought the internationalization and, in particular, Europeanization of right-wing thought. Like Schmitt, they abandoned the nation-state (and industrial society) as an appropriate framework for politics.

From the French *Nouvelle Droite* to the Italian *Lega Nord*, their ideologists all aimed at an 'integral Europe' – a vision which variably included elements of populism, extreme versions of communitarianism, sometimes referred to as localism, and, frequently, federalism.[1] The common denominator of all these currents, however, was a belief in primordial, integral and homogeneous ethnic groups – a vision that often widened into a pan-European vision of a federation of ethnic political entities. Despite its sometimes decidedly pagan and anti-statist character, this transnational nationalist movement in favour of a 'European rebirth' frequently had recourse to Schmitt's thought. It shared with Schmitt a desire for the revitalization of European elites and the re-entry of Europe into 'great politics'.[2] Benito Cereno was to take control of the ship again.

New Right thinkers all held that a Europe divided between the superpowers had lost its capacity for distinguishing its own real friends and enemies and therefore any autonomous political role. Such a role was necessary because of Europe's distinctive cultural identity, which was in danger of being obliterated by a one-world, American-inspired 'monoculture'. From the beginning, anti-Americanism was a central element of New Right ideology – an element that would be strengthened after the end of the Cold War.[3] Like so many right-wing parties and movements in post-war Europe, protagonists of the New Right justified their drive towards political division and exclusion with the claim that they and their compatriots were ultimately *victims*.

Revising the Fascist Legacy: The Integralist Imagination

There were significant differences between various national versions of the New Right. Nevertheless, they became part of a common movement by virtue of a number of shared core beliefs. They all learnt lessons from the first New Right, the *Nouvelle Droite* of the French theorist Alain de Benoist. De Benoist, a highly eclectic and esoteric thinker, stood in the tradition of French fascist thought and its concept of integral nationalism.[4] Faced with the fact that the extreme Right in post-war France seemed unable to rely on old models of political mobilization, he added distinctive ideological elements to this long home-grown tradition. In particular, he held that all political conflicts had to be interpreted along cultural lines. He raided the human sciences, from anthropology to psychiatry, in order to bolster claims about the endurance of cultural and ethnic differences. Culture was supposed to replace class as a sign of difference in increasingly socially homgeneous European societies – and these societies as a whole were called upon to defend their cultural distinctiveness against non-European foreigners both inside and outside.[5] This distinctive ideology of 'ethnic pluralism' demanded drawing clear lines according to ethnic and cultural differences. The emphasis on preserving particularity – as opposed to a supposedly aggressive egalitarianism and universalism, which led to an uncontrolled mixture of peoples and thereby annihilated particular traditions – made New Right thought akin to forms of philosophical conservatism. It also became philosophically compatible with versions of postmodernism, as New Right theorists constructed a universal 'right to difference'.

There was then a premium on proving Europe's particularity – for the sake of which de Benoist and his followers established a whole range of research institutes, regular conferences and journals, with such high-minded names as the *Groupement de récherche et d'études pour la civilisation européenne* (Research Group for the Study of European civilisation). The conclusion of most of these investigations was that European distinctiveness was grounded not so much in the Judeo-Christian tradition, which, after all, had blurred Europe's identity with its universalism, but in Europe's pagan past. Therefore New Right thinkers would eagerly debate such esoteric questions as 'Are the old gods returning?' – returning, that is, to a Europe steeped in universalist decadence, in order to restore its integral and primordial Indo-European character.

The New Right's concept of the political was cultural in a double sense. Culture marked out the essential political tensions – but the path to political power was also via culture. The *Nouvelle Droite* had been conceived in the heady atmosphere of the Parisian May '68 – when it seemed obvious that profound political changes in post-war Europe would not end, but begin with culture. Taking a lesson from Antonio Gramsci and his theory of cultural hegemony as well as the eighteenth-century *sociétés de pensée*, de Benoist and his followers sought to engage in what they called 'metapolitics'.[6] Rather than entering party politics directly (let alone using paramilitary groups or constructing broad-based fascist movements), the New Right sought to infiltrate the media and the education system and thereby gain the intellectual high ground. Only then would its cultural power be translated into winning actual elections. Nothing less was required than a complete transvaluation of values, and a new unitary European consciousness.

Thus, extreme philosophical conservatism did not translate into radical, political action driven by national myths, as with the original fascists. Neither did New Right thinkers rest content with the kind of political quietism that technocratic conservatives had advocated. Rather, they took seriously what technocratic conservatives had ignored to their detriment: culture, which in the long run could be infused with nationalist patterns of thought and might then pave the way for a return of radical political action. In the eyes of French New Right thinkers, Schmitt's friend–enemy distinction was a presupposition of such radical political action. According to Julien Freund, Schmitt's most important French pupil and eventually a New Right theorist, it remained what André Gide had called a *banalité supérieure* that political action depended on the prior identification of the enemy.[7]

Yet another Revolt against the Modern World

Schmitt was by no means the main inspiration for the 'integralist insurgency'. Sources for New Right thinkers were self-consciously pagan and anti-Christian thinkers like Oswald Spengler, Nietzsche and Julius Evola – with whom Schmitt continued friendly relations after the War and who unsuccessfully tried to have Schmitt's post-1945 books published in Italian.[8]

Baron Evola in particular became a patron saint for the various New Rights. He was no less complex or contradictory a figure than Schmitt in the history of right-wing European political thought.[9] Evola fought in the First World War, and then started his proper intellectual life as a Dadaist, reading his avant-garde poetry to the accompaniment of music by Schönberg and Bartók in the Cabaret Grotte dell'Augusteo, Italy's version of Zürich's Café Voltaire, the birthplace of Dada.[10] He then turned into a committed esoteric, engaging in what he called 'trans-rational studies' of the mythic and the occult. He finally came out in full *Revolt against the Modern World*, as the title of his most important and influential work of 1934 announced.[11]

In *Revolt*, he argued that the last two thousand years had been a process of involution, that is, decline and decadence, for Europe. This process had accelerated with the Renaissance and, in particular, the French Revolution. To redeem itself, Europe had to recover what he called 'spiritual virility' and return to a hierarchical, organic political order. This, in a nutshell, was Evola's doctrine of integral Traditionalism. It resonated more, however, with right-wing German thinkers such as Gottfried Benn than with Evola's fellow Italians.

Evola felt much closer to German National Socialism than Italian Fascism, which, he thought, had not succeeded in implementing its ideas. Evola was a committed antisemite and tried to spread his ideas in Nazi Germany with the help of Alfred Rosenberg. However, he always couched his theories in the language of cultural anthropology, rather than plain biological racism – which is why the official guardians of Nazi ideology resisted his plans to publish in German, even when he had Mussolini's personal support. The Baron remained loyal to Mussolini until the very last days of the Republic of Salo.

After the War, Evola – who had never belonged to the Fascist Party – took up a role in Italian intellectual life not altogether dissimilar from Schmitt's in Germany. He was an inspiration – and an oracle – for many young right-wing thinkers, activists and even terrorists. They would flock to his Rome apartment on Corso Vittorio Emmanuelle to listen to his ruminations on Nordic races, Hindu mythology and even the 'metaphysics of sex'.[12]

Evola's lasting contribution to New Right thought was his focus on the pagan and the primordial, his self-consciously European perspective and his stress on hierarchical, organic communities. He opened up an ideological perspective from which nationalism (and the nation-state) appeared as part and parcel of the modern world that was to be rejected. Instead, pre-modern forms of political community such as empires or federations of communes had to be the goals for Europe if it was to regain the sources of 'spiritual virility'.

This search for a revitalization of European elites in the context of a new geopolitical order provided a bridge to Schmittian thought. In so far as New Right thinkers, especially in Germany, promoted a specifically political theory, they drew extensively on Schmitt's ideas – or creative misinterpretations thereof, which in turn often reflected peculiar national traditions. The Italian *Nuova Destra*, for instance, attempted to use Schmitt's thought to bolster their ideal of a new organic community based on a 'new anthropology', 'substantive values' and even a new concept of the political – steadfastly ignoring Schmitt's reservations about the philosophy of values.[13] For the most part, however, such ideas never became concrete in terms of actual institutional change – except for the call to hold more plebiscites.[14]

What resulted from the fusion of fragments of Schmittian theory with the more mythical strands of New Right thought were often highly idiosyncratic ideological mixtures. The Italians, for instance, developed Evola's

esoteric concerns into a full-blown fascination with myths, fantasy literature and even science fiction – which hardly went together with Schmitt's
coldly analytical insights into the nature of the political. Yet, there it was:
C. Schmitt joined J. R. R. Tolkien as an ideological staple for the *Nuova
Destra*, and New Right thinkers would unite for seminars on Schmitt's political thought in *Campi Hobbit*.[15]

In Schmitt's Shadow: The German New Right

The German New Right, not surprisingly, chose Schmitt – and, above all,
Ernst Jünger – as guiding lights in their battle against what they saw as the
liberal democratic pieties of the Federal Republic. The prime magazine of
the German New Right, *Junge Freiheit* [Young Freedom] provided ample
space for the unfolding of what one might call the 'Schmitt subculture' –
books by and about Schmitt were reviewed extensively, and Schmitt's friends
and pupils were regularly celebrated.[16]

Yet, it was not clear what, beyond an obvious aesthetic fascination with
the secret world of San Casciano, New Right thinkers actually derived from
their readings of Schmitt. Like some of Schmitt's immediate post-war
pupils, they offered a rather paradoxical image of West Germany. On the one
hand, they tended to view the Federal Republic as a weak state colonized by
special interests inside and by the Americans from the outside. On the other
hand, the Republic was viewed as a state ruled by a seemingly all-powerful
enemy of liberal intellectuals who controlled the media and public discourse. In short, the excessively liberal German state, while persecuting its
internal enemies under the banner of 'political correctness', was unable to
determine its real enemies on the outside. This became particularly problematic, as the world returned from the 'global state of exception' of the
Cold War to the normality of a more complex 'pluriversum' of political
spaces.

In many ways, the New Right adopted the legacies of the resentment-
driven radical conservatism of Armin Mohler – rather than sharpening
their own political analyses with Schmittian tools, in the way, for instance,
Altmann had done in the 1960s. A self-conscious realism, for which New
Right thinkers coined the term 'political verism', was a matter of attitude and
even aesthetics rather than a matter of offering genuine answers to the 'concrete political situation'.[17] It was not surprising, for instance, that what appeared in the eyes of New Right thinkers to be the dystopia of a civil society

founded on the principles of civic participation and publicity disqualified itself on the grounds of being 'unaesthetic'.[18]

Since the German New Right also chose the path of 'metapolitics', it was not irrelevant that their intellectual leaders aimed at a rehabilitation of Schmitt as a *cultural* figure and of the aesthetics of a hardened political realism in general. Power was, after all, to be gained through revising cultural idioms and wider political vocabularies first. Like Schmitt himself, New Right thinkers subscribed to a form of conceptual realism – the belief that the power to determine the content of concepts would sooner or later bring reality into line with one's conceptual scheme. Sometimes, however, conceptual realism seemed to border on magical realism. New Right intellectuals put all their faith in capturing political language, rather than addressing political issues.

The New Right in general took up Ernst Nolte's distinction between 'liberal' and 'liberalistic'.[19] They claimed the former label and defended their own contributions in the name of, if nothing else, freedom of expression. 'Liberalistic' named the representatives of a system whose limits they recognized but which they still defended in increasingly dogmatic and even 'evil' ways. Schmitt's concerns about weak-willed liberalism and Arnold Gehlen's reservations about domestic morality sheltered from the hard choices of real politics could then all be projected onto the 'system'.

However, apart from such rather transparent exercises in gaining 'discursive hegemony', there were also more profound pieces of antiliberalism. The essay *Anschwellender Bocksgesang* [Rising Song of the Goat – an allusion to Greek Tragedy] by the writer Botho Strauß offered the most prominent – and most perceptive – manifesto for the German New Right (although ultimately it was more of a premonition than a manifesto, inspired by what Strauß called a 'terror of foreboding').[20] Self-consciously playing with a vocabulary of cultural pessimism, Strauß chided the West for having lost its historical memory, any understanding of history as tragic and any sense of the limits to human agency – especially ecological limits. In a piece that was ultimately more indebted to Heidegger and Jünger than Schmitt, he also claimed that the substance of Western societies, in the absence of real political threats and challenges, had been sapped by 'democratism', 'liberal-libertarian self-centredness', the shallow satisfactions of prosperity and the 'socialization of suffering and happiness'. As with Heidegger and Evola – and the French and Italian New Rights – Strauß called upon an elite to consciously reappropriate and refashion the *longue durée* of the European past and even 'mythic time' – as opposed to the total domination of the present and what he called the 'dictatorship of the temporary' in liberal societies.

The gesture of elitist, lonely defiance of the liberal, shallow public sphere was as familiar in the Conservative Revolution, the movement of right-wing nationalist intellectuals in the 1920s, as it was in the various counter-public spheres of the 1950s. Strauß's opposition to diluting stark oppositions, his desire for immoderation and the heroic stance of disdaining the 'masses' or even the 'enlightened masses' – these were not so much political or even metapolitical positions (let alone concepts), but rather aesthetic attitudes. Such attitudes proved attractive for a significant number of younger intellectuals – but had little to do with genuinely Schmittian politics. The liberal pupils and even the liberal enemies of Schmitt in the 1950s and 1960s had done more to modernize his thought than his self-proclaimed disciples on the New Right. For proposals to translate Schmittian thought into constitutional politics during the 1980s and 1990s, observers of the fortunes of Schmittian prescriptions had to look further south.

Integral Federalism

One of the most theoretically sophisticated visions of an integral Europe was propounded by Gianfranco Miglio, a professor (and, for 29 years, rector) at Milan's Catholic University – *la Cattolica* – and later the chief ideologist of the Northern League.[21] He had been instrumental in re-introducing Schmitt into Italian political thought in the early 1970s and continued to portray him an as inexhaustible classic wherever he could.[22] He was also a leading activist in the *Grupo di Milano* for constitutional reform in the 1980s and early 1990s. The Milan Group advocated a directly elected prime minister and a strong president as the guardian of the constitution – although their proposals did not include a plebiscitary legitimation for the president. They also sought a strengthening of the constitutional court and generally emphasized the need to limit pluralism and to relativize parliamentarism. Milgio's ideas found much resonance in the Italian press. Eventually they were even debated by the socialist party and the post-fascist Italian Social Movement (which was to take the name *Alleanza Nazionale* in 1994).

Even before the implosion of the Italian political system in the early 1990s, Miglio had begun to move in a different theoretical direction. Rather than wanting to strengthen central power, he developed into an opponent of Italian statism tout court.[23] Miglio based this position on what he perceived, like Schmitt, as the end of European statehood. Instead of a strong state, he came to advocate the vision of a federal Italy – with the federal units or 'macro-regions' based on cultural criteria. This advocacy was preceded by the admission that the Italians were simply not a homogeneous people, with the most important split running between the Northern 'bourgeois' and the Southern 'Mediterraneans'. A proper federation of three separate regions in the north, centre and south, Miglio thought, would take account of this fact, but would also have to include a real right to secession in order to make federalism genuine.[24] The Swiss federation served as a model, alongside much older entities such as the Hanseatic cities.

Throughout, Miglio was concerned to rectify what he regarded as the preponderance of Hans Kelsen's pure theory of law in Italian constitutional thought – for which Schmitt was one of the obvious antidotes. In an interview Miglio went so far as to claim that unfortunately Kelsen with his conception of democracy as compromise had exercised too much of an influence in Italy – and that this stress on accommodating oneself and living with compromise could probably be explained by Kelsen's Jewish background.[25]

One of Miglio's most eager students turned out to be Umberto Bossi, the leader of the Northern League. He came to call for fiscal federalism alongside integral, that is, cultural, federalism, while also adding a heavy dose of anti-immigration rhetoric. Most importantly, he took up the idea of a northern macro-region, to be called 'Padania'. The *Lega Nord* managed to enter a right-wing governing coalition with Silvio Berlusconi at its head, first in 1994 and then again in 2001. Miglio was elected a Northern League senator in 1992, but fell out with Bossi two years later, allegedly because Bossi had denied him the post of Minister of Institutional Reform. Miglio himself, who had hoped to be the moral guide and conscience of the party, claimed that Bossi had betrayed the true principles of federalism and went on to found a group that he felt represented a truly federal solution for Italy.[26]

Miglio did not see a significant break in his intellectual trajectory. In the tradition of Italian realism going back to Pareto, Mosca and, of course, Machiavelli, he had always been distrustful of parliamentarism. His relentlessly realist analysis of the state and its power had not changed either – but the recommendations which followed from it had been reversed, as the age of statehood itself came to an end. Miglio denied that he had ever been what he called an 'integral decisionist', that is, an advocate of a 'transcendental import' behind the decision.[27] Rather, he increasingly supported the market as a means of stabilizing political arrangements: federalism, pluralism and freely negotiated contracts between diverse political entities were to be the conceptual building blocks of a new post-statist Italian politics. It was only consistent, in the end, that Miglio had Henry David Thoreau's essay on civil disobedience translated into Italian. Libertarianism and the Italian politics of ethnic resentment apparently went together effortlessly.

A Transatlantic Meeting of Minds
Curiously enough, many of the characters and concerns of the European New Rights ultimately came together across the Atlantic. Since the 1970s Schmitt had left a deep impression among a new generation of American scholars. These scholars often felt that emigrants like Otto Kirchheimer and Franz Neumann, who had been Schmitt's left-wing students in the 1920s, had somehow suppressed the truth about the Crown Jurist and thereby the truth about their own intellectual origins.[28] New York-based scholar George Schwab pioneered the American discovery of Schmitt. In the 1960s he wrote a dissertation on Schmitt's rule during the final phase of the Weimar Republic, for which he even resided in Plettenberg for a number of months. He strenuously denied any continuity in Schmitt's work before and after 1933, and played down Schmitt's anti-semitism. The dissertation was repeatedly rejected by Kirchheimer and Schwab had to write another dissertation on a different topic. Eventually, however, his work appeared with Schmitt's main German publisher.[29]

This interpretation of Schmitt as a contemporary classic who had defended Weimar to the last fused with a new interest in Schmitt among scholars associated with the 'Journal of Critical Thought', *Telos*, based in New York's Greenwich Village. *Telos* had originally been a conduit for Frankfurt School theory into the American New Left. However, during the 1980s, *Telos* intellectuals shifted towards a curious ideological mixture of communitarianism, populism and federalism on the one hand and anti-statism and anti-nationalism on the other – a mixture not that different from the one propounded by the later Miglio. *Telos* took Gramsci, Schmitt and Miglio as major inspirations to conceive a vision of a federation of organic communities against a liberal, statist 'technocracy' administered by a 'new class' of politicians, bureaucrats and tenured academics. Like Schmitt and the European New Rights they held that the era of the nation-state was at an end, and that in any case, the nation-state had been an agent of homogenization and oppression.

The antidote to a 'totally administered world' was a federation of organic and democratic communities – a vision indebted as much to de Benoist's ethnic pluralism as to early American federalist thought. This opposition was ultimately one between universalist and homogenizing liberalism and particularist and organic democracy – an absolute opposition which the writers in the pages of *Telos* reiterated time and again with reference to Carl Schmitt. In particular, Schmitt's thought was supposed to compensate for the lack of a political and, in particular, a state theory in Marxism.[30]

Beginning with a special issue in 1987 under the title 'Enemy or Foe?', almost every *Telos* issue became a 'special issue on Schmitt', mainly devoted to faithful Schmitt exegesis.[31] At the same time, the journal began publishing articles by de Benoist and Miglio, alongside rather conventional articles on Walter Benjamin and other Frankfurt School topics.[32] This bizarre ideological mixture caused alarm in Germany, where liberals became concerned about a broad Schmitt renaissance in the United States, prepared through a 'preventive historical de-nazification' by Schwab and others.[33] As had happened in Germany, alarmism and resentment fed on each other. The logic of mutual, polemical unmasking came to characterize the international Schmitt-reception, and the North American one in particular.[34]

Just how peculiar was the path traversed by the *Telos* intellectuals from the Frankfurt School to the New Right?[35] Certainly a normative abyss separated one from the other, and yet, the concern with preserving particularity in the face of an abstract liberal universalism that eradicated difference and genuine subjectivity could potentially unite philosophical conservatives and parts of the Left. According to the editors of *Telos*, 'being always exceeds thought', and 'the elimination of the resulting residue by Enlightenment ideology' would lead to an 'ungrounded rationalism articulated through instrumental reason that can accommodate any political agenda'.[36] The only appropriate response was to ground thinking in a 'pre-rational and pre-conceptual dimension that has become occluded or forgotten': among Wittgenstein's 'forms of life', Heidegger's Being, Dewey's experience, Adorno's mimesis or indeed: Schmitt's concrete orders.[37]

Both the Left and the New Right, then, sought resources against what they saw as the homogenization and instrumentalization of human beings in a 'totally administered' world in which Enlightenment humanism had turned into an ideology of oppression.[38] The New Right(s) and *Telos* sought such resources in traditions and organic communities – without revealing much about where exactly such integral resources were to be found. 'Postmodern populism' appeared animated by idealized (and abstract) images of community, and unable to formulate concepts of practical political action, except for a kind of global cultural protectionism. Allusive calls for a vitalist overcoming of 'an age of collective decadence and luxurious nihilism' remained without any clear addressee.[39] Whether an old Right obsessed with social integration and stability or a New Right obsessed with integrity and particularity – the sources of both integration and integrity often remained obscure or downright mythical.

Part III
Schmitt's Globalization:
Drawing the Lines

Whoever says globalization wants to deceive.

Josef Isensee

. . . as Hegel correctly says, weapons convey the substance of the fighter himself.

Carl Schmitt, 1938

The 1990s were symmetrical like no other decade in the twentieth century. They began with an American-led war in the name of international liberal order and ended with another. They also began and ended with a seeming triumph of philosophical liberalism – most directly expressed by Francis Fukuyama, Kojève's distant pupil, in *The End of History* and *The Great Disruption*.[1] Both appeared to provide world-historical apologias for the successful exercise of American power. *The End of History* announced nothing less than that liberal, capitalist democracy was the answer to the human condition. Capitalism was the final word in economics, since it maximized prosperity, while liberalism was the final word in politics in that it satisfied the human need for individual dignity and mutual recognition. The former was expressed in the 'Washington consensus' on economic policy of the early 1990s, the latter crystallized in global humanitarianism, which ultimately made the West go to war at the end of the decade.

Schmitt would have easily recognized this twofold development as an apparent liberal displacement of the political into the economic and the ethical. The exercises in what was often referred to as liberal 'endism' could easily be unmasked with Schmittian insights or *Ideologiekritik*. Accordingly, the seemingly universalist claims in ethics and economics were merely means to achieve specific Western interests – if necessary, by violent means. They could also only be sustained because the fundamental problem of political order had been solved – through the dominance of the one remaining, albeit largely liberal superpower. That power would adhere to international law during normal times, but, when feeling threatened, could simply suspend it in a moment of sovereign decision.

None of this, however, explained why Schmitt, as the theorist of the friend-enemy distinction, experienced such a renaissance after the truly global Cold War division into friends and enemies had effectively disappeared. Could the reason have been as simple as that with the disappearance of liberalism's enemy, Communism, the internal homogeneity of the West weakened – and therefore new sources of social cohesion and political stability had to be found? This, after all, had been the very problem which had preoccupied Schmitt's German pupils. Or was Schmitt's role confined to that of a particularly perceptive – but perhaps not very constructive – critic of supposed liberal hypocrisies and self-deceptions?

Liberal Self-deceptions: Hypocrisy, Perversity, Complicity

From the perspective of the Left, the displacement of politics into ethics and economics was itself ethically wrong. In some – never fully explained – manner liberal ethics and economics were complicit in producing the very violence which commerce and moral conversation were meant to overcome. According to Slavoj Žižek, the liberal world order not only amounted to a 'post-political suspension of the political' and a 'reduction of the state to a mere police-agent servicing the (consensually established) needs of market forces and multiculturalist tolerant humanitarianism'.[2] Paradoxically, it was in fact the global multiculturalist management of 'unity in difference' and the formation of a rationalist consensus around humanitarian principles itself that produced apparently irrational and contingent outbreaks of cruelty and violence. The fateful coalition of 'enlightened technocrats' and 'liberal multiculturalists', who made up the 'post-political liberal establishment', supposedly suppressed the political in the sense of 'litigation' and 'antagonism'.[3] But, or so the argument went, only if those still excluded by the rationalist consensus of the liberal establishment could assert their humanity, would the political itself break through the 'emerging post-political logic which progressively precludes the dimension of universality at work in politicization proper'.[4] Globalization in a liberal image, then, was presented as, above all, a false form of universalism, which displaced the properly political – and therefore postponed proper political emancipation – in the name of ethics and economics. Conversely, a true universalism shone forth precisely in the struggle against hypocritical or even self-deceptive prescriptions for liberal tolerance and social therapy.

It remained unclear, however, what form the political was supposed to take here. In his examples of properly political action, Žižek, for instance, wavered between the notion of 'litigation' and, the 'excessive "irrational" whim' of skinhead violence and the verbal struggle for universal recognition by 'African-American single unemployed lesbian' mothers. Litigation suggested an adversarial, but ultimately rule-governed relationship, the latter forms appeared more like cries for help. What form, then, was conflict to take here – violent or non-violent; part of liberal democratic procedures; or extraparliamentary action? No answers were forthcoming. One certainty remained, however. If the political was foreclosed '*in the post-political universe of pluralist negotiation and consensual regulation*', it would return as Schmittian 'ultra-politics' – 'the radicalization of politics into the open warfare of Us against Them'.[5] Consequently, Schmitt would remain '*crucial in detecting the deadlocks of post-political liberal tolerance*' – a danger and a diagnostician at the same time.[6]

Schmitt's appearance in the writings of the post-Marxist Left showed to what extent the Left had run out of conceptual resources to rally against an apparently triumphant liberalism. It also betrayed a theoretical paucity in that resistance against liberalism could only be thought through rather random examples, instead of a proper model of political action. The Left simply lacked the theoretical language for an alternative model of social reality, instead staking its critique almost exclusively on an alleged hidden complicity of liberalism with antiliberalism. Fragments of Schmittian thought were deployed in this rearguard antiliberal struggle, but, arguably, Schmittian *Ideologiekritik* all by itself would prove impotent.

On a rather different part of the ideological spectrum, Schmitt's arguments against a pernicious moralization of *international* affairs also appeared to resonate in 'realist' approaches to world order after the Cold War. Samuel Huntington, in arguably the most prominent perspective on international relations in the 1990s, diagnosed the inscription of new friend-enemy relations on the global map.[7] Huntington argued that philosophical universalism, liberal internationalism and humanitarianism could all be equated with a form of Western imperialism, much as Schmitt had suggested half a century earlier. As in Schmitt's (and, to some extent, Koselleck's writings), morality seemed to have stealthily crossed the border between prudent statecraft and a reckless 'ethics of conviction', thereby contaminating a previously safe Hobbesian division of labour between the state and civil society. In short, global humanitarianism, aiming at a 'global civil society', was the latest example of what Koselleck had called the hypocrisy of the Enlightenment – and the moral critique of a permanently divided mankind necessarily produced a permanent crisis, if not the dangers of outright global civil war.[8]

Not surprisingly, Schmitt's arguments against universalism were recovered by those nostalgic for a non-discriminating, state-based concept of war. In a world in which soldiers could no longer be automatically assumed to be the legitimate carriers of weapons, and in which borders of all kinds became increasingly blurred and often replaced by fuzzy frontiers, there seemed a desperate need to re-erect structures – and to re-establish separations. Not surprisingly, there were frequent calls for a comprehensive re-territorialization of conflict. In particular, those diagnosing a new world disorder argued that states not only made war possible – they also made peace possible.[9] Immanuel Kant – unlike his liberal followers in the present – had understood that perpetual peace had to be built on the foundation of discrete and stable republics. Instead, the present promoters of peace were inadvertently creating a world of partial, overlapping or shifting sovereignties, in which semi-autonomous, semi-legal entities existed alongside failed states and de-facto protectorates. Legally and conceptually, these new political spaces were located in a seemingly permanent twilight zone between war and peace. Then there was a further periphery in which any legitimate authority had vanished and where the combined forces of globalization and civil war appeared to be crushing entire populations. It was no accident that failed states turned into breeding grounds for terror.

Strange coalitions emerged between peace activists who accused the West of hypocrisy and conservatives who sought to retain a purely state-based, 'non-discriminating' concept of war. For instance, visitors to wartime Belgrade would be treated to a curious ideological mix of left-wingers turned conservative, such as the Austrian writer Peter Handke, geopolitical 'realists' who dreamed of an integral Europe alongside a 'Eurasian bloc' defined against Islam, and adherents of an old-fashioned sacrificial nationalism. In particular, Aleksander Dugin, the foremost Russian theorist of a 'Eurasian bloc', drew on Schmitt and, even more so Evola to conjure up a new myth of Eurasian superiority over Anglo-American liberalism.

The diverse defenders of difference could find common ground in the opposition to a moral universalism always already tainted by the messiness of actually existing international politics. All subscribed to a philosophical or anthropological – as opposed to political – conservatism. This conservatism rejected the liberal logics of self-interest and human equality qua identity. A liberal order focused on mere survival would create 'an anaemic spectacle of life dragging on as its own shadow'.[10] Often the default option for Left and Right in this scenario was a defence of the nation-state – either as the only reliable agent of political protection in an increasingly dangerous international world, or as the only ultimate framework for preserving cultural particularity.

The point is not that there were no good reasons to question political action undertaken in the name of liberal universalism. But allusions to Schmitt simply came to fill theoretical (and even empirical) voids left by the suspicion of hypocrisy (by Left and Right), of perversity (by the Right), and complicity (by some thinkers of the Left). According to the latter's arguments, liberalism was secretly depending on its apparently worst enemies as a suitable contrast to its own values, thereby providing social cohesion. Thus, it could be concluded that 'our pluralistic and tolerant liberal democracies remain deeply "Schmittian"'.[11]

What appeared to be an ongoing series of 'global police actions', however, left even relatively sympathetic observers uneasy about the apparently overstretched claims of liberal universalism. Liberal intentions simply appeared too mixed for their own good and every post-imperialist liberal intervention which was at least partially vindicated made it all the more obvious that it was for reasons of *Realpolitik* that the West did not intervene in other places.[12] The more moralized global politics became, the more its residue of immorality became plain to see.

Liberal universalists partly made themselves vulnerable to charges of hypocrisy, perversity and complicity by cautiously justifying the new wars as a foreshadowing of a future 'world domestic politics' in which interventions would indeed become a matter of policing. In the meantime, NATO, not the United Nations, would act as the trustee of a future global civil society, providing theoretical mediation between morality, law and power, which could tip over into liberal imperialism at any moment, and for which no clear moral boundaries could as yet be specified. Not surprisingly, Jürgen Habermas, intensely aware of the ambiguities of militant universalism and humanitarianism, defended the Kosovo war by making a pre-emptive strike against those of its critics who were drawing on Schmitt.[13]

Schmitt's arguments against speaking 'in the name of humanity' also came back into fashion. During the Kosovo War, European intellectuals frequently quoted Schmitt's 'Whoever says "humanity" wants to deceive' to unmask 'military humanitarianism' as a façade for NATO's power politics.[14] The dark side of humanitarianism, in the eyes of the anti-moralizers, was the tendency to cast the enemies out as 'inhuman' – and to unleash total, as well as potentially unending, war on them.[15] War from the safety of high altitudes seemed to deny the opponent any recognition and rob him of his dignity as a legitimate adversary.[16] With the help of new technology, policing in the name of liberal universalism had reached new altitudes of hypocrisy (or perhaps self-deception) which even Schmitt could not have foreseen. Such a war, the critics claimed, could also not be contained in the way that wars fought for 'one's own people and concrete territory' could be. Humanitarian wars lacked legitimacy and were limitless at the same time. They could count on little national support from within the intervening countries, but they had to go to the limit of destroying the enemy, once the enemy had become demonized as standing outside humanity. As a British general admitted, in the 1990s demonizing the enemy had indeed become a precondition for deploying ground forces 'among the people', that is, in the confusing ethnic civil wars at the end of the century. Moreover, war was now not only 'among the people', but also took place under the watchful (and, in the eyes of many military men and women, moralizing) eye of the media.

Terror, Political Theology and the Liberal Conscience

Among the people, in turn, ethnic partisans, that is, 'telluric', conservative partisans in the Schmittian sense were hiding. These partisans and other irregular combatants were increasingly difficult to distinguish from traditional clans and their codes of feudal enmity, 'military entrepreneurs' or even members of organized crime syndicates. In short, another moral and political boundary appeared to become blurred. The threat of total war through nuclear weapons seemed to have passed – but on a limited national or even subnational scale, total war, in which the line between combatants and non-combatants had effectively been erased, became a real possibility again. No wonder, Schmitt's thoughts on the partisan were resurrected in dealing with the 'irregular'.[17]

It was not only partisans defending their home territory – a phenomenon familiar from the Second World War and the struggles for decolonization – who characterized the post-Communist era. It was also a new kind of terrorist threat which combined perfectly rational use of supposedly 'neutral' technological means with apparently apocalyptic ends.[18] The new terrorists, rather than defending their own territory, had themselves become de-territorialized. They appeared as 'uprooted partisans' with neither concrete political bases nor concrete political interests.[19] Operating through global networks, they were as faceless and elusive as the forces of globalization and imperialism which the terrorists apparently held responsible for the destruction of genuine religious and moral life. Unlike the partisans whose irregularity was predicated on the regularity of normal army operations which they hoped to emulate one day, the irregularity of the terrorists seemed both permanent and absolute. In the absence of concrete political goals, neither peace treaties nor a return to political normality – let alone any form of political mediation – seemed possible.

Yet, while being de-territorialized, the new terrorists were capable of using technology and entirely new theatres of violence to attack the territory of the one remaining superpower and self-appointed guarantor of a liberal international order. The very tools the West had created were now turned against it – a fact which brought to mind Schmitt's dictum that the enemy embodied the question mark for our own civilization. At the same time, this dictum seemed to be superseded by an altogether new logic. The weak themselves, it seemed, had become the weapons of the weak. In this case, the Hegelian idea that the weapons conveyed the substance of the fighter himself seemed both paradoxically confirmed and strangely prescient, as substance and weapon had become identical. Politics became reduced to bodies hurtling through time and space, while the target – or the apparent question for the enemy – simply became the individual who happened to be in the wrong place at the wrong time in a complex post-industrial society.[20]

This new constellation of rationality of means and apparent irrationality of ends, as well as the complete de-territorialization of terrorists and the re-territorialization of targets, opened a new chapter in the relation of space and political order, which Schmitt had examined up until the 1970s. Traditional concepts of enmity such as amity lines seemed no longer applicable in a situation where further boundaries and distinctions evaporated. Not only was there no longer a clear separation between military and civilian targets (a separation that had already been blurred in the Second World War), the enemy had also appeared from within.[21] Partisans had felt like fish in the water 'among the people', that is, a homogeneous *Volk* determined to preserve its particularity – the new terrorists, however, could become invisible in highly diverse, liberal Western societies.

Most importantly, symbolic, even apocalyptical politics seemed to have replaced comprehensible strategic calculation. The idea of the duel as a model for international conflict had been buried for good. Also, the liberal logic of self-preservation no longer applied to the enemy in a situation of fundamentally asymmetric conflict. The potential self-annihilation of the enemy had simply not been part of a Schmittian scheme of enmity. Neither had Schmitt foreseen that enemy forces might become completely decentralized. Through the much-debated 'death of distance' the Schmittian politics of mass presence, in which the real presence of the people or a Caesarist figure was crucial, became replaced by a politics of virtual representation, outside traditional political space and even outside conventional notions of political time. Yet, such a world, characterized by uncertainty, ambiguity and the invisibility of the enemy, was also likely to provoke Schmittian reactions – either in the sense of an antimodern paranoia or in the sense of liberals losing their nerve, as had sometimes been the case in 1970s Europe.

In response to acts of terror, a minority of liberals advocated police work and a strengthening of the international rule of law. More often, however, terror provoked an oscillation between stressing supposedly substantial liberal values like freedom and preserving liberal neutrality in the face of non-liberal, but non-violent cultures. This back-and-forth – a pattern familiar from Schmitt's critique of liberalism – also facilitated the proliferation of more or less deadly metaphors like 'war on terrorism' as well as ambiguous images like 'balancing liberty and security'. A whole new political and legal language blurred traditional distinctions such as that between criminal and prisoner of war, a distinction now erased through the category of 'unlawful combatant'. Moreover, new and ill-defined doctrines such as 'pre-emptive intervention' and 'anticipatory self-defence' were likely to trouble the liberal conscience for years to come, as they partially eroded the very system of international relations that had been constructed after the Second World War.

However, these new doctrines and the potential destruction of international law would not necessarily invite criticism along Schmittian lines. After all, an open hegemonic unilateralism that claims liberalism's naked power to remake the world in its own image is less vulnerable to charges of hypocrisy – its global sovereign ambition is plain to see. It was also an embarrassment for liberals who had hoped for the liberal superpower to act as a trustee for a future cosmopolitan legal order.[22] Liberal values and international liberal legality could diverge, after all. It is worth bearing in mind perhaps that in the end Schmitt had good arguments against the philosophy of values – but resigned himself to the self-sustaining strengths of legality. Perhaps liberals also had to adopt arguments about perversity with regard to the liberal superpower. After all, it is possible to act in the name of a liberalism that, through those very acts, will lose its character.

Zones of Indistinction

Schmittian arguments became a powerful weapon to criticize the new world order or the new 'Empire' from the Left.[23] For the Left, the deterioration and crisis of the rule of law, which was increasingly undermined through legal exceptions declared by unaccountable executives, was still best diagnosed by Schmitt's text from the 1920s. His diagnosis, however, now applied both to domestic and international law – which were supposedly both sustained by 'police power' and kept in a 'permanent state of exception'.[24]

The more sophisticated thinkers influenced by Schmitt agreed with his diagnosis that the connection between order and localization had broken down – but they complemented this diagnosis with a new focus on biopolitics, the politicization of bodies and 'bare life', which Michel Foucault had first theorized. According to Antonio Negri and Michael Hardt, who drew on the heritage of the *Marxisti Schmittiani*, the new *nomos* of the Earth was not constituted by a separation into sovereign great spaces, as Schmitt would have wished. Rather, it was a truly global, fluid network of international institutions, the media, non-governmental organisations, workers and migrants. This new regime no longer knew a political or economic 'outside' nor recognised traditional conceptions of sovereignty, let alone possess an imperial centre which could be geographically located. It resembled a sea without shores, ever shifting, and could not be understood with traditional geopolitical notions of expansion and contraction. The chief ideologues of this Empire were said to be John Rawls – the foremost proponent of Kantian liberalism in the twentieth century – and Niklas Luhman, who offered an account (and a moral justification) of the complex, but self-stabilizing societies of liberal capitalism.[25]

It was precisely in the crevices and gaps between a seemingly all-encompassing international legal and economic liberal order that the conflation of law and violence characteristic of traditional sovereignty came to be located. Such 'zones of indistinction', in which the lines between inside and outside, as well as force and law, had all been blurred, were said increasingly to characterize the new world order. Such zones were populated by Albanian refugees in Italian football stadiums, Taliban fighters in Guantanamo Bay and the stateless persons held in the *zones d'attentes* at international airports. Thus such *camps* had replaced the nation-state as the real *nomos* of the Earth. Such sites saw a permanent, willed state of exception, in which distinctions between the stateless, criminals, prisoners of war and enemy combatants had become completely erased. According to Giorgio Agamben who developed Schmitt's *nomology* furthest, 'the old trinity composed of the state, the nation (birth), and land' had constituted the nation-state *nomos*.[26] This trinity had now broken apart. Denationalization, dislocation and the disintegration of state structures meant the blurring of determinate spaces with clear juridical rules and the emergence of zones in which old liberal distinctions between public and private and between norm and fact had been blurred.

Such a world was decisively not post-political, as the supposedly liberal vision of dissolving politics into ethics and economics might have suggested. But the relevant divisions were no longer between inside and outside, or national and non-national. Rather, divisions between what Hardt and Negri called 'the multitude', employing a concept of Henry Kissinger's favourite philosopher, Spinoza, and the oppressive, but amorphous apparatus of Empire, ran *inside* Empire itself. The multitude was then asked to engage on a global scale in precisely the strategies of resistance that had failed in the Italy of the 1970s. An amorphous constituent power of the wretched of the Earth was to overcome the hegemony of Empire from within and establish an ill-defined global 'Republic', which supposedly would then also no longer know an 'outside'.

For Negri's friend Agamben, it was precisely the attempt finally to eradicate all divisions and exclusions, and thereby create a people fully identical with itself, that had led to the catastrophes of the twentieth century. Any effort to eliminate the fractures of the body politics – and therefore politics itself – would only lead to a *hyperpoliticization* – and therefore exacerbate 'the civil war that divides the people and the cities of the earth'.[27] In other words, the critique of the Enlightenment critique, which had always led to crisis, returned in the latest diagnoses of the new global civil wars.

Whether the Left was aware of the fact that it opposed a supposedly hypocritical universalism with a theory that was anti-universalist through and through, remained an open question. It also remained unclear whether the Left was celebrating the return of open international conflict because *anything* was preferable to the triumph of the global market, or whether the inevitably conflictual nature of politics had to be reasserted. Marxists in particular often seemed to blur the line between working for a different, more just globalization and merely destroying whatever appeared under the auspices of the American hegemony, whether it happened to be human suffering or human rights. Unable to live with the enduring 'organized hypocrisy' and 'legal fictions' of the international order, some seemed to wish for the great, immediate cataclysm, rather than live with the ambiguities of piecemeal progress in a highly complex and highly mediated world.[28] Schmitt's apocalyptic vision that almost *anything* was preferable to liberalism had apparently invaded the Marxist imagination – and often made it into a form of messianism.

As the spatial structures of politics became reconfigured in unpredictable and unsettling ways, the craving for a return to the 'episteme of separation' increased.[29] This craving united forces on the Left and the Right – but it was doubtful whether Schmitt's theories offered either side more than the satisfactions of nostalgia. He might have been right in diagnosing some of the West's enduring hypocrisies and even been a 'forecaster of our American-headquartered world order'. Yet for those unwilling to despair or give in to the temptations of the apocalyptic temperament little seemed to follow from his diagnosis.[30] A new world, as Schmitt would have been the first to acknowledge, needs new concepts and new distinctions. A world in which even civilian airspace had become part of the battlefield could not be understood with a normative model drawn from early modern Europe. But as long as the Left continued to lack an alternative idea of social reality, it would be all the more likely that it would have to resort to rusty and double-edged Schmittian swords in its battle against global capitalism.

Radical Democracy: Chercher le Peuple

The 1990s also saw a profound crisis of parliamentarianism and traditional party systems.[31] With the end of the friend–enemy relation to Communism, party systems based on excluding Communists and Socialists collapsed in Italy, Japan and Canada. In the US, populism experienced a resurgence, while Europe not only saw the rise of xenophobic protest parties, but also the emergence of the ideology of the 'Third Way' with its decidedly illiberal streaks.[32] Liberalism remained dominant ideologically, but like any dominant ideological formation, it united its enemies and made for strange political bedfellows. Many of the discontents of consensus politics drew on Schmitt's thought – but could not decide whether they wanted to treat Schmitt as a diagnostician or as a danger.

For an ideologically exhausted and disoriented Left, 'democracy' became the new socialism. Democracy, it seemed, was the only political value that could be salvaged from the collapse of the Soviet Union and its satellites, and which, at least nominally, neoliberalism's theoretical assault on Social Democracy had left intact. Democracy became a 'Social Democratic minimum', a last plank of consensus, on which 'Third Way' intellectuals and unreconstructed Keynesian socialists could agree. However, where Third Way thinkers talked about 'democracy' as being essentially about individual consumer choice – a concept appropriated from the neoliberals – socialists and European Social Democrats would argue for a concept of collective economic choice or defend a corporatist version of capitalism.

For left-wing theorists, 'radical democracy' became a watchword, as they resurrected the Marxist – and Schmittian – opposition between liberalism and democracy. None of the proponents of radical democracy, however, could explain what was truly radical about it. Its advocates sought to retain constitutionalism, basic rights and practices commonly associated with the principle of representation. None sought unmediated popular decisions in substantial spheres of political life. They *did* stress the centrality of conflict and the necessity to keep conflicts open, rather than 'suppress' them through liberal rationalism or a compromise between economic interests. But they appeared to overlook that democracy has always been a synonym for contained conflict, with revisability of all decisions a central feature and depending on the extent of constitutionalization. The claim drawn from Schmitt that the constitution itself could become a political battlefield in extreme situations of total politicization was factually correct – but it was unclear what followed from this normatively. A strategy of conscious politicization was not much of an addition to the Marxist manual of class struggle – and the Schmittian view that the people always retained their right to alter the constitution could work for and against social progress. 'When the consensus melts away and the constitutional text becomes another battlefield in an interpretative war of manoeuvre' anything can happen, with democracy as one – but only one – possible outcome.[33]

There was also a profound irony here. Democracy used to be a means to achieve socialism and a constituent of the achieved socialist society for the Second and Third Internationals – now 'radical democracy' seemed merely a means to salvage the remains of the welfare state. In other words, changing a political decision-making mechanism was confused with particular political outcomes in social and economic policy. It was not local experiments in direct democracy which excited radical democrats – it was the large-scale strikes in France in 1995, where, supposedly, a politics of real, immediate mass presence re-emerged. In the name of 'the people' the workers seemed to defy a globalization administered by large Anglo-American pension funds set on reconstructing continental Europe in the image of an economy governed by shareholder value. Essentially, the Left sought to resurrect the state understood as an entity with considerable sovereignty over its economic policy.[34] Left-wing thinkers had gone in search of 'the people' – and found the state.

It was another profound irony that Schmitt, the theorist of the containment of mass democracy, was now put in the service of a politics of real mass presence for the sake of social welfare. Few on the Left noticed that such an appropriation of statism was self-defeating – just as the Left often charged liberals with having moved to the right since the 1980s, some on the Left would now follow them in a more rightward direction through falling back on a conservative belief in the strong state.

Another Struggle for Liberal Stability

It was not only warfare and welfare that exercised Schmitt's readers after 1989. Among North American scholars, Schmitt's critique of liberalism was of central interest. David Dyzenhaus, in what was probably the most ingenious use of Schmittian thought, argued that the debate between Kelsen, Hermann Heller and Schmitt during the last years of the Weimar Republic could be fruitfully mapped onto the dilemmas of the Anglo-American liberalism of Rawls and Ronald Dworkin.[35] For Schmitt, Dyzenhaus argued, liberalism was neither an ideology which wholeheartedly subscribed to the neutrality of the state vis-à-vis individual citizens' visions of the good life, nor a fully-fledged worldview. Liberalism oscillated between these poles, depending on the degree of pluralism and social stability in any given society at any given point.

According to Dyzenhaus, Schmitt had correctly diagnosed the flaws in Kelsen's *Pure Theory of Law*. Kelsen, in turn, had identified the worst aspects of Schmitt's legal theory. The extremes met, however, in the sense that both Schmitt and Kelsen viewed politics as a sphere of the irrational. Schmitt responded to this irrationality with the sovereign decision which created order out of nothing, whereas Kelsen sought to keep his theory uncontaminated with politics – and thereby left the rule of law at the mercy of a primacy of power politics.

Dyzenhaus claimed that only the Social Democrat Hermann Heller had a solution to liberalism's crisis during Weimar. By offering his sociologically oriented, Social Democratic theory, he incorporated the most significant insights of Schmitt and Kelsen, while criticizing Schmitt's primacy of the sovereign and Kelsen's apolitical positivism. Dyzenhaus then mapped these debates onto the current constellation in Anglo-American liberalism. Since the 1970s, when questions of social justice monopolized the attention of liberal political theorists, the question of the stability of a political order had become more troubling. John Rawls, the pre-eminent exponent of liberal political philosophy in the post-war world, had initially conceptualized his theory *sub species aeternitatis*, taking a stable political framework and a liberal political culture for granted.[36] In the 1990s he revised the theory in the light of the emerging realities of multiculturalism and the increasing value pluralism of Western societies. To preserve the stability of a liberal order, Rawls had shifted towards an 'overlapping consensus', to which citizens holding diverse conceptions of the good, whether of a religious or metaphysical nature, could all subscribe. Rawls's liberalism had also become explicitly 'political' in the sense that it limited itself to questions of public life and built on political principles which were already explicitly or implicitly recognized in Western countries. Liberalism, according to Rawls, did not see itself as a 'comprehensive conception of the good' capable of answering ultimate metaphysical questions. It was merely ordering political life. Critics, however, contended that liberalism had covertly become 'political' in a Schmittian sense. Liberalism either asserted itself against any serious political challenge by claiming its metaphysical truth and by positing its values as absolute, thereby abandoning its promise of neutrality, or else seemed helpless against its opponents – that was the essential dilemma which Schmitt had correctly identified. Liberalism, in its latest American incarnation, only allowed a limited range of privatized conceptions of the good in a homogeneous liberal society – or else had to subscribe to a relativist 'pure theory' akin to Kelsen's. In either case, liberalism would fail to live up to its own ideals – and in either case, liberalism had no use for democracy other than securing pre-ordained liberal values.

Dyzenhaus then presented Habermas as a kind of democratic *deus ex Germania* who could compensate the democratic deficits of Anglo-American liberalism, as long as his theories could be made more concrete with the help of Heller's sociologically inflected views on law. With Habermas and Heller, Dyzenhaus contended, liberalism could become both properly political and democratic, without falling into the paradoxes of neutrality which Schmitt had identified. Instead of placing liberal morality into the hands of Supreme Court judges, as Dworkin and, to some extent, Rawls, had supposedly done, Habermas made morality retreat into the liberal rules securing democratic deliberation. Such deliberation would make reasonable political outcomes highly likely.[37] Thus, legality and legitimacy, liberalism and democracy could be achieved at the same time – but democracy had to be given primacy over liberalism if the Schmittian critique of liberalism was to be disarmed. Liberalism did not have to lead into an abyss from which only a Führer could save the demos – on the contrary, liberalism should let itself fall into the abyss of democracy, open itself to deliberation with its opponents and allow debate about its own principles. Instead of limiting the area open to political debate further and further through the juridification (and moralization) of politics, liberals should consciously widen the sphere of the political. Such a 'repoliticization' should also extend to economic issues – which is where Dyzenhaus and the radical democrats met on common ground.

Giving democracy primacy over liberalism seemed to be on the one hand another attempt to stress economic democracy and on the other a theoretical trust in the demos that tended to dismiss all liberal fears about the political as necessarily anti-democratic. However, there seemed to be a number of other sources of such fears – from Judith Shklar's 'liberalism of fear', grounded in the historical memory of the catastrophes wreaked by the 'primacy of the political' at certain points during the twentieth century to the anxieties about populism which characterized the views of Isaiah Berlin.[38] Moreover, not every group intent on questioning liberal orthodoxy had to be antiliberal *per se*. Like the liberal theorists he criticized, Dyzenhaus seemed simply to assert the 'fact of pluralism' without much further sociological analysis. Feminists and multiculturalists did not question liberalism's concern with liberal order and political stability, but merely some of the limits which liberalism set on the public expressions of 'the private' and diverse conceptions of the good. Casting doubt on the liberal account of the self was not equivalent to denying the value of a liberal political order. Washington is not Weimar.

Dyzenhaus seemed to make the same argumentative move that German liberal constitutional thinkers had made in the 1950s: they abandoned positivism and adopted Heller and other theorists of social integration as intellectual patron saints for a legal theory which included a heavy dose of sociology. Ironically, this move only became necessary for Anglo-American theorists because liberals had imported Kant into American political thought and, it seemed, had made political theory a branch of moral philosophy.[39] Dyzenhaus's and others' criticism of liberalism via Schmitt was ultimately a critique of a Kantian liberalism strongly committed to the principle of neutrality, a liberalism that also split the political world into one of pure values and impure interests. But it was far from obvious that liberalism and Kantianism made for the best theoretical marriage, or that Kantian liberalism was necessarily best equipped to deal with new practical challenges to the liberal order. Rather than reverting to Schmitt, internal critics of liberalism might have explored other liberal traditions. Rawls, and in particular Dworkin, were easy targets for certain Schmittian criticisms – but only because they had strayed far into moral philosophy from a more sceptical and pragmatic liberal tradition.

Schmitt had become relevant because he was one of the most acute diagnosticians of the potential dilemmas (and hypocrisies) associated with neutrality – yet, the Schmittian idea that politics has to go all the way down all of the time hardly followed from the criticisms of neutrality. In any event, neutrality was slowly being removed as a central plank of liberal theory. In the end, Rawls pointed out that neutrality had been a misleading concept and should be abandoned.[40] It promised more than liberalism could possibly deliver.

Simply put, liberalism cannot be neutral about liberalism – this triviality had been forgotten during the past decades, when the apparent domination of liberal thought in Anglo-American academic political philosophy led to a certain liberal self-satisfaction. During the reign of what has been called 'high liberalism', there was a premium on conceptual refinements, rather than an engagement with the more institutional aspects of political life.[41] But politics is not a branch of moral philosophy, nor can it be reduced to questions of distribution, although it is not as if these questions played no role in politics. Living with – and working with – the tension between morality and institutional politics is the real challenge, which both Schmitt's followers and self-satisfied liberals tend to avoid.

Among liberal thinkers, then, Schmitt continued to play a paradoxical role. He was presented as an acute diagnostician of liberalism's contradictions and weaknesses. In particular, Schmitt's thought could be employed to unmask the limits of liberal neutrality and liberalism's hypocritical efforts to 'limit the political' more generally. At the same time, liberalism had to be protected from Schmitt's aggressive caricaturing of liberal principles and his plainly malicious distortions. Finally, Schmitt's case was itself a warning example of where liberalism's unresolved dilemmas might lead.[42] Among liberals and critics sympathetic to liberalism, Schmitt's double role as a diagnostician and as a danger continued.

Another Encounter with Schmitt: Weak Politics and Democracies to Come

It seemed only a matter of time before postmodernists and poststructuralists would appropriate a thinker who had apparently anticipated many of their concerns. Not surprisingly, this engagement was fragmented, halting and sometimes ironic. More importantly, it was a series not only of *rendevouz manqués*, but also of *rendevouz ratés*, as postmodernists either could not make up their minds about Schmitt or seriously misunderstood the Crown Jurist. The notorious inability to formulate a postmodern politics was ultimately confirmed by the postmodern encounter with Schmitt.

Postmodernists became interested in Schmitt firstly because he had stressed the violence, arbitrariness and illegitimacy at the heart of every foundation of state and law. The dilemmas of constitutional foundations were of particular interest after 1989.[43] Yet, if anything, 1989, and the processes of democratization since, seem to prove that while on some level power will come before law, the Schmittian vision of a wilful, decisionist reassertion of political forces – whether the people or a Caesarist leader – is not a necessary corollary of major political transformations. These transitions were not 'groundless', that is, without initial normative justification. The velvet revolutions could rely on a velvet underground of roundtables and pre-existing forms of legitimacy and political organization which enabled a more peaceful and pluralist transition to democracy.[44] The fact that the revolutions would still devour their own children and at least partially fall victim to power politics did not by itself confirm a bleak Schmittian view of political foundations.

The metaphysical – as opposed to political – foundations of the Enlightenment itself also came under renewed attack when read through Schmitt's lens. Schmitt had supposedly exposed the Enlightenment's ignorance of 'hostility' and the sheer violence inherent in any politics – a fact that eventually led the Enlightenment itself to violence and hostility.[45] But it was at least questionable whether such a critique of the Enlightenment – after Foucault and the Frankfurt School – was really in need of Schmittian thought.

Postmodernists stressed the 'antinomial nature' of politics, or what they referred to as its sheer 'brokenness', as well as the enmity always present in political life. Liberals, or so they charged along Schmittian lines, reduced the political to the ethical or the economic, thereby neglecting not only its essential autonomy, but also its often tragic elements.[46] They emphatically did not want to make enmity a foundational principle of politics, as Schmitt had done, and found fault with Schmitt for having advanced another 'metaphysical theory' of politics. But they still used Schmitt's insights as a way of breaking what they perceived as the rationalist back of liberalism. Schmitt became the direct opposite of the antimodern theologian German interpreters had made him out to be. Instead, he was at heart an Enlightenment foundationalist – or even fundamentalist – whose insights could be selectively appropriated and normatively reversed.

To arrive at a postmodern theory of democracy, these thinkers argued that Schmitt's portrayal of Romanticism simply had to be turned on its head normatively. The fragmentary, the ironic and the 'variation' were said to be the characteristics of 'postmodern democracy'. The self and the body politic were both described as the site of 'democratic reconciliation', where a 'higher third' would reconcile conflicting claims and parties. In that sense, Schmitt's *Political Romanticism*, considered by some postmodernists as 'undoubtedly one of the greatest political texts written in this century', became a prescription for an (ill-defined) 'aesthetic politics'.[47]

Poststructuralists sought to re-inject 'conflict' into a liberal theory which supposedly repressed difference and conflict in the name of a rationalist consensus. Liberal political philosophy, which, according to Žižek, was necessarily defensive by nature, was a vain 'attempt to de-antagonize politics by formulating the clear rules to be obeyed so that the agonistic procedure of litigation does not explode into politics proper'.[48] However, the critics of Habermas and, in particular, of Rawls, never clarified how conflict was to be dealt with in their models of a radically pluralist democracy. By caricaturing the epistemological claims of liberalism, they could portray themselves as both more practical in recognizing the conflictual nature of politics, and as more tolerant in truly allowing diversity in the public sphere. Like the German modernizers and anti-moralizers after 1945, Chantal Mouffe argued that Schmitt's theories could be used to remedy the blind spots of liberalism and to resist the moralization of politics, which 'liberalist fundamentalism' supposedly entailed. None of this, however, answered the question of how disagreements were actually dealt with in a regime of what was called 'agonistic pluralism'.[49] The proponents of agonistic pluralism never clarified whether they were still committed to some notion of public or mutual justification in politics, or whether such justification would be banned as an instance of oppressive liberal rationalism.

It was a valid point against the proponents of rational consensus as a basis of political legitimacy that such consensus would always retain an element of contingency and that no final 'closure' was either possible or desirable. It was equally valid to point towards the productive tensions between the logic of a universalist liberalism and the logic of democracy. Universalist liberalism challenged all forms of exclusion, while democracy, at least on a Schmittian reading, necessarily entailed a frontier and a moment of closure to form a political unit as the basis of legitimacy. Yet, this supposed paradox of liberal democracy presented a problem only for those who vastly overstated liberalism's epistemological and moral claims. Instead of asking which stance was appropriate in the face of the tensions between liberalism and democracy, the critics went on caricaturing leading liberal theorists.

Time and again, a gap opened for such proponents of radical democracy between the critique of liberalism and the kind of politics that was expected from transcending the horizon of liberalism. The fact that commonly agreed procedures for dealing with conflicts could not do away with conflict altogether hardly proved that proceduralism suppressed conflict – rather, as with the Left more generally, postmodernists would have liked to have seen *different* kinds of conflicts. The fact that politics could never be contained in the Supreme Court – as Dworkin supposedly wished – or the seminar room – as Habermas might have hoped – did not prove that politics would have to be returned to the real presence of the people on the streets.

Finally, Derrida also sought to deconstruct Schmitt's oppositions between concrete and abstract, public and private, as well as the purity and impurity of his concept of the political. He treated Schmitt respectfully as a modern 'political expert' (in quotation marks, to be sure). He also speculated about Schmitt's 'sincerity' and whether Schmitt had seen himself as a mere 'diagnostician'. His own position, however, remained vague. He claimed that

we seem to be confirming – but not by way of deploring the fact, as Schmitt does – an essential and necessary depoliticization. This depoliticization would no longer be the neuter or negative indifference to all forms of the social bond, of the community, of friendship. On the other hand, through this depoliticization, which would only apply to the fundamental and dominant concept of the political, through this genealogical deconstruction of the political (and through it to the democratic), one would seek to think, interpret and implement another politics, another democracy.[50]

Derrida, in the end, obliquely opted for a cautious reformism that was prepared to work with the moral materials at hand, including the hypocrisies and mixed motivations in present-day politics. He claimed that 'the crime against humanity would be to disdain currency, however devalued, illusory or false it might be; it would be to take counterfeit money for counterfeit . . . The crime would be not to do everything in one's power to change it into gold – that is, into virtue, morality, true friendship.'[51]

The point is not that postmodernists and poststructuralists inadvertently became Schmittians – their bets on Schmitt as a force for the renewal of democracy were carefully hedged with many disclaimers. But the 'weak theory' that emerged from postmodern attempts at weak, non-metaphysical thinking was truly too weak to sustain any politics discernibly different from reformist, Social Democratic versions of liberalism.[52] In many ways, the postmodernists seemed to fit the characterization of Romantics which Schmitt had once given. They were opposed to the 'rationalism' of the liberals, but also against making enmity the foundation of political identity – instead they sought to find an ill-defined and ever-elusive 'higher third'. Mixing metaphysics and politics – supposedly the cardinal sin of the Enlightenment – was replaced with a mixture of aesthetics and politics. Schmitt's own criticism of Romanticism remained the strongest claim against such a mixture which, not just according to Schmitt, was in danger of resulting in a form of decisionism – even if that decisionism, as in Derrida's version, paradoxically was supposed to lead to political reflectiveness, ill-defined 'ethical consequences' and the ever elusive, never fully achieved 'democracies to come'.[53]

A Post-heroic Age? Beyond Nation, State – and Political Death

As bounded space becomes increasingly hard to determine, Schmitt's longing for form – including, perhaps, its aesthetic overtones – will resonate more and more with the discontents of globalization.[54] Yet, which new principles of political division and self-division will ultimately come to structure the brave new world of globalization, if it is not to remain an uncontrolled proliferation of 'zones of indistinction'? *Quis separabit?*

A new political divide seems to open up between cosmopolitans and those left in (or put in) their own place. A 'global class', it appears, will increasingly confront the rest of humanity – and be subject to the charge of hypocrisy, if it espouses a liberal universalism that cannot in any way match the experiences of the less successful.[55] Yet, even apart from the question of its availability to the wretched of the Earth, cosmopolitanism as a form of liberal universalism has been attacked for its apparent incapacity to generate real attachments, strong motivations and properly political action. Schmitt, irrespective of his personal nationalist sentiments, seemed to have spelled out the final logic of the nation-state, that 'paranoid monster of modernity' (Edgar Morin), and its capacity to generate all three. The nation-state could create identity through assertion against others, and even make the citizen sacrifice himself for the sake of the nation. Liberal defenders of nationalism stress that it is still true that nothing outside of the nation seems to be worth dying for, and that the nation remains the most universally legitimate value in political life – thereby making Schmitt's criterion the litmus test for real political unity.

Yet, it is no longer true that political subjects find nothing outside the nation-state worth dying for – self-sacrifice, as the new terror demonstrated, has also become de-nationalized and de-territorialized. The real question remains whether it is liberal democracy which will suffer from the weakening of the nation-state, as long as liberal cosmopolitanism appears impotent as a form of politics. Democracy still seems to live – perhaps die – with the nation-state. Irony and utility, the ultimate weapons of liberalism, had eventually managed to contain a highly mediated form of politics within the nation-state. Nevertheless, the apparent connection between philosophical liberalism and a permanently divided world – which had troubled Aron – has become fragile. There are no guarantees that once it has been completely broken, the result will be a global philosophical liberalism.

Those trying to transcend the nation-state, or so it seems, will somehow have to find a response to the nation-state's ability to call on the ultimate, lethal loyalty of its citizens. Yet, it is unlikely that one will ever see the tomb of the unknown post-nationalist. Liberal cosmopolitanism, it seems, can only become effective if it makes common cause with a military humanitarianism – which will always be vulnerable to Schmittian charges of hypocrisy – or if it somehow escapes Schmitt's mortal logic of sovereignty and political unity altogether. The emergence of still fragile transnational public spheres is one hopeful sign in this direction – but, for now, a total escape from a Schmittian logic in the international sphere seems highly unlikely. Above all, those trying to transcend that logic will have to be careful not to lose their nerve in the face of inevitable setbacks. It will always be more comforting to fall back on the supposedly safe truths of political realism and power politics, than to keep faith with the slow practical advancement of liberal universalism. Even for realists, however, the *verità effectuale della cosa* is a world in which apparently 'soft factors' such as human rights and other liberal norms of political legitimacy have hardened into real causes.

Schmitt's ultimate challenge to philosophical liberals will perhaps be this: can a 'post-heroic' age create new, supranational identities without enmity or even some form of homogeneity? Can multiple, overlapping loyalties gain a minimum stability, or will they collapse in the face of the ultimate logic of siding between mortal friends and enemies? Is a political logic beyond *sovereignty* conceivable? And finally, short of Kojève's universal homogeneous state, is a social contract or a 'community of fate' conceivable that does not include death?[56]

Afterword

The liberal is not liberal through himself, but he becomes more and more liberal as a decisive . . . opponent of antiliberalism: He passes for liberal, he has earned prestige as a liberal, he is – in his public office – craving prestige and consequently becomes liberal in an ever more inconsiderate manner. He is contradicting the antiliberal, permanently proclaiming himself, highly irritable inside, in closest proximity to the antiliberal.

Botho Strauss[1]

Schmitt does not belong to one clearly discernible era of modern European politics. Rather, he was a thinker during a time of transition – and a thinker *of* the transition, in particular the transition from a European to a post-European age. He attempted to contain change, and change in the direction of democracy in particular, by suggesting models of the state as essentially static, substantial and authoritarian. These attempts largely failed. The same goes for his attempt to make the political 'form' of the *Reich* into a historical agent of restraint. No less a failure, finally, was his attempt to dissociate the political from political forms altogether and make it a carrier of meaning and substance. Neither the state, with its representation of an idea or a spiritual reality, nor radical forms of political action, could restore any sense of genuine legitimacy. In the end, Schmitt capitulated before what he perceived as the triumph of legality over legitimacy, of function over substance.

What did not change during all the decades of Schmitt's thinking about politics was the belief that genuine legitimacy would necessarily imply the possibility of meaningful enmity. Only enmity would ever endow human life with dignity and moral seriousness. Schmitt took this injunction so

seriously that he would threaten 'woe to someone who has no enemy, because I will be his enemy on Judgement Day'.[2] Yet, no political form emerged
that could have embodied proper enmity in a way that did not end in political and moral catastrophe. Perhaps the very preoccupation with a kind
of enmity that was not merely a fact but a value precluded a more realistic
view of politics by a thinker frequently – but falsely – lauded for his 'realism'.

Schmitt was right about one of his numerous self-characterizations:
often he let political phenomena approach him, rather than subjecting
them to a pre-conceived philosophical system. This did not imply pure passivity, let alone objectivity, as Schmitt sometimes claimed. The concepts
Schmitt brought to bear on these phenomena – or wrested from political
reality, according to his self-presentation – were morally loaded. They were
also supposed to mobilize, and to divide others into friends and enemies.

However, the problems and peculiar perspectives on politics identified
by Schmitt transcended his own times and his own political prescriptions.
Schmitt's pupils and adversarial successors took on these problems, and
often adopted his perspective – for the sake of advocating particular policies or to gain a better vantage point to defend Schmitt's declared enemy,
liberalism. Variously, Schmitt's thought made for lingering doubts, proved
a lightning rod or served as a litmus test – to mix metaphors for a moment.

Many of those who sought to learn from Schmitt after 1945 wanted to recast liberalism as a chastened ideology. These 'learning liberals' aimed to
modernize Schmitt's positions by stripping his theories of all longing for
historical substances and other apparently anti-modern sentiments. But
'modernization', they felt, also implied the need to justify liberal modernity
both philosophically and historically. Such justifications came in the form
of more or less subtle narratives of conflict, loss and compensation. They
also included arguments for disagreement and division as inevitable characteristics of the modern world. Schmitt immunized his adversarial successors against liberal triumphalism once and for all. He also challenged them
to continuously rethink and recalibrate the relationship between substance
and subjectivity in the circumstances of modernity.

Others sought a conscious de-moralization of politics – in the name of an
often hidden morality, which could take liberal, but also antiliberal forms. In
most cases, however, there was agreement that political disagreements could
not be reduced to moral disagreements – and that the liberalism which
followed from this recognition had to be a prudential, sceptical liberalism

that relieved citizens from at least some of the burdens of disagreement. Modernity, as an age of neutralizations and depoliticizations, was at least partially endorsed, rather than deplored.

Thus, the post-war development of German political thought – and, to some extent, political thought in other European countries – can usefully be described as a process of liberalization.[3] What has to be borne in mind, however, is just how complex, paradoxical and conflict-ridden this process was. And just how easily a 'defensive panic' could break through into seemingly normal liberal politics.

In the same vein, it is important to remember the complex and conflict-ridden process in which philosophical conservatism was 'deradicalized'.[4] Philosophical conservatism – under the conditions of twentieth-century mass democracy – did not find a sustainable model of political action. Schmitt's 'intellectual adventures' in the antechambers of power were one cautionary example of how radical action for conservative goals could end in moral and political catastrophe. Ultimately, Schmitt probably recognized that the quest for substance and concrete order had only resulted in a variety of fake legitimacies. What conservatives often referred to as an ideal of 'organic construction' had turned out to be a fraud – and, in many cases, even a matter of self-deception.

After the War, Schmitt vacated more and more political positions, often leaving his closest disciples to defend concepts he had already abandoned.[5] Resignation in the face of the apparently frictionless functioning of liberal legality was, after all, Carl Schmitt's last word. But Schmitt and other conservatives certainly held on to many of their original *philosophical* and anthropological positions. The idea of restraint, or carefully managed change – supposedly *the* conservative political prescription – was only one of the ways in which these positions were translated into practical politics. Besides restraint and resignation, the dream of sovereign political action, sometimes driven by a 'defensive panic', sometimes driven by the longing for a 'politics of the grand gesture', broke through.[6] Philosophical conservatives might have changed their politics – but they did not change philosophically. Perhaps that is all that can be hoped for in the more comprehensive process of liberalization.

For Schmitt, the twentieth century saw the end of the European state and Europeans' conspicuous failure to replace it with substantial, truly sovereign forms of 'political unity'. His post-war adversarial successors did not always fully share this melancholic perspective, but almost all took on the struggle to find a new, stable and legitimate kind of liberal order. For German legal and political theorists this was a particular preoccupation, as traditionally a great deal had been expected from the state by way of social integration and even ethical guidance. Much previous German thinking on the state had betrayed a desire to dignify the state with metaphysical foundations. For the most part, German political and legal theorists had also approached the state from the perspective of the administration. During much of the nineteenth and twentieth centuries there used to be what one might call a primacy of the executive. At the same time, German theorists were particularly prone to dissociate democracy and the rule of law, or constitutional liberalism.

Schmitt restrained, inadvertently hastened and eventually resigned himself to the dismantling of this 'German view of the state'. At the provisional end point of this development, the state had become merely 'the self-description of the political system' (although the stress on the executive might not have weakened quite as much, in Luhmann's case in particular). Reference to the state has played less and less of a role even in Schmitt's own scholarly field, *Staatsrechtslehre*. In constitutional law, the 'argument from the state' has not only become less powerful – it has also become much less frequent.[7] With melancholy or delight, public lawyers and political thinkers have had to register the 'dethronement of state sciences by constitutional jurisdiction'.[8] In other words, independent, substantial doctrines of the state have been replaced with the labour of interpreting the decisions of the Constitutional Court. It was not that all of Schmitt's points and problems had been answered – but new political and legal languages were either redescribing them in fundamental ways or superseding them altogether.

Nevertheless, the anxiety about the depletion of moral sources for social cohesion has hardly been exorcised. The struggle for stability in the aftermath of the twentieth-century European 'Thirty Years War' is over.[9] But the dangers of struggling too hard for stability and for certainty in politics remain. The widespread admiration for Franco's and Salazars' regimes in post-war Europe testifies to a deeply ingrained desire to freeze society in an authoritarian frame. The strong state, and similar forms of 'concrete order', remained *the* temptation even for many relatively liberal thinkers after 1945. The cataclysmic events at mid-century had made them into what the Germans call *Stabilitätsnarren* – fools for stability.

Schmitt could never decide (he had difficulty deciding in general, like many decisionists) whether liberalism was a matter of weakness or hubris. On the one hand, liberals' attempt to dissolve the political into ethics and economics would fail. On the other hand, liberalism also was an ideology of human self-affirmation and self-empowerment – grounded in what Schmitt called an 'activist metaphysics'. Liberalism, in short, is either too meek or too mighty and missionary.

There is an antiliberal affect. Affective antiliberalism will draw on both – contradictory – intuitions about liberalism as meek and missionary. It is also intimately connected to the aesthetics of antiliberalism. The relationship between Schmitt and aesthetics goes deeper than the questions of style I alluded to at the beginning of this volume. Ever since Walter Benjamin's famous 'Work of Art in the Age of Mechanical Reproduction', it has become a commonplace that a dangerous liaison between aesthetics and politics should be thought of as an aestheticization *of* politics. Yet – and this is the peculiarity of Schmitt's 'craving for meaning in politics' – the desire for an autonomous politics from which all moral concerns have been expunged can also take on an aesthetic dimension. An aestheticization of *autonomous* politics as the 'vitalist dream of Great Politics' is no less directed against liberal modernity, which, after all, does allow for the – albeit limited – subjection of politics to morality, than a fascist spectacle which seeks to overwhelm the senses for the sake of total mobilization.[10]

Schmitt asked too much from politics in terms of meaning, and yet he asked too little in terms of morality. Rather than living with the tension between the autonomous demands of power on the one hand, and moral justification on the other, Schmitt dissolved the tension by opting for a politics cleansed of morality. This politics at the same time produced a kind of existential meaning through struggle. Conservatives who see Schmitt as a 'Hobbes of the twentieth century' who was simply preoccupied with political order, miss this point no less than Schmitt's admirers on the Left who believe that an emphasis on conflict will lead to a more democratic politics.

It is true that liberalism systematically denies certain political passions and satisfactions – passions which perhaps can only be satisfied in public and through 'Great Politics'. It cuts itself off from sources of meaning which depend not just on public, but on political life. Liberalism reduces aesthetics to a private or, at least in the narrow sense, apolitical experience. There are cravings and sentiments that liberalism will simply not be able to accommodate.[11]

What, in the end, is to be learnt from Schmitt's legacies and the manifold liberal responses to them in post-war Europe? At the risk of uttering a *superbanalité*: liberalism was originally a theory of political and socio-economic transition. Constant, Madame de Staël and Tocqueville were preoccupied with the challenge of managing the transition from a feudal society to a liberal constitutional state. With Bentham, Mill and others, liberalism became a narrative, centred on notions of progress and rationality. Finally, in the twentieth century, liberalism was given expression, above all, as the moral philosophy of a just and well-ordered society. Despite recent attempts to render liberalism explicitly political, that is, sensitive to questions of political stability, liberalism in Anglo-American academia remains primarily a highly abstract modelling device, centred on moral questions *sub specie aeternitatis*.[12]

One lesson, at least of the German Schmitt reception, appears to be that a chastened liberalism has to be historically conscious and, if possible, include an apologia for nothing less than modernity, in its liberal version, itself. The narratives told by Schmitt's adversarial successors were not so much narratives of progress as of losses honestly faced and the limited and always endangered legitimacy of the modern age. In contexts which demand liberalization, rather than the refinement of 'high liberalism', philosophical liberalism has to be given political and historical expression rather than being presented as a moral philosophy. It will then be in a better position to cope with, 'contradiction, complexity, diversity, and the risks of freedom'.[13]

The central paradox of post-war chastened liberalism – the insight that liberalism cannot guarantee, let alone generate its own preconditions – has lost none of its relevance. It demands, in the end, a contingent and precarious form of universalism which has to be approached and vindicated historically. Such a liberalism has to give an account of liberalization – a concept that needs to be reclaimed from political languages which reduce politics to economics. That account must be neither linear nor imperialist, but a credible story about the struggle for liberal order. In the end, 'political difference is of the essence of politics'.[14] The more that difference is dealt with, rather than denied, the more liberalism faces up to the facts not merely of pluralism, but also of historical competition and contingency, the more acceptable it might become even for those suspicious of liberal modernity. Thus liberalism announces the desire to share existence – and to engage in charitable struggle – with the enemy.

Notes

Introduction

1. José Ortega y Gasset, *The Revolt of the Masses* (1930; New York: Norton, 1957), 76.
2. Jacob Taubes, *Ad Carl Schmitt: Gegenstrebige Fügung* (Berlin: Merve, 1987), 11. The term 'liberal modernity' serves here to indicate the problem of multiple modernities (including fascist modernities). Liberal modernity, on a very broad Weberian reading, would be characterized not least by science, rationalized law and bureaucracy as well as liberal representative institutions, and, finally, rationalized religion and ethics, which allow for a priority of the right over the good. I am indebted to Peter Ghosh for many discussions on this point.
3. Jürgen Habermas, *Politisch-Philosophische Profile* (Frankfurt/Main: Suhrkamp, 1971), 64.
4. Rüdiger Altmann, 'Staatsdenker mit linken Epigonen: Carl Schmitt – Ein fruchtbares Ärgernis', in: *Deutsche Zeitung*, 6 July 1973.
5. The list of Schmitt's direct or indirect interlocutors could be extended considerably. In fact, inspired by Heinrich Meier's brilliant reconstruction of Schmitt's 'hidden dialogue' with Leo Strauss, there has been a tendency to construct ever more hidden – and in fact sometimes completely inaudible – dialogues, especially between Schmitt and thinkers whose politics one dislikes. Ironically, this inflation of dialogues only plays into the hands of the Schmittians who have tried to prove over and over again Schmitt's status as a classic of political thought who could not be ignored by any major twentieth-century thinker. My account here is problem-driven, rather than person-centred.
6. Ulrich K. Preuss, 'Political Order and Democracy: Carl Schmitt and His Influence', in: Chantal Mouffe (ed.), *The Challenge of Carl Schmitt* (London: Verso, 1999), 155–79; here 155.
7. Hasso Hofmann, 'Was ist uns Carl Schmitt?', in: Hans Maier, Ulrich Matz, Kurt Sontheimer and Paul-Ludwig Weinacht (eds.), *Politik, Philosophie, Praxis: Festschrift für Wilhelm Hennis zum 65. Geburtstag* (Stuttgart: Klett-Cotta, 1988), 545–5, and Bernhard Schlink, 'Why Schmitt?', in: *Constellations*, Vol. 2 (1996), 429–41.
8. Henning Ottman, 'Carl Schmitt', in: Karl Graf Ballestrem and Henning Ottmann (eds.), *Politische Philosophie des 20. Jahrhunderts* (Munich: R. Oldenbourg, 1990), 61–87; here 61.
9. Gopal Balakrishnan, *The Enemy: An Intellectual Portrait of Carl Schmitt* (London: Verso, 2000), 261.
10. For an invaluable documentation of this more or less secret reception, see Dirk van Laak, *Gespräche in der Sicherheit des Schweigens: Carl Schmitt in der Geistesgeschichte der frühen Bundesrepublik* (Berlin: Akademie, 1993).
11. Carl Schmitt, *Glossarium*, ed. Eberhard Freiherr von Medem (Berlin: Duncker & Humblot, 1991), 117.
12. Ernst-Wolfgang Böckenförde, "Die Entstehung des Staates als Vorgang der Säkularisation" in *Recht, Staat, Freiheit: Studien zur Rechtsphilosophie,*

Staatstheorie und Verfassungsgeschichte (Frankfurt/Main: Suhrkamp, 1991), 92–114; here 112.

13. Wilhelm Hennis, 'Zum Problem der deutschen Staatsanschauung', in: *Vierteljahrshefte für Zeitgeschichte*, Vol. 7 (1959), 1–23.

14. This study is problem-oriented in a number of ways: it assumes that much of Schmitt's thinking was problem-driven. It also assumes that the political problems Schmitt raised transcend both his own answers and his own times. But it finally assumes that no part of Schmitt's own oeuvre is unproblematic – an isolation (or sanitization) of certain parts is impossible, even if distinctions can be drawn between his basic philosophically conservative positions and his changing prescriptions for practical politics.

15. If anything, Schmitt's thought is *polycentric*, to use a felicitous phrase of Theodor Paleologu's.

16. See also Stephen Toulmin, *Cosmopolis: The Hidden Agenda of Modernity* (Chicago: University of Chicago Press, 1990).

17. Schmitt's opening quote of this introduction is a good example of his tendency to hint at secret connections, which might or might not have been there.

18. As Nicolaus Sombart has pointed out, this 'double talk' not infrequently had the effect of a 'double bind'. See Nicolaus Sombart, *Jugend in Berlin 1933–1943: Ein Bericht* (Frankfurt/Main: Fischer, 1996), 258.

19. Peter Stirk, 'Carl Schmitt's Völkerrechtliche Grossraumordnung', in: *History of Political Thought*, Vol. 20, No. 2 (1999), 357–74; here 360.

20. Jünger to Schmitt, 13 and 14 October 1930, in: Helmuth Kiesel (ed.), *Ernst Jünger-Carl Schmitt: Briefe 1930–1983* (Stuttgart: Klett-Cotta, 1999), 7.

21. George Kateb, 'Aestheticism and Moral-ity: Their Cooperation and Hostility', in: *Political Theory*, Vol. 28, No. 1 (2000), 5–37; here 9.

22. Egon Vietta, 'Raum, Ort und Recht', in: *Frankfurter Allgemeine Zeitung*, 11 April 1953.

23. Karl Heinz Bohrer, *Die Ästhetik des Schreckens: Die pessimistische Romantik und Ernst Jüngers Frühwerk* (Munich: Hanser, 1978), 293–4.

24. Joachim Schickel, *Gespräche mit Carl Schmitt* (Berlin: Merve, 1993), 11.

25. Helmut Quaritsch, *Positionen und Begriffe Carl Schmitts*, 2nd edn. (Berlin: Duncker & Humblot, 1989), 12 and 23.

26. Murray Forsyth, 'Carl Schmitt: The Concept of the Political', in: Murray Forsyth and Maurice Keens-Soper (eds.), *The Political Classics: Green to Dworkin* (Oxford: Oxford UP, 1996), 78–99; here 79, and Robert Hepp's contribution to the discussion after Ellen Kennedy's paper, in: Helmut Quaritsch (ed.), *Complexio Oppositorum: Über Carl Schmitt* (Berlin: Duncker & Humblot, 1988), 257–8.

27. Schmitt to Mohler, 16 October 1948, in: *Carl Schmitt – Briefwechsel mit einem seiner Schüler*, ed. Armin Mohler with the cooperation of Irmgard Huhn and Piet Tommissen (Berlin: Akademie, 1995), 35.

28. Jacques Derrida, *Politics of Friendship*, trans. George Collins (London: Verso, 1997), 107.

29. *Ibid.*

30. For instance Chantal Mouffe, *The Return of the Political* (London: Verso, 1993).

31. One Schmitt reception beyond the scope of this study is Hans Morgenthau's invention of a particular American subject of 'international relations'. On this subject, see Martti Koskenniemi, *The Gentle Civilizer of Nations: The Rise and Fall of International Law 1870–1960* (Cambridge: Cambridge UP, 2002), 413–509, and William E. Scheuer-

man, *Carl Schmitt: The End of Law*
(Lanham: Rowman & Littlefield, 1999),
225–51.
32. See Charles S. Maier, 'Consigning the
Twentieth Century to History', in:
American Historical Review (June
2000), 807–31, and Mary Kaldor, *New
and Old Wars: Organized Violence in a
Global Era* (Stanford: Stanford UP,
1999).
33. A. James Gregor, *The Faces of Janus:
Marxism and Fascism in the Twentieth
Century* (New Haven: Yale UP, 2000),
123, and, in particular, Alan Ingram,
'Alexander Dugin: geopolitics and neofascism in post-Soviet Russia', in: *Political Geography*, Vol. 20 (2001), 1029–51.
34. On this reading, for instance, Burke was
a philosophical conservative, but in
most relevant respects a political liberal. Schmitt read him as a liberal and a
romantic – defensibly, as philosophical
conservatism and romanticism share
certain affinities. Schmitt's closest
double was Joseph de Maistre – or at
any rate the de Maistre whom Schmitt
invented in the early 1920s. I shall return to this topic in Part I.
35. This, to some extent, explains the affinities between Schmitt and some of his
'partisan doubles on the other side of
the European civil war', such as Lukács
and Benjamin. The phrase is Gopal Balakrishnan's in 'The Age of Identity?', in:
New Left Review, no. 16 (2002), 130–42;
here 133. In that sense, John P. McCormick has been right to identify Schmitt
as a 'Critical Theorist of the Right'. See
John P. McCormick, *Carl Schmitt's Critique of Liberalism: Against Politics as
Technology* (Cambridge: Cambridge
UP, 1997).
36. For irony and utility as features of liberal modernity, see Benjamin Constant,
'The spirit of conquest', in: *Political
Writings*, ed. and trans. Biancamara
Fontana (Cambridge: Cambridge UP,
1988), 51–83; here 55.

37. Schmitt often used the hard-to-trans-
late German concept *Geschichtsmäch-
tigkeit*, an approximate gloss of which
would be 'power to shape history'.

**A German Public Lawyer in the
Twentieth Century**

1. Paul Noack, *Carl Schmitt: Eine Biogra-
phie* (Berlin: Ullstein, 1996), 21.
2. As Schmitt once put it in a typically
revealing and at the same time self-
mystifying statement: 'I went through
everything, and everything went
through me'. Carl Schmitt, *Ex Captivitate Salus* (Cologne: Greven, 1950), 92.
3. Carl Schmitt, *Gesetz und Urteil: Eine
Untersuchung zum Problem der Rechts-
praxis* (1912; Munich: C. H. Beck, 1968).
4. Ingeborg Villinger, *Carl Schmitts Kul-
turkritik der Moderne: Text, Kommentar
und Analyse der 'Schattenrisse' des Johannes Negelinus* (Berlin: Akademie,
1995).
5. Carl Schmitt-Dorotić, *Politische Romantik* (Munich: Duncker & Humblot,
1919), 77.
6. György Lukács, review of *Political Romanticism* in: *Archiv für die Geschichte
des Sozialismus und der Arbeiterbewegung*, Vol. 8 (1928), 307–8. After the War,
Lukács came to subsume Schmitt under
the 'destruction of reason' and called
Political Romanticism 'pre-fascist'.
7. Carl Schmitt, *Der Begriff des Politischen:
Text von 1932 mit einem Vorwort und
drei Corollarien* (1963; Berlin: Duncker
& Humblot, 1996), 12 and 11.
8. Carl Schmitt-Dorotić, *Die Diktatur:
Von den Anfängen des modernen Sou-
veränitätsgedankens bis zum prole-
tarischen Klassenkampf* (Munich:
Duncker & Humblot, 1921).
9. In Schmitt's view, the constitution was
the perfectly liberal constitution the
Germans had never had in the nineteenth century – but it was deeply problematic for the post-liberal age of mass
democracy in the 1920s. Therefore, even

10. Ernst Huber to Carl Schmitt, 21 February 1940 (HStAD RW 265–6270/1).
11. Reinhard Mehring, *Carl Schmitt zur Einführung* (Hamburg: Junius, 1992), 72–80.
12. Carl Schmitt, *Verfassungslehre* (1928; Berlin: Duncker & Humblot, 1970), 227.
13. Carl Schmitt, *The Crisis of Parliamentary Democracy*, trans. Ellen Kennedy (1923; Cambridge, Mass.: MIT Press, 1985), 9.
14. *Ibid.*
15. *Ibid.*
16. *Ibid.*, 11, with the translation modified.
17. *Ibid.*, 9.
18. Carl Schmitt, 'Die politische Theorie des Mythus', in: *Positionen und Begriffe im Kampf mit Weimar – Genf – Versailles* (Berlin: Duncker & Humblot, 1988), 9–18.
19. *Ibid.*, 11.
20. *Ibid.*, 15 and 17.
21. *Ibid.*, 16.
22. *Ibid.*, 17.
23. Carl Schmitt, 'Wesen und Werden des faschistischen Staates', in: *Positionen und Begriffe*, 109–15; here 110.
24. *Ibid.*, 115.
25. *Ibid.*, 47–9 and 79.
26. Carl Schmitt, 'Absolutismus (1926)', in: Carl Schmitt, *Staat, Großraum, Nomos: Arbeiten aus den Jahren 1916–1969*, ed. Günter Maschke (Berlin: Duncker & Humblot, 1995), 97.
27. Schmitt, *Verfassungslehre*, 79.
28. *Ibid.*, 78.
29. *Ibid.*, 144. Also *Verfassungslehre*, 81 and 79.
30. Schmitt, *Verfassungslehre*, 204.
31. *Ibid.*, 51.
32. *Ibid.*, 205.
33. *Ibid.*, 207.
34. *Ibid.*, 205.

35. *Ibid.*, 209–10.
36. *Ibid.*, 210.
37. Carl Schmitt, *Römischer Katholizismus und politische Form* (1923; Stuttgart: Klett-Cotta, 1984).
38. Schmitt, *Verfassungslehre*, 214.
39. Carl Schmitt, *The Concept of the Political*, trans. George Schwab (Chicago: University of Chicago Press, 1996), 26–7.
40. *Ibid.*, 28.
41. Jünger to Schmitt, 13 and 14 October 1930, in: *Ernst Jünger – Carl Schmitt*, 7.
42. Robert Musil, *The Man without Qualities*, trans. Sophie Wilkins and Burton Pike (London: Picador, 1997), 404–5. Linking this passage with Schmitt's thought was suggested to me by Friedrich Balke, 'Weimarer Intellektuelle und die neue Ordnung des "Zivilverstandes": Das Beispiel Carl Schmitts', in: Wolfgang Bialas and Georg G. Iggers (eds.), *Intellektuelle in der Weimarer Republik*, 2nd ed. (Frankfurt/Main: Peter Lang, 1997), 71–90.
43. No wonder that Jünger could write to Schmitt a few years later, with a sense of relief, that 'we are slowly leaving modernity behind us,–every new act becomes somehow more exciting'. See Jünger to Schmitt, 4 July 1934, in: *Ernst Jünger – Carl Schmitt*, 36.
44. Schmitt, 'Das Zeitalter der Neutralisierungen und Entpolitisierungen', in: Schmitt, *Positionen und Begriffe*, 122.
45. Whether Schmitt was opposed to the Nazis, and not just the KPD, remains a fiercely contested issue. He drew a stark distinction between the two in his defence of the Reich in Leipzig, and the warning not to vote for the NSDAP in a July 1932 newspaper article, which Schmitt later claimed reflected his intentions, was in fact added by the editor. For contending views, see Gabriel Seiberth, *Anwalt des Reiches: Carl Schmitt und der Prozess 'Preußen contra Reich' vor dem Staatsgerichtshof* (Berlin:

Duncker & Humblot, 2001) and Dirk Blasius, *Carl Schmitt: Preußischer Staatsrat in Hitlers Reich* (Göttingen: Vandenhoeck & Ruprecht, 2001).

46. Others shared the illusion that the Prussian state council would play a real role in governing. Jünger urged Schmitt to investigate the workings of the state council of the First French Empire, 'over which Napoleon presided personally'. See Jünger to Schmitt, 17 August, 1933, in: *Ernst Jünger – Carl Schmitt*, 16.

47. Carl Schmitt, 'Der Führer schützt das Recht', in: Schmitt, *Positionen und Begriffe*, 199–203.

48. Carl Schmitt, *Staat-Bewegung-Volk: Die Dreigliederung der politischen Einheit* (Hamburg: Hanseatische Verlagsanstalt, 1934).

49. Most importantly, Schmitt took the idea of *superlegalité* from Hariou. Hauriou was a Catholic liberal (after all, an impossibility for Schmitt), and Schmitt not so much adopted, as radicalized Hauriou's ideas. I have benefited from conversations with Olivier Beaud on this point.

50. Carl Schmitt, *Über die drei Arten des rechtswissenschaftlichen Denkens* (Hamburg: Hanseatische Verlagsanstalt, 1934).

51. Michael Stolleis, *Geschichte des öffentlichen Rechts in Deutschland*, Vol. 3 (Munich: C. H. Beck, 1999), 316.

52. W. Sommer quoted by Michael Stolleis, 'Im Bauch des Leviathan: Staatsrechtslehrer im Nationalsozialismus', in: *Recht im Unrecht: Studien zur Rechtsgeschichte des Nationalsozialismus* (Frankfurt/Main: Suhrkamp, 1994), 126–46; here 138.

53. Franz Neumann, *Behemoth: The Structure and Practice of National Socialism* (London: Victor Gollancz, 1942), 5. This point can be exaggerated, however. As Schmitt himself explained after the War, the belief of the German bureaucrats, the *Beamten*, in the legitimacy of

legality, 'technical discipline' and 'frictionless functioning' was an important factor in making them follow Hitler and his policies. Any account of the Third Reich that did not pay special attention to the role of the bureaucracy and the jurists would be distorted. See the appropriately labeled section 'legality and bestiality' in Wolfgang Reinhard, *Geschichte der Staatsgewalt: Eine vergleichende Verfassungsgeschichte Europas von den Anfängen bis zur Gegenwart* (Munich: C. H. Beck, 1999), 475–9.

54. Stolleis, *Geschichte*, 317.

55. See also Raphael Gross, *Carl Schmitt und die Juden: Eine deutsche Rechtslehre* (Frankfurt/Main: Suhrkamp, 2000).

56. Aurel Kolnai, *The War against the West* (London: Victor Gollancz, 1938), 146.

57. Jacques Maritain, *Le crépuscule de la civilisation*, 3rd ed. (Montréal: Éditions de l'Arbre, 1944), 51–61.

58. Ilse Staff, *Staatsdenken im Italien des 20. Jahrhunderts: Ein Beitrag zur Carl Schmitt-Rezeption* (Baden-Baden: Nomos, 1991), 12.

59. According to Günter Maschke, *Der Tod des Carl Schmitt* (Vienna: Karolinger, 1987), 99.

60. Carl Schmitt, *Der Leviathan in der Staatslehre des Thomas Hobbes: Sinn und Fehlschlag eines politischen Symbols* (Hamburg: Hanseatische Verlagsanstalt, 1938).

61. Carl Schmitt, 'Die Auflösung der europäischen Ordnung im "International Law" (1890–1939)', in: Schmitt, *Staat, Großraum, Nomos*, 372–87; here 381–3.

62. *Ibid.*, 372.

63. *Ibid.*, 377.

64. *Ibid.*, 284.

65. *Ibid.*, 285.

66. *Ibid.*, 290.

67. Carl Schmitt, *Die Wendung zum diskriminierenden Kriegsbegriff* (Munich: Duncker & Humblot, 1938).

68. Schmitt, 'Raum und Großraum', 251.

69. Carl Schmitt, 'Die Raumrevolution: Durch den totalen Krieg zu einem totalen Frieden', in: Schmitt, *Staat, Großraum, Nomos*, 388–91; here 390.

70. Schmitt first presented his theories of great spaces at a meeting at the Kiel Institute of Politics and International Law on April 1 1939. On March 15 Hitler had given the command for the Wehrmacht to enter what was dismissively called the *Resttschechei*.

71. Andrew Gyorgy, 'The Application of German Geopolitics: Geo-Sciences', in: *American Political Science Review*, Vol. 37 (1943), 677–86; here 682.

72. Ulrich Herbert, *Best: Biographische Studien über Radikalismus, Weltanschauung und Vernunft 1903–1989* (Bonn: J. H. W. Dietz Nachfolger, 1996), 271–2.

73. Carl Schmitt, 'Großraum gegen Universalimus', in: Schmitt, *Positionen und Begriffe*, 295–302.

74. *Ibid.*, 295.

75. Schmitt, *Verfassungslehre*, 57.

76. Carl Schmitt, 'Völkerrechtliche Großraumordnung mit Interventionsverbot für raumfremde Mächte: Ein Beitrag zum Reichsbegriff im Völkerrecht', in: Schmitt, *Staat, Großraum, Nomos*, 269–371; here 294.

77. *Ibid.*, 272.

78. Not surprisingly, given Schmitt's antisemitism, he contended that it had been the Jews, as 'a people without their own soil', who had supposedly advanced such an empty or neutral notion of space. See *ibid.*, 317.

79. Schmitt, 'Der Reichsbegriff im Völkerrecht', 309.

80. *Ibid.*, 311.

81. *Ibid.*, 310.

82. Schmitt, 'Völkerrechtliche Großraumordnung', 301.

83. Herbert, *Best*, 274.

84. *Ibid.*, 306.

85. Dan Diner, *Weltordnungen: Über Geschichte und Wirkung von Recht und Macht* (Frankfurt: Fischer, 1993), 77.

86. Gyorgy, 'The Application of German Geopolitics', 686.

87. Christian Tilitzki, 'Die Vortragsreisen Carl Schmitts während des Zweiten Weltkriegs', in: Piet Tommissen, *Schmittiana*, Vol. 6 (Berlin: Duncker & Humblot, 1998), 191–270.

88. Carl Schmitt, *Land und Meer: Eine weltgeschichtliche Betrachtung* (Leipzig: Reclam, 1942), 76.

Masks and Mirrors

1. Carl Schmitt, 'Welt großartigster Spannung', in: *Staat, Großraum, Nomos*, 513–17.

2. At least according to Alvrao d'Ors and Günter Maschke. See Alvaro d'Ors, 'Das "Glossarium" von Carl Schmitt', in: Piet Tommissen (ed.) *Schmittiana: Beiträge zu Leben und Werk Carl Schmitts, Vol. 7* (Berlin: Duncker & Humblot, 2001), 219–75; here 222.

3. In fact, apart from Schmitt, only Otto Koellreutter and Reinhard Höhn remained permanently banned after 1945. Koellreutter became honorary president of the Federation of Victims of De-nazification, whereas Höhn founded an 'academy for leadership' in Bad Harzburg.

4. While an increasingly subtle picture of the 1950s has emerged in recent scholarship, which revises the picture of a simple silence or repression tout court, the fact remains that in public law silence and repression do sum up the situation well beyond the 1950s.

5. In fact it was only in 2000 that the Association of German Professors of Public Law finally debated its own past. See Horst Dreier, 'Die deutsche Staatsrechtslehre in der Zeit des Nationalsozialismus', in: *Veröffentlichungen der Vereinigung der Deutschen Staatsrechtslehrer*, no. 60 (Berlin: de Gruyter, 2001), 9–72.

6. Jacob Taubes, *Die Politische Theologie*

des Paulus, 2nd ed. (Munich: Wilhlem Fink, 1995), 142.

7. For instance, Erich Kaufmann, 'Carl Schmitt und seine Schule: Offener Brief an Ernst Forsthoff', in: *Deutsche Rundschau*, No. 84 (1958).

8. Richard Schmid, 'Julius Streichers Bewunderer: Der Antidemokrat Carl Schmitt', in: *Die Zeit*, 9 May 1965.

9. Schlink, 'Why Carl Schmitt?'.

10. Schmitt, *Glossarium*, 277.

11. Noack, *Carl Schmitt*, 254.

12. Schmitt, *Glossarium*, 226.

13. *Ibid.*, 256.

14. *Ibid.*, 290.

15. *Ibid.*, 278.

16. Schmitt: *Ex Captivitate Salus*, 80.

17. *Ibid.*, 87.

18. *Ibid.*, 89.

19. *Ibid.*, 89–90.

20. Schmitt, *Glossarium*, 36. On 'Schmitt's Kafka' see also Helmut Lethen, *Verhaltenslehren der Kälte: Lebensversuche zwischen den Kriegen* (Frankfurt/Main: Suhrkamp, 1994), 231–4.

21. Grigoris Ananiadis, 'Carl Schmitt on Kosovo, or, Taking War Seriously', in: Dusan Bjelic and Obrad Savic, *Balkan as Metaphor: Between Globalization and Fragmentation* (Cambridge, Mass.: MIT Press, 2002), 117–61; here 147.

22. Carl Schmitt, 'Entwurf eines "Berichtes" an P. Erich Przywara', in: *Schmittiana*, Vol. 7, 212–18; here 218.

23. Herman Melville, 'Benito Cereno', in: *Billy Budd and Other Tales* (New York: Signet, 1998), 144–226; here 157, and Schmitt, *Ex Captivitate Salus*, 21–2.

24. *Ibid.*, 75.

25. Schmitt, *Glossarium*, 161.

26. Schmitt, *Glossarium*, 165.

27. Carl Schmitt to Luís Cabral de Moncada, 25 June 1948, in: *Luís Cabral de Moncada und Carl Schmitt: Briefwechsel 1943–1973*, ed. Erika Jayme (Heidelberg: C. F. Müller, 1997), 6. In 1951 Schmitt had a brochure printed with the heading 'Carl Schmitt: Nein und Ja', which

quoted major intellectuals making the case for and against Schmitt. Moncada was quoted as saying that 'In the book Ex Captivitate Salus are remarks which would have to shatter a judge of the Nuremberg Tribunal, if one may presuppose a European conscience there'.

28. Bobbio to Schmitt, 20 February 1949, in: 'Der Briefwechsel Schmitt – Bobbio', in: Piet Tommissen, *In Sachen Carl Schmitt* (Vienna: Karolinger, 1997), 113–55; here 118. Bobbio sought to resist Schmitt's lamentations about the end of European statehood – as well as Schmitt's suggestions to celebrate the 300th birthday of *Leviathan*. According to Bobbio, Hobbes, like Machiavelli, had made the mistake of elevating 'effective' reality into a norm.

29. Schmitt to Mohler, 14 April 1952, in: *Carl Schmitt – Briefwechsel mit einem seiner Schüler*, 119.

30. Schmitt to Mohler, 18 July 1952, in: *ibid.*, 129.

31. Elliot Y. Neaman, *A Dubious Past: Ernst Jünger and the Politics of Literature after Nazism* (Berkeley: University of California Press, 1999), 90.

32. Odo Marquard, 'Am Ende, nicht am Ziel', in: *Frankfurter Allgemeine Zeitung*, 23 November 1999.

33. See also Armin Mohler, 'Begegnungen bei Ernst Jünger: Fragmente einer Ordnung', in: Armin Mohler (ed.), *Freundschaftliche Begegnungen: Festschrift für Ernst Jünger zum 60. Geburtstag* (Frankfurt/Main: Klostermann, 1955), 196–206; here 197.

34. Helmut Schelsky, *Die skeptische Generation: Eine Soziologie der deutschen Jugend* (Düsseldorf: Eugen Diederichs, 1957).

35. Quoted by Heinrich Siedentopf, 'Nachruf Roman Schnur', in: *Archiv des öffentlichen Rechts*, Vol. 122 (1997), 141–4.

36. Nicolaus Sombart, *Rendezvous mit dem Weltgeist: Heidelberger Reminiszenzen*

258 Notes to Pages 61–2

1945–1951 (Frankfurt/Main: S. Fischer, 2000).

37. Dan Diner, 'Introduction', in: Dan Diner and Michael Stolleis (eds.), *Hans Kelsen and Carl Schmitt: A Juxtaposition* (Gerlingen: Bleicher, 1999), 9–12; here 10.

38. For instance the following 'sketch' from 1953:

'Einer bleibt übrig (from the Death by Nemesis)

Mord lichtete lustvoll die Scharen verschworener Adepten.
Lustvoller Mord ließ in der Lichtung des Lebens
Einen nur übrig, Liebling der Nemesis,
Auserwählter des Zorns, erhaben durch sein Werk,
Einer blieb übrig. Legal? Legitim?
Ein Katechon verkörpert sich in ihm.
Im Intellektuelkenknäuel ist er, mein Sohn,
Der letzten Position in letzter Situation schlechthinige Transsubstantiation.
Nicht, weil er den Kardinalshut verschmähte,
Nicht, weil er mit Lillian Winstanley Einhörner jagte,
Ein neuer Faust, die Mosel begradigt. . .

Die zölibatäre Bürokratie dekouvrierte,
Bruno Bauer generalisierte,
Erich Kaufmann desintegrierte,
Nicht weil er gegen Severing die Weimarer Verfassung hütete,
Schiller einen Lustmord nachwies,
Kojève enthegelte,
Benito Cereno enträtselte,
Rilke entlarvte,
Von Theodor Däubler träumte. . .

Die politische Theologie revidierte,
Den Weltbürgerkrieg prognostizierte,
Das Freund-Feind-Verhältnis entmoralisierte,
Die Kriminalisierer kriminalisierte,
Nicht wegen dieser oder jener subjektivis-

tischer Occasionalismen,
Begrifflicher, abstrakter, situationsloser Prismen,

Sondern
Weil er der Mann ist,
Der einen Walfisch fing.'
See HStAD RW 265–19160.

39. A story which was first reported in the *Frankfurter Rundschau* and then picked up by *Neues Deutschland* and the *Grey Book* to reveal the fascist character of West Germany. See Nationale Front des Demokratischen Deutschland (ed.), *Grey Book: Expansionist Policy and Neo-Nazism in West Germany: Backgrounds, Aims, Methods* (Dresden: Zeit im Bild, 1967), 124 and 153.

40. See 'Amnestie – Urform des Rechts', in: *Christ und Welt*, 10 November 1949.

41. Lethen, *Verhaltenlehren*, 220–1.

42. Schmitt, *Glossarium*, 275.

43. See for instance Carl Schmitt, 'Im Vorraum der Macht', in: *Die Zeit*, 29 July 1954. Editor Richard Tüngel introduced the piece by writing: 'The great German public lawyer Carl Schmitt is a controversial figure in the Federal Republic. But even his opponents should listen, when he has something astute and unique to say'.

44. *Die Zeit* had initially been modelled on the Nazi paper *Das Reich* and, under the editorship of Richard Tüngel, pursued a nationalist course highly critical of the Allies. Schmitt's reappearance had been prepared through a favourable review penned by Walter Petwaidic von Fredericia, a former Nazi. When Schmitt's first article was published, with a preface by Tüngel, Countess Dönhoff resigned from the paper and began an internship with the *Observer*. After Tüngel's departure, Schmitt developed an obsessive hatred of Dönhoff. See for instance Schmitt to Mohler, 15 July 1962, in: *Carl Schmitt*,

Briefwechsel mit einem seiner Schüler, 319–20, where he offered one of his usual satirical poems about the fact that Charlie Chaplin had received an honorary doctorate from Oxford, whereas Dönhoff had only managed to obtain one from Smith College. See also Gerd Bucerius, 'ZEIT-Geschichte – wie sie uns in Atem hielt', in: *Die Zeit*, 21 February 1966, and Mathias von der Heide and Christian Wagener, '"Weiter rechts von der CDU": Das erste Jahrzehnt der "Zeit"', in: Lutz Hachmeister and Friedemann Siering (eds.), *Die Herren Journalisten: Die Elite der deutschen Presse nach 1945* (Munich: C. H. Beck, 2002), 165–84.

45. Walter Lewald, 'Carl Schmitt redivivus?', in: *Neue Juristische Wochenschrift*, Vol. 3 (1950), 377. Lewald, while recounting Schmitt's record, also claimed that he had a 'right to change'.

In Search of Stability I

1. Rüdiger Altmann, 'Über Stabilität', in: *Abschied vom Staat: Politische Essays* (Frankfurt/Main: Campus, 1998), 153–69; here 153–4.

2. In a letter to Mohler, Schmitt underlined the sentence 'Bonn is known not to be Weimar' and scribbled in the margin: 'Bonn is not even Bonn itself, Bonn is Karlsruhe'. See Schmitt to Mohler, 10 June 1958, in: *Carl Schmitt – Briefwechsel mit einem seiner Schüler*, 247.

3. There is little indication that anything other than financial reasons were behind this publication, however. See Präsident Dr. Haustein [Carl Schmitt], 'Gegenwartsfragen der Verfassung', reprinted in: Klaus Hansen and Hans Lietzmann (eds.), *Carl Schmitt und die Liberalismuskritik* (Opladen: Leske & Budrich, 1988), 171–94.

4. Rüdiger Altmann, 'Die fortdauernde Präsenz des Carl Schmitt', in: *Merkur*, Vol. 45 (1991), 728–34.

5. For instance Hans Lietzmann, 'Vater

der Verfassungsväter? Carl Schmitt und die Verfassungsgründung in der Bundesrepublik', in: Hansen and Lietzmann (eds.), *Carl Schmitt und die Liberalismuskritik*, 107–118.

6. Whether that had more to do with vanity than with historical accuracy, the claim itself paved the way for the acceptance of the constitution by several of Schmitt's students.

7. Another was the provision for a 'constructive vote of no confidence', which only allowed bringing down a government if an alternative government could be installed. Schmitt, however, had not been the only jurist to advocate such a means to prevent the rapid change of governments during Weimar. See Lutz Berthold, 'Das konstruktive Misstrauensvotum und seine Ursprünge in der Weimarer Staatsrechtslehre', in: *Der Staat*, Vol. 36 (1997), 81–94.

8. Carl Schmitt, 'Die legale Weltrevolution', in: *Der Staat*, Vol. (1978), 321–39; here 325.

9. Ernst Forsthoff, *Der Staat der Industriegesellschaft* (Munich: C. H. Beck, 1971), 65.

10. *Ibid.*, 69.

11. Werner Weber, *Weimarer Verfassung und Bonner Grundgesetz* (Göttingen: Karl-Friedrich Fleischer, 1949), 7 and 9.

12. *Ibid.*, 25.

13. *Ibid.*, 31.

14. Karl Loewenstein, 'Militant Democracy and Fundamental Rights I', in: *American Political Science Review*, Vol. 31 (1937), 417–32.

15. *Ibid.*, 424.

16. Karl Loewenstein, 'Militant Democracy and Fundamental Rights II', in: *American Political Science Review*, Vol. 31 (1937), 638–58; here 647.

17. *Ibid.*, 656–7.

18. Preuss, 'Political Order and Democracy'.

19. Ernst-Wolfgang Böckenförde, 'Begriff

und Probleme des Verfassungsstaats', in: *Staat, Nation, Europa* (Frankfurt/Main: Suhrkamp, 1999), 127–40.

20. Michael Stolleis, 'Reluctance to Glance in the Mirror: The Changing Face of German Jurisprudence after 1933 and post-1945', in: Christian Joerges and Navraj Singh Ghaleigh (eds.), *Darker Legacies of Law in Europe: The Shadow of National Socialism and Fascism over Europe and its Legal Traditions* (Oxford: Hart, 2003), 1–18; here 7.

21. Carl Schmitt to Werner Weber, 17th May 1954 (HStAD RW 265–13719).

22. Reinhard Mehring, 'Carl Schmitt und die Verfassungslehre unserer Tage', in: *Archiv des öffentlichen Rechts*, Vol. 120 (1990), 177–204.

23. See in particular Rudolf Smend, 'Verfassung und Verfassungsrecht (1928)', in: *Staatsrechtliche Abhandlungen und andere Aufsätze* (Berlin: Duncker & Humblot, 1994), 119–276.

24. See Smend's succinct summary 'Integrationslehre', in: *ibid.*, 475–81; here 476.

25. Smend distinguished three types of integration: personal, based on leading politicians; functional, based on 'collective forms of life'–political procedures and common forms of political action; and finally factual or *sachliche* integration, which subsumed the 'aims of the state' as well as flags, symbols and national ceremonies – all of which added up to the *Gesamterlebnis* of the state.

26. Rudolf Smend, 'Das Bundesverfassungsgericht', in: *ibid.*, 581–93.

27. Much later both Schmitt and Smend were to be reclaimed by a follower of Schmitt as Catholic and Protestant thinkers respectively for anti-pluralism and anti-positivism. See Hans-Dieter Sander, 'Wie der Pluralismus den Staat zerstört', in: *Die Welt*, 15 February 1982.

28. See Ulfrid Neumann, 'Rechtsphilosophie in Deutschland seit 1945', in: Dieter Simon (ed.), *Rechtswissenschaft in der*

Bonner Republik: Studien zur Wissenschaftsgeschichte der Jurisprudenz (Frankfurt/Main: Suhrkamp, 1994), 145–87.

29. Schlink, 'Why Carl Schmitt?', 435.

30. Carl Schmitt, 'Die Tyrannei der Werte', in: *Säkularisation und Utopie – Ebracher Studien: Ernst Forsthoff zum 65. Geburtstag* (Stuttgart: W. Kohlhammer, 1967), 37–62.

31. *Ibid.*, 46.

32. *Ibid.*, 55.

33. Schmitt to Mohler, 10 April, in *Carl Schmitt – Briefwechsel mit einem seiner Schüler*, 336.

34. Ernst Wolfgang Böckenförde, 'Zur Kritik der Wertebegründung des Rechts', in *Recht, Staat, Freiheit*, 67–91.

35. See for instance Jürgen Habermas, *Between Facts and Norms*, trans. William Rehg (Cambridge, Mass.: MIT Press, 1998), 254–61.

36. Ernst-Wolfgang Böckenförde, 'Entstehung und Wandel des Rechtsstaatsbegriffs', in: *Recht, Staat, Freiheit*, 143–69; here 167.

37. Forsthoff to Schmitt, n.d. (HStAD RW 265–3751).

38. *Ibid.*

39. Werner Weber, *Spannungen und Kräfte im westdeutschen Verfassungssystem* (Stuttgart: F. Vorwerk, 1958).

40. Forsthoff, *Der Staat der Industriegesellschaft*, 72. There Forsthoff also claimed – perhaps prophetically – that 'the unity of Europe is a question of administration, not of the constitution'.

41. Werner Weber, *Die Verfassung der Bundesrepublik in der Bewährung* (Göttingen: Muster-Schmidt, 1957).

In Search of Stability II

1. Forsthoff, *Der Staat der Industriegesellschaft*, 78.

2. Ernst Forsthoff, *Die Verwaltung als Leistungsträger* (Stuttgart: Kohlhammer, 1938). See also Dieter Scheidemann, *Der Begriff Daseinsvorsorge: Ursprung,*

Funktion und Wandlungen der Konzep-tion Ernst Forsthoffs (Göttingen: Muster-Schmidt, 1991).

3. Ernst Forsthoff, 'Verfassungsprobleme des Sozialstaats', in: Ernst Forsthoff (ed.), *Rechtsstaatlichkeit und Sozial-staatlichkeit: Aufsätze und Essays* (Darmstadt: Wissenschaftliche Buchgesellschaft, 1968), 145–64; here 149.

4. *Ibid.*, 159–61.

5. *Ibid.*, 163.

6. *Ibid.*, 164.

7. *Ibid.*

8. See in particular Herbert Sultan and Wolfgang Abendroth, *Bürokratischer Verwaltungsstaat und soziale Demo-kratie: Beiträge zu Staatslehre und Staatsrecht der Bundesrepublik* (Han-nover: O. Goedel, 1955), *Antagonistische Gesellschaft und politische Demokratie: Aufsätze zur politschen Soziologie* (Neu-wied: Luchterhand, 1967) and *Ein Leben in der Arbeiterbewegung* (Frankfurt/Main: Suhrkamp, 1976).

9. Jürgen Habermas, *Strukturwandel der Öffentlichkeit* (Neuwied: Luchterhand, 1962).

10. Forsthoff, *Der Staat*, 74.

11. *Ibid.*, 164.

12. *Ibid.*, 79.

13. *Ibid.*, 164.

14. *Ibid.*, 167.

15. Helmut Schelsky, 'Der Mensch in der wissenschaftlichen Zivilisation', in: *Auf der Suche nach Wirklichkeit: Gesam-melte Aufsätze* (Düsseldorf: Eugen Diederichs, 1961), 439–80.

16. Joseph H. Kaiser, *Die Repräsentation organisierter Interessen* (Berlin: Duncker & Humblot, 1956).

17. *Ibid.*

18. *Ibid.*

19. Joseph H. Kaiser, 'Vorwort', in: *Planung I: Recht und Politik der Planung in Wirtschaft und Gesellschaft* (Baden-Baden: Nomos, 1965), 7–9.

20. Joseph H. Kaiser, 'Einleitung: Exposé

einer pragmatischen Theorie der Pla-nung', in: *ibid.*, 11–34.

21. *Ibid.*, 20.

22. Other members of the Schmitt School remained considerably more cautious about planning. See for instance Ernst Forsthoff, 'Über Mittel und Methoden moderner Planung', in: Joseph H. Kaiser (ed.), *Planung III: Mittel und Methoden planender Verwaltung* (Baden-Baden: Nomos, 1968), 21–38.

23. Kaiser, 'Einleitung', 22–3.

24. Joseph H. Kaiser, 'Europäisches Groß-raumdenken: Die Steigerung geschicht-licher Größen als Rechtsproblem', in: Hans Barion *et al.* (eds.), *Epirrhosis: Festgabe für Carl Schmitt*, Vol. 2 (Berlin: Duncker & Humblot, 1968), 529–48; here 534.

25. *Ibid.*, 548.

26. *Ibid.*

27. James C. Scott, *Seeing like a State: How Certain Schemes to Improve the Human Condition Have Failed* (New Haven: Yale UP, 1998), 4.

28. Gabriele Metzler, 'Am Ende aller Krisen? Politisches Denken und Han-deln in der Bundesrepublik der sechziger Jahre', in: *Historische Zeitschrift*, no. 275 (2002), 57–103.

29. Carl Schmitt, 'Von der TV-Demokratie: Die Aggressivität des Fortschritts', in: *Deutsches Allgemeines Sonntagsblatt*, 28 June 1970.

30. *Ibid.*

31. Rüdiger Altmann, 'Die formierte Gesellschaft', in: *Abschied vom Staat*, 61–70; here 62.

32. *Ibid.*, 65.

33. *Ibid.*, 70.

34. Maschke, *Tod des Carl Schmitt*, 65.

35. Altmann was one of Erhard's advisors. Before he assumed this role, two intel-lectuals close to Schmitt had debated whether the Chancellor should have a 'brain trust'. Ernst-Wolfgang Böcken-förde had been opposed, Altmann had been in favour, although he freely

conceded that the 'indirect powers' ex-
cercised by experts would have
influence at the expense of professional
civil servants and Parliament. See
'Eierköpfe für Erhard? Diskussion um
den Beraterstab des Kanzlers', in: *Die
Zeit*, 22 November 1963.

36. Peter Brügge, 'Rechts ab zum Vaterland',
in: *Der Spiegel*, 15 May 1967. The article
juxtaposed pictures of Schmitt and
Altmann and referred to Schmitt as the
'patron saint of the Grand Coalition'.

37. Ralf Dahrendorf, 'Nach dem Überfluß:
Formierte oder offene Gesellschaft?', in:
bertelsmann texte, No. 4 (1975), 5–20;
here 11.

38. In *Sonntagsblatt*, 20 March 1966.

39. Rüdiger Altmann, 'Späte Nachricht
vom Staat', in: *Abschied vom Staat*, 71–7;
here 72.

40. *Ibid.*, 77.

41. Hermann Lübbe, 'Zur politischen Theorie der Technokratie', in: *Der Staat*,
Vol. 1 (1962), 19–30. *Der Staat* was
meant to be the theoretical voice of the
Schmitt School and was edited by a
number of Schmitt's pupils, in particular Böckenförde and Roman
Schnur.

42. Schmitt himself criticized the theories
of, for instance, Schelsky along similar
lines. Technocratic necessities might
sometimes appear to prescribe solutions, but they could not yield practical
philosophical answers, let alone questions such as *quis judicabit?* See Carl
Schmitt, 'Die vollendete Reformation:
Bemerkungen und Hinweise zu neuen
Leviathan-Interpretationen', in: *Der
Staat*, Vol. 4 (1965), 51–69; here 67.
There Schmitt also defended Hobbes's
'juristic personalism' against any charge
that the philosopher of Malmesbury
was in fact a technocrat.

43. Quoted by Geoffrey Foote, *The Labour
Party's Political Thought: A History*
(London: Croome Helm, 1986), 237.

44. Rüdiger Altmann, 'Carl Schmitt oder

das Ende der Repräsentation', in: *Abschied vom Staat*, 181–7; here 183.

Visions of Global Order

1. George Lichtheim, *Europe in the Twentieth Century* (London: Weidenfeld and
Nicolson, 1972).

2. Carl Schmitt, *Der Nomos der Erde im
Völkerrecht des Jus Publicum Europaeum* (1950; Berlin: Duncker & Humblot, 1997), 15.

3. *Ibid.*, 17.

4. *Ibid.*, 19.

5. *Ibid.*, 36.

6. As Raphael Gross has shown, right-
wing Protestant political theologians
had already developed a notion of Volk-
nomos in the inter-war period. See *Carl
Schmitt und die Juden*, 83–112.

7. Schmitt, *Gespräche über die Macht und
den Zugang zum Machthaber/Gespräch
über den neuen Raum* (1954; Berlin:
Akademie, 1994), 53.

8. *Ibid.*, 38.

9. Schmitt, *Glossarium*, 9.

10. Schmitt, *Nomos*, 266.

11. Schmitt, *Glossarium*, 3.

12. *Ibid.*, 8.

13. Taubes, *Gegenstrebige Fügung*, 24.

14. Many of these myths have been
recounted – and, to some extent, dis-
pelled – in Dominique Auffret's *Alexandre Kojève: La Philosophie, l'État, la fin
de l'Histoire* (Paris: Grasset, 1990).

15. *Ibid.*, 19.

16. Quoted by Michael S. Roth, *Knowing
and History: Appropriations of Hegel in
Twentieth-Century France* (Ithaca: Cor-
nell UP, 1988), 118.

17. See also Vincent Descombes, *Modern
French Philosophy*, trans. L. Scott-Fox
and J. M. Harding (Cambridge: Cambridge UP, 1980), 9–54.

18. According to Armin Mohler in Piet
Tommissen (ed.), *Schmittiana*, Vol. 6
(Berlin: Duncker & Humblot, 1998), 48.

19. Barre in Auffret, *Alexandre Kojève*, 418
and 417.

20. See also the perceptive essay by Galin Tihanov, 'Regimes of Modernity at the Dawn of Globalization: Carl Schmitt and Alexander Kojève', in: Djelal Kadir and Dorothea Löbbermann (eds.), *Other Modernisms in an Age of Globalization* (Heidelberg: C. F. Winter, 2002), 75–93.

21. Alexandre Kojève, *Introduction à la lecture de Hegel: Leçons sur la Phénoménologie de l'Esprit professées de 1933 à 1939 à l'École des Hautes-Études 1902–1968*, ed. Raymond Queneau (Paris: Gallimard, 1947), 435.

22. Schmitt to Jünger, 26 January 1957, in: *Ernst Jünger-Carl Schmitt*, 320.

23. Carl Schmitt, 'Nehmen/Teilen/Weiden: Ein Versuch, die Grundfragen jeder Sozial- und Wirtschaftsordnung vom Nomos her richtig zu stellen [1953]', in: *Verfassungsrechtliche Aufsätze aus den Jahren 1924–1954: Materialien zu einer Verfassungslehre* (Berlin: Duncker & Humblot, 1958), 489–501.

24. Kojève to Schmitt, 16 May 1955; reprinted in, Tommissen (ed.), *Schmittiana*, Vol. VI, 103–7; here 103.

25. *Ibid.*, 104.

26. *Ibid.*

27. Kojève to Schmitt, 11 July 1955, in *ibid.*, 110–1; here 110.

28. Kojève to Schmitt, 16 May 1955, in *ibid.*, 105.

29. Alexandre Kojève, *Outline of a Phenomenology of Right*, trans. Bryan-Paul Frost and Robert Howse; ed. Bryan-Paul Frost (Lanham: Rowman & Littlefield, 2000). The full legal implications of Kojève's thought are lucidly explained in the introductory essay by Frost and Howse.

30. Schmitt to Kojève, 7 June 1955, in *ibid.*, 108–10; here 108.

31. Auffret, *Alexandre Kojève*, 305.

32. Schmitt to Kojève, 109.

33. Schmitt to Kojève, 113.

34. Kojève to Schmitt, 115. See also Tihanov, 'Regimes of Modernity', 85.

35. A profoundly playful and self-consciously provocative man, Kojève probably quite purposefully exaggerated his differences with Schmitt in their correspondence. After all, in 1945, in preparation to his work as a diplomat, Kojève had outlined a scheme of multiple empires, each animated by different fundamental principles – a scheme in certain respects not dissimilar to Schmitt's conception of *Grossräume*, as empires were also to be based on particular concepts. In this 'sketch', France was supposed to be the leading part of an empire spiritually and intellectually based on 'Latinity' and geographically centred on the Mediterranean. The spiritual affinities of the members of the Latin Empire were centred on an appreciation of beauty and the art of living. The 'humanization of leisure' was a particularly important project for humanity as a whole. See Alexandre Kojève, 'L'Empire Latin: Esquisse d'une doctrine de la politique française (27 août 1945)', in: *La regle du jeu*, Vol. 1. No. 1 (1990), 89–123.

36. Lutz Niethammer (in collaboration with Dirk van Laak), *Posthistoire: Has History come to an End?* (London: Verso, 1993),

37. Carl Schmitt, 'Dem wahren Johann Jakob Rousseau: Zum 28. Juni 1962', in: *Zürcher Woche*, 29 June 1962. Schmitt continued: 'Rousseau himself was no player either. His ideal was a democracy which proves itself in severe frugality. Such ideals, which amount to a renunciation of consumption are also outdated nowadays. Not even the Albanians would permanently put up with something like this.'

38. Ernst Jünger, *Der Weltstaat: Organismus und Organisation* (Stuttgart: Klett, 1960), 9.

39. *Ibid.*, 31.

40. *Ibid.*, 73.

41. Strauss to Kojève, 22 August 1948, in: Leo Strauss, *On Tyranny*, eds. Victor Gourevitch and Michael S. Roth (Chicago: University of Chicago Press, 2000), 236.

42. *Ibid.*, 238.

43. *Ibid.*

44. See also Richard Tuck, *The Rights of War and Peace: Political Thought and the International Order from Grotius to Kant* (Oxford: Oxford UP, 1999), 226–34.

45. Aron to Schmitt, 14 January 1954 (HStAD RW 265–517). For the relationship between Schmitt and Aron in general, see Piet Tommissen, 'Raymond Aron face à Carl Schmitt', in: Piet Tommissen (ed.), *Schmittiana*, Vol. 7, 111–29. Aron had supervised the thesis of Julien Freund, a former Resistance fighter and subsequent Schmitt pupil, on 'the essence of the political' – a thesis which Aron supposedly would have wanted to write himself in one form or another. Freund had initially been supervised by Jean Hyppolite, who, after he had realized that Freund centred his argument on the friend-enemy distinction, had recommended that Freund rather approach Aron. At the defence, Hyppolite concluded his intervention with the words: 'If you are right, nothing remains for me but to commit suicide'. The *rapporteur* at the defence, Paul Ricoeur, was almost equally critical, but all examiners commended Freund for his 'courage'. See Nicolas Baverez, *Raymond Aron: Un Moraliste au Temps des Idéologies* (Paris: Flammarion, 1993), 325–6. See also Julien Freund, *L'essence du politique* (Paris: Sirey, 1965) and Gary Ulmen, 'Reflections of a Partisan: Julien Freund (1921–1993)', in: *Telos*, No. 102 (1995), 3–10.

46. According to Piet Tommissen in *Schmittiana*, Vol. 6, 92. See also Raymond Aron, *Mémoires* (1983; Paris: Julliard, 1993), 94–101.

47. Théodor Paléologue, 'Carl Schmitt et Alexandre Kojève: Une anecdote, une conférence et autres miettes', in: *Commentaire*, No. 87 (Autumn 1999), 567–73; here 568.

48. Raymond Aron, *Le spectateur engagé: Entretiens avec Jean-Louis Missika et Dominique Wolton* (Paris: Julliard, 1981).

49. Raymond Aron, *Mémoires* (1983; Paris: Julliard, 1993), 650.

50. Tommissen, 'Raymond Aron face à Carl Schmitt', 125.

51. Letters from Freund to Aron, Archives Privées Raymond Aron, *carton* no. 38 and *carton* no. 206. Aron had written to Freund on 17 April 1967: 'En toute franchise, je n'envisage pas de collaborer au volume en l'honneur de Carl Schmitt. Vous savez quelle est mon attitude en ces sortes de questions. Je ne juge personne et je laisse à d'autres le soin de prononcer des condamnations catégoriques. Tout de même, j'ai vécu la période des années 30 et je ne puis pas oublier le rôle que Carl Schmitt a joué, volontairement ou involontairement, consciemment ou inconsciemment. Mon admiration pour la personne est grande et j'ai entretenu avec lui des relations intermittentes depuis la guerre, mais la collaboration à un volume de ce genre est un hommage à une personalité, hommage que je ne puis pas malgré tout lui rendre'. *Ibid.*

52. Raymond Aron, *Paix et guerre entre les nations* (Paris: Calmann-Lévy, 1962).

53. The expression 'icy clarity' is François Mauriac's. Quoted in Tony Judt, *The Burden of Responsibility: Blum, Camus, Aron and the French Twentieth Century* (Chicago: University of Chicago Press, 1998), 164.

54. Aron to Schmitt, 1 October 1963 (HStAD RW 265–521).

55. Aron also seemed to view Schmitt's theory of land and sea with considerable scepticism. Schmitt had sent Aron 'a poem by Goethe from 1812 – a

tremendous anticipation of the *terrane* counter-position to Mackinder's maritime position'. The poem about Napoleon, 'Ihro der Kaiserin von Frankreich Majestät', ended with the lines:

Nur Meer und Erde haben hier Gewicht;
Ist jenem erst das Ufer abgewonnen,
Daß sich daran die stolze Woge bricht,
So tritt durch weisen Schluß, durch Macht-
gefechte
Das feste Land in alle seine Rechte.

Aron replied: 'Les vers de Goethe sont impressionnants, mais dès lors que l'empire continental se confond avec la parfaite tyrannie, je me sense, pour mon compte, converti, à la mer'. Schmitt noted in the margins: 'Il n'y a pas de "convertir"; il s'agit d'un fait élémentaire, vis-à-vis lequel toute convertibilité évanait et s'évanait'. Schmitt to Aron, 18 March 1954, Archives Privées Raymond Aron, carton no. 208, and Aron to Schmitt, 26 March 1954 (HStAD RW 265–518). Of course, the implication could be that for Schmitt, on an 'elemental level', the Jew Aron had to be with the 'sea powers' in any case.

56. Aron to Schmitt, 14 January 1954 (HStAD RW 265–517).
57. Aron to Schmitt, 1 October 1963.
58. Raymond Aron, *Penser la guerre, Clausewitz, Vol. 2: L'âge planétaire* (Paris: Gallimard, 1976), 217.
59. *Ibid.*, 215.
60. *Ibid.*, 218.
61. Judt, *The Burden*, 149.
62. Aron to Freund, 5 February 1964, Archives Privées Raymond Aron, carton no. 206.
63. Freund to Aron, 3 February 1964, *ibid.*
64. Raymond Aron, *In Defense of Political Reason: Essays by Raymond Aron*, ed. Daniel J. Mahoney (Lanham: Rowman & Littlefield, 1994), 84.
65. For an analysis of Aron in this light, see Stephen Launay, *La pensée politique de*

Raymond Aron (Paris: Presses Universitaires de France, 1995).
66. Tuck, *The Rights*, 227–8.
67. *Ibid.*, 229.
68. Quoted by H. H. Gerth and C. Wright Mills, *From Max Weber: Essays in Sociology* (London: Routledge, 1995), 71–2. See also Robert Latham, *The Liberal Moment: Modernity, Security, and the Making of the Postwar International Order* (New York: Columbia UP, 1997).
69. See also Carl Schmitt, 'Die legale Weltrevolution: Politischer Mehrwert als Prämie auf juristische Legalität und Superlegalität', in: *Der Staat*, Vol. 17 (1978), 321–39.

Schmitt and his Historians

1. See Nicolaus Sombart's entertaining memoirs *Rendezvous mit dem Weltgeist*, 193.
2. For a thorough account of how this effort failed, see Steven P. Remy, *The Heidelberg Myth: The Nazification and Denazification of a German University* (Cambridge, Mass.: Harvard UP, 2002).
3. Sombart, *Rendezvouz*, 228.
4. *Ibid.*, 196. Koselleck, on the other hand, recollects that he did in fact address Schmitt's stance towards the Jews. Schmitt apparently claimed that his was a case of anti-Judaism, not antisemitism (conversation with author).
5. *Ibid.*, 202–3.
6. *Ibid.*, 196.
7. *Ibid.*, 203.
8. *Ibid.*, 270.
9. Kesting to Schmitt, 8th March 1950 (HStAD RW 265–7465).
10. Van Laak, *Gespräche*, 273.
11. Nicolaus Sombart, *Pariser Lehrjahre 1951–1954: Leçons de Sociologie* (Frankfurt/Main: Fischer, 1996), 418–26. Apparently, they did not talk about Schmitt.
12. Sombart, *Rendezvous mit dem Weltgeist*, 269, and Kesting to Schmitt, 22 September 1950 (HStAD RW 265–7467).

13. Reinhart Koselleck, *Critique and Crisis: Enlightenment and the Pathogenesis of Modern Society* (1959; Oxford: Berg, 1988) and Hanno Kesting, *Geschichtsphilosophie und Weltbürgerkrieg: Deutungen der Geschichte von der Französischen Revolution bis zum Ost-West-Konflikt* (Heidelberg: C. Winter, 1959).

14. Carl Schmitt's review can be found in *Das Historisch-politische Buch*, Vol. 7 (1959), 300–1.

15. Jürgen Habermas, 'Verrufener Fortschritt – verkanntes Jahrhundert: Zur Kritik der Geschichtsphilosophie', in: *Merkur*, Vol. 14 (1960), 468–77. The very fact that Habermas then decided to omit this reference from the version of the review reprinted in *Political-Philosophical Profiles* prompted Henning Ritter, son of Joachim and one of Schmitt's admirers at the *Frankfurter Allgemeine Zeitung*, to suggest a connection between Habermas's and Schmitt's thought – a suggestion which Habermas in turn countered by writing that it was Koselleck's own 'liberalization' which had prompted him to drop the reference. Such was the dynamic of mutual unmasking in matters Schmittian.

16. Friedrich Wilhelm Graf, 'Die Macht des Schicksals entschuldigt gar nichts: Auch eine Theorie des Partisanen: Wie Reinhart Koselleck die Geschichte überlistet', in: *Frankfurter Allgemeine Zeitung*, 1 November 1999. See also the laudatory remarks by Schmitt disciple Günter Maschke in 'Der Intellektuelle als Agent des Bürgerkriegs: Zur Neuausgabe von Reinhart Kosellecks Studie "Kritik und Krise"', in: *Frankfurter Allgemeine Zeitung*, 16 April 1974. Remarkably, the book was translated into Spanish quite quickly, and published by Opus Dei. See *Critica y crisis del mundo burgués*, trans. Rafael de la Vega (Madrid: Rialp, 1965). Koselleck might have been inspired to adopt this title by a passage in Schmitt's *Donoso Cortés in gesamteuropäischer Tradition*. Incidentally, in the early 1930s, Brecht and Benjamin had planned a journal entitled 'Krise und Kritik' – a telling reversal. See Erdmut Wizisla, ' "Windschiefes", "Grüppchenhaftes" und "selbstverständliche Bedeutung": Das Zeitschriftenprojekt "Kritik und Krise" (1930/31) aus der Sicht Ernst Blochs und die Edition der Dokumente', in: Klaus Garber and Ludger Rehm (eds.), *Global Benjamin* (Munich: Wilhelm Fink, 1999), 801–9. For Schmitt's discussion of the dynamics of critique and crisis, see also *Glossarium*, 23 September 1947, 17.

17. Reinhart Koselleck, *Kritik und Krise: Eine Studie zur Pathogenese der bürgerlichen Welt* (1959; Frankfurt/Main: Suhrkamp, 1997), 123.

18. Kesting, *Geschichtsphilosophie*, ix.

19. *Ibid.*, ix.

20. *Ibid.*, 6.

21. *Ibid.*, 14.

22. *Ibid.*, 19.

23. *Ibid.*, 21.

24. *Ibid.*, 24.

25. *Ibid.*, 25.

26. See also Reinhard Mehring, 'Karl Löwith, Carl Schmitt, Jacob Taubes und das "Ende der Geschichte"', in: *Zeitschrift für Religions- und Geistesgeschichte*, Vol. 48 (1996), 231–48, and Jeffrey Andrew Barrash, 'The Sense of History: On the Political Implications of Karl Löwith's Concept of Secularization', in: *History and Theory*, Vol. 37 (1998), 69–82. Arguably, Löwith's book had itself been an indirect attack on Schmitt. Kesting sent Schmitt his translations, expecting Schmitt to add 'the last polish'. See Kesting's letter to Schmitt from 26 September 1949 (HStAD RW 265–7463).

27. See also Reinhart Koselleck, 'Über die Verfügbarkeit der Geschichte', in: *Vergangene Zukunft: Zur Semantik*

geschichtlicher Zeiten (Frankfurt/Main: Suhrkamp, 1989), 260–77.

28. Kesting, *Geschichtsphilosophie*, 22.

29. Von Lask, *Gespräche*, 281–2.

30. Roman Schnur, 'Weltfriedensidee und Weltbürgerkrieg 1791/92', in: *Der Staat*, Vol. 2 (1963), 297–317; here 299.

31. *Ibid.*, 304.

32. *Ibid.*, 303.

33. *Ibid.*, 307.

34. *Ibid.*, 308.

35. *Ibid.*, 311.

36. *Ibid.*, 312–13.

37. *Ibid.*, 315.

38. He also fell under the spell of another master of resentment, albeit of a more aristocratic variety: Arnold Gehlen, under whom he wrote a *Habilitation*.

39. Sombart, *Rendezvous*, 263.

40. Reinhart Koselleck, *Preussen zwischen Reform und Revolution: Allgemeines Landrecht, Verwaltung und soziale Bewegung von 1791 bis 1848* (Stuttgart: Klett-Cotta, 1967). Much later, in the preface to the English edition of *Critique and Crisis*, Koselleck also conceded that a different and more subtle view of the Enlightenment – in particular the inclusion of the English and, above all, Scottish Enlightenments, would have led him to offer a different analysis.

41. It was Schmitt's self-styled 'hostile brother' Jacob Taubes who understood Koselleck's intention, but who, in the spirit of Benjmain, also pleaded for a reintroduction of apocalyptic thought into an analysis of the present. See Jacob Taubes, 'Geschichtsphilosophie und Historik: Bemerkungen zu Kosellecks Programm einer neuen Historik', in: Reinhart Koselleck and Wolf-Dieter Stempel (eds.), *Geschichte: Ereignis und Erzählung* (Munich: Wilhelm Fink, 1973), 490–9.

42. Nicolaus Sombart, *Die deutschen Männer und ihre Feinde: Carl Schmitt – ein deutsches Schicksal zwischen Männer-* *bund und Matriarchatsmythos* (Munich: Hanser, 1991).

43. See also Reinhard Mehring, 'Das Politikum der Kritik: Geschichtstheorie nach Carl Schmitt', in: *Neue Rundschau*, Vol. 111, No. 3 (2000), 154–67.

44. *Ibid.*, 164.

45. See in particular Ernst Nolte, *Der europäische Bürgerkrieg 1917–1945: Nationalsozialismus und Bolschewismus* (Berlin: Propyläen, 1987).

46. G. Krauss, 'Die totalitäre Staatsidee', in: *Die neue Ordnung*, Vol. 3 (1949), 494–508. Krauss claimed that on the ideological battlefield one had to set powerful myth against myth – whereas half-heartedness plus de-nazification was supposedly a recipe for national disaster.

47. Ernst Nolte, *Der Faschismus in seiner Epoche: Die Action française, der italienische Faschismus, der Nationalsozialismus* (Munich: Piper, 1963).

48. Ernst Nolte, *Historische Existenz: Zwischen Anfang und Ende der Geschichte?* (Munich: Piper, 1998).

49. *Ibid.*, 218.

50. But if history is political, then the political is also historical. Christian Meier, perhaps Germany's most respected historian of the ancient world, who was inspired by a number of Schmitt's concepts and in particular by Schmitt's method of concept-formation, famously traced the emergence of the political among the ancient Greeks. Meier understood the political as a distinct area of life, but he also saw it as a form of self-rule. At the same time, he insisted, revealingly, that the Greeks had not had any political theology. See Christian Meier, *Die Entstehung des Politischen bei den Griechen* (1980; Frankfurt/Main: Suhrkamp, 1995) and *Athen: Ein Neubeginn der Weltgeschichte* (Berlin: Siedler, 1993).

51. See also Horst Möller, 'Ernst Nolte und das "Liberale System"', in: Thomas

Nipperdey, Anselm Döring-Manteuffel and Hans-Ulrich Thamer (eds.), *Weltbürgerkrieg der Ideologien: Antworten an Ernst Nolte* (Berlin: Propyläen, 1993), 57–72.

Melancholy Modernism

1. Eventually, Hanover became a branch, supposedly keeping the sacred flame of the original Marxism of the Institute for Social Research throughout the 1970s and 1980s.
2. Quoted by van Laak, *Gespräche*, 197.
3. Ernst Tugendhat, *Philosophische Aufsätze* (Frankfurt/Main: Suhrkamp, 1992), 9.
4. Van Laak, *Gespräche*, 193.
5. Like Koselleck, Ritter and his students were concerned to understand the specificity of modernity through its peculiar conceptual languages – which resulted in the monumental *Historical Dictionary of Philosophy*. Schmitt had been invited to contribute, but declined. See Joachim Ritter, Karlfried Gründer and Rudolf Eisler (eds.), *Historisches Wörterbuch der Philosophie*, 10 Vols. (Basel: Schwabe, 1971–).
6. Jürgen Seifert, 'Joachim Ritters "Collegium Philosophicum": Ein Forum offenen Denkens', in: Richard Faber and Christine Holste (eds.), *Kreise – Gruppen – Bünde: Zur Soziologie moderner Intellektuellenassoziationen* (Würzburg: Königshausen & Neumann, 2000), 189–98; here 191. According to Seiffert, it was – ironically – this very openness which eventually led members of the *Collegium* to adopt a sort of decisionism as the idea that conversation has to stop somewhere. In the same vein, he claims, they developed a hostility to Habermas's theory of communicative action. See *ibid.*, 193.
7. Spaemann in Claus Leggewie, *Der Geist steht rechts: Ausflüge in die Denkfabriken der Wende* (Berlin: Rotbuch, 1987), 159.

8. Joachim Ritter, *Hegel und die französische Revolution* (1965; Frankfurt/Main: Suhrkamp, 1972), 21.
9. Seifert, 'Joachim Ritters "Collegium Philosophicum"', 190.
10. Ritter, *Hegel*, 45–8.
11. *Ibid.*, 48–9. See also Dieter Groh and Ruth Groh, 'Vize-Glück im Unglück? Zur Entstehung und Funktion der Kompensationsthese', in: *Merkur*, Vol. 44 (1990), 1054–66.
12. Joachim Ritter, *Metaphysik und Politik: Studien zu Aristoteles und Hegel* (Frankfurt/Main: Suhrkamp, 1969), 338.
13. Joachim Ritter, 'Die Aufgabe der Geisteswissenschaften in der modernen Gesellschaft', in: *Subjektivität: Sechs Aufsätze* (Frankfurt/Main: Suhrkamp, 1974), 105–40.
14. Van Laak, *Gespräche*, 196.
15. On Böckenförde in general see Reinhard Mehring, 'Zu den neu gesammelten Schriften und Studien Ernst-Wolfgang Böckenfördes', in: *Archiv des öffentlichen Rechts*, Vol. 117 (1992), 449–73, and Olaf Köppe, 'Politische Einheit und pluralistische Gesellschaft: Ambivalenzen der Verfassungstheorie Ernst-Wolfgang Böckenfördes', in: *Kritische Justiz*, Vol. 30 (1997), 45–62.
16. Ernst-Wolfgang Böckenförde, *Demokratie und Repräsentation: Zur Kritik der heutigen Demokratiediskussion* (Hannover: Schriftenreihe der Niedersächsichen Landeszentrale für politische Bildung, 1983), 26–7.
17. *Ibid.*, 30 and 24.
18. *Ibid.*, 14.
19. *Ibid.*, 20.
20. Ernst-Wolfgang Böckenförde, 'Der Begriff des Politischen als Schlüssel zum staatsrechtlichen Werk Carl Schmitts', in: Quaritsch (ed.), *Complexio Oppositorum*, 283–99.
21. Robert Hepp in *Complexio Oppositorum*, 310.

22. Odo Marquard, 'Eine Philosophie der Bürgerlichkeit', in: *Neue Zürcher Zeitung*, 5th April 2003.

23. Odo Marquard, *Abschied vom Prinzipiellen* (Stuttgart: Reclam, 1981), 15.

24. Odo Marquard, *Schwierigkeiten mit der Geschichtsphilosophie: Aufsätze* (Frankfurt/Main: Suhrkamp, 1982), 13.

25. Odo Marquard, 'Der angeklagte und der entlastete Mensch in der Philosophie des 18. Jahrhunderts', in: *Abschied vom Prinzipiellen*, here 47–51.

26. *Ibid.*, 57.

27. Marquard, 'Homo compensator', in: *Philosophie des Stattdesssen: Studien* (Stuttgart: Reclam, 2000), 11–29.

28. 'Mut zur Bürgerlichkeit', in: *Focus*, 7 November 1994.

29. Jan Ross, 'Skepsis zum Wohlfühlen', in: *Berliner Zeitung*, 26 February 1998. It was also older, cold-eyed conservatives which viewed concepts such as relief and compensation with scepticism. See for instance Rüdiger Altmann's satirical 'Die große Ent-Entung', in: *Frankfurter Allgemeine Zeitung*, 28 December 1957, in which he claimed that 'today the capacity for relief is the foundation of legitimacy', and that 'alienation relates to relief in the way freedom relates to leisure'.

30. Henning Ritter, 'Entwegt', in: *Frankfurter Allgemeine Zeitung*, 26 February 1988.

31. Van Laak, *Gespräche*, 276.

32. Marquard, quoting Hermann Krings, in Quaritsch (ed.), *Complexio Oppositorum*, 442.

33. Hermann Lübbe, 'Carl Schmitt liberal rezipiert', in: Quaritsch (ed.), *Complexio Oppositorum*, 428–40.

34. Hermann Lübbe, 'Aneignung und Rückaneignung', in: Georg Kohler and Heinz Kleger (eds.), *Diskurs und Dezision: Politische Vernunft in der wissenschaftlich-technischen Zivilisation – Hermann Lübbe in der Diskussion*

(Vienna: Passagen, 1990), 335–71; here 340.

35. *Ibid.*, 343.

36. *Ibid.*, 341.

37. Lübbe, 'Carl Schmitt', 431.

38. See also, Hermann Lübbe, 'Zur Theorie der Entscheidung', in *Collegium Philosophicum: Studien Joachim Ritter zum 60. Geburtstag* (Basel: Schwabe, 1965), 118–40.

39. Eckard Bolsinger, 'Was ist Dezisionismus? Rekonstruktion eines autonomen Typs politischer Theorie', in: *Politische Vierteljahresschrift*, Vol. 39 (1998), 471–502.

40. Robert Spaemann, *Zur Kritik der politischen Utopie: 10 Kapitel politischer Philosophie* (Stuttgart: Klett, 1977), 69.

41. Robert Spaemann, *Philosophische Essays: Erweiterte Ausgabe* (Stuttgart: Reclam, 1994), 6.

42. *Ibid.*, 7.

43. Robert Spaemann, *Der Ursprung der Soziologie aus dem Geist der Restauration: Studien über L. G. A. de Bonald* (Munich: Kösel, 1959). Berlin quoted by Darrin M. McMahon, *Enemies of the Enlightenment: The French Counter-Enlightenment and the Making of Modernity* (New York: Oxford UP, 2001), 9.

44. *Ibid.*, 84–5.

45. *Ibid.*, 89.

46. Spaemann, *Philosophische Essays*, 10–11.

47. Spaemann in Leggewie, *Der Geist*, 149.

48. Spaemann, *Philosophische Essays*, 71–2.

49. Spaemann in Leggewie, *Der Geist*, 164.

50. *Ibid.*, 153.

51. *Ibid.*, 165.

Don Carlos in Iberia

1. A copy of the letter is at HStAD RW 265–12874.

2. See also Richard Faber, *Lateinischer Faschismus: Über Carl Schmitt den Römer und Katholiken* (Berlin: Philo, 2001).

3. Ernst Niekisch, 'Über Carl Schmitt', in: *Augenblick*, No. 4 (1956), 8–9.

4. Pedro Carlos Gonzáles Cuevas, 'Carl Schmitt en España', in: Dalmacio Negro Pavón (ed.), *Estudios sobre Carl Schmitt* (Madrid: Veintiuno, 1996), 231–62; here 234.

5. Maschke, *Der Tod des Carl Schmitt*, 79.

6. Manuel Fraga Iribarne, *En busca del tiempo servido* (Barcelona: Planeta, 1987), 25. Fraga, sometimes dubbed 'Spain's greatest political survivor', was probably Schmitt's most important follower in politics. He had held top positions under Franco, had been vice-president of the first post-Franco government, had founded the Alianza Popular (which later dissolved into the Partido Popular) and eventually became president of Galicia, a position he still occupies at the time of writing. He also held chairs in political science, served as head of the *Instituto de Estudios Políticos* and provided introductions to texts by Donoso Cortés. In a 1963 interview with Schmitt's friend Johannes Gross, a highly influential journalist in post-war West Germany, Fraga also claimed with reference to his 'Freund und bewunderter Meister' that Franco had initially established a 'dictatorship with constituent power', but that that there had to be a transfer to 'normal institutions . . . the institutions of the traditional Spanish monarchy'. A copy of 'Interview der Woche' is at HStAD RW 265–19091. While Minister of Information, Fraga was also explicitly attacked as a 'disciple of Carl Schmitt, not along ago the fascist theorist of the Führerstaat'. See Jorge Semprun, 'Burgos', in: *Le Monde*, 15 October 1964.

7. 'Herlich Wilkommen Herr Professor', in: *La Voz de Galicia*, 1 June 1960. Augustín José Menéndez, 'From Republicanism to Fascist Ideology under the early Franquismo', in: Joerges and Ghaleigh (eds.), *Darker Legacies of Law in Europe*, 337–60; here 351. Schmitt himself claimed that 'Santiago is super-credibly [sic] beautiful; whoever does not know it, should not talk about Europe'. Schmitt to Mohler, 2 July 1958, in: *Carl Schmitt – Briefwechsel mit einem seiner Schüler*, 249. Galicia was also an area for the *Auseinandersetzung zwischen Land und Meer*. See Schmitt to Mohler, 6 July 1958, *ibid.*, 250.

8. Enric Jardí, *Eugeni d'Ors: Obra i Vida* (Barcelona: Edicions dels Quaderns Crema, 1990), 240.

9. Menéndez, 'From Republicanism to Fascist Ideology', 345, and Stanley G. Payne, *The Franco Regime 1936–1975* (London: Phoenix, 2000), 240–1.

10. See also the laudatory speech on the occasion by M. Fraga Iribarne, 'Carl Schmitt: el hombre y la obra', in: *Revista de Estudios Politicos*, No. 122 (1962), 5–36. At that time, Conde had already been offered a 'golden exile' as a diplomat after rising ideological tensions within the regime. He capped his second career as Spanish ambassador to West Germany, where he died in 1974. See Menéndez, 'From Republicanism to Fascist Ideology', 349.

11. Pablo Lucas Verdu, 'Die Entwicklung der Staatstheorie in Spanien seit 1945', in: *Der Staat*, Vol. 2 (1963), 227–44.

12. Menéndez, 'From Republicanism to Fascist Ideology', 347.

13. See for instance, Raúl Morodo, *Los orígines ideológicos del franquismo: Acción Española* (Madrid: Alianza, 1985), 114–15, 116 and 141. *Acción Española* arguably did more than any other ideological publication to form Franco's worldview. See Pedro Carlos González Cuevas, *Historia de las Derechas Españolas: De la Ilustracíon a Nuestros Días* (Madrid: Biblioteca Nueva, 2000), 364–5.

14. José María Beneyto, *Politische Theologie als politische Theorie: Eine Unter-

suchung zur Rechts- und Staatstheorie Carl Schmitts und zu ihrer Wirkungsgeschichte in Spanien (Berlin: Duncker & Humblot, 1983), 26.

15. Francisco Javier Conde, *Teoría y sistema de las formas políticas* (Madrid: Instituto de Estudios Políticos, 1944), 76. See also Beneyto, *Politische Theologie*, 28.

16. Menéndez, 'From Republicanism to Fascist Ideology', 354.

17. Beneyto, *Politische Theologie*, 25.

18. Menéndez, 'From Republicanism to Fascist Ideology', 354.

19. For an overview, see Benjamin Rivaya, *La Filosofía del derecho en el franquismo* (Madrid: Centro de Estudios Constitucionales, 1998).

20. Stanley G. Payne, *A History of Fascism, 1914–1945* (Madison: The University of Wisconsin Press, 1995), 266, and Payne, *The Franco Regime*, 413. In the end, the 'national Catholicism' advocated by Acción Española provided more of the principles underlying the actual regime than the Falange.

21. Jerzy W. Borejsza, *Schulen des Hasses: Faschistische Systeme in Europa* (Frankfurt/Main: Fischer, 1999), 225.

22. *Ibid.*, 226.

23. Menéndez, 'From Republicanism to Fascist Ideology', 354.

24. Beneyto, *Politische Theologie*, 24.

25. Elías Díaz, *Pensamiento Español en la Era de Franco, 1939–1975* (Madrid: Tecnos, 1983), 31–2.

26. Schmitt truncated Virgil's *Magnus ab integro saeclorum nascitur ordo*, which is commonly translated as 'a mighty order of ages is born anew'. For Schmitt's rather casual use of classical references, see Annette Rink, *Das Schwert im Myrtenzweige: Antikenrezeption bei Carl Schmitt* (Vienna: Karolinger, 2000).

27. *Ibid.*, 33–7.

28. Beneyto, *Politische Theologie*, 39–43, and Payne, *The Franco Regime*, 438.

29. See also Rockwell Gray, *The Imperative of Modernity: An Intellectual Biography*

of *José Ortega y Gasset* (Berkeley: University of California Press, 1989). More specifically, there was the mid-century debate between Laín Entralgo and Calvo Serer about 'España como problema' versus 'España sin problema'. See Díaz, *Pensamiento Español*, 52–8.

30. Carl Schmitt, *Donoso Cortés in gesamteuropäischer Interpretation* (Cologne: Greven, 1950). See also Beneyto, *Politische Theologie*, 22.

31. Manuel Fraga Iribarne, *How Spain Is Governed* (Madrid: Diplomatic Information Office, 1950), 117.

32. Moreover, Schmitt's closest pupil in the 1930s, Günther Krauss, had actually fought in the Spanish Civil War and had 'audiences' with Franco in the post-war period. See for instance the report about his meeting with Franco on 27 February 1974, which Krauss sent to Schmitt, at HStAD RW 265–20356. According to Krauss, his main contribution to the conversation consisted in advising Franco not to abolish the death penalty.

33. In fact, the Spanish case was more complicated, since, according to Schmitt, only the Spanish *amor mortis* had allowed the country to stand the test of civil war. It would be worthwhile to analyze to what extent there was a 'cult of death', an almost inevitable part of anti-liberalism, in Schmitt's thought. See Schmitt, *Glossarium*, 266.

34. See Winfried Martini, *Das Ende aller Sicherheit: Eine Kritik des Westens* (Stuttgart: Deutsche Verlags-Anstalt, 1954). Schmitt also tried to have the book translated into Portuguese by the Portuguese propaganda ministry, praising the book as a 'most interesting and intelligent critique of Western democracy'. See letter by Schmitt to Cabral de Moncada, 10 December 1954, in: *Luís Cabral de Moncada und Carl Schmitt*, 29. Martini then in turn promoted an apologetic view of Schmitt's past. See

for instance Winfried Martini, 'Carl Schmitt und die Weimarer Verfassung', in: *Frankfurter Allgemeine Zeitung*, 19 July 1963. This advocacy of authoritarian Spain and Portugal was not an isolated phenomenon. See, for instance, Theodor Maunz's essay in *Salazar et son Oeuvre* (Lisbon: S. N. I., 1956), 9–24. In this publication by the Portuguese propaganda ministry Maunz lauded the stability of an authoritarian presidentialism, which had failed in Germany in the early 1930s. Portuguese success in this matter was based on the harmony between parliament and the presidential system. See *ibid.*, 11–12. Maunz also praised the will embodied in the constitution to avoid 'extreme individualism' and 'dangerous massification'. *Ibid.*, 17. Most curiously, perhaps, he also applied (and transformed) Schmitt's mythology of land and sea, claiming that countries which 'leaned against a continent' and had far-reaching goals on the 'world seas' needed harmony and stability in domestic affairs. In general, however, the supposed fact remained that 'just as the sea is mysterious, so the politics and the life of the state of sea powers are covered with a mysterious veil for land-based peoples'. *Ibid.*, 23. See also Rudolf Walter, ' "Sowjetspanien" und "Advokatenrepublik": Spaniens Bürgerkrieg als Versuchsfeld für Geschichtsapologetik – In bundesdeutschen Medien galt Franco bis in die siebziger Jahre hinein als ehrenwerter Antikommunist der ersten Stunde', in: *Freitag*, 13 July 2001.

35. Axel Schildt, *Zwischen Abendland und Amerika: Studien zur westdeutschen Ideenlandschaft der 50er Jahre* (Munich: R. Oldenbourg, 1999).

36. This stance was most prominent in the 'Journal for European Thought', *Merkur*, which, despite its claim to disavow all 'ideologies', became the platform for traditional literary criticism and published international exponents of the *Abendland* ideology, most prominently Ortega y Gasset and T. S. Eliot. Schmitt initially published in *Merkur*, until Ernst Robert Curtius and Theodor W. Adorno, among others, protested to the editor, Hans Paeschke.

37. Axel Schildt, *Konservatismus in Deutschland: Von den Anfängen im 18. Jahrhundert bis zur Gegenwart* (Munich: Beck, 1998), 217–18.

38. Armin Mohler, *Die konservative Revolution in Deutschland 1918–1932: Grundriss ihrer Weltanschauungen* (Stuttgart: F. Vorwerk, 1950).

39. Armin Mohler, *Die französische Rechte: Vom Kampf um Frankreichs Ideologienpanzer* (Munich: Isar, 1958) and *Die Fünfte Republik: Was steht hinter de Gaulle?* (Munich: Piper, 1963). In the former, Mohler advocated a renewal of France from the periphery through a *Nouvelle Droite*, which would draw on France's pagan traditions. Concepts such as 'the elementary', 'the origins', 'the wilderness' and 'the irrational' were supposed to play a central part in this renewal of a Right, which would explode France's 'ideological armour' without 'hurting the substance'. See *Die französische Rechte*, 62, 68 and 23.

40. Armin Mohler, *Was die Deutschen fürchten: Angst vor der Politik – Angst vor der Geschichte – Angst vor der Macht* (Stuttgart: Seewald, 1966), 130.

41. *Ibid.*, 207–12.

42. *Ibid.*

43. Mohler, *Was die Deutschen fürchten*, 195 and 199.

44. *Ibid.*, 49.

45. Martin Greiffenhagen, *Das Dilemma des Konservatismus in Deutschland* (Frankfurt/Main: Suhrkamp, 1986), 341–6.

46. There is the possibility that Schmittian thought played some role in the founding of the Fifth Republic via the writings of René Capitant. Capitant had

studied (and praised) Schmitt in the early 1930s; he later became a representative of 'left-Gaullism' and served as education minister as well as justice minister. See Gwénäl Le Brazidec, *René Capitant, Carl Schmitt: Crise et Réforme du Parlementarisme: De Weimar à la Cinquième République* (Paris: L'Harmattan, 1998).

47. Schmitt, 'Von der TV-Demokratie'.

48. *Ibid.*

49. See the remarks by Calvo Serer about 'España sin problema' quoted in Díaz, *Pensamiento Español*, 58.

50. See also Fernando Rosas (ed.), *Vom Ständestaat zur Demokratie: Portugal im Zwanzigsten Jahrhundert* (Munich: Oldenbourg, 1997), which discusses the primacy of the political under Salazar.

51. Schmitt's self-interpretation was fleshed out by one of his Spanish friends in one of the many Festschriften for Schmitt. Enrique Tierno Galván completely omitted the obviously central question of slavery from his account of Melville's novel, portraying Cereno instead as the 'myth of Europe'. See Tierno Galván, 'Benito Cereno oder der Mythos Europa', in: Barion *et al.* (ed.), *Epirrhosis*, 345–56. Tierno Galván had a much more ambivalent relation to Schmitt's politics as such. He was an opponent of the Franco regime and became the socialist mayor of Madrid in 1979.

52. Taubes, *Gegenstrebige Fügung*, 15.

The Partisan in the Landscape of Treason

1. Schickel, *Gespräche*, 9. See also Joachim Schickel (ed.), *Guerilleros, Partisanen: Theorie und Praxis* (Munich: Hanser, 1970).

2. See also Monika Faßbender and Klaus Hansen (eds.), *Feuilleton und Realpolitik – Ralf Schroers: Schriftsteller, Intellektueller, Liberaler* (Baden-Baden: Nomos, 1984).

3. Rolf Schroers, *Der Partisan: Ein Beitrag*

zur politischen Anthropologie (Cologne: Kiepenheuer & Witsch, 1961).

4. van Laak, *Gespräche*, 252.

5. *Ibid.*, 252.

6. Hans Grünberger, 'Die Kippfigur des Partisanen. Zur politischen Anthropologie von Ralf Schroers', in: Herfried Münkler (ed.), *Der Partisan: Theorie, Strategie, Gestalt* (Opladen: Westdeutscher Verlag, 1990), 42–60.

7. *Ibid.*, 59.

8. *Ibid.*, 45.

9. Carl Schmitt, *Theorie des Partisanen: Zwischenbemerkung zum Begriff des Politischen* (1963; Berlin: Duncker & Humblot, 1995).

10. See also Herfried Münkler, 'Guerillakrieg und Terrorismus', in: *Gewalt und Ordnung: Das Bild des Krieges im politischen Denken* (Frankfurt/Main: Fischer, 1992), 142–75.

11. Schmitt, *Theorie*, 14. Needless to say, this account could be substantially questioned in light of subsequent historical scholarship.

12. *Ibid.*, 48.

13. *Ibid.*, 14.

14. On this point see also Michael Walzer, *Just and Unjust Wars: A Moral Argument with Historical Illustrations* (New York: Basic Books, 1991), 179.

15. Schmitt, *Theorie*, 17.

16. *Ibid.*

17. *Ibid.*, 15.

18. See also Uday Singh Mehta, *Liberalism and Empire: A Study in Nineteenth-Century British Liberal Thought* (Chicago: University of Chicago Press, 1999).

19. Helmut Ridder, 'Schmittiana II', in: *Neue politische Literatur* No. 2 (1967), 137–45.

20. Ernst Jünger, *Der Waldgang* (Frankfurt/Main: Klostermann, 1951), 120–1.

21. Aron, *Penser la guerre, Clausewitz, II*, 213. According to Aron, Schmitt had committed 'stunning errors' in applying Clausewitz's doctrines. In reply, Robert

Hepp, one of Schmitt's right-wing followers, wrote a devastating review – which included antisemitic overtones – of Aron's Clausewitz book, in which he accused the French thinker of having rendered Clausewitz liberal and harmless. Aron responded and also wrote to Schmitt that Hepp's article had 'approached the level of personal injury'. See Robert Hepp, 'Der harmlose Clausewitz', in: *Zeitschrift für Politik*, Vol. 25 (1978), 390–429, Raymond Aron, 'Verdächtiger Anwalt: Bemerkungen zu Robert Hepps Rezension', in: *Zeitschrift für Politik*, Vol. 26 (1979), 284–308. See also *Raymond Aron*, 432. It is debatable whether either Schmitt or Aron provided a faithful rendering of Clausewitz. See Beatrice Heuser, *Reading Clausewitz* (London: Pimlico, 2002).

22. At other points, Schmitt seemed to suggest that human beings, even those nominally in possession of power, had become merely a 'prosthesis' of the atom bomb, 'a part of the technical and social apparatus which produces the atom bomb and applies it'. See Schmitt, *Gespräch*, 27.

23. Margret Boveri, *In der Landschaft des Verrats* (Hamburg: Rowohlt, 1956). See also Christian Tilitzki, 'Margret Boveri und Carl Schmitt – ein lockerer Briefkontakt', in: Piet Tommissen (ed.), *Schmittiana*, Vol. VII (Berlin: Duncker & Humblot), 281–308.

24. Carl Schmitt, 'Clausewitz als politischer Denker: Bemerkungen und Hinweise', in: *Der Staat*, Vol. 6 (1967), 479–502; here 485.

25. *Ibid.*, 488.

26. And it was then also no accident that Rolf Schroers entitled the controversial article in which he congratulated Carl Schmitt on his ninetieth birthday 'In the Landscape of Treason'. See Ralf Schroers, 'In der Landschaft des Verrats: Zum 90. Geburtstag von Carl Schmitt (11. VII. 1978)', in: *Merkur*, Vol. 32 (1978)

735–8. There Schroers lauded Schmitt as a thinker who 'lived and lives in the state of exception'.

27. Schmitt, *Theorie*, 65–70.

28. *Ibid.*, 83–7.

29. *Ibid.*, 80.

30. Aron sensed this hidden homage and was adamant that he found the analogy Schmitt drew between Salan and General von York 'unacceptable'. See Aron, *Penser la guerre*, 210. Aron also criticized Schmitt for having omitted – rather tellingly – references to the various forms of resistance to the Nazis.

31. And as the brother-in-law of the sister of Gudrun Ensslin, who later was part of the Baader-Meinhof gang.

32. 'Die Versuchung, Amok zu laufen', in: *Süddeutsche Zeitung*, 18 September, 1998 and Lorenz Jäger, 'Gelehrter ohne Amt: Zum sechzigsten Geburtstag von Günter Maschke', in: *Frankfurter Allgemeine Zeitung*, 16 January 2003.

33. Communication with author.

34. He also became the German translator of the then world-famous Cuban poet and *cause celèbre* Heberto Padilla, whom Castro had put in jail for writing lyrics that could be interpreted as critical of the regime.

35. Günter Maschke, *Kritik des Guerillero: Zur Theorie des Volkskriegs* (Frankfurt/Main: S. Fischer, 1973) and *Das bewaffnete Wort: Aufsätze aus den Jahren 1973–93* (Vienna: Karolinger, 1997). Maschke also introduced Sun-Tzu to a German audience in the early 1970s. See Sun-Tzu, *Die dreizehn Gebote der Kriegskunst* (Munich: Rogner & Bernhard, 1972).

36. In particular see his 'Die Geburt der Guerilla aus dem Geist der Revolution', in: *Kritik des Guerillero*, 15–33.

37. *Ibid.*, 28.

38. Maschke, *Das bewaffnete Wort*, 193. At the same time, Maschke exhibited a healthy contempt for West German mainstream conservatism. See, Günter

Maschke, 'Auf der Suche nach dem Konservatismus: Zu einer Tagung der Evangelischen Akademie Hannover,' in *Frankfurter Allgemeine Zeitung*, 23 February 1973.

39. 'Die Versuchung'.

40. He also founded a publishing house which carried titles by Eliade and Drieu La Rochelle alongside books by Regis Débray and Agnes Heller. Its slogan was 'A good library does not reveal the convictions of the owner'. It was intended specifically to change a 'landscape of treason and of suspicion'.

41. Subsequently, he was hired by the Peruvian military academy to teach philosophy as part of the fight against *Sendero Luminoso*, the Shining Path guerillas.

42. Herfried Münkler, 'Partisanen der Tradition', in: *Der Monat*, No. 282 (1982).

43. Walter Laqueur, *Guerila: A Historical and Critical Study* (New Brunswick: Transaction, 1998).

44. *Ibid.*, 386.

45. *Ibid.*, 396.

46. Schmitt, 'Dem wahren Johann Jakob Rousseau'.

47. Which is not to deny the essential differences between Schmitt and Jünger. Schmitt's disciples were eager to stress this difference: Kesting claimed in a letter to Schmitt that Schroers had become a victim of his admiration for Jünger, whose figure of the 'worker' he sought to replace with the partisan. For Schmitt, the worker would transform himself into the player. Robert Hepp, on the other hand, was jubilant that 'Ihre jungen Freunde sind jedenfalls hell begeistert, weil sie endlich etwas in der Hand haben, was nicht nach Wald-, Wasser- und Wiesengängen riecht'. Thus a line was drawn, with the two dandies Jünger and Kojève on one side, and Schmitt on the other. See Kesting to Schmitt, 30 January 1962 (HStAD RW 265–7489) and Hepp to Schmitt, 22 January 1964 (HStAD RW 265–5996).

48. Aron, *Penser la guerre*, 218.

Dangerous Labyrinths

1. According to a letter Schmitt wrote to Piet Tommissen. Quoted by Tommissen, 'Erster Einstieg in zwei Desiderate der Carl-Schmitt-Forschung', in: Dietrich Murswiek, Ulrich Storost and Heinrich A. Wolff (eds.), *Staat – Souveränität – Verfassung: Festschrift für Helmut Quaritsch zum 70. Geburtstag* (Berlin: Duncker & Humblot, 2000), 565–602; here 573. In fact, however, the term was polemically opposed to the use Bakunin had made of the expression against Giuseppe Mazzini in 1871. See Mikhail Bakunin, 'The Political Theology of Mazzini', in: *Selected Writings*, ed. Arthur Lehning, trans. Steven Cox and Olive Stevens (New York: Grove, 1974), 214–31. Earlier uses go back to the Stoa and Varro. For a useful general introduction see Heinrich Meier, 'Was ist Politische Theologie? Einführende Bemerkungen zu einem umstrittenen Begriff', in: Jan Assmann, *Politische Theologie zwischen Ägypten und Israel* (Munich: Carl Friedrich von Siemens Stiftung, 1992), 7–19.

2. Quoted by Tommissen, 'Erster Einstieg', 574.

3. Erik Peterson, *Der Monotheisumus als politisches Problem: Ein Beitrag zur Geschichte der politischen Theologie im Imperium Romanum* (Leipzig: Hegner, 1935), reprinted in: *Theologische Traktate* (Munich: Kösel, 1950), 45–147. On Peterson, see also Barbara Nichtweiß, *Erik Peterson: Neue Sicht auf Leben und Werk*, 2nd edn. (Freiburg: Herder, 1994).

4. Peterson, *Der Monotheismus*, 95.

5. Towards the end of the 1960s, Peterson's thesis was partially taken up by a number of left-wing theologians and critics. They accepted Peterson's discrediting of monotheism, but denied a strict separation between politics and theology. Instead, they claimed that the dogma of

the trinity was critical of power and domination – and therefore could serve as the basis of a decidedly left-wing political theology. See Helmut Peukert (ed.), *Diskussion zur 'Politischen Theologie'* (Mainz: Matthias-Grünewald, 1969) and Jürgen Moltmann, *Der gekreuzigte Gott: Das Kreuz Christi als Grund und Kritik christlicher Theologie* (Munich: Chr. Kaiser, 1972).

6. Marianne Kesting, 'Begegnungen mit Carl Schmitt', in: Piet Tommissen (ed.) *Schmittiana*, Vol. 4 (Weinhelm: VCH 1994), 93–118.

7. Schmitt to Julien Freund, 18 February 1970, quoted by Piet Tommissen, 'Einstieg', 577.

8. Schmitt to Jünger, 19 October, 1971, in: *Ernst Jünger – Carl Schmitt*, 379.

9. Meier, 'Was ist Politische Theologie?', 14.

10. Hans Blumenberg, *The Legitimacy of the Modern Age*, trans. Robert M. Wallace (Cambridge, Mass.: MIT Press, 1983). One needs to examine the various German editions to follow the changes Blumenberg made in response to Schmitt's criticisms.

11. Robert B. Pippin, 'Blumenberg and the Modernity Problem', in: *Idealism as Modernism: Hegelian Variations* (Cambridge: Cambridge UP, 1997), 265–85; here 266. In particular, the modern age genuinely overcame the gnosis – a difficult argument which Pippin succeeds in reconstructing in a lucid manner.

12. Pippin, 'Blumenberg and the Modernity Problem', 272.

13. See also the discussion in Ruth Groh, *Arbeit an der Heillosigkeit der Welt: Zur politisch-theologischen Mythologie und Anthropologie Carl Schmitts* (Frankfurt/Main: Suhrkamp, 1999), 156–84.

14. Hans Blumenberg, *Die Legitimät der Neuzeit* (Frankfurt/Main: Suhrkamp, 1966), 60.

15. *Ibid.*, 59.

16. *Ibid.*

17. *Ibid.*, 60.

18. *Ibid.*

19. Schmitt, *Politische Theologie II*, 111.

20. *Ibid.*, 113.

21. *Ibid.*, 124.

22. *Ibid.*, 125.

23. Blumenberg, *Die Legitimität*, 515–23.

24. Hans Blumenberg to Carl Schmitt, 7 August 1975 (HStAD RW 265–1498).

25. Hans Blumenberg to Carl Schmitt, 24 March 1971 (HStAD RW 265–1495).

26. *Ibid.*

27. Hans Blumenberg, *Säkularisierung und Selbstbehauptung: Erweiterte und überarbeitete Neuausgabe von 'Die Legitimität der Neuzeit', erster und zweiter Teil* (Frankfurt/Main: Suhrkamp, 1974), 117.

28. *Ibid.*

29. *Ibid.*, 118.

30. Odo Marquard, 'Entlastung vom Absoluten: In memoriam Hans Blumenberg', in: *Philosophie des Stattdessen*, 108–20.

31. See also Werner Köhne, 'Zeitzeugenschaft im Verborgenen: Der Philosoph als Seismograph der geistigen Situation der Zeit', in: Franz Josef Wetz and Hermann Timm (eds.), *Die Kunst des Überlebens: Nachdenken über Hans Blumenberg* (Frankfurt/Main: Suhrkamp, 1999), 409–25.

32. Hans Blumenberg, *Arbeit am Mythos*, 2nd edn. (1979; Frankfurt/Main: Suhrkamp, 1981), 433–604.

33. *Ibid.*, 597.

34. Richard Faber, 'Von der "Erledigung jeder Politischen Theologie" zur Konstitution Politischer Polytheologie: Eine Kritik Hans Blumenbergs', in: Jacob Taubes (ed.), *Der Fürst dieser Welt: Carl Schmitt und die Folgen* (Munich: Fink, 1985), 85–99; here 99.

35. Max Horkheimer quoted in *ibid.*, 99.

36. Hermann Lübbe, 'Aspekte der politischen Philosophie des Bürgers', in: *Philosophie nach der Aufklärung: Von der Notwendigkeit pragmatischer*

Vernunft (Düsseldorf: Econ, 1980), 211–22; here 216.

37. Hermann Lübbe, 'Politische Theologie als Theologie repolitisierter Religion', in: Taubes (ed.), *Der Fürst dieser Welt*, 77–84.

38. Robert Spaemann, 'Funktionale Religionsbegründung und Religion', in: *Philosophische Essays*, 208–31.

39. Odo Marquard, 'Lob des Polytheismus', in: *Abschied vom Prinzipiellen*, 91–116.

40. Odo Marquard, 'Aufgeklärter Polytheismus – auch eine politische Theologie?', in: Taubes (ed.), *Der Fürst dieser Welt*, 77–84; here 83.

41. Ernst-Wolfgang Böckenförde, 'Politische Theorie und politische Theologie: Bemerkungen zu ihrem gegenseitigen Verhältnis', in: Taubes (ed.), *Der Fürst dieser Welt*, 16–25.

42. *Ibid.*, 24.

43. Ernst-Wolfgang Böckenförde, 'Das Ethos der modernen Demokratie und die Kirche', in: *Hochland*, Vol. 50 (1957/58), 4–19.

44. Rober Spaemann, 'Für und wider eine politische Theologie', in: *Westdeutscher Rundfunk*, 1 and 2 November 1969.

Dangerous Liaisons

1. Volker Neumann, 'Carl Schmitt und die Linke', in: *Die Zeit*, 8 July 1983.

2. Bahman Nirumand, 'Die Avantgarde der Studenten im internationalen Klassenkampf', in: *Kursbuch*, No. 13 (1968), 1–17; here 1, as well as Oskar Negt, 'Studentischer Protest – Liberalismus – "Linksfaschismus"', in: *ibid.*, 179–89.

3. Noack, *Carl Schmitt*, 293.

4. Arguably, Schmitt also took a particular interest in the student movement because the students had made Walter Benjamin into one of their icons. The students had rediscovered Benjamin's Marxist side, which, they argued, had been suppressed by Theodor Adorno and other members of the Frankfurt School. Schmitt followed some of the radical student publications, and avidly underlined and commented on discussions of Benjamin. If Benjamin's legacy could be subject to such fundamental revision by a new generation, why should not Schmitt's own *oeuvre* come to be seen in a different light – especially when Schmitt felt that he had also been a victim of manipulation by left-wing scholars? On Schmitt's interest in New Left publications on Benjamin, see also Helmut Lethen, 'Unheimliche Nähe: Carl Schmitt liest Walter Benjamin', in: *Frankfurter Allgemeine Zeitung*, 16 September 1999.

5. Schmitt to Jünger, 13 August 1970, in: *Ernst Jünger – Carl Schmitt*, 375.

6. Ingeborg Maus, *Bürgerliche Rechtstheorie und Faschismus: Zur sozialen Funktion und aktuellen Wirkung Carl Schmitts* (Munich: Wilhelm Fink, 1976).

7. Altmann, 'Die formierte Gesellschaft', 46.

8. Wilhelm Bleek, *Geschichte der Politikwissenschaft in Deutschland* (Munich: C. H. Beck, 2001), 355, and Johannes Agnoli, 'Das deutsche '68: Theoretische Grundlagen und historische Entwicklung einer Revolte', in: *1968 und die Folgen, Gesammelte Schriften*, Vol. 5 (Freiburg: Ça ira, 1998), 258–9.

9. Johannes Agnoli and Peter Brückner, *Die Transformation der Demokratie* (Frankfurt/Main: Europäische Verlagsanstalt, 1968), 10.

10. *Ibid.*, 17.

11. *Ibid.*, 26.

12. *Ibid.*, 25.

13. *Ibid.*, 24.

14. Hans Kelsen, *Vom Wesen und Wert der Demokratie* (1929; Tübingen: Mohr, 1981), 30–1.

15. Agnoli and Brückner, *Die Transformation*, 18 and 21.

16. *Ibid.*, 48.

17. *Ibid.*, 29.

18. *Ibid.*, 53.

19. *Ibid.*
20. *Ibid.*, 20.
21. *Ibid.*, 11.
22. Georges Sorel, *Reflections on Violence,* trans. T. E. Hulme (New York: Peter Smith, 1941).
23. In retrospect, Habermas as well as German political scientists and school teachers were blamed for having corrupted the youth through such an idealized image of democracy. See for instance Kurt L. Schell, 'Repressive Toleranz, strukturelle Gewalt: Vordenker von '68', in: *Frankfurter Allgemeine Zeitung,* 6 February 2001.
24. Agnoli and Brückner, *Die Transformation,* 48–9.
25. Bernard Manin, *The Principles of Representative Government* (Cambridge: Cambridge UP, 1997), 208.
26. *Ibid.*, 21.
27. Bernd Rabehl, 'Von der antiautoritären Bewegung zur sozialistischen Opposition', in: Uwe Bergmann, Rudi Dutschke, Wolfgang Lefèvre and Bernd Rabehl (eds.), *Rebellion der Studenten oder Die neue Opposition* (Reinbek: Rowohlt, 1968), 151–78; here 156.
28. Agnoli, *Die Transformation,* 16.
29. *Ibid.*, 13.
30. *Ibid.*, 154. This thesis was advanced by Herbert Marcuse.
31. Agnoli, 'Das deutsche '68', 261.
32. *Ibid.*, 263.
33. Detlev Claussen, Bernd Leineweber, Ronny Loewy, Oskar Negt and Udo Riechmann, 'Einleitung', in: Hans-Jürgen Krahl, *Konstitution und Klassenkampf: Zur historischen Dialektik von bürgerlicher Emanzipation und proletarischer Revolution: Schriften, Reden und Entwürfe aus den Jahren 1966–1970* (Frankfurt/Main: Verlag Neue Kritik, 1971). 'Einleitung', 7.
34. Ulrich K. Preuß, in: Siegward Lönnendonker (ed.), *Linksintellektueller Aufbruch zwischen 'Kulturrevolution' und 'Kultureller Zerstörung': Der SDS in der*

Nachkriegsgeschichte (1946–1969): Ein Symposium (Opladen: Westdeutscher Verlag, 1998), 255.
35. Claussen, Leineweber, Loewy, Negt and Riechmann, 'Einleitung'.
36. Gerd Koenen, *Das rote Jahrzehnt: Unsere kleine deutsche Kulturrevolution 1967–1977* (Hamburg: Kiepenheuer & Witsch, 2001), 185–6.
37. Agnoli, 'Das deutsche '68', 263.
38. Koenen, *Das rote Jahrzehnt,* 128.
39. In general, see Giuseppa Vacca, *Politica e Teoria nel Marxismo Italiano 1959–1969: Antologia Critica* (Bari: De Donato, 1972).
40. Staff, *Staatsdenken,* 190–1.
41. *Ibid.*, 192.
42. *Ibid.*, 193.
43. Staff, 18, Mario Tronti, 'Su Schmitt. "Le categorie del politico"' and *Sull'autonomia del politico* (Milan: Feltrinelli, 1977). 1972 also saw the publication of the Italian translation of *The Concept of the Political.* See Carl Schmitt, *Le categorie del 'politico': Saggi di teoria politica,* eds. Gianfranco Miglio and Pierangelo Schiera (Bologna: Il Mulino, 1972).
44. Staff, *Staatsdenken,* 197.
45. It is important to stress, however, that these thinkers always remained a tiny minority and were consequently also referred to as *la sinistra minoritaria.*
46. In his obituary of Schmitt in the Italian Communist newspaper Tronti argued that he wanted to be for Schmitt what Marx had been for Hegel. See his 'Dentro il Leviatano', in: *L'unità,* 24 April 1985.
47. Staff, *Staatsdenken,* 200.
48. Italian leftist and liberal thinkers could agree that Schmitt's distinctions no longer did justice to the social complexity of post-industrial societies towards the end of the twentieth century. See, for instance, Gianni Vattimo, 'Inventò la politica di amico-nemico', in: *La Stampa,* 17 April 1985.

49. Michael Hardt, 'Introduction: Laboratory Italy', in: Paolo Virno and Michael Hardt (eds.), *Radical Thought in Italy: A Potential Politics* (Minneapolis: University of Minnesota Press, 1996), 1–10; here 5.

50. Norberto Bobbio's unique (and eminent) position in post-war Italian political theory was due not least to the fact that he embodied both traditions. See also his interview about Schmitt 'La norma e la bestia', in: *Rinascita*, 27 April 1985.

Terror, States of Emergency and Liberal Secessions

1. Iring Fetscher, Günter Rohrmoser *et al.*, *Ideologien und Strategien* [*Analysen zum Terrorismus*, Vol. 1] (Opladen: Westdeutscher, 1981).

2. The best account of the RAF remains Stefan Aust, *The Baader-Meinhof Group: The Inside Story of a Phenomenon* (London: Bodley Head, 1987).

3. Fetscher, Rohrmoser, *Ideologien und Strategien*, 44–5.

4. RAF, 'Stadtguerilla und Klassenkampf', reprinted in: Oliver Tolmein, *Vom Deutschen Herbst zum 11. September: Die RAF, der Terrorismus und der Staat* (Hamburg: Konkret Literatur, 2002), 110–43; here 113.

5. Meinhard Schröder, 'Staatsrecht an den Grenzen des Rechtsstaates: Überlegungen zur Verteidigung des Rechtsstaates in außergewöhnlichen Lagen', in: *Archiv des öffentlichen Rechts*, Vol. 103 (1978).

6. Golo Mann, 'Quo usque tandem?', in: *Die Welt*, 7 September 1977.

7. See for instance Ernst-Wolfgang Böckenförde, 'Verhaltensgewähr oder Gesinnungstreue? Sicherung der freiheitlichen Demokratie in den Formen des Rechtsstaats', in: *Frankfurter Allgemeine Zeitung*, 8 December 1978. Böckenförde argued that since the Basic Law united legality and legitimacy, the defence of the constitution also had to be entirely on the basis of the legal order, not through examinations of the political convictions of particular citizens suspected of harbouring 'sympathy' for terrorism.

8. See in particular Ulrich K. Preuss, *Legalität und Pluralismus: Beiträge zum Verfassungsrecht der Bundesrepublik Deutschland* (Frankfurt/Main: Suhrkamp, 1973).

9. *Ibid.*, 26.

10. *Ibid.*, 29.

11. *Ibid.*, 30.

12. Ingeborg Maus, *Bürgerliche Rechtstheorie und Faschismus: Zur sozialen Funktion und aktuellen Wirkung der Theorie Carl Schmitts* (Munich: Wilhelm Fink, 1976).

13. One of the first and most insightful presentations of this position had been by Herbert Marcuse, 'Der Kampf gegen den Liberalimus in der totalitären Staatsauffassung', in: *Zeitschrift für Sozialforschung*, Vol. 3, No. 2 (1934), 161–94. The idea of Schmitt as an 'authoritarian liberal' has been developed most recently by Renato Cristi, *Carl Schmitt and authoritarian liberalism: Strong State, Free Economy* (Cardiff: University of Wales Press, 1998).

14. Ulrich K. Preuß, 'Die latente Diktatur im Verfassungsstaat: Zum 95. Geburtstag von Carl Schmitt', in: *tageszeitung*, 12 July 1983.

15. For a concise account of the development of the emergency statues and constitutional changes required for them – and a critique with many references to Schmitt – see Dieter Sterzel (ed.), *Kritik der Notstandsgesetze* (Frankfurt/Main: Suhrkamp, 1968).

16. For instance Ernst-Wolfgang Böckenförde, 'Der verdrängte Ausnahmezustand: Zum Handeln der Staatsgewalt in außergewöhnlichen Lagen: Carl Schmitt zum 90. Geburtstag gewidmet',

in: *Neue Juristische Wochenschrift*, Vol.
31 (1978), 1881–90.

17. *Der Ernstfall* [Schriften der Carl-
Friedrich-von-Siemens-Stiftung]
(Berlin: Propyläen, 1979).

18. 'Pankraz, Carl Schmitt und das "crisis
management"', in: *Die Welt*, 14 April
1980.

19. Hans-Dietrich Sander, 'Wenn Moskau
zum Golf durchbricht: Das Münchner
Symposium über die Kriterien des
Ernstfalls', in: *Die Welt*, 23 February
1980 and Malte Buschbeck, 'Solo für
Carl Schmitt: Zum Abschluß der "Ern-
stfall"-Vortragsreihe in der Siemens-
Stiftung', in: *Süddeutsche Zeitung*, 26
July 1978.

20. *Ibid.*

21. According to Josef Isensee, in: Quaritsch (ed.), *Complexio Oppositorum*,
603.

22. Buschbeck, 'Solo für Carl Schmitt'.

23. Roman Schnur, 'Die Wanzen vom
Mond aus betrachtet: Zoonpolitische
Observationen', in: *Die Welt*, 23 March
1977.

24. Hermann Lübbe, 'Freiheit und Terror',
in: *Merkur*, 1977.

25. Jens Hacke, 'Skepsis und Kompensa-
tion: Rückblick auf eine liberalkonser-
vative Intellektuellengeneration in der
Bundesrepublik', in: *Vorgänge*, Vol. 40,
No. 4 (2001), 18–27.

26. Luigi Manconi, 'The Political Ideology
of the Red Brigades', in: Raimondo Cat-
anzaro (ed.), *The Red Brigades and Left-
Wing Terrorism in Italy* (London:
Pinter, 1991), 115–43.

27. Henner Hess, 'Italien: Die ambivalente
Revolte', in: *Angriff auf das Herz des
Staates: Soziale Entwicklung und Terror-
ismus*, Vol. 2 (Frankfurt/Main:
Suhrkamp, 1988), 9–166; here 53–9.

28. To what extent there really were a full-
fledged 'double state' and 'double loyalties' remains highly controversial –
what is beyond doubt are the prepara-
tions on the Right for a coup. For recent

interpretations, see Jens Petersen, 'Der
Feind steht fest: Was ist an Italien so
zerbrechlich?', in: *Frankfurter Allgemeine Zeitung*, 6 April 2001, Alessandro
Silj, *Malpaese: criminalita, corruzione e
politica nell'Italia della prima Repub-
blica, 1943–1994* (Rome: Donzelli edi-
tore, 1994).

29. Geoffrey Eley, *Forging Democracy: The
History of the Left in Europe, 1850–
2000* (New York: Oxford UP, 2002),
409.

30. Santiago Carrillo, *Eurocomunismo y
Estado* (Barcelona: Editorial Crítica,
1977). For Tronti's retrospective reflections on his political thought between
'Carl and Karl', see Mario Tronti, *La
politica al tramonto* (Turin: Einaudi,
1998).

31. Schmitt, 'Die legale Weltrevolution'.

32. *Ibid.*, 322.

33. Schmitt also used this occasion to
reaffirm his supposed role as defender
of Weimar – whose warnings had been
ignored by the 'sceptical' and 'ironic' attitude of (supposedly liberal) 'interpreters' of the Weimar constitution. See
ibid., 333.

34. *Ibid.*, 329.

35. For an analysis of the Italian case from
a left-wing perspective, see Paolo Per-
sichetti and Oreste Scalzone, *La révolu-
tion et l'État: Insurrections et
"contre-insurrection" dans l'Italie de
l'après-68: la démocratie pénale, l'État
d'urgence* (Paris: Dagorno, 2000).

36. Wolfgang Schieder, 'Carl Schmitt und
Italien', in: *Vierteljahrshefte für Zeit-
geschichte*, Vol. 37 (1989), 1–21; here 11.
See also Robert Lumley, *States of
Emergency: Cultures of Revolt in Italy
from 1968 to 1978* (London: Verso, 1990).

37. Wilhelm Hennis, Peter Graf Kiel-
mannsegg and Ulrich Matz (eds.),
*Regierbarkeit: Studien zu ihrer Prob-
lematisierung*, 2 Vols. (Stuttgart: Klett-
Cotta, 1977–1979).

38. Schmittians were of little importance in

the rise of neo-liberalism, but there were some links nonetheless. For instance, the political theorist and historian of political thought Gottfried Dietze, who had been heavily influenced by Schmitt in his interpretation of the American founding and the tensions between liberalism and democracy, presented a paper at the infamous conference of the neo-liberal Mont Pelerin Society in Chile, alongside Friedrich von Hayek. See, for instance, his *Liberalism Proper and Proper Liberalism* (Baltimore: Johns Hopkins University Press, 1985) and 'Nachfahre des Hobbes: Amerika diskutiert das Werk von Carl Schmitt', in: *Die Welt*, 19 September 1980.

39. Scott, *Seeing like a State*.
40. Reinhard, *Geschichte der Staatsgewalt*, 337.
41. *Ibid.*
42. In analogy to *Landnahme*, Schmitt now theorized the *Industrienahme*.
43. *Ibid.*, 336.
44. *Ibid.*
45. Reinhart Koselleck, 'Zur historisch-politischen Semantik asymmetrischer Gegenbegriffe', in: *Vergangene Zukunft: Zur Semantik geschichtlicher Zeiten* (1970; Frankfurt/Main: Suhrkamp, 1989), 211–59.

The Death (and Strange Rebirth) of Carl Schmitt

1. Jünger to Schmitt, 17 July 1983, in *Ernst Jünger–Carl Schmitt*, 456.
2. Noack, *Carl Schmitt*, 302.
3. Kurt Sontheimer, 'Der Macht näher als dem Recht: Zum Tode Carl Schmitts', in: *Die Zeit*, 19 April 1985.
4. Dolf Sternberger, 'Irrtümer Carl Schmitts: Bemerkungen zu einigen seiner Hauptschriften', in: *Frankfurter Allgemeine Zeitung*, 1 June 1985 and 'Was ist ein politischer Klassiker?', *Frankfurter Allgemeine Zeitung*, 9 July 1988. The former piece was a direct re-

sponse to Maschke's obituary mentioned below.

5. Habermas. 'The Horrors of Autonomy', 138.
6. Ellen Kennedy, 'Carl Schmitt und die "Frankfurter Schule" – Deutsche Liberalismuskritik im 20. Jahrhundert', in: *Geschichte und Gesellschaft*, Vol. 12 (1986), 380–419.
7. Rolf Wiggershaus, *Die Frankfurter Schule: Geschichte, theoretische Entwicklung, politische Bedeutung* (Munich: dtv, 1993), 598–628.
8. Jürgen Habermas, 'Vom öffentlichen Gebrauch der Historie', in: *Die Zeit*, 7 November 1986.
9. Quaritsch (ed.), *Complexio Oppositorum* and Hofmann, 'Was ist uns Carl Schmitt?', 545–6. The Speyer congress was followed by more left-wing and liberal gatherings in Gummersbach in 1987 and Kassel in 1988.
10. Maschke, *Der Tod des Carl Schmitt*.
11. Hofmann, 'Was ist uns Carl Schmitt?', 547.
12. Michael Stolleis, 'Die Jünger am Grabe', in: *Rechtshistorisches Journal*, Vol. 6 (1987), 247–50.
13. See for instance Rüdiger Altmann and Johannes Gross, 'Was bleibt von Carl Schmitt? Verfassungslehre als politische Wissenschaft', in: *Frankfurter Allgemeine Zeitung*, 4 October 1986.
14. Helmut Schelsky, 'Der "Begriff des Politischen" und die politische Erfahrung der Gegenwart', in: *Der Staat*, Vol. 22 (1983), 321–45.
15. *Ibid.*, 332.
16. *Ibid.*, 337.
17. William Rasch, *Niklas Luhmann's Modernity: The Paradoxes of Differentiation* (Stanford: Stanford UP, 2000), 10. This is now the best introduction to Luhmann's thought in English.
18. See Niklas Luhmann, *Politische Theorie im Wohlfahrtsstaat* (Munich: Olzog, 1981), 22. The posthumously published *Die Politik der Gesellschaft*, ed. André

Kieserling (Frankfurt/Main: Suhrkamp, 2000) summarizes Luhmann's views on politics.

19. Quoted by Thomas Wirtz, 'Entscheidung: Niklas Luhmann und Carl Schmitt', in Albrecht Koschorke and Cornelia Vismann (eds.), *Widerstände der Systemtheorie: Kulturtheoretische Analysen zum Werk von Niklas Luhmann* (Berlin: Akademie, 1999) 175–97, here 175–6.

20. The question of the proximity of Luhmann and Schmitt is examined in a number of contributions in Kai-Uwe Hellmann and Rainer Schmalz-Bruns (eds.), *Theorie der Politik: Niklas Luhmanns politische Soziologie* (Frankfurt/Main: Suhrkamp, 2002).

21. Matthias Beyerle, 'Die Vollendung des staatstheoretischen Nihilismus', in: *Der Staat*, Vol. 36 (1997), 163–87. Forsthoff had already been shocked by Luhmann's apparently complete elimination of the state in a letter to Schmitt from October 1969. There he also stressed the need for a phenomenological, rather than a sociological method. See HStAD RW 265–3934.

22. Niels Werber, 'Von Feinden und Barbaren: Carl Schmitt und Niklas Luhmann', in: *Merkur* Vol. 49 (1995), 949–57.

23. Heinrich Meier, *Carl Schmitt, Leo Strauss und 'Der Begriff des Politischen': Zu einem Dialog unter Abwesenden* (Stuttgart: Metzler, 1988).

24. Bernd Rüthers, *Entartetes Recht: Rechtslehren und Kronjuristen im Dritten Reich* (Munich: C. H. Beck, 1988).

25. Schlink, 'Why Carl Schmitt?', 438.

26. Thomas Wirtz, 'Heillose Arbeit am Begriff: Carl Schmitt und die Politische Theologie', in: *Merkur*, Vol. 53 (1999), 651–6.

27. Heinrich Meier, *Die Lehre Carl Schmitts: Vier Kapitel zur Unterscheidung politischer Theologie und politischer Philosophie* (Stuttgart: J. B. Metzler, 1994).

28. Schmitt, *The Concept of the Political*, 28–9.

29. Groh, *Arbeit an der Heillosigkeit*, 13.

30. Armin Mohler, 'Begegnungen bei Ernst Jünger: Fragmente einer Ortung', in: Armin Mohler (ed.), *Freundschaftliche Begegnungen: Festschrift für Ernst Jünger zum 60. Geburtstag* (Frankfurt/Main: Vittorio Klostermann, 1955), 196–206; here 198.

31. Ernst-Wolfgang Böckenförde, 'Auf dem Weg zum Klassiker: Carl Schmitt in der Diskussion: Politische Theologie als Fluchtpunkt seines Werkes', in: *Frankfurter Allgemeine Zeitung*, 11 July 1997. Böckenförde's position was directly opposed by Bernd Rüthers in 'Retter vor dem Antichrist? Carl Schmitt als politischer Theologe', in *Frankfurter Allgemeine Zeitung*, 28 November 1997. Rüthers, like many other observers, pointed out that Schmitt's political theology was incompatible with official Catholic doctrines and reiterated that the personalized Schmitt discussion was at heart a debate about the role of jurists during Weimar and the Third Reich.

32. Hofmann, 'Was ist uns Carl Schmitt?', 551.

Integral Europe and the Rise of the European New Right(s)

1. Douglas R. Holmes, *Integral Europe: Fast-Capitalism, Multiculturalism, Neofascism* (Princeton: Princeton UP, 2000).

2. Note the title of the German New Right journal *Elemente – Für eine europäische Wiedergeburt.*

3. Alain de Benoist claimed that 'the main enemy for us will be bourgeois liberalism and the Atlantic-American Occident, which has one of its most dangerous surrogates in European Social Democracy'. Quoted by Manfred Baldus, 'Carl Schmitt im Hexagon: Zur Schmitt-Rezeption in Frankreich', in:

Der Staat, Vol. 26 (1987), 566–86; here 578.

4. For some of the main sources of the *Nouvelle Droite*, see in particular Alain de Benoist, *Vu de Droite: Anthologie critique des idées contemporaines* (Paris: Copernic, 1978). Schmitt's ideas are discussed at 216–19. De Benoist had taken positive notice of Schmitt early on – see his review of *La Notion de Politique* in *Valeurs Actuelles*, 13 March, 1972.

5. Pierre-André Taguieff, 'From Race to Culture: The New Right's View of European Identity', *Telos*, Nos. 98–9 (1994), 99–125.

6. Baldus, 'Carl Schmitt im Hexagon', 576.

7. Freund had initially been a reference point for de Benoist and others, but eventually, he came to publish articles on decisionism and other Schmittian topics in *Nouvelle Ecole* and other New Right journals himself. The expression *banalité supérieure* is originally André Gide's to denote an idea of genius that will come to seem obvious as soon as a genius has expressed it.

8. Julius Evola, *Lettere di Julius Evola a Carl Schmitt: 1951–1963*, introduction by Antonio Caracciolo, trans. Lucia Bartolucci (Rome: Fondazione Julius Evola, 2000). See also Thomas Sheehan, 'Myth and Violence: The Fascism of Julius Evola and Alain de Benoist', in: *Social Research*, No. 48 (1981), 45–73.

9. See also his autobiography *Il cammino del cinabro* (Milan: All'insegna del pesce d'oro, 1972).

10. Interestingly enough, he never disowned his Dadaist beginnings – after all, Dada represented an assault on the rationalist liberalism of bourgeois life. See Richard H. Drake, 'Julius Evola and the Ideological Origins of the Radical Right in Contemporary Italy', in: Peter Merkl (ed.), *Political Violence and Terror: Motifs and Motivations* (Berkeley: University of California Press, 1986), 61–89.

11. Julius Evola, *Rivolta contro il mondo moderno* (Milan: Ulrico Hoepli, 1934).

12. Julius Evola, *Metafisica del sesso* (Rome: Atanor, 1958).

13. Staff, *Staatsdenken*, 230–41.

14. *Ibid.*, 237.

15. The journal *Trasgressioni*, for instance, published articles about Tolkien side by side with articles by Schmitt, de Benoist and Günter Maschke. See also Lorenzo Papini, *Radici del Pensiero della Nuova Destra: La Riflessione Politica di Alain de Benoist* (Pisa: Giardini, 1995), 127–30.

16. Klaus Kriener, 'Plettenberg-Freiburg-Potsdam: Über den Einfluss Carl Schmitts auf die *Junge Freiheit*', in: Helmut Kellershohn (ed.), *Das Plagiat: Der völkische Nationalismus der Jungen Freiheit* (Duisberg: DISS, 1994), 181–213. The paper also celebrated its five-year anniversary in Plettenberg to honour Schmitt.

17. Karlheinz Weissmann, 'Herausforderung und Entscheidung: Über einen politischen Verismus in Deutschland', in: Heimo Schwilk and Ulrich Schacht (eds.) *Die Selbstbewußte Nation: "Anschwellender Bocksgesang" und weitere Beiträge zu einer deutschen Debatte* (Berlin: Ullstein, 1994), 309–26.

18. *Ibid.*, 313.

19. Reinhart Maurer, 'Schuld und Wohlstand: Über die westlich-deutsche Generallinie', in: *Die Selbstbewußte Nation*, 69–84.

20. Both Strauß, 'Anschwellender Bocksgesang', in: *Die Selbstbewußte Nation*, 19–40; here 26.

21. See Gioergio Ferri, *Gianfranco Miglio: Storia di un Giacobino Nordista* (Milan: Liber, 1993).

22. Gianfranco Miglio, 'L'ultimo dei "classici"', in: *Sole-24 ore*, 17 April 1985.

23. Gianfranco Miglio and Marcello Veneziani, *Padania, Italia: Lo stato nazionale è soltanto in crisi o non è mai esistito?*, ed. Marco Ferrazoli (Florence:

Casa Editrice Le Lettere, 1997), 14–15. There Miglio also claimed that the nation-state had been born to 'make true war', but that such wars were no longer possible. Of course, this did not exclude future conflicts among 'post-nationalist protagonists'. The conflict '*amicus-hostis*' would also play a part in the constitution of the 'macro-regions'. See *ibid.*, 17 and 68. At the same time, he remained deeply sceptical about the process of European unification. See *ibid.*, 25–42.

24. Gianfranco Miglio and Augusto Barbera, *Federalismo e secessione: Un dialogo* (Milan: Mondadori, 1997).

25. Gianfranco Miglio, *Una Costituzione per i prossimi trent'anni: Intervista sulla Terza Republica a cura di Marcello Staglieno* (Bari: Laterza, 1990), 31.

26. For Miglio's own account of the falling out, see *Io, Bossi e la Lega: Diario segreto dei mei quattro anni sui Carrocio* (Milan: Mondadori, 1994).

27. See also Carlo Lottieri, 'Gianfranco Miglio (1918–2001)', in: *Telos*, No. 122 (2002), 101–10.

28. He was soon followed by Joseph Bendersky, who wrote the first biography of Schmitt. Joseph Bendersky, *Carl Schmitt: Theorist for the Reich* (Princeton: Princeton UP, 1983). These works were either ignored or received a hostile reaction from the mainstream of American political science which saw Schwab and Bendersky as unreconstructed apologists – a charge that was not entirely fair in Bendersky's case.

29. George Schwab, *The Challenge of the Exception: An Introduction to the Political Ideas of Carl Schmitt between 1921 and 1936* (Berlin: Duncker & Humblot, 1970).

30. See also Norberto Bobbio, 'Is there a Marxist Theory of the State?', in: *Telos*, No. 35 (1978), 5–16.

31. Special Issue on Schmitt, *Telos*, 1987.

32. De Benoist and the Telos authors also converged on a federalist vision of Europe as a 'community of communities', drawing on Althusius and repudiating Hobbes and Bodin. See for instance Alain de Benoist, 'What is Sovereignty?', in: *Telos*, No. 116 (1999), 99–118.

33. Dieter Haselbach, 'Die Wandlung zum Liberalen: Zur gegenwärtigen Schmitt-Diskussion in den USA', in: Hansen and Lietzmann (eds.), *Carl Schmitt und die Liberalismuskritik*, 119–40.

34. Like so many post-war Schmittians in Germany, the *Telos* authors also seemed driven by resentment of established academics, and the supposed hypocrisy of mainstream liberals.

35. The New Right had always claimed that Left and Right were becoming exhausted as political categories, and that it was necessary to move beyond Left and Right. Alain de Benoist, for instance, was adamant that the old Left and old Right 'worship the same god: the cult of performance, efficiency and profit'. See Alain de Benoist, 'End of the Left-Right Dichotomy: The French Case', in: *Telos*, No. 102 (1995), 73–89; here 86.

36. Paul Piccone and Gary Ulmen, 'Uses and Abuses of Carl Schmitt', in: *Telos*, No. 122 (2002), 3–32; here 25.

37. *Ibid.*, 25.

38. Paul Piccone, the editor of *Telos*, claimed that capitalism eroded its own preconditions, as subjectivity was systematically eroded. Attempts by the system to reconstruct subjectivity artificially would then necessarily fail. Right and Left responses to this process met with contempt by *Telos* intellectuals. In particular, the 'kathechontic role' of 'neo-conservative ideology' was 'merely to contain the growth of the existing bureaucratic apparatus by deploying the rhetoric of a faded classical liberalism', while the Left was 'even more conservative than the Right' in that it continued to support illegitimate

state interventionism. See Jorge Raventos, 'From the New Left to Postmodern Populism: An Interview with Paul Piccone', in: *Telos*, No. 122 (2002, 133–52, in particular 139).

39. Piccone and Ulmen, 'Uses and Abuses', 32.

Schmitt's Globalization

1. Francis Fukuyama, *The End of History and the Last Man* (London: Hamish Hamilton, 1992) and *The Great Disruption: Human Nature and the Reconstitution of Social Order* (London: Profile, 1999).
2. Slavoj Žižek, 'Carl Schmitt in the Age of Post-Politics', in: (ed.), *The Challenge of Carl Schmitt*, 18–37; here 30.
3. *Ibid.*, 34.
4. *Ibid.*, 30.
5. *Ibid.*, 35.
6. *Ibid.*, 35.
7. Samuel P. Huntington, *The Clash of Civilizations and the Remaking of World Order* (New York: Simon & Schuster, 1996).
8. Istvan Hont, 'The Permanent Crisis of a Divided Mankind: "Contemporary Crisis of the Nation State" in Historical Perspective', in: *Political Studies*, Vol. 42 (1994), 166–231.
9. Michael Howard, *The Invention of Peace: Reflections on War and International Order* (London: Profile, 2000), 103.
10. Slavoj Žižek, *Welcome to the Desert of the Real: Five Essays on September 11 and Related Dates* (London: Verso, 2002), 90.
11. *Ibid.*, 110.
12. David Rieff, 'A New Age of Liberal Imperialism?', in: *World Policy Journal*, Vol. 16, No. 2 (1999), 1–10.
13. Jürgen Habermas, 'Bestialität und Humanität: Ein Krieg an der Grenze zwischen Recht und Moral', in: *Die Zeit*, 29 April 1999.
14. Danilo Zolo, *Invoking humanity: war,*

law, and global order (London: Continuum, 2002). The original Italian volume appeared in 1999.

15. William Rasch, 'Menschenrechte als Geopolitik: Carl Schmitt und die völkerrechtliche Form der amerikanischen Hegemonie', in: Dirk Baecker, Peter Krieg and Fritz B. Simon (eds.), *Terror im System: Der 11. September und die Folgen* (Carl-Auer-Systeme, 2002), 130–58.
16. Karl Otto Hondrich, 'Der Westen irrt', in: *Frankfurter Allgemeine Zeitung*, 24 April 1999. See also Michael Ignatieff, *Virtual War: Kosovo and Beyond* (London: Chatto & Windus, 2000).
17. Ulrich Raulff, 'Die Irregulären: Die Truppen im Kosovo und das Gesetz des Partisanen', in: *Frankfurter Allgemeine Zeitung*, 18 June 1999.
18. Interpretations of the terrorist attack on the World Trade Center and the Pentagon in the German press drew extensively on Schmitt in trying to come to terms with the new logic of world conflict. See for instance Andreas Krause, 'Wir stehen bereit – aber wofür? Viel Feind, viel Gemeinschaft: Deutschland stürzt sich ins Ungewisse', in: *Berliner Zeitung*, 15 September 2001.
19. See also Henning Ritter, 'Der Feind: Terror ohne Territorium, Vernichtung als Programm', in: *Frankfurter Allgemeine Zeitung*, 19 September 2001.
20. Seyla Benhabib, 'Ende aller Unterscheidung', in: *Die Zeit*, 17 September 2001.
21. *Ibid.*
22. Jürgen Habermas, 'Was bedeutet der Denkmalsturz? Verschließen wir nicht die Augen vor der Revolution der Weltordnung: Die normative Autorität Amerikas liegt in Trümmern', in: *Frankfurter Allgemeine Zeitung*, 17 April 2003.
23. Michael Hardt and Antonio Negri, *Empire* (Cambridge, Mass.: Harvard UP, 2000), 16.
24. *Ibid.*

25. *Ibid.*, 13–14.
26. Giorgio Agamben, *Homo Sacer: Sovereign Power and Bare Life*, trans. Daniel Heller-Roazen (Stanford: Standford UP, 1998).
27. *Ibid.*, 180.
28. Stephen D. Krasner, *Sovereignty: Organized Hypocrisy* (Princeton: Princeton UP, 1999). See also Gopal Balakrishnan, 'The Book on Schmitt', in: *Boston Review* (Summer 2001).
29. Maier, 'Consigning the Twentieth Century to History'.
30. Balakrishnan, 'The Book on Schmitt'.
31. Alan Ware, 'The Party Systems in the Established Liberal Democracies in the 1990s: Is this a Decade of Transformation?', in: *Government and Opposition*, Vol. 30 (1995), 312–26.
32. Ralf Dahrendorf, 'The Third Way and Liberty', in: *Foreign Affairs*, Vol. 78, No. 5 (1999), 13–17.
33. Balakrishnan, 'The Book on Schmitt'.
34. David Dyzenhaus, 'Putting the State Back in Credit', in: Mouffe (ed.), *The Challenge of Carl Schmitt*, 75–91.
35. David Dyzenhaus, *Legality and Legitimacy: Carl Schmitt, Hans Kelsen and Hermann Heller in Weimar* (Oxford: Oxford UP, 1997).
36. John Rawls, *A Theory of Justice* (Oxford: Oxford UP, 1971).
37. Habermas, *Between Facts and Norms.*
38. Judith Shklar, 'The liberalism of fear', in: Nancy Rosenblum (ed.), *Liberalism and the Moral Life* (Cambridge, Mass.: Harvard UP, 1989).
39. Michael Freeden, *Ideologies and Political Theory: A Conceptual Approach* (Oxford: Oxford UP, 1996), 226–75.
40. John Rawls, *Political Liberalism* (1993; New York: Columbia, 1996), 191. Rawls also discussed Schmittian objections to his theory in the preface at lxii.
41. John Tomasi, *Liberalism beyond Justice: Citizens, Society, and the Boundaries of Political Theory* (Princeton: Princeton UP, 2001).
42. Renato Cristi, in an intuitively implausible fashion, claimed that Schmitt himself was an authoritarian, antidemocratic liberal. Like Dyzenhaus, he deduced liberalism's need to open itself to democracy from Schmitt's case. See Christi, *Carl Schmitt and authoritarian liberalism.*
43. Jacques Derrida, 'Force of Law: The Mystical Foundation of Authority', in *Cardozo Law Review*, vol. 11 (1990), 919–1046, and Bonnie Honig, 'Declarations of Independence: Arendt and Derrida on the Problem of Founding a Republic', in: *American Political Science Review*, Vol. 85 (1991), 97–113.
44. For attempts to build on this notion of a pluralist founding, see Ulrich K. Preuß, *Revolution, Fortschritt und Verfassung: Zu einem neuen Verfassungsverständnis* (Frankfurt/Main: Fischer, 1994), 84–8 and Andrew Arato, *Civil Society, Constitution, and Legitimacy* (Lanham: Rowman & Littlefield, 2000).
45. Pierre Saint-Amand, 'Hostile Enlightenment', in: Jean-Joseph Goux and Philip R. Wood (eds.), *Terror and Consensus: Vicissitudes of French Thought* (Stanford: Stanford UP, 1998), 145–58.
46. See for instance F. R. Ankersmit, *Aesthetic Politics: Political Philosophy Beyond Fact and Value* (Stanford: Stanford UP, 1996).
47. *Ibid.*, 127.
48. Žižek, 'Carl Schmitt in the Age of Post-Politics', 29.
49. See in particular Chantal Mouffe's *The Return of the Political* and *The Democratic Paradox* (London: Verso, 2000).
50. Derrida, *Politics of Friendship*, 104.
51. *Ibid.*, 275.
52. Gianni Vattimo, *Il Pensiero debole* (Milan: Feltrinelli, 1988).
53. See also Christian Schwaabe, 'Liberalismus und Dezisionismus: Zur Rehabilitierung eines liberalen Dezisionismus im Anschluß an Carl Schmitt, Jacques

Derrida und Hermann Lübbe', in: *Jahrbuch Politisches Denken 2001* (Stuttgart: J. B. Metzler, 2001), 175–201.

54. Maier, 'Consigning the Twentieth Century to History', 817.

55. Of course, not every cosmopolitan in the sociological sense turned out to be a universalist in the normative sense. And not every universalist in the normative sense turned out to be a liberal universalist in any sense. Both liberalism and antiliberalism could go global. See also Ralf Dahrendorf, *Auf der Suche nach einer neuen Ordnung: Vorlesungen zur Politik der Freiheit im 21. Jahrhundert* (Munich: C. H. Beck, 2003).

56. Howard, *The Invention of Peace*, 100.

Afterword

1. Botho Strauss, 'Anschwellender Bocksgesang', 23.

2. Schmitt, *Ex Captivitate*, 90.

3. Mark Lilla, 'The Other Velvet Revolution: Continental Liberalism and its Discontents', in *Daedalus*, Vol. 123, No. 2 (1994), 129–57, and Ulrich Herbert, 'Liberalisierung als Lernprozeß: Die Bundesrepublik in der deutschen Geschichte – eine Skizze', in: Ulrich Herbert (ed.), *Wandlungsprozesse in Westdeutschland: Belastung, Integration, Liberalisierung* (Göttingen: Wallstein, 2002), 7–49.

4. Jerry Z. Muller, *The Other God That Failed: Hans Freyer and the Deradicalization of German Conservatism* (Princeton: Princeton UP, 1997).

5. As was recognized by his sharper pupils – see Rüdiger Altmann's remarks in Quaritsch (ed.). *Complexio Oppositorum*, 602.

6. Judith Shklar, *Ordinary Vices* (Cambridge, Mass.: Harvard UP, 1984), 243.

7. Christoph Möllers, *Staat als Argument* (Munich: C. H. Beck, 2000). To this day, the Right prefers to speak of *Staatsrechtslehre*, whereas the Left is more likely to refer to *Verfassungsrechtslehre*.

8. Bernhard Schlink, 'Die Entthronung der Staatsrechtswissenschaft durch die Verfassungsgerichtsbarkeit', in: *Der Staat*, Vol. 28 (1989), 161–72.

9. See also Toulmin, *Cosmopolis*.

10. Lutz Koepnick, *Walter Benjamin and the Aesthetics of Power* (Lincoln: University of Nebraska Press, 1999), 12.

11. Which is not to say that liberals cannot go some way in meeting the cravings of what has sometimes been called 'reasonable Romantics'. See Nancy L. Rosenblum, *Another Liberalism: Romanticism and the Reconstruction of Liberal Thought* (Cambridge, Mass.: Harvard UP, 1987).

12. Bernard Williams, 'From Freedom to Liberty: The Construction of a Political Value', in: *Philosophy and Public Affairs*, Vol. 30 (2001), 1–24; here 3, and Richard A. Posner, *The Problematics of Moral and Legal Theory* (Cambridge, Mass.: Harvard UP, 1999). I am also indebted to Michael Freeden on this point.

13. Judith Shklar, *Ordinary Vices*, 5.

14. *Ibid.*, 4–5.Abendroth, Wolfgang, 78.

Index